REDUCTION, EXPLANATION, AND REALISM

REDUCTION, EXPLANATION, AND REALISM

Edited by

DAVID CHARLES
AND
KATHLEEN LENNON

CLARENDON PRESS · OXFORD
1992

Oxford University Press, Walton Street, Oxford OX2 6DP
Oxford New York Toronto
Delhi Bombay Calcutta Madras Karachi
Petaling Jaya Singapore Hong Kong Tokyo
Nairobi Dar es Salaam Cape Town
Melbourne Auckland
and associated companies in
Berlin Ibadan

Oxford is a trade mark of Oxford University Press

Published in the United States
by Oxford University Press, New York

British Library Cataloguing in Publication Data
Data available

Library of Congress Cataloging-in-Publication Data
Reduction, explanation, and realism / edited by David Charles and
Kathleen Lennon. p. cm.
Includes bibliographical references and index.
1. Reductionism. 2. Philosophy of mind. 3. Ethics. 4. Life
sciences—Philosophy. 5. Social sciences—Philosophy. 6. Physical
sciences—Philosophy. 7. Explanation. 8. Realism. I. Charles,
David (David Owain Maurice) II. Lennon, Kathleen.
B835.5.R43 1992 149—dc20 91-37585
ISBN 0–19–824273–5
ISBN 0–19–875131–1 (Pbk)

Typeset by Best-set Typesetter Ltd., Hong Kong
Printed and bound in
Great Britain by Bookcraft (Bath) Ltd.,
Midsomer Norton, Avon

CONTENTS

vi   *Contents*

NOTES ON THE CONTRIBUTORS

JUSTIN BROACKES is a Fellow in Philosophy at Oriel College, Oxford. He has published on Hume, Descartes, metaphysics, and the mind.

JOHN CAMPBELL is a Fellow in Philosophy at New College, Oxford. He has published on issues in the philosophy of mind and language, and on metaphysics.

QUASSIM CASSAM is a Fellow in Philosophy at Wadham College, Oxford. He has published on Kantian metaphysics and the philosophy of mind.

DAVID CHARLES is a Fellow in Philosophy at Oriel College, Oxford. He is the author of *Aristotle's Philosophy of Action* (London, 1984) and has published on the philosophy of mind and ancient philosophy.

ADRIAN CUSSINS is Assistant Professor at the University of California at San Diego. He has published articles in the philosophy of language and the philosophy of mind.

JAMES GRIFFIN is a Reader in Philosophy at Oxford University. He is the author of *Wittgenstein's Logical Atomism* (Oxford, 1964) and *Well Being* (Oxford, 1988), and has written widely on issues in moral and political philosophy.

JENNIFER HORNSBY is a Fellow in Philosophy at Corpus Christi College, Oxford. She is the author of *Actions* (London, 1980) and has published on questions in the philosophy of mind and language. She is currently working on feminist topics and the philosophy of biology.

FRANK JACKSON is Professor of Philosophy at Monash University, Australia. He was formerly Professor of Philosophy in the Research School of Sciences at the Australian National University. He is the author of *Perception* (Cambridge, 1977) and *Conditionals* (Oxford, 1987).

KATHLEEN LENNON is a Lecturer in Philosophy at the University of Hull. She is the author of *Explaining Human Action* (London, 1990) and works in the philosophy of mind, philosophy of social science, and feminist theory.

BRIAN LOAR is Professor of Philosophy at the University of Southern California. He is the author of *Mind and Meaning* (Cambridge, 1981) and papers in the philosophy of mind and the theory of meaning.

CYNTHIA MACDONALD is a Lecturer in Philosophy at the University of Manchester. She has published in the areas of philosophy of mind and metaphysics. Her recent book *Mind–Body Identity Theories* (London, 1989) is in Routledge's Problems of Philosophy Series.

GRAHAM MACDONALD is co-author with Philip Pettit of *Semantics and Social Science* (London, 1981), edited *Perception and Identity: Essays Presented to A. J. Ayer* (London, 1979), and co-edited, with Crispin Wright, *Fact, Science and Morality* (Oxford, 1986). He is presently completing a book, *Special Explanations*, which argues the case for non-reductive monism in biology, psychology, and sociology.

DAVID PAPINEAU is Professor of Philosophy of Science at King's College, London. He has published articles on the philosophy of mind, epistemology, and causation, and is the author of *For Science in the Social Sciences* (London, 1978), *Theory and Meaning* (Oxford, 1979), and *Reality and Representation* (Oxford, 1987).

PHILIP PETTIT is Professor of Social and Political Theory, Research School of Social Sciences, Australian National University, Canberra. He is the author of a number of books including, most recently, *Not Just Deserts: A Republican Theory of Criminal Justice*, with John Braithwaite (Oxford, 1990). He works on the foundations of psychology and social theory and in political philosophy.

PETER SMITH is Senior Lecturer in Philosophy at the University of Sheffield, editor of *Analysis*, and co-author, with O. R. Jones, of *The Philosophy of Mind* (Cambridge, 1986). He is currently working on a series of papers on the philosophical implications of chaos.

MICHAEL SMITH currently teaches in the Department of Philosophy at Monash University, Australia, having taught previously at the University of Oxford and Princeton University. He is the author of *The Moral Problem*, as well as several papers in ethics and moral psychology.

Introduction

Kathleen Lennon and David Charles

For many years there was a widespread belief amongst philosophers in a variety of different areas that the projects of making certain phenomena intelligible or of vindicating the legitimacy of certain modes of explanation required their reduction to phenomena whose intelligibility was considered less problematic or to explanations whose value was assured. Reduction was regarded as the only alternative to accepting as dualists the existence of mysterious entities or kinds, or else to rejecting the reality of these problematic phenomena.[1] In recent years, however, there has been an attempt to articulate a position which does not fit either of these two alternatives. In a number of areas explicitly *anti-reductionist* views have been proposed, which are both realist and non-dualist, laying claim, for instance, to a respectable materialism. Biologists working in evolutionary theory argue that there is no precise physical property or relation correlated with the evolutionary property of 'fitness'.[2] Theorists of social science resist the reduction of social facts and social explanations to individualist ones.[3] Some writers on secondary qualities challenge both the possibility of primary quality correlates for secondary qualities and the ability of any putative correlate to capture the necessarily participatory nature of the secondary quality.[4] Perhaps the areas which have been given the most philosophical attention concern the relation between the mental and the physical and

[1] See e.g. B. Loar, *Mind and Meaning* (Cambridge: Cambridge University Press, 1981), ch. 1. Also D. Parfit, *Reasons and Persons* (Oxford: Oxford University Press, 1984), 210 and 240.

[2] A. Rosenberg, 'The Supervenience of Biological Concepts', *Philosophy of Science*, 45 (1978).

[3] D. H. Ruben, *The Metaphysics of the Social World* (London: Routledge & Kegan Paul, 1985).

[4] See C. McGinn, *The Subjective View: Secondary Qualities and Indexical Thoughts* (Oxford: Oxford University Press, 1983). G. McCulloch, Reply to Peter Smith, 'Subjectivity and Colour Vision', *Proceedings of the Aristotelian Society*, Supp. Vol. 61 (1987).

the moral and the non-moral. In the psychological case anti-reductionists have challenged reductionist strategies in both their classical physicalist and contemporary functionalist versions.[5] In moral philosophy the claim that our practices of ascribing moral predicates can be understood without the need to assume the existence of objective moral properties has been strenuously resisted by moral realists.[6]

What is distinctive about these modern anti-reductionist strategies is that they are avowedly anti-dualist. While defending the autonomy of the particular discourses with which they are concerned, they none the less accept some form of *supervenience* or dependence claim, grounding such discourses in underlying materialist or naturalist ones.[7] It is the coherence and success of these anti-reductionist claims which constitute the principal focus of the papers in this collection.

1. WHAT IS REDUCTION?

Reductionist accounts aim to show that where we thought we had two sets of concepts, entities, laws, explanations, or properties, we in fact have only one, which is most perspicuously characterized in terms of the reducing vocabulary. Within the class of proposed reductions with which we shall be concerned there is little attempt to effect a translation of one discourse into another.[8] (It is, none the less, an important issue whether

---

[5] D. Davidson, 'Mental Events', in *Essays on Actions and Events* (Oxford: Oxford University Press, 1980). J. McDowell, 'Functionalism and Anomalous Monism', in E. Lepore and B. McLaughlin (eds.), *Actions and Events: Perspectives on the Philosophy of Donald Davidson* (Oxford: Blackwell, 1985). K. Lennon, 'Anti-reductionist Materialism', *Inquiry*, 27 (1984).

[6] See the contemporary debate between S. Blackburn and J. McDowell, e.g. S. Blackburn, 'Moral Realism', in J. Casey (ed.), *Morality and Moral Reasoning* (London: Methuen, 1971); J. McDowell, 'Values and Secondary Qualities', in T. Honderich (ed.), *Morality and Objectivity: A Tribute to J. L. Mackie* (London: Routledge & Kegan Paul, 1985).

[7] Such a formulation may suggest that the categories of the 'natural' or the 'material' or 'physical' are themselves unproblematic. This is not, however, the case. James Griffin raises problems for the category of the natural in his paper in the volume. See also the paper by David Charles. Also P. Snowdon, 'On Formulating Materialism and Dualism', in J. Heil (ed.), *Cause, Mind and Reality: Essays Honouring C. B. Martin* (Dordrecht: Kluwer Academic Publishers, 1989).

[8] An important exception to this is found in some contemporary functionalist thought, where attempts are made to 'explicate' mental concepts

certain anti-reductionist arguments tell against the reduction of properties, or only against reduction of concepts.) Moreover, within these reductionist projects it is not, in general, sufficient to establish that the *particulars* from one level are identical with or constituted out of particulars individuated at some more fundamental level of theory. Defending token-identity claims of this kind has indeed formed an important component in some materialist projects.[9] But the strength and nature of such claims depends on the criteria of event-identity which their proponents adopt. If we follow Kim,[10] the identity of particular events requires the identity of their constitutive properties. Attention then shifts to conditions for property identity. If we accept Davidson's account of event-identity,[11] identity of particular events does not require property identity. But this leaves unresolved the relation of the distinct characteristics of the events and the explanations in which they feature. Either way, the key concern for the reductionist remains the reduction of laws, explanations, and, for those who admit them into their ontology, properties.

As classically discussed in the philosophy of science, reduction is a relation between causal explanatory theories. The motivation for these reductions is to defend the primacy of physical explanation. Many would accept (1) that social and psychological events are (in some sense) constituted out of physical events, (2) that physical explanation is complete, i.e. that all physically characterizable events are susceptible to explanation in terms of physically sufficient causes, and (3) that there are causal explanations employing social and psychological vocabulary. But if so, they need to give an account of how the causal explanations at each level of description interconnect. Since we need to rule out overdetermination, it

in an extensional way. See Loar, *Mind and Meaning*. However, in Hilary Putnam's original defence of functionalism mental properties were reduced to functional ones *without* an explication of intentional discourse by means of extensional functional discourse. See *Philosophical Papers*, ii: *Mind, Language and Reality* (Cambridge: Cambridge University Press, 1975).

[9] Davidson, 'Mental Events'.

[10] J. Kim, 'Events as Property Exemplifications', in M. Brand and D. Walton (eds.), *Action Theory* (Dordrecht: Reidel 1977).

[11] D. Davidson, 'The Individuation of Events', in Davidson, *Essays on Actions and Events*.

can seem that the only way to do this is to accept reduction. We also are required to explain how the predictions made from within each explanatory structure march in step. Without reduction this can appear 'a miraculous coincidence'. (In the present volume this issue is discussed in the papers by Adrian Cussins, Graham Macdonald, and David Papineau.) Other motivations for seeking a reduction have their origin in a view of causation which has been regarded by some as a scientific orthodoxy. This is the view that real causation takes place at the physical level. Macrocausal links are constituted out of causal links between microparticles in which the principle of conservation of energy is maintained. Where this is interpreted as the need for a vindication at the microlevel of causal generalizations at the macrolevel, macrocausal laws are seen as 'essentially derivative from laws governing the micropro-cesses'.[12] Again reduction appears to be required.

In Ernest Nagel's famous account,[13] the reduction of a theory consisted in its *derivation* (or approximate derivation) from another more fundamental theory. Interesting cases arise when the vocabularies of the two theories are distinct. Then re-duction can only proceed by means of a 'condition of connect-ability', relating the terms of the theory to be reduced with terms already present and playing a role in the reducing science. Such a condition is satisfied by means of 'bridge laws', nomological biconditionals, linking the terms of each theory. Nagel, moreover, imposed the further important condition that such biconditionals should link terms at the higher level to terms which are already individuated and play a role in the reducing science. Such a condition would rule out the possi-bility of the reducing side of the biconditional consisting merely in a disjunction, without any theoretical unity at the reducing level between its components.

Is derivability a sufficient condition for reduction? It may ensure that different theories march in step, but it does not by itself guarantee that the higher-level theories are reductively equivalent to the lower-level ones. One concern is with the

[12] G. Macdonald, 'Modified Methodological Individualism', *Proceedings of the Aristotelian Society*, 86 (1985–6).
[13] *The Structure of Science* (London: Routledge & Kegan Paul, 1961), ch. 11.

interpretation of the bridge laws. If they are simply empirical nomological correlations they will need support from further theory, on which the higher-level laws will also depend. Nagel explicitly restricted his discussion to the reduction of theories and avoided considerations of an ontological kind concerning the relation between the kinds or properties linked by his connectability conditionals. Other theorists, however, addressed the issue of the interpretation of the bridge laws, and in general treated them as claims of reductive identity between the properties or kinds picked out at each level of theory. For them Nagel's further proviso took an ontological form as the requirement that there be a genuine property at the reducing level. The criterion for property identity became nomological coextensiveness, together with a requirement that the reducing property causally explains the phenomena explainable by means of the property to be reduced.[14] When we discovered that lightning was static electricity in specified circumstances, our theory of electricity could explain all the effects of lightning. There was simply no room for the suggestion that we might have two, coexisting, distinct kinds of entity.

To speak of a theory being reduced is to privilege the descriptions at the reducing level. One reason for this may be the greater generality of the lower-level laws. Those involved in a successful reduction will fit into a body of theory of which the higher-level laws are simply one manifestation in a particular set of conditions. This greater generality might enable, for example, the whole of biology to be derived from chemistry and physics, but not vice versa. For some writers the more fundamental nature of the reducing theory is ensured by its being closer to a characterization of the basic or real causal mechanisms.

We can, therefore, summarize the classical conditions for the scientific reduction as requiring: (1) the derivation of higher-level laws, (2) the discovery of nomological biconditionals linking the terms of each theory, (3) the presence of genuine properties at the reducing level, (4) the causal explanation in terms of the reducing theory of the phenomena explained by

---

[14] H. Putnam, 'On Properties', in *Philosophical Papers*, i: *Mathematics, Matter and Method* (Cambridge: Cambridge University Press, 1975).

the reduced theory, and (5) a reason for giving privileged status to the reducing descriptions. (For a further discussion of classical reduction and its variants see the paper by Peter Smith.)

Reflection on scientific reduction suggests conditions which must be met by successful reductions elsewhere. Reductive relations have been proposed between properties whose primary location is not exclusively within scientific explanations, e.g. the moral to the 'natural' or psychological (see the papers by James Griffin and Michael Smith); secondary qualities to primary ones (see the paper by Justin Broackes); being a subject to being a bundle of interconnected experiences (see the papers by Quassim Cassam and John Campbell). The question arises, in such cases, of both the necessity and sufficiency of the conditions required for scientific reduction. In some areas the primary motivation has been to fit problematic properties into our favoured metaphysical framework. Such metaphysical reductions could be proposed without any commitment to integrate explanations at the two levels. These proposed reductions might accept conditions (2) and (5), but not the others. However, it could be argued that such positions have not moved beyond establishing mere correlations unless the requirement of shared explanatory work is accommodated. But where this condition is accepted, a further issue arises over non-causal explanations. Some have doubted whether purposive explanations in psychology, biology, and social science are of an exclusively causal kind (see the papers by Graham Macdonald, and Frank Jackson and Philip Pettit). If a proposed reduction needs to accommodate all the explanatory work at the higher level, then condition (4) will need to be adjusted to allow for any non-causal explanation. Differences on these matters lead to disagreements over whether certain positions count as reductive.[15]

2. ANTI-REDUCTIONIST STRATEGIES

The conditions for successful reduction serve to indicate the diverse forms that anti-reductionist challenges may take. It has

[15] It is, of course, partly stipulative what theories we are going to call 'reductions', but the guiding concern is that of monism.

been argued that in different areas some of these conditions cannot be met. The point most commonly made against the reductionist is that of *multiple realization*. This set of considerations, popularized by functionalists in the philosophy of mind, is designed to show that there is no one individualist, physiological, or natural property which is nomologically coextensive with each social, psychological, or moral one. Think of the many different ways in which nations can go to war, individuals can fear reprisals, and systems can be unjust. Simply pointing to multiple realization, however, is not sufficient to guarantee the anti-reductionist point (see the paper by Peter Smith). For it might be possible to form a disjunction of the different kinds of base property on which the higher-level property may rest and argue that it is such a disjunction that forms the basis for the reducing property.[16] In resisting this suggestion philosophers have argued that not *any* disjunction can generate a genuine reducing property.[17] Should the disjunction be shapeless from within the resources of the lower-level theory, no genuine reduction has been achieved. There would be shapelessness of this kind if the disjunction consisted simply of a (potentially infinite) list of lower-level properties, where the criterion for deciding what should be included required the employment of the higher-level predicates. Thus, for example, it might be argued that the many different naturalistic descriptions which apply to different heroic actions will be shapeless unless we apply the ethical predicate 'heroic'. If shapelessness of this type is found, there is no way within the lower-level theory of unifying the disjunction which underlies the higher-level property. Such a disjunction is to be rejected as the basis for a genuine property because it displays no explanatory unity. The shapelessness of the underlying properties in respect to those at a different level is discussed in a number of papers in the volume (Justin Broackes in relation to secondary qualities, James Griffin in relation to moral properties, Kathleen Lennon in consideration

[16] See J. A. Fodor, 'The Special Sciences: The Disunity of Science as a Working Hypothesis', *Synthese*, 28 (1974).
[17] Nagel, *The Structure of Science*; also H. Putnam, *Representation and Reality* (Cambridge, Mass.: MIT Press, 1988), 78. D. M. Armstrong, *A Theory of Universals* (Cambridge: Cambridge University Press, 1978).

of intentional properties). This claim is at its most plausible when we have a principled reason to believe that the classificatory schemes at each level of description proceed on radically diverse principles. (See Kathleen Lennon and Cynthia Macdonald for a discussion of these principles in the intentional case, James Griffin in the moral one.) In any event, it is not possible to establish shapelessness simply by producing a list of multiple bases. The resources of our classificatory schemes are complex, and there may be some level of abstraction within them, by means of which the disjuncts can be unified. This is the functionalist strategy within philosophy of mind. Functionalists reject reduction of psychological kinds to categorical physical kinds because of multiple realization, but argue instead for their reduction to extensional functional kinds. If such functional kinds can be characterized within the resources of physical theory, the reduction of the psychological to the physical remains possible.

A second anti-reductionist strategy exploits the requirement that any reducing property must be able to do the *explanatory work* of the property it is reducing. In certain areas it is claimed that this requirement is not met. Where the explanatory work is of a causal kind, such a strategy requires the truth of the claims of shapelessness mooted above. For if higher-level properties are needed for autonomous causal explanatory work, reference to such properties is required to establish nomological regularities and support conditional and counterfactual claims which cannot be captured at lower levels of description. Many anti-reductionists make such claims. Without higher-level categories, they argue, some nomological generalizations would not be capturable. (See Jackson and Pettit.) To argue for autonomous causal explanations at levels which fail to reduce is to resist the dichotomy—either overdetermination or reduction—which was the basis of many reductionist claims. But it also requires engagement with the thought, which motivated some reductionists, that the real causal work is done at the physical level, and that everything above that is merely epiphenomenal. Brian Loar, in this volume, challenges the possibility of there being genuine causal explanations at levels which fail to reduce within a framework which is a physicalist one. Jackson and Pettit, in this volume, argue for different kinds of causal explanatory work, allowing for autonomous explanations at higher levels while respecting the primacy of the physical. Other writers have been less convinced that real causal explanation is only found at the physical level, emphasizing that causal explanation is in general interest-relative and that the appropriate level is that level that we would find intelligible.[18] Much of the argument here clearly rests on which notions of causation and causal explanation are to be employed.

Many anti-reductionists point to distinctive non-causal explanatory work done by our higher-level kinds. Reference to intentional states, it is claimed, provides explanations in which things are made intelligible by being revealed to be, or approximate to being as they rationally ought to be'. Evaluative properties have their home in explanations which display our responses as 'merited by' or appropriate to our situation. Both kinds of property are anchored in a project by which we 'attempt to understand ourselves'[19] in a way that transcends the intelligibility which causal explanations can offer. These explanations, it is argued, cannot be captured at the physical level because they depend on normative relations which are not to be found within physicalist vocabulary. (See the papers by Kathleen Lennon and Cynthia Macdonald.) James Griffin examines the role evaluative thoughts play in practical deliberation, which (he claims) could not be accommodated if values were mere projections of desire. Michael Smith also points to justificatory work which would not be possible if what is desirable were reduced to what is desired.

A variant on the claim that higher-level properties are required as the basis for distinctive explanatory work is found in the articles by Quassim Cassam and Cynthia Macdonald. Here the anti-reductionist strategy involves the consideration of the conditions under which a certain kind of thought can exist or be rendered coherent. The argument is that these conditions would be violated if certain proposed reductions were successful. For Cynthia Macdonald the conditions required for the ascription of semantic content rule out the reduction of mental states to internal physical states. Quassim

[18] See H. Putnam, 'Philosophy and our Mental Life', in Putnam, *Mind, Language and Reality*.
[19] McDowell, 'Values'.

Cassam uses similar arguments to resist the suggestion that we can capture what is distinctive of a subject of experience in an impersonal way, for we cannot capture in an impersonal way the constraints on 'I'-thoughts which are constitutive of subjecthood. (See also the related paper by John Campbell.)

These arguments are independent of claims of shapelessness. For even if nomologically coextensive properties could be found, the lower-level discourse would be without the resources to capture the required explanatory work. However, the anchorage of these higher-level properties within such distinctive explanatory projects is one of the principled reasons for suggesting that nomological coextensiveness is unlikely to be found. Outside the intentional and moral domains theorists point to the existence of teleological explanatory structures in biology and social science which appear to be capturable only within the vocabulary of the higher-level discourse. (See papers by Graham Macdonald, Jackson and Pettit.)

A third strand of anti-reductionist argument exploits neither the phenomenon of shapelessness nor the claim that the higher-level properties do distinctive explanatory work. Rather it points to the presence of some essential feature of certain higher-level kinds which is not reflected at the proposed reducing level, for instance their perspectivity or subjectivity. The major recent source of these arguments is the writings of Thomas Nagel.[20] Nagel argues that our psychological kinds contain features which are essentially perspectival, and consequently essentially subjective. These features, he claims, necessarily resist capture within the non-perspectival and objective framework of physical science. For Nagel it is of the essence of our experiences that they involve a point of view of this type; we cannot grasp what it is to have an experience of a certain kind without adopting that point of view. What is involved in grasping that certain physical facts obtain does not require us to adopt a particular point of view. Therefore, he concludes the mental cannot be reduced to the physical. Following Nagel, writers have argued for the essential perspec-

---

[20] 'What Is it Like to Be a Bat?', in T. Nagel, *Mortal Questions* (Cambridge: Cambridge University Press, 1979) and *The View from Nowhere* (New York and Oxford: Oxford University Press, 1986).

tivity not only of psychological kinds, but also of secondary qualities and values.[21]

Nagel's view has been challenged. Christopher Peacocke has argued that the subjective participatory character of certain kinds is a reflection of their mode of presentation, rather than an essential feature of the kind. The charge here is that Nagel has confused concept and quality.[22] Others have questioned whether it is legitimate to move from the claim that a certain position is required to grasp the nature of a kind to the conclusion that the kind itself is essentially perspectival in a way that undermines its objectivity.

In different areas a variety of anti-reductionist arguments have been both employed and challenged. Although the themes of many of the articles in this volume are anti-reductionist, some of the problems inherent in these strategies are explored.

3. REALISM

There are two further major issues which need to be faced by anyone who accepts some form of anti-reductionist argument. The first of these is whether to adopt a realist or non-realist attitude to the properties which fail to reduce. The second, within a context which is avowedly materialist or naturalist, is of how to conceive of the relation between the two levels of discourse, for which a reductionist account has been rejected (addressed in Section 4).

To be a realist concerning a level of discourse is to accept that its statements are true or false and that its names and (perhaps) its predicates refer to genuine entities and properties. Discussions of reduction within the philosophy of science saw the reduction of higher-level explanations and kinds as simultaneously a vindication of their truth and of their reality. Here a distinction was drawn between reduction of theories and their replacement or elimination. Where the latter occurs, we no longer accept the explanations they offer or believe in the

[21] J. McDowell, 'Values', McCulloch, Reply to Peter Smith, 'Subjectivity and Colour Vision'; and McGinn, *The Subjective View*.

[22] 'No Resting Place: A Critical Notice of *The View from Nowhere*, by Thomas Nagel', *Philosophical Review*, 98 (Jan. 1989).

existence of the kinds they sought to individuate. (Given that reductions can be approximate and our knowledge of natural kinds can develop and change, the distinction between reduction and replacement is not always clear-cut, but the distinction is none the less of great importance.) If we accept anti-reductionist arguments, the vindication of our explanations and kinds afforded by reduction is no longer available to us. How then are we to respond to the claim that if reduction is not available, the reality of the properties to which we appear to refer is in doubt? Paul Churchland,[23] amongst others, argues that where our psychological kinds fail to reduce, we should decompose them into as many properties as there are distinct bases, and provide an explanation in terms of these. Our current psychological categories are eliminated. Not all anti-realists are eliminativists in Churchland's mode. Sometimes it is recommended that we maintain a certain discourse for pragmatic purposes, without accepting the reality of the kinds it evokes. Instrumentalists within the philosophy of mind view the interpretation of organisms as intentional systems as dependent on a stance we adopt towards them, which assists predictions and interactions; but no more than that. Brian Loar, in this volume, is sceptical of the coherence of a realist anti-reductionist position which avoids both instrumentalism and dualism of a non-materialist kind.

In the debate between realists and non-realists the issue of explanation again occupies a central position. In moral philosophy, Simon Blackburn takes an anti-reductionist attitude to moral predicates because of the shapelessness of the relevant naturalistic base. He none the less argues against the *reality* of moral properties on the grounds that, if we work with a conception of the world which lacks such properties, we can satisfactorily explain anything which we might invoke such properties to explain, including our moral phenomenology, the quasi-realistic form of our moral discourses, and our ability to project irreducible moral predicates.[24] John McDowell, in

---

[23] P. M. Churchland, 'Eliminative Materialism and Propositional Attitudes', *Journal of Philosophy*, 78 (1981); *Matter and Consciousness* (Cambridge, Mass.: MIT Press, Bradford Books, 1986).

[24] 'Moral Realism'.

response, accepts this argument only in so far as *causal* explanation goes.[25] There are, however, other explanatory tasks (see the discussion in Section 2 above), for which reference to evaluative properties is essential. The issue of realism is particularly acute for those anti-reductionists who base their position on the existence of non-causal explanations. Within philosophy of science the genuineness of properties which do causal explanatory work is accepted. Thus, the task for a realist anti-reductionist there is to show that such causal work is done and done autonomously, and that it is not a mere epiphenomenal offshoot of real causal work done at the base level (see the paper by Brian Loar). However, the case of non-causal explanations is more problematic. If, as many theorists argue, a role in genuine explanations guarantees the reality of a kind, it is necessary to establish the genuineness of the non-causal explanation. (An instrumentalist would argue that merely by adopting the intentional stance we can make the behaviour of machines intelligible to ourselves.) This debate is made more complex by the fact that many of the properties whose reality is challenged appear to possess essentially perspectival characteristics. It is therefore important not to impose conditions for believing in their reality which are appropriate only to scientific properties of a radically different kind.

The debate between realism and instrumentalism is linked with the issue, explored below, concerning the kind of grounding or dependency required between higher-level properties and properties at a naturalist or physicalist level of description. Writers in this volume differ in the extent to which they are impressed by reductionist motivations. For some the failure of classical reduction leaves us with the urgent task of characterizing an intelligible grounding for higher-level properties on a privileged base. Without such a grounding the *reality* of such irreducible properties remains fragile. (See papers by Charles, Cussins, and Loar.) For others, of whom Jennifer Hornsby is an example, the status and reality of higher-level properties is established within their own sphere of discourse, and does not require legitimization from below in order to establish their reality.

[25] 'Values'.

4. SUPERVENIENCE

In recent years materialists who wished to resist full-fledged reduction have often characterized their materialism in terms of the claim that mental properties are supervenient on physical properties. Such a supervenience claim was initially articulated as a claim of indiscernibility. Thus Davidson wrote: 'Mental characteristics are in some sense dependent, or supervenient, on physical characteristics. Such supervenience might be taken to mean that there cannot be two events alike in all physical respects but differing in some mental respect, or that an object cannot alter in some mental respect without altering in some physical respect.'[26]

The notion of supervenience has also been invoked in discussing the relation of natural and moral characteristics, of physical and biological properties, and of colour-free to coloured features. In Davidson's formulation, indiscernibility in all physical respects between two events required indiscernibility in all mental respects. Kim claimed that in this case the presence of certain physical properties would be sufficient for the presence of certain mental properties, a claim requiring the backing of supervenience generalizations.[27] (This claim and the strength of the *modalities* involved in Davidson's account are both matters of debate: see the paper by David Charles.) Davidson's characterization of supervenience linked predicates attributed to individual events, but the relation can be characterized without assuming his event ontology. At its most *global*[28] the relation connects families of properties or predicates. Worlds indiscernible in physical respects are indiscernible in mental respects. At its most *local* supervenience links differential mental (or other higher-level) characteristics to a more restricted range of physical (or other lower-level) characteristics.

Claims of supervenience are capable of two different kinds of interpretation appropriate to different positions regarding the

---

[26] *Actions and Events*, 214.

[27] J. Kim, 'Supervenience and Nomological Incommensurables', *American Philosophical Quarterly*, 15 (1978).

[28] G. Currie, 'Individualism and Global Supervenience', in *British Journal for the Philosophy of Science*, 35 (1984).

reality of the higher-level properties.[29] On one view if we discover indiscernibility, for instance in the physical properties of a world or situation, we are required to attribute indiscernible mental *predicates* to them. Within this *ascriptive form of supervenience*, we are not committed to regarding the relevant mental predicates as picking out genuine properties. So this view is compatible with adopting a non-realist view of mental properties. The source of the necessity attaching to supervenience claims lies in *our* project of justifiable psychological attribution, and not in a genuine metaphysical relation independent of that project. This necessity is intelligible to us because of the goals we set ourselves in making psychological attributions. It depends basically on our concepts and practices. Such a notion of supervenience goes hand in hand with a form of anti-reductionism which is non-realist about certain higher-level properties. It has been advocated most commonly by theorists examining the relation between evaluative and non-evaluative descriptions.[30] Theorists who follow this approach need to explain why our practices of psychological explanation, moral evaluation, or colour perception require us to apply our predicates in such a way that supervenience holds. And this explanation must be given without essentially involving the thought of, for example, physical properties fixing mental or moral properties as part of the order of the world in a way which is independent of our practices.

An alternative to ascriptive supervenience is to construe the supervenience claim in such a way that the indiscernibility of, for example, all physical properties of a world or situation necessitates indiscernibility with respect to their mental properties. Accepting this view, *ontological supervenience*, requires us to adopt a realist view of the higher-level properties in question. But it also demands that we see the necessity invoked not as dependent solely on our practices or concepts, but as a feature of the world. Nor is the necessity involved, in general, taken to be that of efficient causation. For if it were, mental properties would exist 'over and above' physical properties

---

[29] See J. Klagge, 'Supervenience, Ontological and Ascriptive', *Australian Journal of Philosophy*, 66 (1988).
[30] Cf. Blackburn, 'Moral Realism'.

in a way which appears to require an objectionable form of property dualism.

Those who espouse ontological supervenience as a way of characterizing their physicalism or naturalism often advance the further thesis that claims expressed in the discourses of morality, psychology, or sociology are 'true in virtue of'[31] the truths of physics, or natural science (or whatever in their view forms the ontological base). The intention here is to capture both the dependency of the higher-level properties on those at the lower level, and their determination by them. These 'true in virtue of' claims go beyond claims of mere indiscernibility in several respects. Firstly, mere indiscernibility leaves open the possibility of mental properties existing in a world with no physical properties (a possibility which seems genuine for at least unchanging higher-level properties). It depends on the strength of our materialism whether we wish to exclude this possibility in all worlds, or only in those with our kinds of mental state[32] or which share our natural laws. In any event its exclusion constitutes an addition to the bare indiscernibility claim. When we have made such an addition, the occurrence of at least some base properties sufficient for those at a higher level is necessary for the occurrence of any higher-level pro-perties. These ontological claims also embody an asymmetry which is intended to reflect an ontological bias in favour of the base property. It is not an adequate recognition of such an asymmetry to say that physical indiscernibility yields mental indiscernibility but not vice versa. For even if there were two-way indiscernibility, the ontological asymmetry would still be present. For some writers this is adequately captured by the recognition that mental properties cannot occur without physical ones but not vice versa. Others make the different point that the base properties have greater generality or ex-planatory power. For still others, however, this asymmetry reflects the fact that the occurrence of higher-level properties may be *rendered intelligible* on the basis of the lower-level ones, but not vice versa. For such writers these intelligibility claims are required to justify realism concerning the higher-level

---

[31] From H. Field, 'Conventionalism and Instrumentalism in Semantics', *Nous*, 9 (1975).

[32] See Snowdon, 'On Formulating Materialism and Dualism', 143.

properties. (A discussion of these claims and the degree or nature of the intelligibility required is found in the papers by Charles and Cussins.)

When we are considering 'true in virtue of' claims we need to distinguish between the general and the particular. We might argue that *in general* sentences ascribing (certain types of) psychological properties are true in virtue of the truth of sentences ascribing (certain types of) physical state. We might also make the *particular* claim that, on a given occasion, the truth of a given psychological ascription is true in virtue of the truth of a given physical ascription. In the latter case we might talk of the instantiation of the psychological properties as being grounded in that of the relevant physical properties. In the absence of alternative occurrent physical bases sufficient to ground the psychological ascription, the given physical base is both necessary and sufficient for the instantiation of the psychological properties. The difference between general and particular (type and token) claims yields different strengths of intelligibility demand.

The move to these more robust claims of dependency and determination appeals to theorists who are impressed by the force of reductionist arguments, but who none the less reject reduction. The arguments in question primarily concern cases where the higher-level properties are invoked in causal explanation. The challenge from the reductionist is to provide an account which both respects physicalism and rules out overdetermination and the existence of 'miraculous coincidences'. Are the ontological claims mooted above adequate to do this? In a given instance, where the 'true in virtue of' relation holds, the instantiations of the properties at each level are interdependent. The necessity and sufficiency of the psychological antecedents of a given act can thereby be made compatible with the existence of physical conditions sufficient for the bodily movement it involves, without overdetermination (but see the challenge in Brian Loar's paper). Is this all that is required? Many writers argue that it is not. In this volume Adrian Cussins, Graham Macdonald, and David Papineau suggest that this leaves the coincidence of *generalizations* at the two levels in need of explanation. For Macdonald and Papineau this further explanation is given by an appeal to evolution. Others have demanded that the required intelligibility constraints should make manifest how the causal explanatory work done at the higher level is based on the causal explanatory work at the lower level. (For a consideration of this requirement see the papers by Cussins and Charles.) The strength of the relevant intelligibility demands remains controversial. Differences on these matters motivate a *range* of positions all distinct from the picture of the unity of science which attracted classical reductionists.

If we do not accept that certain higher-level properties have a role within causal explanation, insistence on the necessity of a 'true in virtue of' relation remains undermotivated. Our metaphysical bias may be satisfied by a global indiscernibility claim, with an added asymmetry (perhaps explicated in terms of the greater generality of the base properties). James Griffin in his paper expresses scepticism regarding naturalist claims which go beyond supervenience of this global kind. With regard to value properties, he suggests that if we try to isolate the non-evaluative features which are *relevant* to our evaluative descriptions so as to form one side of the supervenience conditionals, we encounter insuperable difficulties. For without an evaluative concept we are unable to detect just what features are relevant.

These are clearly important issues, whose resolution leads to very different forms of anti-reductionism. At this point the precise form of anti-reductionist position to be adopted depends on more general views about the reality of the higher-level properties, the nature of the supervenience or 'true in virtue of' relations to be invoked, and the kinds of intelligible link demanded between the different levels of discourse. These are the issues which need to be addressed and clarified if the currently fashionable anti-reductionist strategies are to prove successful. For without this, appeal to relations of supervenience, and its more robust variants, may merely hold out the false hope that there can be a realist view of certain higher-level properties which avoids reduction (see Brian Loar's paper in this volume).

K.L.
D.C.

July 1990

1

Modest Reductions and the Unity of Science*

Peter Smith

1

The unity of science, conceived of as a programmatic ideal, is now widely held to be indefensible. Jerry Fodor's slogan 'The Disunity of Science as a Working Hypothesis'[1] is characteristic; the very idea of unity is often dismissed as symptomatic of an unjustified physicalist imperialism. And plainly, if we build enough into the programmatic ideal, then we can undoubtedly ensure that it must fail to be realized. What I want to argue here, however, is that there is a conception of the unity of science, more modest than some but still far from trifling, which remains untouched by representative arguments for disunity. In a little more detail: I will first make some outline remarks about varieties of reductionism (for intertheoretic reductions are the stuff of unity). These remarks will then motivate a certain core conception of unity;[2] this will have to be sketched with a broad brush—but the outline will, I hope, be

* A distant ancestor of this paper was read at the Bradford Workshop on Reductionism in September 1988, and later versions were read to groups at Sheffield, Durham, and York. I am indebted to the discussions on these occasions, and also to Tim Crane, O. R. Jones, Gregory McCulloch, and Hugh Mellor

[1] J. A. Fodor, 'Special Sciences: The Disunity of Science as a Working Hypothesis', *Synthese*, 28 (1974); repr. in J. A. Fodor, *Representations* (Brighton: Harvester Press, 1981), 77–115.

[2] Perhaps I should stress at the outset that my concern is with the unity of *science*; I distinguish this from the more all-embracing 'scientistic' idea of the unity of all knowledge—the idea, that is, that *any* body of purportedly fact-stating doctrine must, if it is to be defensible, in some sense reduce to science (ultimately to physics). For present purposes I can leave the question whether, for example, moral discourse is fact-stating but irreducible entirely up for grabs.

recognizable and contentful. We need to distinguish the core ideal from one standard way of filling it out, which we can call the 'strong interpretation'. I readily concede, along with the majority camp, that on the strong interpretation, a general unity thesis would indeed be quite unrealistically strong: but while the strong interpretation may rightly be held to be objectionable, that doesn't in itself damage the core programmatic ideal. Too many have rushed from legitimate worries about the strong interpretation to a blanket condemnation of the very idea of unity. And that is quite unjustified.

2

In his classic discussion in *The Structure of Science*, Ernest Nagel wrote 'Reduction . . . is the explanation of a theory or a set of experimental laws established in one area of enquiry, by a theory usually though not invariably formulated for some other domain.'[3] Reductions in this very general sense are evidently always good things to have, and are often mandatory. If we can explain why theory T_2 holds (or at any rate, holds as well as it does) by appeal to theory T_1, then that is by any standards a worthwhile theoretical achievement. And if theory T_2 makes claims about some domain for which some more inclusive theory T_1 already purports to give a reasonably comprehensive causal account, then maintaining both theories together will indeed require that the applicability of T_2 can be explained in terms of T_1.

To take a familiar example. Classical Mendelian theory gives us a good initial understanding of the patterns of heredity by postulating a genetic basis for inherited characteristics: and if this theory isn't to invoke embarrassingly magical powers, then genes need in some way to be realized in the biological materials involved in reproduction. However, molecular biology plausibly purports to have the resources to give us an adequate account of the causal workings of those biological materials. We need, therefore, to reconcile the success of genetic theory with the pretensions of molecular biology: and we have a

[3] E. Nagel, *The Structure of Science* (London: Routledge & Kegan Paul, 1961), 338.

problem on our hands unless we can explain in terms of T_1 (molecular biology) how it can be that T_2 (classical genetics) is more or less roughly true. The scandal here would not be reductionism—in the current wide sense—but the failure of a reductionist research programme: fortunately, the programme is a resounding success.

For a second example, consider common-sense psychology. This delivers a rough-and-ready understanding of the grounds of intelligent human behaviour: yet neuroscience, very broadly construed, already aims to give us an adequate account of the causal operation of our behavioural control system. And what ensures that the predictions of our causal-explanatory T_1 (neuroscience) will march in step with the deliverances of T_2 (common-sense psychology)? We have another interface puzzle[4] unless we can explain how, in the light of the neuro-biological facts, folk psychology as an explanatory framework can also be applicable and more or less true. Here too, it is not reductionism but rather the prospect of the failure of any reductionist research programme that should be worrying—and, fortunately, announcements of necessary failure by the Churchlands and others seem far too hasty.

These last remarks will of course seem quite excessively tendentious unless it is remembered (1) that 'reduction' is still being used in Nagel's initial very broad sense, according to which the essence of a reduction is simply an explanation in terms of one theory of why another theory works, and (2) that explanations can come in a variety of flavours. There is no necessary implication, for example, that the mode of explan-

---

[4] 'But why is there any greater problem about how my body can obey both psychological and neurophysiological laws than there is about how it can obey the laws of both (say) mechanics and genetics simultaneously?' Because obeying the laws of mechanics *and* genetics just requires exhibiting together suitable patterns of mechanical and genetic properties, where these properties are in a good sense quite independent: but not so with psychology–neurobiology. Some properties which engage with psychological causal explanations (e.g. the property of an action's being an *arm-raising*) require for their instantiation the instantiation of properties which engage with neurobiological explanations (e.g. the property of a movement's being an *arm-rising*). Hence, unlike the mechanics–genetics case, the predictions of a psychological theory could in principle be at variance with those of some neuroscientific theory; so the requirement that the theories 'march in step' is indeed non-trivial.

ation in question has to involve type–type correlations or
identifications between kinds recognized by the two theories.
Nor is there any necessary implication that explaining the applicability of T_2 in terms of an underlying theory T_1 must
mean that T_1 absorbs, supersedes, or eliminates the reduced
theory T_2. Where we *can* smoothly identify ontologies across
theories and handle T_2-explanations as special cases of T_1-
explanations—i.e. where we do have a simple theoretical
unification—then we have what might well be called a *strong*
reduction. Such full-blooded cases of reduction are great when
we can get them: however, as is familiar, theories in the
special sciences frequently resist this kind of thoroughgoing
ontological and explanatory subsumption. But that certainly
does not eliminate all possibilities of reduction in our initial
broad sense; there remains considerable room for more modest
styles of explanation of why certain theories work as well as
they do—and also considerable intellectual pressure to provide
such explanations.

3

Perhaps regrettably, the term 'reduction' has commonly come
to be reserved in the literature for cases of what I just called
strong reduction. It will therefore help to have some more
colourless jargon to hand; so let's henceforth call an explanation in terms of theory T_1 of why theory T_2 works as well as it
does an *explanatory interfacing* of T_2 to T_1. I must immediately
say a little more by way of clarification about the sources of the
pressure to provide such explanatory interfacings.

   It would be wrong, of course, to speak as if neuroscience (for
example) confronts common-sense psychology with another,
much better, way of explaining just the same patterns of
events. If that *were* the situation, then we would indeed be
faced with the unpalatable options of either strong reduction or
elimination. But neuroscience cannot pretend to explain the
patterns that psychology discerns. Explanation is contrastive:
the fundamental form of an explanation is *that p (rather than q_1,
q_2, . . .) explains why r (rather than s_1, s_2, . . .)*, and explanatory
frameworks are in part constituted by the taxonomies of rel-

evant contrasts that they acknowledge. Since neuroscience is simply blind to the taxonomies involved in the explanations of common-sense psychology, it cannot hope to explain, for example, why Alice wrote a cheque, rather than paid cash or used a credit card; it can only yield explanations of (say) why Alice's fingers moved in these trajectories rather than those.

So the pressure to provide an explanatory interfacing between a theory T_2 and some more sweeping theory T_1 does not arise, in the general case, because T_1 already explains exactly what is explained by T_2 (if that means that T_1 already explains the same contrastive patterns as T_2). But suppose, as is often the case, that we can regard T_2 as reclassifying phenomena for which there is already a sufficiently comprehensive causal account at least potentially available at the level of T_1. Suppose, in other words, that we hold that there are causal mechanisms fairly well described in terms of T_1, mechanisms which generate the events that are redescribed and re-explained by T_2. Then the question is pressing: how in that case do the causal mechanisms, discerned at the level of T_1 and thus specifiable without any reference to T_2, come to generate the new patterns discerned by T_2 explanations?

To continue with the example where T_2 is psychology and T_1 neuroscience: Alice's hand movements are, we take it, causally generated by various cellular changes in her musculature, which are triggered by signals from the nervous system that are in turn generated by events in her motor cortex . . . where the causal mechanisms involved operate at the microlevel according to biochemical causal laws which make no mention of the mind (the same biochemical laws that operate quite generally, and equally govern happenings in mindless organisms). We don't pretend, of course, that the conjunction T_1 of our best current neuroscientific theories can deliver a fully correct causal story about the antecedents of Alice's action. And we need not make any play either with the idea of a possible future neuroscience which will be ideally 'complete' (whatever that exactly might mean).[5] It is enough that we take

---

[5] For some discussion of the difficulties in handling the related idea of a complete physical theory compare D. Papineau, 'Why Supervenience?', *Analysis*, 50(2) (1990), 66–71, and T. Crane, 'Why Indeed? Papineau on Supervenience and the Completeness of Physics', *Analysis*, 51 (1991), 32–7.

it that T_1 is broadly on the right lines, that is, is *adequate* in the sense that there actually are causal mechanisms generating the movements of Alice's hands which are roughly as our current T_1 says they are, and which do not involve additional causal ingredients of some radically different kind to those countenanced in T_1. If we do indeed take our current neuroscience to be causally adequate in that modest sense, then we are already faced with the question: how come that the underlying causal mechanisms generate patterns of behaviour such that psychology can get a quite different explanatory grip on the same phenomena? If, modulo worries about determinism, all God needed to do to fix that Alice's fingers moved as they did was to rig up the underlying broadly physical causal workings, how come that her resulting movements can also be seen as actions susceptible to a different kind of explanation? What we need here, in a phrase, is an explanatory interfacing of psychology to neuroscience.

There is a similar pressure to provide an explanatory interfacing in turn between neuroscience and more basic physical science. Changes in cells, for example, are changes in complexes whose parts are subject to physical causal laws, parts whose causal interactions suffice to produce the overall behaviour at cell level—or so at any rate we are inclined to believe. But if that is so, if T_1 (in this case, the physics of atoms) is an adequate shot at describing the causal mechanisms actually generating cell behaviour, then how come that we can also successfully deploy T_2 (now neurobiology) with its distinctive taxonomy of functional types?

4

I have here gestured towards two rather inclusive stages in a project that can be cut finer: developing the project in more detail, we might seek (for example) to interface the study of neural structures with the biology of neurones, interface that with the biochemistry of cell components, and that in turn with the physics of large molecules, which in turn is to be interfaced with the physics of atoms . . . I will return to say a little more about this overall project later (Section 7), but for the moment it should be emphasized that what drives the project is *not* some radical physicalist prejudice. If radical physicalism is the doctrine that in some sense there are only atoms in the void— that the only genuine entities, properties, and facts are the entities, properties, and facts recognized by fundamental physics—then it is precisely a *denial* of such a physicalism that gives rise to the pressure for explanatory interfacings. It is just because we want to take entirely seriously the explanatory pretensions of psychology (for example), that we stand in need of some account of how it is that its explanatory structures work as well as they do, applied as they are to causal complexes, the operation of whose crucial parts are already adequately described by neuroscience. If there is a driving prejudice at work here, it is not radical physicalism but a principle, P, to the effect that the behaviour of wholes is in general causally produced by the behaviour of the parts, so that our explanatory stories about wholes must be consonant with our stories about the causal mechanisms constituted by their parts. Even Tim Crane and D. H. Mellor in their recent anti-physicalist manifesto allow that 'facts about parts often explain facts about wholes'.[6] But the key principle that concerns me is better expressed in terms of *causation* rather than *explanation*; and it is worth noting that, though Crane and Mellor deny that the principle about parts/wholes explanation holds in general, their listed exceptions do not sabotage the use to which I want to put principle P.

Crane and Mellor offer three considerations. They first claim that 'if we take the quantum mechanical description of a quantum ensemble to be complete . . . the superposition principle entails that its properties will not be a function only of those of its isolated constituents plus relations between them'.[7] But whatever the general force of this point (particularly against strong Nagelian reduction claims), worries engendered by quantum mechanical considerations can be side-stepped in the present context. Maybe the constituents of certain quantum mechanical wholes cannot strictly be regarded as *parts* whose causal behaviour can be understood in isolation and which can

[6] T. Crane and D. H. Mellor, 'There Is No Question of Physicalism', *Mind*, 99 (1990), 185–206, 190.
[7] Ibid.

be seen as combining to fix the behaviour of the wholes: in other words, the part/whole distinction may well not (so to speak) go all the way down. But no matter: it goes down far enough to take us to items which are the province of physics– chemistry (e.g. those large protein molecules which are parts of cells which are parts of motor nerves which are parts of the muscle assembly which are parts of my arm which are parts of *me!*); and the doings of such parts causally suffice for the macrophysical behaviour which it is the business of sciences other than physics to explain. So the requirements for explan- atory interfacings of the kinds we mentioned earlier can remain in place whatever we say at the quantum level.[8]

Crane and Mellor's second point is that physics is sometimes 'positively *macro*reductive: Mach's principle, for example . . . makes the inertial mass even of microparticles depend on how matter is distributed throughout the universe'.[9] True: but Mach's principle obviously does not go any way towards showing that (say) the facts about the mass of my parts (and their binding energies) do not fix the facts about the mass of my body.

They offer a third, more humdrum, line of argument. Con- sider a gas sample, whose volume is suddenly halved at constant temperature.

If the gas is ideal, Boyle's law entails that when its pressure settles down again it will be twice what it was. That law does not dictate all the interim behaviour of the sample's molecules—except that it must be such as will eventually double the sample's pressure. That much of their behaviour is determined—and thereby explained—*macrore- ductively* by a law governing the sample as a whole.[10]

Mostly true again. But this plainly doesn't cut against the notion that the microcausal interactions, this time of a gas, causally suffice to produce the macrobehaviour (exemplified as pressure and temperature). Indeed, how else is the gas supposed to get back into equilibrium at increased pressure

---

[8] There are, of course, further pressures (not based on simple part/whole considerations) for requiring explanatory interfacings within physics, between quantum and classical theories.
[9] Ibid.
[10] Ibid. 190–1.

but via the myriad microcausal interactions? And once a micro-theory of gases is up and running, the agreed fact that Boyle's law retains some explanatory clout itself requires explanation by reference to the microfacts—which is precisely what is provided by that familiar explanatory interfacing of the classical gas laws with statistical mechanics.

To fend off a possible misunderstanding, the claim is not that Boyle's law is suspect until the explanatory interfacing is found. If anything it is the other way about. We may be entitled to be a lot more confident in Boyle's law than in any microtheory: and we may reasonably treat it as a constraint on any acceptable microtheory that it delivers the macrolaw at least approximately (which is, I suppose, a 'macroreductive' constraint). Hence the claim, to repeat, is only that where we *do* have a going microtheory, we should require it to be comprehensible in the light of that theory how it is that our relevant macrotheories work as well as they do.

In sum, then, whatever the relevance of Crane and Mellor's points about Mach's principle and quantum physics to global physicalist theses about explanation, they do not matter for our mid-scale concerns when worrying about (say) how the physics–biochemistry and the psychology of humans fit together. And while examples like that of Boyle's law may remind us that not all genuine explanation operates at the microlevel, that was never in doubt—and the point remains that when an ensemble of microparts conforms to macrolaws, we can plausibly require an explanatory interfacing to show how the patterns recognized by the macrolaws are generated by the microcausal interactions.

5

I have already noted that the term 'reduction' has come to be reserved for strong reductions, i.e. explanatory interfacings where one theory simply subsumes the ontology and explana-tory resources of another (so that T_2 is revealed as just a special application of T_1). And it is in turn widely supposed that reductions properly so-called (i.e. the strong ones) will conform to the official model that Nagel himself goes on to endorse. As is entirely familiar, Nagel argues that a reductive explanation of T_2 in terms of T_1 should consist in a straight deduction of T_2 from T_1 plus type–type bridge principles:[11] and on the face of it, if we have a straight deduction, we can expect full-blooded explanatory subsumption.

But matters are in fact much more complex; and we certainly should not treat Nagel's attempt at a formal analysis within the tight constraints of his official DN-model of explanation as a proprietary definition of the very notion of reduction. Let's dub those reductive explanations which do strictly conform to the DN-model 'Nagel-reductions'. Then it is worth noting that (1) even among paradigm strong reductions, very few are strictly Nagelian. Conversely (2), even in the rare cases where we do have a Nagelian reduction, that needn't deliver us a strong reduction in any good intuitive sense.

Point (1) is conclusively established in a series of classic papers from Paul Feyerabend's 'Explanation, Reduction and Empiricism',[12] through to Clifford Hooker's 'Towards a General Theory of Reduction'.[13] Thus, the explanation in relativistic terms of why classical mechanics works as well as it does (and likewise the explanatory interfacing of physical optics to electromagnetic theory, or of classical thermodynamics to statistical mechanics) cannot proceed via a deduction of the old theory from the new, because in each case the theory-pairs are not even consistent. The explanatory strategy in such cases is therefore to provide within the more embracing new theory T_1 an *analogue* T^* of the basic laws of the old theory T_2; i.e. we construct a T^* such that (a) T_1 plus certain conditions C entails T^*, and (b) the internal structural relations and observational implications of T^* correspond sufficiently to those of T_2. Because (a) echoes the official Nagelian requirement on reductions, i.e. that T_2 itself be deducible from T_1 plus additional assumptions, we can call such explanatory interfacings 'quasi-

---

[11] *The Structure of Science*, ch. 11.

[12] P. K. Feyerabend, 'Explanation, Reduction and Empiricism', in H. Feigl and G. Maxwell (eds.), *Minnesota Studies in the Philosophy of Science*, iii (Minneapolis, Minn.: University of Minnesota Press, 1962); repr. in P. K. Feyerabend, *Realism, Rationalism and Scientific Method* (Cambridge: Cambridge University Press, 1981).

[13] C. Hooker, 'Towards a General Theory of Reduction', *Dialogue*, 20 (1981), 38–60, 201–35, 496–529.

Nagelian'. And because of the slackness of the idea of 'sufficient correspondence' in (*b*), there will be a variety of quasi-Nagelian cases, depending on the degree of parallelism between the explained theory and the analogue embedded in the new explaining theory. Where the correspondence is very tight, this enables a charitable cross-theoretic identification of objects, stuffs, properties, etc., and a relatively full-blooded reduction may ensue. For example, in the physical optics–electromagnetic theory case, we have a rather tidy explanatory interfacing, which sustains an identification of light rays with electromagnetic radiation—an identification whose character shows what it is about the nature of light rays that brings it about that they have the properties attributed them by physical optics. At the other extreme, there are cases where the correspondence is at its most shaky and fragmentary, e.g. when we explain why the phlogiston theory worked as well as it did by matching claims about de-phlogisticated gas with claims about oxygen, etc. Here the parallelism between old theory and new theory is merely vestigial, and we consequently have an example of 'explimination' (to use Ronald Yoshida's happy coinage[14]); we explain the partial successes of the old theory while simultaneously eliminating commitment to its ontology. In many quasi-Nagelian cases, however, the correspondence between old and new is neither so tight as to sustain unqualified cross-theoretic identification, nor so loose as to make straight elimination of the old ontology a comfortable option. For instance, should we say that the atomic theory of matter shows that classical continua really *are* gappy ensembles of molecules, or does it rather show that there are no continua, thus eliminating them in favour of the gappy ensembles? Well, say what you will about the intermediate cases: the crucial point is that (in quasi-Nagelian cases) readiness to identify ontologies cross-theoretically should sway with smoothness of modelling—the closer the analogue theory T^* corresponds in structure and observational implications to the old theory T_2, the more apt it is to say that T_1 reveals the real nature of the objects and properties postulated by T_2.

[14] R. M. Yoshida, *Reduction in the Physical Sciences* (Halifax, NS: Dalhousie University Press, 1977).

I will not delay further over point (1), for it should by now
be entirely familiar (though the bald assumption that true
reductions are Nagelian continues to surface in the literature).[15]
The converse point (2) is much less frequently remarked. So it
is worth emphasizing that even in cases that approximate most
closely to the official Nagelian story, reductions need not entail
the supersession or effective redundancy of the explanatory
resources of the 'reduced' theory as articulated in its own
terms. In other words, even the most Nagelian reductions need
not be strong reductions.

Consider elementary fluid mechanics. Textbooks come near
to regimenting this as an axiomatic theory: roughly speaking,
you begin from Newton's laws of motion, the laws of classical
thermodynamics, and the special assumption that you are
dealing with a substance that deforms continuously under
the application of shear stress, no matter how small the stress
may be. From this basis, various results are derived—first
(say) Laplace's equation for incompressible irrotational flow
or the equation for the speed of propagation of normal
shock waves, then (more excitingly) equations modelling
slightly more complex flows, such as Lorenz's model for a
certain system with thermal convection. Now suppose you can
use the molecular theory of the fluid state to show why the
special assumption of axiomatized fluid mechanics concerning
continuous deformation under shear stress holds as well as it
does. Then the basic principles of elementary fluid mechanics
will be constructible within a composite of the molecular theory
of matter, Newton's laws, plus thermodynamics. That would
certainly count as an explanatory reduction by quasi-Nagelian
standards (indeed it comes unusually close to the strict Nagelian
ideal); yet, for all that, it does not give us a case of theoretical
supersession or redundancy in any realistic sense. For even
the modest excitements of elementary fluid mechanics, the
development of its distinctive concepts and strategies, the
characteristic mathematical problems, are all (so to speak) well
downstream from the basic assumptions: and warranting the
basic assumptions of fluid mechanics by reference to a molecular theory of the fluid state just doesn't help us significantly

---

[15] See e.g. D. Owens, 'Levels of Explanation', *Mind*, 98 (1989), 59–79, 62.

with the downstream problematic. The point becomes vivid when we consider slightly more complex fluid systems, e.g. those modelled by the Lorenz equations. The discovery that such systems exhibit regular but non-periodic behaviour, the development of the idea of chaotic dynamical systems, the consequent work on fluid systems which settle on to chaotic attractors—all this current theoretical turmoil, with its own explanatory strategies, is untouched by remarking that the underlying basic principles of fluid mechanics are themselves derivable from more fundamental theories. Explanatory inter-facing here, even by means of a Nagelian deduction of the basic principles of fluid mechanics, is quite evidently not tantamount to theoretical supersession.

Now, I imagine that the underlying molecular theory of the fluid state can in fact provide a pretty uniform account of why it is more or less true of a large range of stuffs in normal circumstances that they deform continuously under shear stresses. However, it could have turned out that the reasons why water and oil (say) deform continuously were quite dif-ferent; yet fluid mechanics—in so far as it is the study of what water and oil have in common in virtue of their continuous deformability—would have cheerfully ignored the microstruc-tural divergence. In other words, so far as fluid mechanics is concerned, the fluid state could have been multiply realizable relative to the microtheory of matter. This 'don't care' attitude to the possibility of multiple realization is characteristic, as Fodor has emphasized, of the 'special sciences', and marks a kind of autonomy from the details of more basic science. The classical macrotheory of fluids, in particular, has a considerable degree of research autonomy from any microtheory; and this autonomy is surely not in the least compromised if it happens to turn out (as I presume it does) that there is in fact a fairly uniform explanation of the continuous deformability of fluids, and so a particularly simple, almost-Nagelian, reduction is available.

Only the most extravagantly formalistic conception of scien-tific theorizing could sustain the thought that basic principles are everything, and all else is mere mathematics; but if this absurd formalism is abandoned, there is no route from the claim that the basic assumptions of some area of science are (near enough) explanatorily reducible by Nagel's formal criterion to the conclusion that we have thoroughgoing theoretical supersession or absorption. So, we do need to divorce the ideas of such absorption from the core sense of reduction, i.e. the explanatory interfacing of theories. In the case of fluid mechanics, the postulated almost-Nagelian intertheoretic reduction shows that our macrotheory of fluids is consonant in its basic principles with our microtheory plus other well-entrenched theories (and also has the means to explain areas of breakdown of the classical macrotheory). So we do not have interface problems—there is no mystery at all about why the developed apparatus of fluid mechanics works as well as it does: for the basics do not float free from our underlying more fundamental theories. Had it had turned out that there is a scattered variety of microstructures for fluids, then we would have needed a corresponding variety of reductive interfacings showing why the key assumption of continuous deformability obtains more or less in each type of case. But, either way, the macrotheory can retain a distinctive problematic and (as we move away from elementary consequences of the basic assumptions) we may allow the possibility of interesting and fruitful research—e.g. the investigation of chaotic flow—whose techniques are *sui generis*.

6

I have argued, then, that even in the limiting case where the explanatory interface between T_2 and T_1 is almost-Nagelian, it doesn't follow that T_2 is immediately rendered explanatorily superfluous. The point of course holds *a fortiori* in cases where the interfacing is more complex.

Consider, to take a first type of example, a high-level theory—e.g. an ecological theory—that essentially invokes functional types and deploys purposive explanation. There is no prospect of extracting purposive explanations from lower-level causal laws plus bridging correlations in the Nagelian style. In fact, Jonathan Bennett has a nice argument[16] which

---

[16] J. Bennett, *Linguistic Behaviour* (Cambridge: Cambridge University Press, 1976), §22.

aims to show precisely that where a generalization *is* Nagel-reducible to a straight mechanistic causal law via type–type bridge principles, then it cannot be a genuinely teleological law. However, given that we do not want to countenance brutely emergent teleology (e.g. we do not want it to be just an independent new fact about the world, undetermined by all the microfacts, that these moths are so coloured in order to camouflage them from predators), then we will need to show in some way or another how the higher-level explanatory framework can possibly be legitimate. We need, in a phrase, a non-Nagelian explanatory interfacing (a 'modest reduction', if you like) of the teleological to the non-teleological.

As is familiar, an elegant solution emerges if we take a selectionist view of teleology. We can say (crudely) that the purpose of the moth's particular colour is to camouflage it from predators just if the capacity to camouflage is part of the explanation of this moth having the colour it has. But how can this be? Well, the capacity to camouflage can indeed be part of the explanation of the colour in the context of a Darwinian story concerning the selection for and survival of moths with that colour. Against the background of a microbiological understanding of the mechanisms of hereditary variation, this selectionist underpinning of the story about the function of the moth's colour enables us to understand how teleological categories can be applicable to a world constituted by physical items governed ultimately by non-teleological causal laws. I do not insist (at least here) that you buy the selectionist account: but some such explanatory interfacing is plausibly required of us if we are to avoid the intellectual discomfort of brutely emergent teleology. And the selectionist story will certainly do to illustrate the key point that there is conceptual room for modest reductions, i.e. styles of explanatory interfacing that fall short of being Nagelian (or even quasi-Nagelian) reductions.

For a second kind of example where we will arguably encounter non-Nagelian explanatory interfacings, I want briefly to consider qualitative dynamics (though within the confines of the present paper, I can only gesture towards an intriguing area).

There are various ways, classically, of describing a particular dynamical system. Take first the case of an idealized pendulum, a simple harmonic oscillator. We can fully describe the system by giving its displacement and velocity at some initial time t_0, together with the appropriate parameter (in this case, the length of the pendulum) which fixes the equation governing the evolution of the system over time. But it can be illuminating to give a more abstract representation of the system, representing the trajectory of the pendulum as a closed ellipse in a two-dimensional phase space (plotting angular displacement against momentum). In this simple example, however, the two forms of description of the system map neatly on to each other; in particular, systems that are similar in terms of their initial boundary conditions and/or the parameters determining their dynamical equations will have similar trajectories in phase space.

Contrast the case of an iron pendulum suspended over three magnets arranged in a triangle (a familiar desk-top toy). Again, allowing certain idealizations, we can fully describe the system by setting down initial conditions, plus various parameters (the pendulum's length, strength of the magnetic fields, the damping constant for air resistance, etc.); all these, fed into the appropriate general equation for a damped pendulum moving in a magnetic field, will determine its trajectory. Alternatively, we can give a more abstract representation of the motion in phase space—since the system is damped by air resistance, the pendulum's trajectory in phase space will wind in a more or less complex way towards one of three point 'attractors', representing the three final stationary states where the pendulum hovers over one magnet or the other. Now, what is fascinating about this simple toy is that there is no general correlation at all between settings of the initial position and velocity and the character of its phase space trajectory. In other words, we can tweak the initial settings by arbitrarily small amounts, and the system can keep flipping from a 'finishes over magnet A' trajectory to a 'finishes over magnet B' trajectory and back again: thus, in some regions, between any two 'goes off an A trajectory' starting-points, however close, there will be a 'goes off on a B trajectory' starting-point. This means that if we take, so to speak, a snapshot at time t_0, what appear as systems of just the same type in terms of their initial settings (i.e. systems which have the *same* initial parameters within the limits of observational error, however finely set) can in fact be completely different when described in terms of their qualitative geometrical behaviour in phase space. So classifications of these pendulum systems in terms of phase space trajectories can cross-cut their classification in terms of initial settings.

Dynamical systems exhibiting this kind of radical cross-cutting between the similarity classes induced by representations in terms of initial-state-plus-equations and qualitative phase space representations are paradigms of *chaotic* systems (though our particular example is not in fact a very exciting one, since in this case the long-term behaviour of the system is so simple—the pendulum just settles down stably on to one of three point attractors: still, it suffices to illustrate the point about cross-cutting). Such systems are deterministic, since the initial state fixes the later trajectory, but quite unpredictable, because the best we can do in practice is fix the initial state to within a certain margin of error; and within that margin of error, there will be some initial states that lead to one type of trajectory, and others to a quite different type of trajectory. The impossibility of even rough prediction based on imperfect knowledge of initial settings means that qualitative studies (of phase space trajectory types, and of the attractors on to which a particular system's trajectories can settle) become our prime means of understanding chaotic systems. However, because of cross-cutting, there is (in the general case) no way that we can Nagel-reduce the categories characteristic of the qualitative geometrical study of phase space dynamics to the more familiar similarity-kinds of initial-state-plus-equations dynamics.

Now, the existence of qualitative dynamical studies of chaotic systems implies that, *if* explanatory interfacings must be Nagel-reductions, *then* even modern dynamics is quite fragmented, with some parts incapable of being interfaced to the familiar and basic initial-states-plus-equations dynamics. But rather than detach, we should contrapose: we need here to allow for another kind of non-Nagelian explanatory story which (like the selectionist story about teleology) will elucidate how a radically cross-cutting but theoretically useful taxonomy can apply, given that the underlying basic laws are as they are.

7

To draw some threads together: Consider briefly the somewhat messy interfacing of classical genetics with molecular biology. This has been significantly disruptive of classical concepts; the most fruitful work on genetics even at the more abstract level is now thoroughly informed by detailed knowledge of the relevant microtheory, and the research programme of molecular genetic theory has pretty well absorbed its classical predecessor. It is probably this sort of case (a rather typical 'strong reduction') that many tend to think of as a paradigm of a theoretical reduction, where the reduced theory is no longer left with anything much by way of autonomous explanatory resources. And it is often supposed that Nagel's official DN-model of reductions fits this kind of case well.

However, we noted (Section 5) that many strong reductions are at best quasi-Nagelian, and also that Nagel-reductions need not be strong. Further (Section 6), reductions—in Nagel's initial broad sense of an explanation in the light of one theory why another theory works as well as it does—may be neither strong nor even quasi-Nagelian. That is to say, the explanatory interfacing of theory T_2 to theory T_1 need not involve type–type identities, need not impugn T_2's research autonomy or entail theoretical subsumption in any strong sense, nor need it be inconsistent with the fact that T_2 deploys a quite distinctive style of explanation.

The demand to provide at least such modest reductions may often be compelling, for in many cases it is arguable (Sections 3 and 4) that we need to be able to see, given the T_1 facts, how some other theory T_2 can hold good of the domain in question. Moreover—and here at last is the pay-off!—*modest reductions can still subserve the old programmatic aim of demonstrating unity*, i.e. of showing how science hangs systematically together, with higher-level theories being shown to have application in virtue of lower-level facts, with basic physics presumably at the most fundamental level of the hierarchy.[17] If we can explain,

---

[17] The traditional programme implies, of course, an ordered hierarchy. Suppose psychology were interfaced downwards to biology, and that in turn to chemistry, and that in turn to quantum mechanics—but that quantum mechanics could itself only be understood by importing psychological

ultimately in terms of relevant physical facts, why a given theory can be successfully applied (within limits), then—even if it resists full-blooded ontological and explanatory reduction to physics—the theory is thereby shown to be consonant with a fundamental intuition driving traditional doctrines of the unity, namely that there is a good sense in which fixing the physical facts fixes everything.

To amplify a little, consider the teleological case again. Such explanations are well entrenched in biology and ecology, and certainly appear to have a respectable role. Suppose it had turned out (and the idea is not incoherent) that the teleological facts are brutely emergent; suppose it had turned out that there is no accounting for the teleological facts by reference to isolable facts about the constituent parts of the biological systems they involve. Then, since the teleological facts dealt with in biological science would sit loose to the microfacts of chemistry and physics, there would (in a very evident sense) be a consequent disunity of science. Needless to say, a vast amount of productive work has been driven by a reluctance to countenance *this* kind of disunity, and by the desire to explain somehow or other why higher-level patterns obtain in virtue of lower-level facts.[18] For example, the research assumption of much work in the ecological sciences is (of course) that the existence of functionally adapted teleological systems is something which can be explained ultimately in terms of micro-biological mechanisms and the selectionist forces operating on them; and this modestly reductive research assumption is thoroughly vindicated by the resounding successes of work based upon it.

A core part of the traditional programmatic ideal of unity (i.e. the fundamental antipathy to disunity) is captured by the

categories ('it is *conscious* observation that collapses the wave-packet'). That would be unity of a kind, but not unity as standardly conceived.

[18] It must be emphasized again that explanatory interfacings are not supposed to make the 'reduced' theory more secure, epistemically or ontologically. We may rightly be more confident that all is well with our molecular chemistry than with our quantum mechanical account of the chemical bond; and in turn we may rightly be more confident of the 'classical' quantum theory of the atom than we are of the latest flavour of quark theory. The search for explanatory interfacings is not a search for foundations, but the attempt to get our various levels of theory to hang together.

thought that this sort of unification by explanatory interfacings can be more systematically brought off. Now, so understood, the ideal is notably more modest than the positivist or strong interpretation of unity, according to which all science can be *strongly* reduced to physics (or, what is mistakenly thought to be the same thing, *Nagel*-reduced to physics). If the old dream of being able to deduce all scientific laws from one 'ever more adequate grand scheme'[19] is construed in Nagelian terms, then there is indeed no hope of realizing it. But, as we have noted, explanatory interfacings may be achieved where even *quasi*-Nagelian reductions are not available. And, while relatively modest, the idea that we can unify by means of modest reductions is very far from nugatory. It is certainly not an a priori truth that this ideal can be achieved to any interesting extent: adherence to a global or partial programme for the unity of science by modest reductions involves high-level empirical assumptions warranted, if at all, by their results in prompting successful research. And, leaving aside the question of modal status, it is quite possible to doubt whether the claim that modest unity can be achieved is even plain true. What I do want to argue, however, is that modest unity claims—construed as claims about the possibility of understanding how higher-level theories are applicable by providing modest reductions—are not vulnerable to various arguments which allegedly establish serious disunity.

8

Consider first Fodor's seminal paper 'Special Sciences'. Fodor quite explicitly adopts the strong interpretation, and takes the hypothesis of the unity of science to be the hypothesis that all science reduces to physics in Nagel's official sense of 'reduce'.[20] I have already readily conceded that this would be an over-strong doctrine; though, given the influence of Fodor's

---

[19] The phrase is from H. Feigl, 'Physicalism, Unity of Science and the Foundations of Psychology', in H. Feigl, *Inquiries and Provocations*, ed. R. Cohen (Dordrecht: Reidel, 1981), 315, quoted by Crane and Mellor, 'There Is No Question of Physicalism', 188.

[20] Fodor, 'Special Sciences', 128.

paper, it is perhaps worth remarking that his arguments for this conclusion are not in fact particularly weighty. He relies on two key examples.[21] The first concerns Gresham's law; and Fodor makes much play with the obviously true point that the monetary transactions to which Gresham's law applies can involve quite disparate physical monetary tokens (gold, cash, cheques, strings of wampum, or whatever). So, he argues, there is going to be no predicate of physics lawfully coextensive with 'is a monetary exchange'; and hence no type–type reduction of Gresham's law to physics. But surely this is a rather thumping *ignoratio elenchi*. The traditional positivist programme would aim to reduce economic facts (like other social facts) to psychological facts in the first instance. And the suggestion would be that different participants in monetary exchanges, while no doubt shuffling different physical tokens, would share certain relevant beliefs and desires—and it is in virtue of *these* shared states, which in turn are to be reduced to physical states, that Gresham's law holds (and not, of course, in virtue of facts about the shuffled tokens). So Fodor's first anti-reductionist argument seems off target. His second argument concerns the non-reducibility of psychology to neurophysiology, and he offers a quick jab with the now familiar multiple realization point. But again, Fodor's version is *too* quick; after all, neurophysiology is a complex business, involving many different levels of description of neural architecture and functioning—and you cannot infer from the conceivability of the multiple realization of mental states at one level that there isn't a higher and more abstract level of functional neural description which identifies a state plausibly type-identical to the mental state.

However, let us happily concede Fodor's conclusion that the strong positivist interpretation of the unity of science is too strong. What really interests me is what Fodor does with the conclusion. For he takes it that, once we have rejected the agreed positivist dream that all science is full-bloodedly Nagel-reducible to physics, then the most that a reasonable physicalist can require is the truth of token identity theories. But absolutely not so; any physicalist worth his salt will insist that,

[21] Ibid. 133–8.

where a low-level theory interfaces with a higher-level theory, we should be able to use the lower-level theory to explain why the basic assumptions of the high-level theory actually obtain. For if, as a physicalist, you hold that all events fall under physical causal laws, then it will be quite unsatisfactory for you also to allow the higher-level laws just to float free; for then why should these higher-level laws happen to produce correlations between events which, token by token, also fall under some physical causal law or other? What makes it more than a miracle that two events which are correlated by a higher-level law also happen conveniently to get correlated by the lower-level physical laws they also fall under? The physicalist needs to understand the unity here.

Suppose we grant for the sake of argument what is in fact disputable, namely that the explanatory interfacing between different-level theories will standardly sustain token identity claims; still, token identity claims are typically only an ingredient or side consequence of such explanatory reductions, and are not explanations in themselves. To help see the point, note that it seems to make sense to suppose that we might achieve a relatively a priori argument for token identities among the events described by two theories (an argument like Davidson's for anomalous monism, for example), without thereby deriving any understanding at all of just how the two theories interface (a point often made, in effect, by Davidson's critics). So, contrary to Fodor, the serious physicalist cannot really rest content with unaugmented token identity claims; he also needs to understand just *how* the higher-level theory can be true given (as he sees it) the ultimately physical constitution of the world—in a phrase, the physicalist will seek to unify science by explanatory interfacings, ultimately taking us down to physics.

There is a similar point to be made about David Owens's more recent 'Levels of Explanation'. Here, Owens seeks to give physics a certain causal primacy while not granting any special status to physical explanations, arguing that 'the primacy of physics does not entail the hegemony of physical explanation'.[22] He defends a (rather Fodorian) thesis of causal pervasion to

---

[22] 'Levels of Explanation', 60.

the effect that, if the occurrence of a (non-physical) S_1 event explains the occurrence of an S_2 event, then there will be subvenient physical states, P_1 and P_2 respectively, such that P_1 is causally relevant to, *but does not necessarily causally explain*, P_2. Although there are problems with this way of putting it,[23] the basic idea that explanations in higher-level theories are not neatly tracked by corresponding explanations at the physical level is surely right. However, while Owens presents his arguments as a thorough reconciliation of the conviction that physics is basic with the obvious fact that science is partitioned into a number of explanatorily autonomous disciplines, in fact his position poses a serious problem for the physicalist. Just as a physicalist cannot rest content with unaugmented token identity theses, so the physicalist who prefers to operate with notions of supervenience rather than identity cannot rest content with an unaugmented thesis of causal pervasion: for the question will be pressed—how can it be that S-explanations are genuine explanations, yet do not track physical explanations, although S-type occurrences are supervenient on the physical facts? Causal pervasion without modest reductions will just be mysterious, so Owens's physicalist is still required to be a unifier.

Consider finally John Dupré's paper 'The Disunity of Science'.[24] Again, his target is essentially the Nagelian formal analysis of reduction, and again the illicit conclusion is that, since there are areas of science which are not Nagel-reducible to physics, any serious idea of the unity of science must be rejected.

Dupré's main example of a non-Nagel-reducible piece of high-level theory is drawn from ecology, and concerns the oscillations in the populations of predators and prey (say, Canadian lynxes and hares). The populations of certain predators and their prey can exhibit cyclical oscillations—for example, the hare population increases dramatically; lynxes thereby do better, breed more successfully, and the population of predators dramatically increases; life gets much tougher for the hares, whose population consequently begins to decline,

[23] See K. Neander and P. Menzies, 'David Owens on Levels of Explanation', *Mind*, 99 (1990), 459–66.
[24] *Mind*, 92 (1983), 321–46.

leading to starving lynxes and a consequent reduction in their population; freed from such a high level of predation, the hare population dramatically increases again, starting off the cycle again. Now, it is an elementary programming task to simulate simple ecologies of this sort with various computer models. And even very crude models roughly reproducing the observed fluctuations are highly informative: typically, they are extremely sensitive to the fixing of parameters such as rates of reproduction and the average time a lynx can survive without a square meal. A relatively stable ecology can be transformed by very small adjustments into a wildly oscillating one, or even into a catastrophic one (in which the lynxes are so successful that they wipe out all the hares, and so die of starvation). But can this sort of simple modelling exercise teach us anything about the unity of science?

Dupré in fact misses a possible trick here; he could have noted that very simple population models actually provide standard examples of chaotic dynamical systems (and so perhaps, as we suggested, the qualitative study of such systems can illustrate a certain kind of Nagel-irreducibility). However, he takes a quite different line. His argument is that the heavily idealized ecological modelling talks of the average propensities for breeding and hare-catching of the average lynx, and that these are not the sort of property apt for type-identification with (say) the actual physical properties of particular lynxes; for no particular lynx may be exactly average in the requisite respects. But this line of thought really does not seem to carry much weight. The modelling process essentially involves a move from talking about real populations exhibiting normal biological variance to talking about imagined homogeneous populations of individuals who each share what are in fact the average characteristics of the real population. Does this really show a radical discontinuity between what's going on in ecological modelling and the study of real individual lynxes? (What about those simple calculations in statistical mechanics in which we pretend that we are dealing with a homogeneous population of molecules, each with the average characteristics of the molecules in the sample of real gas? Should we say that this illuminating kind of modelling is equally inimical to the unity of science?)

I cannot imagine that even Nagel would feel particularly embarrassed by this sort of case. We needn't pause to consider how best to tinker with a quasi-Nagelian formal criterion of reduction to get it to cover the reduction of quasi-nomic generalizations covering the average lynx. For what is quite clear in the ecological case is that we can explain in lower-level terms why the assumptions built into the modelling approximate to the truth. And (given what is non-trivial, that we can also show mathematically that the modelling is reasonably stable in that the qualitative behaviour of a population whose propensities statistically scattered around the average would be much like the homogeneous population), we could therefore explain in terms of lower-level facts why the modelling works as well as it does. In short, there would seem to be no conceptual difficulty of principle in giving an explanatory interfacing with biology and the like for Dupré's ecological modellings (even if the mathematics is non-trivial). And indeed in this case it wouldn't just be physicalist prejudice that was offended by the thought that such an interfacing was impossible (irreducible biological facts, for example, are one thing, irreducible average lynxes quite another!). In short, then, Dupré's key example causes no problems for the notion of the unity of science understood as I have suggested that it should be.

2

Irreducibility and Teleology*

David Papineau

How do such 'special sciences' as psychology, economics, genetics, pharmacology, meteorology, and so on relate to physics? There is currently a widespread consensus among analytic philosophers on this question. Namely, that we should be *physicalists* but *non-reductionists* about the special sciences.

We can take physicalism here to mean the *supervenience* of the special on the physical: if two situations are physically identical, then they must be psychologically (and so on) identical too. Non-reductionism means that any given psychological state will be *variably realized* at the physical level: no common physical property will characterize all instances of any given psychological property. (To avoid unnecessary repetition, I shall sometimes refer to psychology as the typical science. But, unless I say otherwise, my points are intended to apply to the other special sciences as well.)

In this paper I want to show that it is not as easy to combine physicalism with non-reductionism as current orthodoxy supposes. There is an internal tension in this combined position which has received little attention in the literature. I shall argue that this tension can be resolved only for those special sciences that have a teleological underpinning.

1. AN UNEXPLAINED COINCIDENCE

The view I have doubts about is most clearly expressed in Jerry Fodor's 'Special Sciences'.[1] (Donald Davidson's influential

© David Papineau 1992

* I would like to thank David Owens for a number of useful suggestions about an earlier draft of this paper, and the participants at the Reduction Workshop in Bradford in September 1988 for many helpful comments

[1] *Synthese*, 28 (1974).

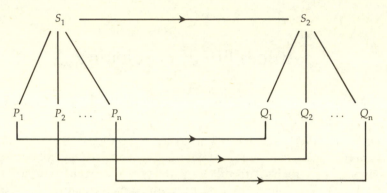

FIG. 2.1. *Fodor's relation between special sciences and physics*

views about psychology also combine physicalism with non-reductionism. But it is important for my purposes that Davidson denies that psychology is any kind of *science*. I shall say something about Davidson in the next section.)

Fodor has a picture of the relation between a typical special science and physics (see Fig. 2.1). S_1 and S_2 are special science categories, and $S_1 \rightarrow S_2$ a special science law. The P_is and Q_is are physical categories, which subvene S_1 and S_2, but don't reduce them: S_1 can be realized by different P_is on different occasions, and S_2 can similarly be realized by different Q_is. Whichever P_k realizes S_1 on a given occasion, however, will lead, by the physical law $P_k \rightarrow Q_k$, to a corresponding Q_k which realizes S_2.

My difficulty with this picture is this. If the different P_is have nothing physically in common, as required by the non-reducibility of S_1, then how come they all give rise to Q_is which *do* have something in common, namely that they are all realizations of S_2? Why should such heterogeneous Ps always yield Qs with this homogeneous feature? (True, Fodor allows that *some* P_ks might not lead to Q_ks that subvene S_2, in order to explain the fact that special science laws typically have exceptions. But this won't affect my basic argument. I shall return to this point in the next section.)

Contrast the kind of situation Fodor has in mind with one where physical reduction *is* possible, such as the standard example in which the classical gas laws, which deal with the temperatures, pressures, and volumes of gases, are reduced by kinetic theory to the basic dynamics of molecular movement. At first sight it might not be clear how this kind of case differs from Fodor's picture. After all, aren't there lots of *different* ways the molecules can be moving around in a gas at a given temperature, thus giving us a heterogeneity of P_is for the S_1 of temperature? But, even so, there is still something physically in common between all those different P_is, namely that the molecules have a given mean kinetic energy. It is this commonality that then enables us to explain such things as why an increase in temperature at constant volume always results in an increase in pressure.

Reducibility to physics does not involve the absurdly strong requirement that the instances of the reduced category should share *all* their physical properties. The requirement is only that there should be *some* physical property present in all and only those instances, which then allows a uniform physical explanation of why those instances always give rise to a certain sort of result.

But that's precisely what we don't have in the Fodor picture. If there's nothing physically in common among the P_is, then there's no possibility of any uniform explanation of why they all give rise to Q_is which subvene S_2. And that's what I find puzzling.

Imagine that the temperatures and pressures of gases were always determined by their internal molecular motions, and temperature increases always led to pressure increases, but yet it was impossible to explain this in terms of basic physics. I take it that this would be incredible. But that's what Fodor is asking us to believe about the other special sciences.

It is worth emphasizing that I am not accusing Fodor's picture of inconsistency, but only of incredibility. It is *possible* that every P_i which realizes S_1 should also just happen to be a P_i that yields a Q_i that subvenes S_2. However, if this were so, it would be the kind of coincidence that cries out for explanation. In general, if a certain kind of result always appears in certain specified circumstances, then we expect there to be some explanation in terms of laws. Fodor's picture, however, commits us to the existence of such a generalization, but denies that it can be explained. I think we ought to reject Fodor's picture rather than accept this.[2]

I am appealing here to a principle that general patterns demand explanations in terms of laws. Some of you might have doubts about the scope of this principle. In particular, you might doubt whether patterns whose formulation requires *special* terminology (that is, patterns like 'every physical *realization of* S_1 leads to a physical state *which subvenes* S_2') need to be explained in terms of *physical* laws. Why shouldn't such patterns simply be explained, you might ask, by the *special* law $S_1 \rightarrow S_2$? However, I would prefer to postpone discussion of this issue until Section 4. My strategy there will be to show that, even if this doubt is reasonable, it won't help the irreducibility of the special sciences. More specifically, my strategy will be to show that the special sciences commit us not just to special patterns that can't be physically explained, but also, underlying those special patterns, to purely physical patterns that can't be physically explained. And this, I shall claim, is certainly in tension with their irreducibility. But it will be easier to explain all this after I have made a number of further initial points.

2. LAWS IN THE SPECIAL SCIENCES

If the argument of the last section does indeed identify a tension in Fodor's way of combining physicalism and non-reducibility, a number of different resolutions are open.

One possibility would be to give up physicalism. If you denied that special categories even supervene on physical categories, then that would immediately remove any pressure towards reduction. For, without supervenience, the physical consequences of the physical accompaniments of S_1 wouldn't

---

[2] For other versions of this argument, see D. Papineau, 'Social Facts and Psychological Facts', in G. Currie and A. Musgrave (eds.), *Popper and the Human Sciences* (Dordrecht: Nijhoff, 1985); J. Searle, *Minds, Brains and Science* (London: BBC, 1984; Cambridge: Cambridge University Press, 1985); G. Macdonald, 'The Possibility of the Disunity of Science', in G. Macdonald and C. Wright (eds.), *Fact, Science and Morality* (Oxford: Blackwell, 1986).

even share the common property of subvening S_2, and so there wouldn't be anything left for the reduction to explain.

I shall not consider this option any further in this paper. We surely don't want to allow that two worlds can be psychologically different even though physically identical. This would be tantamount to accepting dualism. Even less do we want to allow that two situations can differ genetically, or pharmacologically, or meteorologically, without differing physically.[3]

Another line of response would be to give up non-reducibility. You could allow that Fodor's picture was in general adequate, but then conclude that, since physicalism is true, reduction must follow. This is the view I shall adopt for those special sciences that lack any teleological underpinning.

A third form of response would be to add something to, or subtract something from, Fodor's model of the special-physical relation, in such a way as to remove the tension. For example, when I eventually argue that the teleological underpinning characteristic of some special sciences accounts for their being non-reducible even though supervenient, this will then resolve the tension by adding a teleological element to Fodor's picture.

In this section, however, I want to examine the possibility of resolving the tension by subtracting something from Fodor's picture. In particular, I want to consider what happens if we drop the Fodorian assumption that psychology is a science.

Note that my argument for a tension between physicalism and non-reducibility made essential appeal to the existence of lawlike generalizations at the level of the special sciences. The problem with Fodor's model was: why are the heterogeneous physical realizations of S_1 always followed by states which subvene S_2? But this is only a problem if S_2 *does* always follow S_1: if it doesn't, then the consequences of S_1's realizations won't any longer share the puzzling commonality of always subvening S_2.

So the proposed argument, that you can't have physicalism without reducibility, only applies to special categories that enter into lawlike generalizations. It probably doesn't apply

---

[3] In my paper 'Why Supervenience?', *Analysis*, 50(2) (1990), I investigate exactly why we don't want to allow such things, and I use the answer to explain how 'physics' should be understood in connection with issues of supervenience and reduction.

to aesthetic categories, for instance. It seems plausible that aesthetic categories supervene on physical categories: two situations can scarcely differ aesthetically if they are physically identical. But since it also seems likely that aesthetic categories, such as 'beautiful' or 'tragic', don't enter into any serious lawlike generalizations, there need be nothing puzzling about the failure of aesthetic categories to reduce to the physical. If there are no generalizations framed in aesthetic categories in the first place, then there is no need for physical reductions of those aesthetic categories to explain those generalizations.

However, you can only resist reductionism in this way if your denial of special laws is whole-hearted. Fodor holds that the laws of the special sciences have exceptions, and takes it to be a virtue of his model that it can explain this: his thought is that some of the Q_is which follow from the realizations of S_1 won't subvene S_2, and that in those cases we'll get exceptions to the $S_1 \rightarrow S_2$ law. But, still, Fodor continues to hold that S_1 *usually* leads to S_2, or *tends to* lead to S_2, or some such. And this in itself will be puzzling, just as before, unless the realizations of S_1 *usually* have a common physical characteristic to explain why their physical consequences *usually* subvene S_2.

So, by denying that the laws of his special science are exact, Fodor can resist the argument for an exact reduction. But he still faces an argument for an approximate reduction, as long as his special science contains approximate laws. There is, I think, a general pattern here. By weakening the extent to which a special science contains general truths, you can weaken the extent to which its categories have to be reducible to physics. But you can only avoid reductionist conclusions completely by denying that the special categories enter into general lawlike patterns at all.

By way of further illustration, consider a suggestion made by Davidson. In general Davidson is sceptical whether serious laws can be framed in psychological terminology. However, in his paper 'Hempel on Explaining Action'[4] Davidson offers the suggestion that the generalizations involved in explaining actions are always *person-specific*. We can know that Jim, say,

---

[4] In D. Davidson, *Essays on Actions and Events* (Oxford: Clarendon Press, 1980).

will buy an ice-cream when he wants one, will lose his temper if he thinks someone has been rude to him, and so on. But at the same time there are other people of whom these things aren't true. And so, even if we can know a law which applies to Jim, this doesn't mean that there are psychological laws ranging over people in general.

My immediate concern here is not to evaluate this ingenious suggestion, but just to point out that the reductionist argument still gets some grip on even this minimalist Davidsonian conception of psychology as a generalizing science. Davidson still holds that it is a general truth that if Jim wants an ice-cream, he buys one. And this itself would be mysterious unless there is at least a uniform physical realization of Jim wanting an ice-cream.[5] Perhaps this amount of reduction isn't much. But it's still something, given that even Jim's wanting an ice-cream can in principle be realized by different physical states in different instances of Jim wanting an ice-cream. Once more, the moral is that, in so far as generalizations of any kind are admitted in a special science, to that extent there will be an argument for a corresponding amount of reduction.

As it happens, I find Davidson's minimalist view of psychology implausible. I think that our ability to predict human responses testifies to our implicit grasp of a truly general, even if essentially approximate, psychological folk science. This is not the place to defend this view, however. My arguments are more concerned with the question of what follows *if* there are laws in psychology and other special sciences, than with whether there are actually any such laws. Still, it will smooth my exposition to assume psychological laws henceforth. Readers who are unhappy with this assumption can reinterpret my subsequent arguments hypothetically, as addressing the issue of what consequences would follow from such laws, if there were any.[6]

---

[5] In fairness to Davidson, it should be noted that he takes the relevant generalizations to be *dispositional* as well as person-specific. This raises further issues, which I discuss in the next section.

[6] This is in fact the attitude to the suggested argument for reduction adopted by Searle in *Minds, Brains and Science*. Searle doesn't endorse the premiss that the special sciences contain laws. Rather he views the suggested argument as a *reductio* of that premiss: if there were special laws, then the categories of the special sciences would have to be reducible to physics; and so, since the

3. FUNCTIONALISM AND DISPOSITIONS

There is one obvious way in which S_1 could be variably realized and yet there be no mystery about a general law linking S_1 and S_2. Namely, if S_1 were a *dispositional* term, *defined* as the state of being disposed to give rise to S_2 in appropriate circumstances. In that case there wouldn't be any further need to explain, via some physical reduction of S_1, *why* the different realizations of S_1 all give rise to S_2: giving rise to S_2 is precisely what makes those different states all count as realizations of S_1 in the first place.

It is possible that this conception lies behind the widespread acceptance of Fodor's picture. Fodor, and many other contemporary philosophers, favour *functionalist* definitions of special categories in general, and of psychological categories in particular. Functionalism is the view that special categories can be defined as states that enter into specified *structures of causes and effects*. This is an addition to the Fodorian model as laid out so far, in that it adds a specific account of the nature of special categories to the general picture of the special-physical relationship. And, in connection with present purposes, it is an addition that promises to dissolve the tension between physicalism and non-reducibility, by assimilating the categories of the special sciences to dispositional notions.

However, even if we add functionalism to Fodor's picture, problems remain. The basic difficulty is that functionalist concepts aren't so much dispositional concepts as *theoretical* ones. Functionalism defines special categories not just as states which produce certain effects, but rather as states which enter into a certain structures of causes *and* effects. According to a functionalist picture of psychology, for example, pain will be defined not just as the state that characteristically causes avoidance behaviour, but also as the state that characteristically *results* from bodily damage; again, the belief that there is an ice-cream in front of me will be defined not just as the state that characteristically causes me to reach out if I want an ice-cream, but also as the state that characteristically *results* from my looking at an ice-cream with my eyes open. In general, in

categories of the special sciences clearly aren't reducible to physics, there can't be any special laws.

terms of Fodor's diagram, functionalist definitions of S_1s generally allude to their resulting from S_0s, as well as to their causing S_2s.

This now means that the argument against S_1 being variably realized once more goes through as before. We can put it like this: if the various realizations of the state which arise *from* S_0 have nothing physically in common, then how come they all alike give rise *to* S_2? If the various realizations of the state which arises when people look at an ice-cream have nothing in common, how come they all alike lead to their reaching out for it?

The presence of S_0 as an independent criterion for the presence of an S_1, independent of S_1's effects, means that we can't any longer simply account for S_1's realizations all yielding S_2 by saying that's what *makes* them realizations of S_1. For now something else also makes them realizations of S_1, namely, that they arise from S_0.[7]

It is perhaps worth pointing out that I am not here raising any difficulty for fuctionalism understood merely as the claim that psychological states can be defined in terms of structures of causes and effects. The problem I am worried about arises only when functionalism in this sense is combined with the thesis that psychological states are variably realized. So I would have no argument against a functionalist who insisted that our *concept* of pain is a concept of a state with certain perceptual causes and behavioural effects, and not a concept of any specific physical state. My concern is only to point out that, unless there *is* a specific physical state which generally realizes pain, albeit an unknown one, it would be a mystery why those

---

[7] Some philosophers suggest that psychological generalizations are analytic, on the grounds that failures of psychological prediction always reflect on the initial conditions, and not on the psychological generalizations themselves (see J. Haldane, 'Understanding Folk', *Proceedings of the Aristotelian Society*, Supp. Vol. 62 (1988), §4). I have my doubts about this view: after all, wouldn't it be *better* to let the failures reflect on the psychological generalizations, given that we use them to predict? But let that pass. Even if psychological generalizations *per se* are analytic, the problem raised by the variable realizations of psychological states is still present. For the suggested argument will still apply to non-analytic regularities of this form: *apparent* satisfaction of the initial conditions usually leads to the predicted result. These regularities will still be puzzling if psychological states are variably realized.

perceptual causes are generally followed by those behavioural effects.[8]

A connected point. I am exploring an argument for the conclusion that the categories of the special sciences must be reducible to physics. This is not an argument, however, for the conclusion that the practitioners of the special sciences have to *know* that reduction. For, even if such a reduction is in principle available, you don't necessarily have to know it to have an adequate conceptual grasp of the relevant special categories, and hence be in a position to investigate them empirically. After all, the classical gas laws were well known long before kinetic theory was developed. (This point would be too obvious to be worth making, were it not for my suspicion that many people are attracted to 'functionalism', in the strong sense of variable realizability, because they think that without it the special sciences would be under an unfortunate immediate obligation to produce physical reductions of their categories. But of course there are plenty of other possible justifications for not producing immediate reductions, apart from functionalism in this strong sense.)

David Lewis combines a functionalist account of the meaning of psychological concepts with the view that those states are uniformly realized in any given species.[9] Up to a point this position circumvents the difficulty I am raising. Within any given species, so to speak, there is no puzzle about why the state that arises from S_1 always gives rise to S_2, for by Lewis's own account that state will be a homogeneous physical state which will lead to S_2 as a matter of physical law. However, there does remain a problem across species. If the central states that result from bodily damage in octopuses and dolphins and humans are all so different, how come they all lead to avoidance behaviour? Of course, behavioural or neurophysio-

[8] Thus, for those who think in terms of possible universes, I have nothing against the thought that there are conceptually possible universes in which pain, say, is realized by a different state from the state which realizes it in this world. What would raise my puzzle, however, would be universes *within* which pain was variably realized and yet had uniform effects. (Not that such universes would be impossible. As I observed earlier, my complaint is one of incredibility, not of inconsistency.)

[9] 'Mad Pain and Martian Pain', in N. Block (ed.), *Readings in the Philosophy of Psychology*, i (Cambridge, Mass.: Harvard University Press, 1980).

logical observation of each such species could show us *that* the various central states in question all give rise to avoidance behaviour, that is, could show us *that* all these species had states that fitted the general functionalist definition of pain. But, without further explanation, there would still be a puzzle about *why*, despite their physical differences, the different central states that arise from bodily damage should have the same effects. (By now a solution to this puzzle will no doubt be suggesting itself. Namely, that these states all have the same effect because they have all been naturally selected to produce that effect. But let us leave this solution until Section 6. My current concern is only to establish that there is a puzzle here to be solved.)

The argument of this section is not intended to imply that dispositional concepts in general must be physically reducible. To return to an earlier example, beauty is arguably definable as a dispositional concept, namely, the characteristic of producing a certain kind of response in suitable observers. But, as I said earlier, provided the notion of beauty doesn't enter into any laws (apart, that is, from the definitional 'law' that beautiful objects cause suitable observers to judge they are beautiful), there is no reason to expect beauty to be reducible to physics.

The same point applies to many other dispositional concepts. Redness, for example, is arguably definable as a dispositional characteristic of objects, namely, the characteristic of producing a certain kind of perceptual response in normal observers. But it remains perfectly possible that there is nothing physically in common between all the different objects that produce this response. It is true that if the notion of redness entered into certain kinds of further laws, then there would be reason to expect a reduction. But the mere fact that all red things make normal people see red doesn't itself give reason to expect reducibility.[10]

---

[10] I am here thinking primarily of irreducibility to intrinsic physical characteristics of red objects, such as the molecular constitution of their surfaces (cf. P. Smith, 'Subjectivity and Colour Vision', *Proceedings of the Aristotelian Society*, Supp. Vol. 60 (1987).) But there also seems to me no immediate reason (*pace* Smith) for thinking that redness *must* be reducible even to such relational physical characteristics as transmitting certain wavelengths of light in certain sorts of illumination. Indeed, there arguably isn't even any immediate reason for supposing there *must* be something physically in common even between

Again, the biological notion of fitness is arguably definable as a dispositional characteristic of biological traits, namely, the characteristic of enhancing survival better than alternative traits influenced by the same genetic locus. But it would be wrong to expect just because of this that there will be anything physically in common between different fit traits and the ways they enhance survival.

Of course, if we want to explain the display of a disposition by reference to that disposition itself, as when we explain someone's visually judging something to be red by reference to its redness, or when we explain some trait's selection by reference to its fitness, then we will be committed to the disposition as something more than *just* the property of producing that effect. But this commitment to 'something more' could just be that there is *some* physical basis for the production of the effect. And this commitment can thus leave it open that the physical basis might be different in different instances of the dispositional property.

Let me emphasize the requirements for the irreducibility of a dispositional property. Such irreducibility requires that the property not enter into any substantial non-dispositional laws, that is, that there not be any uniform *cause* for the *different* physical bases of the disposition, nor any uniform *effects* which aren't themselves effects of the purely dispositional definition. These are fairly strong requirements, but I see no reason to suppose that they are not satisfied in plenty of familiar cases. For example, I take it that redness does not in fact have any such uniform causes or uniform effects. There is surely no uniform physical cause for all the different physical bases for redness, nor, arguably, any uniform effect of redness independently of its uniform effect on observers. And similarly with fitness: there is no single cause of all the different physical properties which make different traits fit, nor any uniform effect of those properties apart from their influence on survival.

the way different people *respond* perceptually to red objects: couldn't each person learn *some* physical way of reliably responding to what everybody else called 'red', but with different people doing this in physically different ways? But perhaps this last extreme anti-reductionist conjecture is in tension with the ability of different people to agree in identifying a previously unobserved kind of object as red, even when that kind has nothing except its redness in common with other red objects.

Which is why, once more, there is no reason to expect redness or fitness to be reducible.

We might wonder why dispositional concepts are useful, if they cover a heterogeneity of different physical bases, and have no uniform causes or effects apart from their defining display. However, there are obvious reasons why it might sometimes be useful to classify things together just in virtue of their producing a certain kind of effect. An interior designer doesn't care about the physical constitution of a fabric, nor even about how it was made, but simply about the colour responses it will produce in humans. Again, suppose we are interested in predicting the spread or extinction of some biological trait. All we need to know is its fitness, not its physical nature or its developmental history. If two different traits have the same fitness relative to their competitors, then they will evolve in the same way, whatever the other differences between them.

4. NO COINCIDENCES

My complaint about Fodor's picture has been that it postulates inexplicable coincidences. It commits us to the existence of certain patterns, while denying that those patterns can be accounted for uniformly in terms of physical law. There is nothing of course wrong with the idea of a *local* coincidence, of events falling into significant patterns on a few particular occasions, even though there is no explanation in terms of laws. But *general* coincidences are different: if certain types of event *always* tend to go together, then there must be some causal connection between them, or they must be joint effects of a common cause, or some such. Yet, in the Fodor-type cases, S_1 always goes with S_2, even though at the physical level there is no uniform causal connection between them.

However, as I pointed out at the end of Section 1, even if it is agreed that patterns always require explanation in terms of laws, it isn't clear that patterns which make essential use of *special* terminology ('All realizations of S_1 give rise to realizations of S_2') need to be explained in terms of *physical* laws.

Why shouldn't this pattern just receive the obvious explanation that there is a *special* law that S_1 generally leads to S_2?

My response to this query is to note that the laws of the special sciences don't just relate special categories to other *special* categories. There are also laws relating categories of special sciences to *physical* categories. There are certain physical circumstances that have uniform mental effects, as when, say, I sit on a drawing-pin and feel a pain; and there are certain mental circumstances that have uniform physical effects, as when, say, a competent typist wants to write a certain word and strikes the keyboard accordingly. The point is even more obvious in connection with non-mental special sciences like genetics, pharmacology, etc. Indeed functionalist accounts of the special sciences make explicit and essential use of such 'mixed' laws, in that functionalists hold that the categories of the special sciences are defined by their lawlike relations to each other *and* to their *non-special* causes and effects.

Let us now focus on some special category S_1 which is related to *physical* categories R_0 and R_2 by laws $R_0 \rightarrow S_1$ and $S_1 \rightarrow R_2$. If we continue to suppose that S_1 is variably realized at the physical level by different P_is, then we will be committed to the consequence that whenever any such P_i results from R_0, it will give rise to R_2. And this is surely an inadmissibly inexplicable coincidence. For now we have an unequivocally *physical* pattern, namely, that whatever results from R_0 leads to R_2, and yet, according to Fodor's picture, this physical pattern lacks any uniform physical explanation.

The point can be generalized. Even if a given special category S_1 only appears explicitly in laws linking it to other special categories, these other special categories will eventually be linked by further laws to non-special causes and effects. Which means there will be derived laws linking S_1 itself to those non-special causes and effects. And this, as before, would appear to be an inexplicable coincidence in the absence of a uniform physical reduction for S_1.

5. REDUCTION

One question raised by Fodor's diagram is whether there really is a principled difference between reduction and variable realization: for, given the way Fodor sets things up, why shouldn't we simply disjoin the various P_is which realize S_1, and then say that S_1 reduces to $(P_1 \lor P_2 \lor \ldots P_n)$?

Fodor's answer to this challenge is to insist that this disjunctive property $(P_1 \lor \ldots P_n)$ won't in general be a genuine *natural* physical kind, and the generalization $(P_1 \lor \ldots P_n) \rightarrow (Q_1 \lor \ldots Q_n)$ won't therefore be a genuine *law*. However, Fodor's analysis stops here. As he admits, he has no explicit account of what makes some kinds natural and others not, and so at this point simply rests his case on intuitions.

Other anti-reductionists have adopted a rather more sophisticated approach. Instead of resting their case on intuitions about whether the disjunction $(P_1 \lor \ldots P_n)$ is a natural kind, they have pointed out that the relevant disjunction might be infinitely long, or indeed might not even be finitely specifiable,[11] and that therefore the question of any reductive *explanation* of high-level laws in terms of lower-level ones doesn't even arise.

This more sophisticated line is certainly of technical interest. But I would like to point out that the argument of this paper adds weight to Fodor's simple approach to the question of what *counts* as a reduction (though of course disagreeing with him on when such reductions are *needed*). This is because the argument of this paper shows that even a finite disjunction of different physical states yields enough non-reducibility to be *implausible*.

Imagine that a given disease is produced by well-defined causes (a certain kind of diet, say) and has well-defined symptoms (a certain kind of skin rash, say). But now imagine that we discover there are two quite different physical processes by which the cause leads to the result: in some patients, say, there is a virus acquired from the food, but nothing else wrong, while in others there is no virus, but a certain metabolic deficiency. The obvious question raised by this discovery is 'If the diet causes the disease by two quite different paths, then how come we get the *same* symptoms in both cases?'

With just two alternative paths from cause to effect, we

might be happy simply to accept that the world is just like that, that these two quite different internal mechanisms just happen to have the same symptomatic upshot. But now imagine that there are, say, fifty distinct paths from cause to effect: fifty quite different viruses and deficiencies which people get from the diet in question, but which, despite their differences, all produce the same skin rash. That would surely be quite incredible.

Of course it would be even more incredible if an unspecifiable infinity of different processes resulted from the diet, and yet all produced the same skin rash. But even a finite disjunction seems incredible. And this now yields a non-arbitrary rationale for saying even the finite disjunction isn't a physical natural kind.

In effect I am suggesting that the notion of a reduction is precisely the notion of an account which shows that nothing incredible is happening at the physical level. Fodor says that a finite disjunction is not a reduction because the physical categorization involved isn't 'natural'. I am adding the thought, not available to Fodor himself, that this lack of 'naturalness' resides in the fact that such disjunctions are too heterogeneous for it to be plausible that there should be no further explanation for the disjuncts all producing the same effect.

6. TELEOLOGY AND IRREDUCIBILITY

Despite the argument I have been developing in this paper, I don't in fact think that *psychological* categories are reducible to physical ones. It is high time I explained why not.

By way of an analogy, consider this example. All domestic water heaters contain thermostatic devices which stop the heating when the water gets hot enough. If we denote the threshold temperature by R_0, the thermostat operating by S_1, and the heating stopping by R_2, then we have the generalization, applicable to all domestic devices that heat water, that $R_0 \rightarrow S_1 \rightarrow R_2$. However, there clearly isn't any physical reduction of S_1 here: there are many different kinds of thermostat, with quite different designs and constitutions, and with nothing physically in common apart from their all turning the heater off when the water gets hot enough.

Even so, there is scarcely much of a puzzle here about *why* all the physically different realizations of S_1 produce the common result R_2. The obvious answer is that water heaters are *designed* by people not to burn out, and that's why they all contain thermostats that switch off the heating when the water gets hot enough. We can say the mechanisms in water heaters have been selected by the designers *in order to* switch the water heaters off. That's what the thermostats are there *for*.

Another example. All vertebrates who breed within a fixed location will act towards invaders of that territory in such a way as to frighten off those invaders. Here let R_0 be the invasion of the territory, S_1 the characteristic behaviour, and R_2 the departure of invaders. Then, plausibly, for such animals, $R_0 \to S_1 \to R_2$. Yet there is no physical reduction of S_1: there is nothing physically in common between all the different forms of territorial behaviour displayed by vertebrates, apart from the fact that they all make intruders go away.

But, once more, there is scarcely anything puzzling here. The obvious explanation for the fact that these physically different kinds of behaviour all have the uniform effect of frightening away intruders is that natural selection has favoured those behaviours precisely *because* they frighten away intruders. As in the previous example, the different physical causes have all been selected *in order to* produce that effect.

I favour the 'aetiological' theory of teleological notions like function, purpose, and design.[12] According to this theory, it is appropriate to say that item X has the function of doing Y just in case item X is now present *as a result* of causing Y.[13] The paradigm for the aetiological theory is where X has been *naturally selected* by a mechanism which picks out things that cause Y, as in the case of biological evolution by genetic selection. But the aetiological theory can also be extended to cover artefacts like thermostats, and indeed human actions in general, since human decision-making can itself be thought of

[12] See L. Wright, 'Functions', *Philosophical Review*, 82 (1973), and K. Neander, 'Abnormal Psychobiology', Ph.D. thesis, La Trobe University, Melbourne, 1984.

[13] It is unfortunate that 'function' and its cognates are used both for the teleological notion of causes that are *explained* by their effects, and for the definitional notion of concepts that can be *defined* as elements in a structure of causes and effects. The two ideas are quite distinct.

as a mechanism that selects artefacts and actions because they produce certain effects.

Not everybody agrees about the aetiological account of teleology. Some people will want to put scare quotes around words like 'purpose' and 'design' when they are used in connection with blind mechanisms like genetic natural selection. But we need not spend time on this issue here. For the terminology of 'purposes' is not essential to my central point— namely, that there is nothing puzzling about physically quite different things all having the same effect, if those physical things are all products of some mechanism which selects items *because* they have that effect. Adherents of the aetiological theory will be able to express this point by saying that there is nothing puzzling about the non-reducibility of some special science's phenomena, if those phenomena are there for a purpose. But others can put scare quotes round 'purpose' here if they like.

Let us now consider the specific question of the reducibility of the generalizations of psychology. Here another kind of selection mechanism, different from both biological genetic selection and from intelligent decision-making, becomes relevant. This is selection by individual psychodevelopmental *learning*. There are good general reasons for supposing that individual learning, at least in its early stages, must involve some innate tendency to enhance those neural pathways which lead to certain kinds of result, and to discourage neural pathways which lead to other kinds of result.[14] In this sense learning is itself a mechanism that selects items because they produce certain results.

As with all selection mechanisms, the items between which this mechanism chooses will be relatively random, depending on such things as idiosyncrasies of individual circumstance, or on previous training, or even on genuinely chance occurrences in the brain. (Compare the 'mutations' which are inputs to genetic selection.) From the point of view of learning, the

[14] Cf. D. Dennett, *Content and Consciousness* (London: Routledge & Kegan Paul, 1969), ch. 3.

precise physical nature of the relevant items doesn't matter, provided they produce the right kind of effect.

And this, finally, is why there is no reason to expect there to be anything physically in common between two people when they both believe, say, that there is an ice-cream in front of them, even though this state has similar effects on their behaviour. The physical realizations are likely to be different simply because the inputs to each individual's learning mechanism (the 'mutations') will be relatively random. But we needn't be puzzled about how there can be similarity of effects without the physical commonality, for the one thing that the learning mechanism *will* have ensured is that the different states which arise when different people look at an ice-cream will at least share the feature that they will produce appropriate effects in appropriate circumstances (such as reaching out for it when you are hungry).

The presence of selection in individual learning enables us to understand not only how mental states with common effects can be variably realized in different species, as David Lewis allows, but also how they can be variably realized within the same species. Innate mental states with common effects get to be variably realized in different species in virtue of the fact that genetic natural selection will preserve any genetic mutation with the relevant beneficial effect, where such mutations are likely to be different in different species. Entirely analogously, if each individual contains a learning mechanism which preserves any 'physiological mutation' with certain beneficial effects, and if these physiological mutations are different in different individuals, then the upshot will be that even among conspecifics we will find variable physical realizations of mental states with common effects.

Actually, in the case of the mental state that Lewis himself concentrates on, namely, pain, there *is* a reason to expect uniform realizations within species. For pain is best thought of as *part* of our learning mechanism, rather than as the kind of mental ability that this mechanism *produces*, given that learning selects precisely those mental items that *don't cause pain*. Since our basic ability to learn isn't itself learnt, but a consequence of our genetic endowment, this is then a reason for thinking that pain, and similar basic mental states like hunger, cold, and so on, are uniformly realized within species.[15]

So far in this section I have indicated a way of understanding how various biological and psychological non-dispositional categories might have uniform effects even though variably realized: such variable causes can have uniform effects in virtue of mechanisms which select items because they have that effect. The corollary, however, is that we shouldn't expect non-reducibility in those special sciences where no such selection mechanisms are to hand.[16] This seems to me to include nearly all special sciences apart from biology and psychology. Perhaps there are some rudimentary selection mechanisms in some of the social sciences, in the form of economic or social competition. But there are certainly none in such special physical sciences as meteorology or chemistry. In any case, the general moral should be clear: special categories that aren't products of selection will be reducible.[17]

[15] This point might seem open to dispute. If, within a species, two physically different genes produce exactly the same phenotypic effects in different ways, then both genes will equally be preserved by natural selection. Indeed, short of knowledge of the details of the DNA components, two such genotypes are likely to be counted as one by biologists. This suggests the possibility of two physically different types of pain within one species. However, it seems unlikely that variant physical components in such a complex mechanism as pain would ever have exactly the same selection-relevant effects. This case is different from the case where we're considering different species, for in different species natural selection will favour different physical bases for roughly the same job as long as they have roughly similar effects. But within an interbreeding species there will be direct competition between such physical alternatives, and so such alternatives will both be preserved only if they have an exact selective equivalence.

[16] Why should appeal to selection mechanisms be the *only* way of explaining away non-reducibility? But what else could account for the fact that physically disparate items have the same effect, except some mechanism that picks them out because they have that effect?

[17] Of course, reducibility to *physics* won't be at issue for sciences whose entities are partly psychologically constituted, like sociology or economics, or partly biologically constituted, like demography or epidemiology. For, even if such sciences are reducible to psychology or biology, the selection-based irreducibility of the latter sciences to physics will block the overall reduction. However, the point remains that the absence of selection mechanisms *within* such sciences as sociology or demography will imply that such sciences will at least be reducible to their psychological or biological constituents. The point is illustrated by Fodor's example of Gresham's law (bad money drives out good). Fodor stresses the extreme implausibility of any uniform *physical* realization of such categories as good and bad money. But it is worth noting that there are

7. SELECTIONAL EXPLANATIONS

An obvious question raised by the argument of this paper is the status of selectional explanations themselves. I have argued that in disciplines with a teleological underpinning, such as psychology, we can explain why the disparate physical realizations, P_i, of some given special category, S_1, all have the same effect, R_2, by invoking a selection mechanism which picks out P_is precisely *because* they cause R_2. Implicit here is the general claim that, in systems of the relevant kind, if any P_i causes R_2, then that P_i will tend to be preserved. But what now about *this* general claim? Is it itself reducible to physics? And, if not, doesn't it raise just the same puzzle about variably realized generalizations having common effects with which I started the paper?

I think that some such selectionist generalizations (if P_i causes R_2, then P_i is preserved) *are* physically explainable. Others, however, will be variably realized. But then there will be some more general selection mechanism which in turn explains the existence of the specific selection mechanisms which pick things that cause R_2. What about the generalization implicit in this last explanation (if a selection mechanism picks P_is that cause R_2, then this selection mechanism will be preserved)? Well, either this generalization will be physically explainable, or it will be due to a yet more general selection mechanism which . . . is physically explainable.

So I would say that we can explain patterns that are not themselves physically explainable in terms of selection mechanisms which are, or at least in terms of selection mechanisms whose selection is physically explainable, or . . . and so on. We can have hierarchies of selection mechanisms, with variable realizations at each level until the last. But the last level should always offer a uniform physical story, for until we have such a

obvious *psychological* reductions of these categories, and correspondingly an obvious *psychological* explanation of Gresham's law—as predicted by my argument, together with the fact that there is no economic selection mechanism which selects just those kinds of bad money which will drive out the good. (Incidentally, this point also shows that Gresham's law will be a persuasive example of physical irreducibility only for those who are already persuaded that psychology is physically irreducible.)

uniform physical story the explanatory buck with which I have been concerned in this paper won't have stopped.

Let me give an illustration of the simplest case, where some variably realized pattern $S_1 \rightarrow R_2$ is explained by a physically uniform selection mechanism. Consider some simple biological organism which is capable of learning how to get rid of some given painful stimulus. Different individuals in this species will no doubt learn physically different ways of getting rid of the pain. Then, if we think of the behaviour as S_1, its different real-izations as the P_is, and the disappearance of pain as R_2, we will have the generalization $S_1 \rightarrow R_2$, and this will be variably realized by the different P_is. This is the kind of variable generalization that this paper has argued to be prima facie puzzling. In the current example we can remove this puzzle-ment by invoking the learning process which ensures that, if any P_i causes R_2, that P_i will be preserved. The current issue, however, is what kind of explanation we can give of *this* selectionist fact. But now recall a point made in the last section, that pain and associated learning mechanisms are likely to be innate and so uniformly realized within any given species. If this is right, then a uniform physical explanation for the selectionist generalization will be available. The story will no doubt be complicated. Nevertheless, to postulate that the learning mechanism is uniformly realized throughout the species is precisely to postulate some *physically uniform feedback mechanism* which is triggered by the disappearance of pain, and which then operates to preserve whatever physical behaviour caused that disappearance.

Does this mean that in this kind of case the original be-havioural generalization $S_1 \rightarrow R_2$ will be reducible to physics after all? Only in an extended sense. There is still no uniform *physical* explanation of why the behaviour S_1 generally gets rid of pain, for S_1 is still variably realized at the physical level. Rather, what we can explain physically is why each individual, on receipt of the painful stimulus, performs *some* bit of be-haviour which gets rid of the pain. In effect, what the selec-tionist story allows us to explain is not so much why the behaviour has the effect it does, but rather why each individual is disposed to *some* bit of behaviour with that effect. This explanation does, it is true, imply that all the behaviours in question have the effect they do; but it doesn't do this by identifying a uniform physical reduction for those behaviours; rather it switches to a broader context and instead gives a uniform physical account for each individual having some behaviour with that effect to start with.

Now for a more complicated case. Suppose again that some group of animals have learned some common but variably realized behaviour, but not now because of their innate tendency to avoid pain, but rather because they have all *acquired* a common desire in virtue of their common experience. Suppose, for example, they have all learned to like bananas. I take it that this, analogously to the last example, will lead to their all learning ways (though not necessarily the same ways) of doing such things as getting bananas down from trees. But in this case there *won't* be any uniform *physical* explanation for their all acquiring such behaviour. For, if the desires for bananas are themselves acquired by learning, it is unlikely that those desires will themselves have a uniform physical realization, and so unlikely that the feedback mechanism responsible for learning how to get bananas down from trees will be physically uniform across the different individuals.

Here we need to shift to a yet wider context, and focus on how the desires for bananas were acquired in the first place. At which point we will presumably want to tell a story about a mechanism which selects states (namely, desires) which will cause, and help develop, behaviour which will yield results, such as bananas, which in the organism's experience have been associated with pleasure or the avoidance of pain—where *this* selection mechanism *is* uniformly realized across the species. And this will then, as before, offer a uniform physical explanation not of how the movements each animal performs get it bananas (for there is no uniform physical explanation of *that*), nor even of how each animal has learned some bit of behaviour which gets it bananas (there's no uniform physical explanation of that either), but rather of why each animal has acquired a state which disposes it to learn some bit of behaviour which will get it bananas.

We could go on. Generalizations about suitably experienced individuals seeking out bananas will hold good across species, as well as within them. But this then opens up the possibility that the associated innate mechanism for acquiring desires will be differently physically realized in different individuals who alike seek out bananas, thus undermining the physical uniformity of the story told in the last paragraph. But then we can widen the context even further, and appeal to inter-generational genetic selection, which will then explain these variably realized innate learning mechanisms as themselves selected by the physically uniform process which preserves things which cause survival and the replication of genetic DNA.

I am not of course suggesting that special scientists need to go into all this every time they appeal to some variably realized special generalization in explaining something. The idea that you must explain everything you use in an explanation is obviously self-defeating. Nevertheless, on the metaphysical level, as opposed to the methodological level, it is worth knowing that if we widen the context enough we can in principle always show that any variably realized special generalization is the upshot of some uniform physical process. For if such physical explanations weren't in principle available, it would be incredible that such variably realized generalizations should be true.

3

Reduction and Evolutionary Biology*

Graham Macdonald

1. BACKGROUND

As the demands for the reduction of biology to physics and chemistry seem to have receded into the past, it may appear as though producing new arguments to the same effect is a waste of energy. However, recent arguments against the reductionist claim seem to be misguided; either they settle on weak non-reduction, by which is meant empirical or pragmatic non-reducibility allied to a claim of 'in principle' reducibility, or if they go for 'in principle' non-reducibility their arguments fail to hit the intended target. My diagnosis of this state of affairs is that since supervenience has been seen to be compatible with token–token identity, simply *asserting* that a supervenience relation holds between the special sciences and physics has come to be seen as an easy materialist option. In what follows I will be repeating, briefly, some suggestions why this assertion is unsatisfactory before proceeding to argue that the reason behind the autonomy of biology is that it uses functional explanation.[1] It is, however, only on a certain construal of functional explanation that the conclusion emerges in a way that is consonant with the criticisms of pragmatic non-

* I am indebted to Roger Fellows and Cynthia Macdonald for many discussions on these topics, and to the audience's comments on an original draft given at the Workshop on Reductionism, University of Bradford, September 1988

[1] Dissatisfaction with the standard view has been voiced by John Searle in *Minds, Brains and Science* (London: BBC, 1984; Cambridge: Cambridge University Press, 1985) and by David Papineau in 'Social Facts and Psychological Facts', in G. Currie and A. Musgrave (eds.), *Popper and the Human Sciences* (Dordrecht: Nijhoff, 1985). For a more detailed criticism than is provided here see G. Macdonald, 'The Possibility of the Disunity of Science', in G. Macdonald and C. Wright (eds.), *Fact, Science, and Morality* (Oxford: Blackwell, 1986). The rest of this section is essentially a summary of some of the early sections of this paper.

reducibility, so that construal will be defended before it is shown why it leads to the non-reductionist conclusion. In doing this the distinctive *explanatory* work done by functional explanation should become apparent.

For the purposes of this paper some of the assumptions which form the background to the issue of 'supervenience or reduction' will have to be taken for granted. The principal assumptions are (1) a (physical) monist ontology, and (2) the supervenience of causality on physical causality. To examine (1) in depth would take us into issues which are peripheral to our main concerns. As our concern is with supervenience versus reduction we can take (1) as an assumption which both parties to the debate accept. Accepting (2) involves essentially the same choice: if the events of any special science had causal powers which were not determined by physical causal powers it would be necessary to give up any hope of a reduction and plausible to sacrifice supervenience as well. The possession of independent causal power would presumably mean that there could be change at the supposedly supervening level without accompanying physical change, and that is simply to deny that supervenience holds. Again, (2) is not uncontroversial, but it is an assumption common to reductionists and supervenience theorists, so we can safely take it for granted. Also the precise nature of the supervenience relation will not be examined; nothing much hinges on it in the rest of the paper. All we need is the intuitive account provided by the claim that any two worlds indiscernible with respect to their physical properties will be so with respect to their biological properties. It will emerge that not only does this principle have to be read in spatially global terms (the relevant physical properties must include those instantiated in the organism's environment), but it must also be read as being temporally global. The histories of the two worlds are relevant in deciding on their present biological properties, and this is true even if they share all their present physical properties. This does not prejudge any decision about token–token identity, but that is also an issue not discussed here.[2]

---

[2] The problems for token identity theories are discussed, and solved, in Cynthia Macdonald's 'Weak Externalism and Mind–Body Identity', *Mind*, 99(395) (July 1990).

Previously[3] it has been argued that empirical non-reducibility is an unstable position. The classic statement of what is meant by 'empirical' non-reducibility is that of Fodor.[4] For Fodor it just happens to be the case that a special science may not be reducible to physics, despite the sharing of an ontology. The classification of events which is effected by economic theory, for example, just is radically different from that effected by physical theory. The two sciences both classify physical events, and they both use the same general type of explanation (causal explanation); it may just turn out that the supervening science's classifications will not match up to the physicist's classifications in any way which would make for a reduction. The taxonomies of the two sciences simply diverge. This position we now call the simple taxonomic divergence thesis, or STD for short. Pragmatic non-reduction is a close cousin to STD. Here the claim is that given the finitude of nature it is inevitable that a reduction is in principle possible. Given the assumption of monism, all special science events will be physical events, so for any particular special science its classification of events will range over a finite number of physical events, it therefore being in principle possible to reduce any property of a special science to the disjunction (or disjunction of conjunctions) of physical properties which instantiate it. What prevents the reduction taking place is our lack of relevant knowledge; if we knew the disjunction of physical properties upon which the non-physical property supervened then reducibility would follow. This position is slightly more reductionist than STD but both pragmatic and STD non-reductionism share the assumption that variable realization of the non-physical in the physical is a purely contingent matter, so we will concentrate on the STD version.

The STD thesis is that one can have two types of event, S_1 and S_2, which are such that (1) instantiations of S_1 can cause instantiations of S_2, (2) $S_1 \rightarrow S_2$ is a causal law, (3) both S_1 and S_2 are variably instantiated in different types of physical event, so (4) when S_1 is instantiated in p_1 and S_2 is instantiated in p_2, $p_1 \rightarrow p_2$ is a causal law. The variable instantiation claim is

[3] See my 'The Possibility of the Disunity of Science'.
[4] J. A. Fodor, 'The Special Sciences', *Synthese*, 28 (1974).

meant to rule out the possibility of a reduction; the various types of physical event in which S_1 and S_2 are instantiated are alleged to have nothing relevant in common with one another, so reduction is not feasible. (To have something relevantly common would be to have some causal feature in common which was responsible for the production of the effect, S_2.)

The objection to this picture is fairly simple. It points to the implausibility of the *same* supervening event being realized in physical events that have so little in common. This implausibility is heightened when we note that the supervening event is picked out as causally stable even though it is instantiated in underlying physical events which have no causal similarity. Remember that the supervening events have no causal powers independently of their physical bases. The causal efficacy of the supervening event regularly brings it about that its nomologically related effect occurs, but it does this in virtue of the causality it inherits from its associated physical events (assumption (2) above). The puzzle is how the regularity of the supervening causal process can be based on such irregular physical causes, how the *same* supervening cause can be dependent for its causal powers on such causally *different* physical events. Many instantiations of the causal process whereby S_1 produces S_2 are covered by different physical causal laws, yet it is the case that varied physical causes happen to produce an effect which must instantiate S_2. The wonder is how such causal harmony is achieved.

The resolution of this puzzle is achieved by giving up one part of the STD thesis, that being the insistence that the supervenient explanation be a causal explanation, where this means that the explanation must eschew the essential use of causal laws. If one insists on the essential use of causal laws at the supervening level, and accepts assumption (2), then it would be plausible to see the causal stability of the supervening level reflected in the base from which it derives its causal powers. The contention then will be that this reflection will ensure sufficient similarity amongst the underlying causes for a reduction to be feasible. There will be *some* common physical property which ensures that the supervening causal processes are regular enough to be capturable in a causal law. This physical property will ensure that the right kind of effect occurs, one which will instantiate the supervening effect event, S_2. What one needs to avoid this reductive conclusion is a type of explanation which concentrates on the effect produced. Essentially what is required is a selection of causes *because* they produce the desired effect. Then we can explain the effect as resulting from a cause which was meant to produce just that effect, *no matter what else is true of that cause*. The causes of the relevant effect can be varied; what will be important is that they are there in order to produce the effect.

Talk of 'selecting causes to produce desired effects' can appear mysterious, but it is one of the claims of modern biology that it has eliminated the mystery. My contention is that it is the use of functional explanation in biology which renders it autonomous, and that functional explanation is best explicated via the process of natural selection. This latter claim has recently been the subject of much criticism, so it will be necessary to outline the selectionist account of biological functionality and to defend it against its critics.[5]

2. FUNCTIONALITY: SELECTIONISM AND ITS RIVALS

Depending upon the analysis of 'function' which one prefers, it may well be possible to specify a function for an item without any functionalist *explanation* of how that item came to exist. The two main accounts of 'function' are the aetiological (generally selectionist) account, and the 'goal-directed' (or 'directed systems') account. In the latter one specifies as the function of an item anything that a feature of the item contributes to a goal, regardless of the aetiological background of the item. If one uses a rock in the desert as a sundial, then it has that function, regardless of the fact that its original and continued existence have nothing to do with it performing that function. Sometimes the 'goal' is specified as some behaviour, or capacity, of a containing system, the function of a subordinate part of the system being to enable the containing system to operate in the described manner. Now one point of dispute

[5] Criticisms have been voiced by Alexander Rosenberg in *The Structure of Biological Science* (Cambridge: Cambridge University Press, 1985), and J. Bigelow and R. Pargetter, 'Functions', *Journal of Philosophy*, 84 (1987), 181–96.

within the camp of those who adhere to a goal-direction account of function is whether the goals need to be specified naturalistically, as existing in nature independently of our own interests. The sundial case is clearly one of an assigned function, making functionality dependent on intentionality. With the 'systems' variant of the goals account, the problem is to specify non-arbitrarily which behaviour or capacity of the containing system is relevant for the functional analysis to analyse. Again, the problem is that the choice of a capacity seems to depend upon our interests in a way which makes the choice of any capacity as suitable for functional analysis seem justifiable. This is a major drawback in using this notion of function to underpin functional explanation in biology. We have the strong intuition that biological functions are independent of our interests, that they would have existed even if intentional creatures had not evolved. Unless the goals of the goal-orientated account can be specified in a manner consistent with this intuition it will be a mark against it as an account of biological function.

This means that we are adopting 'explanatory realism' as a reasonable constraint on the acceptance of an analysis of functional explanation. Explanatory realism requires that the explanans be grounded in an objective relation between the events involved in the explanation, where 'objective' means that its instantiation does not entail the existence or non-existence of any intentional (psychological) state.[6] Where the explanation is causal explanation, this will commit us to causal realism, and in the case of functional explanation, functions will have to be construed as existing independently of our psychological states (if one wishes to be realist about intentional explanation the definition provided would have to be suitably amended). This constraint (of explanatory realism) is particularly effective in criticizing those who are defending a supervenient biology against reductionism in a non-instrumentalist fashion, as they must allow that the biological pro-

---

[6] This is Jaegwon Kim's construal of explanatory realism, in J. Kim, 'Explanatory Realism, Causal Realism, and Explanatory Exclusion', in P. French, T. Uehling, Jr., and H. Wettstein (eds.), *Midwest Studies in Philosophy*, xii: *Realism and Antirealism* (Minneapolis, Minn.: Minnesota Press, 1987).

perties, especially functional properties, are truly attributed to biological organisms.

In general, the systems approach is made to appear plausible by first concentrating on the notion of function, and then, sometimes only implicitly, claiming that functions, in this sense, are what gets functionally explained. Very often all this means is that citing a feature as a function is sufficient, or so it is thought, for the explanation of that feature. We will return to this issue when we examine these accounts in more detail. For the present we need to know more about the selectionist, or aetiological, theory of functional explanation.

The essential features of the aetiological account are dependent upon the idea that to attribute a function to an item is to say that the item has that feature or behaviour because it has a certain history; in the past that feature produced certain consequences, those consequences themselves having the effect of reproducing items with that feature. It is this latter aspect which makes the account teleological (or teleonomic). One can say that the item has the relevant property *in order to* produce those consequences. It is because of (some of) its effects that the property is selected for. What the theory of natural selection does is make respectable the apparent purposefulness of the 'in order to'. It does this by showing how environmental pressures on variable items can produce varied reproduction of those items; those items with certain features will become more prevalent because those features have typical effects on the reproductive capacity of the items which bear them. This is all that is needed for the aetiological theory of function. Pared down to its essence a selectionist theory relies on:

1. variability in the items to be selected;
2. selection of some of those items;
3. variable reproduction of the items selected for.

Selection cannot take place if there is no initial variation; the same selection forces operating on a homogeneous population will have no differentiating effect, so one could not say of one property, or set of properties, that it has been selected because of the effects it produces. For a property to be there *in order to* produce certain effects it must also be the case that properties with those causal powers have been selected in the past because they produced those effects. The selection process requires that the causal property interact with salient features of the environment in such a way that other items without that property are seen to 'suffer' some loss as a consequence of their non-possession of the property. Finally, it is because the favoured properties are transmitted to descendants of the items having those features that the present items have these properties. Then it can be said that the property is, or was, functional, its function being to produce those types of effect which lead to its ancestors reproducing items with the property in question.

That is the essence of the aetiological account of functional explanation. Before proceeding to defend it against those who think that it is not doing any explanatory work, it will be useful to give more detail to the main rival to selectionism, the directed systems version. The strength of this account is that it takes as its starting-point the fact of biological complexity and proposes to understand the complex functioning of a biological entity in terms of the working of its parts. The fact of complexity suggests that the systems are goal-directed; and if this is taken for granted, then one can recover what is distinctive of biological explanation, that it invariably cites the effects of causes as explaining why the cause is there. It does this by specifying how a part of the system operates in the production of the goal. Rosenberg puts the general position well:

Organisms have aims and purposes, which their behavior serves; their component parts serve to fulfill these purposes and have functions in meeting the needs of cells, tissues, organs, whole biological organisms, and systems like ant colonies made up of large numbers of individual organisms. Because the objects of biological interest have goals, ends, purposes, and functions, it is incumbent on biology to identify, describe and explain these teleological—end-directed—features. And because biological systems and their components have these teleological features, it is perfectly appropriate to cite and appeal to them in the explanation of biological phenomena. The search for functions seems dictated by the biological facts alone, right down to the level of biochemistry.[7]

---

[7] Rosenberg, *The Structure of Biological Science*, 43.

The problem, as Rosenberg notes, is accounting for the original attribution of goals to the system. After considering and rejecting the selectionist theory (for reasons which we will come back to) he puts forward a version of the directively organized systems (hereafter DOS) approach, which he also characterizes as involving feedback or feed-forward loops. The claim is that functional explanation is legitimate when, taking environment *E*, goal-directed system *S*, its behaviour *B*, and goal *G*, subsystems of *S* can be specified which generate *G* in *E* because they are causally related in the following ways:[8]

1. The state of each subsystem of *S* at *t*, together with the states of the others at *t*, causes the attainment of goal *G* at *t* + 1.

2. The states of each of these subsystems is instantaneously independent of the states of the others at *t*.

3. Each subsystem has only a restricted range of states.

4. If the state of one of the subsystems changes greatly enough at *t*, then, in the absence of changes in the other subsystems at *t* + 1, the whole system *S* will be caused not to attain *G*. But

5. The subsystems are so causally linked that whenever such a great change occurs in one of them at *t*, this change causes changes in the other subsystems at *t* + 2, which together with the initial great change at *t* causes the whole system to attain its goal at *t* + 1.

Crucial to the claimed success of the DOS model of functionality is that it should not presuppose any teleological notions. One cannot say, for example, that clause (5) indicates that subsystems are there *in order to* bring the system back to its goal-directed path whenever deviations from the path threaten the system. The DOS account aims at elucidating functionality in a purely causal way, thereby eliminating the mystery of teleology. For our purposes it is important to note that this approach to teleology in biology is implicitly reductionist. Richard Dawkins commits himself to something like the DOS view (with a qualification which will become important) and names it 'hierarchical reductionism'—the understanding of complex entities via an understanding of the working of their

---

[8] This is a slightly abbreviated version of Rosenberg's as it appears in *The Structure of Biological Science*, 53.

parts.[9] If the parts are complex, one carries on the procedure until one arrives at parts whose workings are immediately intelligible.

A consequence of a DOS account is that it fits naturally with the belief that failure to achieve a reduction is to be put down to 'the sheer complexity of the empirical facts with which biology must deal. Teleology is unavoidable in biology for contingent and nonconceptual reasons.'[10] (This, of course, is what must be argued against if the view of non-reduction as dependent upon the explanatory differences of a discipline is to be upheld.) The DOS approach immediately prompts the following questions: how is the 'goal' of the system to be determined? And how would a DOS differ from a 'purely physical' (i.e. non-biological) system? The second question implicitly connects with a third: what is lost when a functional explanation is replaced by a purely causal explanation? Rosenberg suggests that a sufficient answer to the second question is that it is the independence of the subsystems, combined with the plasticity of the goal attainment, which guarantees the presence of the teleological element which the physical system lacks. However, a DOS, thus characterized, would appear to be neither necessary nor sufficient for functionality. Firstly, 'plasticity' is notoriously difficult to capture in a non-question-begging way. An Aristotelian might say that rocks rolling down hills will display, under some descriptions, plasticity of goal attainment, the goal being to get to the bottom of the hill, their natural resting-place. On the other hand some simple biological organisms might display tropistic behaviour which, again under some description, will be fairly rigid. There is surely no theoretical reason why such rigid biological behaviour should be deemed non-deserving of a functional explanation, why non-plasticity should preclude adaptation (unless 'being an adaptation' is confused with 'being adaptable'). What would be relevant to the functional explanation of the rigid behaviour would be the past history of that organism, how it evolved, why it was preferred to its historical variants and rivals. If a selectionist account can be given of the rigid

---

[9] R. Dawkins, _The Blind Watchmaker_ (London: Penguin Books, 1988), 11–13.
[10] Rosenberg, _The Structure of Biological Science_, 65.

behaviour, the fact of its rigidity would be irrelevant to its functionality. A mutant displaying rigid behaviour may well be fitter than its variants, thus making its descendants more adapted to the environment, and hence functional.

This reasoning naturally takes the aetiological theory for granted, and so could be said to beg the question. What it shows, though, is that the DOS account needs to explain away the intuitions, and more importantly the biological practice, which underlies the aetiological view. What is absolutely crucial to the DOS account is the independent behaviour of the subsystems which cause the system's goal attainment. This is the aspect of organization of the system which gives the appearance of design and function. It also means that the simple parts for which there is no further decomposition into components will not have their typical effects functionally explained. Functionality is simply drained out of the system. This consequence is in itself puzzling. Why should it be impossible for biological simples to have their behaviour functionally explained? On the aetiological account this presents no problem. Provided that the simples reproduce and vary, it will be possible for the environment to favour some over the others, thus conferring on the descendants functionality, regardless of their simplicity or non-plasticity in goal attainment.

A second problem is that it is not impossible that a complicated physical system (the complexity being not due to an evolutionary history) could display the behaviour associated with a DOS. It may display regular behaviour *B* which is brought about by the interaction of its independent parts. It may also just be the case that when there is a change in one part there is compensating change in the other parts and the behaviour *B* is still manifested. (The improbable can happen.) On the DOS account we would have to attribute functionality to the parts. But this shows just how little explanatory work is being done by the attribution of function. Attributing functionality to a part of a system entails only, on this account, that we have a physical system of some complexity. There is nothing that would be lost by simply giving the causal story without any functional elaboration. Functional *explanation* becomes essentially redundant; we are left with a *description* of a certain sort of causal system. One can certainly describe this kind of causal system as being composed of functioning parts, but this description has no explanatory pay-off.

A fall-back position may be to stress the purposiveness of the behaviour associated with the biological DOS (its goal-orientatedness) as opposed to the non-purposiveness of the simply physical DOS. This brings us back to our first question, that of determining how the goal is to be specified in the first place. Unless this can be done in a non-teleological way, the DOS account will not be able to claim success in its aim of making teleology causally respectable. Rosenberg has very little to say about this. He seems to have taken goal-directed behaviour as a datum, giving an analysis of functional explanation as it applies to entities which are goal-directed. Sometimes, however, he seems to suggest that goal-directedness is another name for the typical behaviour of an organism which has complex parts acting independently of one another to cause that typical behaviour. ('Typical' here will have to be cashed out in something like probabilistic terms in order to avoid any question-begging concerning goals, and this is going to be difficult to do. Ruth Millikan notes that many biological entities have as their function behaviour which they may very rarely succeed in accomplishing.[11] Sperm surely have as their function the fertilization of eggs, but since very few of them perform this function, on a probabilistic basis it would be foolhardy to attribute to sperm the function of fertilizing eggs.) If ths is all that is meant by 'goal-directed' then the randomly generated complex physical system will be goal-directed, a result which eliminates any explanatory gain from the attribution of function.

Dawkins suggests that the difference between the biological and the physical can be elaborated in terms of the complexity of the biological, which in turn is cashed out in terms of the improbability of the biological entities existing in a world of biological chance. It is precisely this improbability which does give rise to our perception of function and design, and it is because of it that the argument from design for the existence of a deity who did the designing gets some credence. Dawkins is

[11] R. Millikan, *Language, Thought and Other Biological Categories* (Cambridge, Mass.: MIT Press, 1984).

sufficiently impressed by this complexity (and so improbability) of biological entities that he claims that without Darwin it would not be respectable to be an atheist. What Darwin did was to provide a natural explanation of how such complexity could originate, and he did this via the theory of natural selection. It is here that one can get some purchase on the goals of biological systems. Ultimately these goals have to be tied into the survival and reproduction of those entities for whose behaviour one wants to give a functional explanation. This is a major strength of the aetiological account. The behaviour which gets functionally explained may not happen regularly, but provided it has an evolutionary history in which one can see that it was selected for because it behaved a certain way (even if only rarely), then that behaviour can be functionally explained. The ultimate biological 'goal' of any biological entity is the reproduction of more of its kind. It is only on the aetiological account that this goal can be attributed in a non-question-begging way, and this gives that account a firmer basis than the DOS theory.

Another crucial consideration which bears against the DOS view is that the aetiological account has an easier way of handling malfunctions. It is difficult to see how a DOS account will deal with malfunctions: in general it will not be able to produce judgements about what biological features are there for, and so will have difficulty in saying of any such feature that it is not performing up to scratch. No doubt some story could be cobbled together whereby one would be able to attribute functions, in the suitably attenuated sense, to some complex systems and then proceed to say that other systems 'sufficiently like' the standard ones are malfunctioning if they do not replicate the behaviour of the standard systems in all respects. But this story would get horribly complicated ('standard system' would be very difficult to define, and the respects or behaviour in virtue of which a difference from the standard system would count as a malfunction would be difficult to capture), and would not be as natural as the aetiological alternative, where one has a fairly clear account of the purpose of the trait, and a reasonably clear idea of what would constitute malfunctioning.

It is worth noting at this stage that the aetiological approach does not entail the rejection of a DOS explanation. There is no barrier to a selectionist proceeding beyond the simple-sounding attribution of functionality to a detailed account of the mechanism which produces the adapted feature or behaviour of the organism. Ernst Mayr notes that one finds within biology two very different areas, functional biology and evolutionary biology. The former 'is vitally concerned with the operation and interaction of structural elements, from molecules up to organs and whole individuals' whereas the latter always has in mind the historically orientated question 'How come?'[12] In our terms, those Mayr calls functional biologists are dealing in DOS-style explanations, the evolutionary biologists in selectionist explanations. It is clear that there is no incompatibility between the two concerns: 'how' questions and 'what for' questions can complement one another. The important claim will be that the so-called functional explanations (probably better termed 'structural explanations') take place within the parameters set by the concerns of the evolutionary biologist. The biological units for which the DOS explanations are appropriate are those which are subject to selection pressures.

On this account the evolutionary biologist is interested in ultimate causes, the functional biologist in proximate causes, both being essential for a full understanding of biological phenomena. Our claim now is that the proximate causes which are of interest to the DOS explainer are causes of those phenomena for which the evolutionary biologist has, or hopes to acquire, ultimate explanations. The evolutionary biologist maps out the terrain within which Mayr's functional (our structural) biologist can operate, providing the functional form within which the mechanistic concerns of the DOS explanation can be seen as biologically appropriate. It is *adaptations* for which one needs the structural detail, not just any old physically complicated entity.[13]

[12] E. Mayr, 'Cause and Effect in Biology,' *Science*, 134 (1961), 1502.

[13] The same criticisms concerning the non-explanatoriness of attributions of function can be levelled against Bigelow and Pargetter's dispositional theory of function ('*Functions*'). On this view 'Even before [the disposition] had contributed (in an appropriate way) to survival, it had conferred a survival-enhancing propensity on the creature. And to confer such a propensity, we

3. FUNCTION AND EXPLANATION

The selectionist account of functionality has been subject to a lot of criticism, so before proceeding we had better address the most important of these. There are, roughly, two types of criticism: that which attacks the details of the selectionist account of function and that which addresses the issue of the explanatoriness of the attribution of function. A defence against the important detailed criticisms has been given elsewhere,[14] so in this section I will deal with the issue of explanation, as it is this which is relevant to the topic of reduction.

It is in its concern with adaptations that the strength of the aetiological account resides. It ties in the explanations of how behaviour is proximately caused to the broader concerns of the evolutionary biologist's interest in the apparent appropriateness of the behaviour, this in turn requiring a historical explanation. Although it could be said that a creature is adapted to its environment because it so happens that in that environment it will flourish, the biologists tend to restrict their attribution of adaptations to those features which have come about as a result of a long process of selective pressure. The idea is one of the environment moulding creatures so that they fit into that environment, and that this can happen because of the processes of variation, selection, and inheritance outlined above. As Richard Burian puts it, 'Fleetness is an adaptation of the deer if, and only if, the deer's fleetness has been moulded by a historical process in which relative fleetness of earlier deer helped shape the fleetness of current deer.'[15] Burian argues that it is essential to the proper understanding of Darwin's theory that one connect the concept of adaptation to that of natural selection. It is because adaptations are designed, not accidental, features of organisms that we are entitled to the use of functional explanation.

It is this connection between adaptation and functional

suggest, is what constitutes a function' (p. 192). The relevant question is why it is thought that this use of 'function' explains anything.

[14] An extended discussion of the various detailed criticisms is provided in G. Macdonald, *Special Explanations* (Oxford: Blackwell, forthcoming), ch. 4, §4.3.

[15] R. M. Burian, 'Adaptation', in M. Grene (ed.), *Dimensions of Darwinism* (Cambridge: Cambridge University Press, 1983), 288.

explanation which underlines the explanatory merits of the aetiological account over its rivals. This is ironic in so far as Rosenberg, amongst others, indicts the aetiological view for producing extremely weak explanations: 'It works only by treating all [teleological] claims as equally generic statements about the adaptive course of evolution over the eons.'[16] The second part of Rosenberg's complaint about the explanatoriness of aetiological functionality concerns such explanations' reference to the 'adaptive course of evolution over the eons'. This, he claims, puts too great a distance between the function and its causal determinants.

In seeking and providing a causal explanation, we reflect a widely held scientific conviction that a phenomenon and the forces that determine its occurrence cannot be decoupled, that there cannot be action-at-a-distance. A scientific explanation must cite the chain of causes behind the event to be explained. Selectionist accounts that explain a function in terms of the adaptiveness of paleontologically venerable ancestors fulfill this demand only in the most limited sense.[17]

Jon Elster makes a similar claim against functional explanation:

If the goal of science is to explain by means of laws, there is a need to reduce the time-span between explanans and explanandum—between cause and effect—as much as possible, in order to avoid spurious explanations.[18]

It is difficult to see this complaint as anything but plain prejudice in favour of causal explanation being the only 'proper' explanation in science. If it is in the nature of functional explanation to cite causes (selection pressures) which may have occurred some time before the existence of the trait which is being explained, then it is beside the point to complain that this does not meet the standards appropriate for causal explanation. Note that providing the causal history in the manner desired (citing the chain of causes between the effects of the original selection pressures and the time at which the explanation is being proffered) would only be illuminating if

---

[16] Rosenberg, *The Structure of Biological Science*, 52.
[17] Ibid. 50–1.
[18] J. Elster, *Making Sense of Marx* (Cambridge: Cambridge University Press, 1985), 5.

the chain of causes made a difference to the outcome, to the emergence of the trait being explained. If they did make such a difference, omitting mention of them would render the explanation defective *as a functional explanation*; the explanation would not explain what it set out to explain. If the chain of causes made no such difference, so that the environment was stable and provided no new causes to which the animal adapted, then citing the intervening causes would be explanatorily redundant. The absence of 'new' causes would not imply that nothing happened in the interim, just that nothing of biological note had happened, and this means that what was happening did not change the selection pressures so as to produce different functions. In general, when earlier selection pressures are the only ones which feature in the explanation of a particular trait, the fact of relevant environmental stability is assumed, and there is no explanatory loss in making this assumption.

The complaint about 'equally generic' claims is supported by noting that

Adaptational claims do not explain why in a given case nature has 'chosen' the actual adaptive process over all the other available alternative ways of meeting the same need. Circulation is an adaptation because of the metabolic needs of the organism. These needs could have been met by any of a large number of mechanisms, and indeed in other organisms are met by many other mechanisms that do not involve circulation. . . . the functional attribution, understood . . . as a disguised appeal to evolutionary adaptation, does not give even a hint of the causes that restricted or encouraged the particular sequence that led to the actual manner in which evolutionary needs were met.[19]

It would, indeed, be a cause for complaint if biological explanation were stuck at the level of 'that's there because it is an adaptation'. *But it is of the essence of functional explanation that it allows for the detail to be slotted inside it.* In this respect it is not dissimilar to psychological behaviourist explanation, where one has a stimulus and a response cited in the explanation, with a blank left in the middle, leaving it open to further investigation which mechanisms within the organism are responsible for translating the stimulus into the response. Similarly, functional

---

[19] Rosenberg, *The Structure of Biological Science*, 48.

explanation leaves it open which mechanisms are responsible for the effects which are selected. This is a strength rather than a weakness. It provides a reason why the function can be realized in physically different ways. In other words, it is because the functional explanation prescinds from the detail concerning how the functional effect is produced that it can be autonomous with respect to that detail, and so can naturally lead us to a non-reductionist conclusion concerning biological categories and explanations. We will return to this, but at the moment it is important to see that Rosenberg's accusation of vacuity against functional explanation would be telling only if these explanations were incompatible with the further causal explanations which detailed the mechanisms which performed the function. We have seen that, far from being incompatible, the functional explanations positively invite this further causal elaboration.

Rosenberg's (and Bigelow and Pargetter's) criticism may be read in a slightly different way. It may be acknowledged that causal elaboration of functional claims is permissible, but that, given that the functional claims are made only at the level of generality which has to do with fitness enhancement, the explanatory gain of these claims is negligible. The claim here is that all that functional explanation can explain is the relative proliferation (and decrease) of traits which directly serve survival and reproduction. This ignores both the different levels at which the functional claims can be made *and* the history behind the traits which have evolved to serve those purposes. To take the first point, it is true that the ultimate function of selected traits is to enhance fitness, but the manner in which this is done is gloriously diverse. There are all sorts of proximate functions whose causal effects are directed into the workings of slightly higher-level functions, whose effects in turn may subserve even higher-level functions, until we reach a level at which the effects feed directly into increasing reproduction capacity. The employment of functional explanation for the explanation of proximate functions is vindicated by their effects feeding into the ultimate function, and so the selection processes can be seen to have selected these traits because of those effects.

The second point has been emphasized by Karen Neander in

a recent criticism of Elliot Sober's more restrictive claims for functional explanation.[20] Sober suggested that selection could not explain how individuals could come to have the traits which they did have.[21] What selection does is to choose amongst the traits which are in existence, favouring some at the expense of others. The explanation for the traits possessed by any individual would be simply the causal story instantiated in the genetic processes which produced the trait in that individual. Sober called this latter type of explanation developmental explanation, and the good point he was making was that selection operates on traits already present. One can accept this point, though, and still deny that all that functional explanation can explain is the very general fact concerning the proliferation-rates of the causally explained traits. What Neander points out is that each such trait will have an evolutionary history, the elaboration of which will show how the trait came to have the form it now has. Opposable thumbs did not emerge fully fledged (as it were); there were many mutations, and those which increased opposable thumbness were favoured. A restriction to looking at 'selection of pre-existing traits' has almost an air of saltationism about it. It is as though the traits came into existence formed as they now are, and were then selected for on that basis. Ignoring the more gradual, at times almost imperceptible, changes that took place in order to arrive at the present trait is to ignore a part of the explanation why the trait is what it is. It is because functions can be performed by different mechanisms that attending to the historical detail is important in showing how and why this mechanism evolved into its present form. The central point is that although selection does distribute characteristics, the history of successive distributions shows it as also moulding those characteristics. It will then be in order to explain the shape of your thumb by citing facts about its predecessors' shapes, those facts being more adaptive than the failed rival shapes.

The variability of mechanism *vis-à-vis* function provides a

[20] K. Neander, 'What does Natural Selection Explain? Correction to Sober', *Philosophy of Science*, 55 (1988), 422–6.

[21] E. Sober, *The Nature of Selection* (Cambridge, Mass.: MIT Press, 1984).

defence against a different type of criticism. Elster suggests that once we have provided the mechanism via which the consequence feeds back on to the behaviour being explained, then we have in effect substituted a non-functional (mechanistic) type of explanation for a functional one.[22] The suggestion is that the more we know about the mechanisms, the less we need to know about functions. The increasing knowledge of mechanism would eventually render all functional explanation eliminable. This would only be so if there were a reduction between function and mechanism, and it is precisely the nub of Rosenberg's 'generality' criticism that such a reduction is not likely. Given that different mechanisms can perform the same function, eliminating the level of functional explanation once our knowledge of the mechanisms is complete would be to exclude the possibility of interesting generalizations at the functional level.

This is true even when we descend to the lower levels of functionality. It has been the hope of those who have accepted something like a DOS account of function to eventually reach a level of function at which the function to be performed would be so simple that all talk of function could be eliminated in favour of purely mechanistic explanation. (Similarly, in functionalist-inspired psychological explanation the idea was to provide internal homunculi whose intentional capacity became so limited that it would become transparent how a mechanism could perform such tasks. Intentionality could thus be discharged.) This would be possible if, at this level, there were one-to-one correlation between function and mechanism. It is essential to our non-reductionist concerns that this cannot happen in the required way. The required way is that the correlation be nomic, not merely contingent. In order to be confident that the elimination of functional talk is justified it must be the case that the mechanism–function correlation be projectible; it will not be sufficient just to have discovered that up to now there is a one-to-one correlation, when this empirical fact does not give us confidence that the future will be similar.

It must be a part of the non-reductionist argument that such

---

[22] Elster, *Making Sense of Marx*, 29.

nomic correlations are not available. If we left our argument resting just on the claim that functional explanation captures a level of generality above that of causal explanation, it would leave us open to our own complaints against the simple taxonomic divergence thesis. The reductionist could reasonably ask why the higher-level functions had so little in common with the lower-level causal processes that a reduction to the causal was not available. Are we not just resting content with postulating variable realization? To see why the emphasis on functional explanation goes beyond this we need to see how it will produce explanations which cannot be replicated by causal explanations. There are two aspects to this non-reductionist conclusion, the first underlying the slippage between cause and function (and which also fits in neatly with our earlier argument concerning the problems of simple taxonomic divergence), the second concentrating on the inability of causal explanations to capture the idea of a malfunction.

The problems of the STD thesis centred around the implausibility of there being a supervening and a base property which differed in causal efficacy but which nevertheless produced harmonious effects—i.e. effects which were compatible with the truth of both supervening and base theories. The suggested solution was that to ensure the harmony of outcome the causes would have to be chosen just so that the harmony would occur. As indicated at the time, a selection of causes for this purpose would do the trick, and clearly our selectionist defence of functionality in biology provides the means by which the solution, in the case of biology, is achieved. It is because the causes are selected for the effects which they produce that we can be sure that the required outcome will occur.

To take an example discussed (for different reasons) by Dawkins:[23] different biochemical pathways can lead to the same result. Say the result is the synthesizing of a certain important substance needed by the body for its development. Different steps in the pathway to the synthesis may require different enzymes. In organism X (or species X) the pathway may require enzymes A_1, B_1, and C_1, in organism or species Y, enzymes A_2, B_2, and C_2 are needed. Which enzymes are found

[23] *The Blind Watchmaker*, 171.

will depend upon the contingencies of selection and history. If the species is packed with A_1 and B_1 enzymes there will be strong selection pressures in favour of enzyme C_1 becoming fixed in the population, as opposed to enzyme C_2, and this will be solely because the results produced by the first series of enzymes will be superior to those produced by the mixture. One starts from historical contingencies (which enzymes are present in the species) and selection 'arranges' the rest of the causes so that the right result is achieved. Or so one hopes (selection is neither omnipotent nor infallible).

Now a consequence of this is that the mechanisms which produce the desired effects can be any old mechanisms, provided only that they produce the proper result. They are selected, or, in other words, their function is, to produce that result. Provided that we know that that is their function (which the history of selection will tell us) their causal details are irrelevant to the functional explanation. It could be that in different animals the mechanisms performing the same function could be the same; the point is that it strictly does not matter whether they are the same or not. Even if we discovered that in fact there was a one-to-one correlation between mechanism and function, this would not be sufficient for a reductionist conclusion to be drawn. It is precisely because the biological property's function is specified in terms of its effects that the detail of how the effects are produced is not a candidate for a reduction. It will no doubt be illuminating to us to see how the effects are produced, but the possibility of different mechanisms instantiating the same function will always be present. This possibility is built into the character of functional explanation; it ensures that although causal knowledge will flesh out functional claims, it cannot replace them.

The second aspect of the anti-reductionist argument has to do with the inability of causal explanation to capture the notion of a malfunction. The best illustration of this is given by the example of the human immune system, used, to telling effect, by Mohan Matthen and Edwin Levy.[24] Essentially the story is that our bodies need to repel foreign cells, as these spell

---

[24] M. Matthen and E. Levy, 'Teleology, Error, and the Human Immune System', *Journal of Philosophy*, 81(7) (July 1984).

danger to the health of the organisms which they attack. To do this the immune system must be able to discriminate between the friendly and foreign cells, and this recognition of invaders is achieved via the epitopes, certain shapes, on the surfaces of the antigens (the enemy). Matthen and Levy categorize certain sorts of 'error' which can occur in the identificatory process. In one case which is of particular interest mistakes occur because the foreign epitopes resemble, in crucial aspects, the epitopes of some safe cells, so the *same* causal process which leads to an attack on a correctly identified invader can turn into an attack on self.

Our interest in reduction should lead us to ask whether causal explanation can produce an account of this process as an error (malfunction) in the immune system. Take the causal account of what is going on in the immune system when it goes into operation. An antibody is caused to be attached to a body by the characteristics of the epitope of that body. This causes the system either to multiply antibodies or to exercise tolerance. If more antibodies are formed then they will become attached to the specified epitopes, forming immune-complexes which cause the body to expel those complexes. Now take the case where the epitopes of self and non-self are sufficiently similar for the system to expel those belonging to self. The causal story cannot identify this as a mistake of the immune system, as it is acting in a causally 'proper' manner. The system is acting on the same characteristics of the epitopes as it does when no mistake occurs. If the functional account was reduced to this causal account we would have to identify the function of the immune system in this case as being to destroy self, and that is absurd. The causal explanation could register this as a mistake only if there is provision in it for the notion of 'misidentification'—but that description of what is going on seems to be parasitic on the idea of the 'proper working' of the system. That is, it is a description dependent on the idea of the function of the immune system.

If this is right, then the proposed reduction of the functional explanation of the system to a causal one is a non-starter. The reduction would not yield an account equivalent to that provided by the explanation which makes use of the idea of the goals of the system and sub-processes whereby those goals are achieved. It is impossible to make sense of causal mistakes. Causal explanation has to tailor itself to the requirement of registering what actually happens. If antibodies are caused to attack the 'wrong' epitopes, then the causal generalization must recognize this as part of the causal processes going on. As a result the causal generalization will include a description of all the epitopes to which the particular antibody is caused to attach itself. There is no room within that generalization for the singling out of some causes or effects as being the right or wrong ones. The judgement of rightness or wrongness is available only when the function has been specified. The point here is much the same as that which has been made much of in the case of psychological explanation. There is a normative component embedded in the notions of function and malfunction which cannot be captured if our task is, as it is with causal explanation, to capture causal regularities.

4. BIOLOGY AND FUNCTION

So far we have shown that, on a certain construal of functions and functional explanation, functional explanation cannot be replaced by causal explanation. Functional explanation will use normative concepts not available to causal explanation, and necessarily operates at a level which makes the causal detail strictly irrelevant to its task. This is sufficient, we believe, to justify the conclusion that if functional biology were to operate only with explanation by causal laws, then this would leave it explanatorily impoverished.

There is, though, a remaining question: how much of biology is dependent upon functional explanation? This is clearly an empirical question, one which only the biologists can answer. It is at this point that the question about reduction becomes a contingent matter. On the alternative model of supervenient special sciences, that provided by the simple taxonomic divergence view, the contingency of reduction emerges at a much earlier stage. Because that view places no stress on the requirement that non-causal explanation be the bulwark against reduction, any theory emerges as a candidate for non-reduction. The reverse holds as well: any theory is a candidate for reduction. It is simply up to science to adjudicate the issue; it so happens that some theories will, and others will not, be reducible to lower-level theories.

On our account none of these claims is true. If a theory centrally employs causal explanation ('centrally' to allow for the non-central causal elaboration which can take place in functional biology) then it will be in principle reducible to a lower-level theory (always presuming such a lower level exists). And if a theory is formed with functional concerns in mind, then it will be irreducible. What is empirical is to what extent various domains require explanation by theories which use causal, functional, or intentional explanation. To conclude, it may be worth while recording some biologists' verdicts on the importance of selection, and hence functional explanation, to their subject-matter. A recent rival to all-embracing selectionism is the theory of Motoo Kimura that most molecular evolution is neutral with respect to selection processes, the evolution of molecules being driven by random genetic drift. (My discussion of neutralism is influenced by Mark Ridley's careful examination of the various claims made, and the evidence for and against them.[25]) An important point to notice is that even Kimura does not suggest that all biological evolution is due to selectively neutral causes. It is molecular evolution only that is the subject-matter of his claim. Nor does he deny that those molecular changes resulting in fairly gross differences in organisms will be affected by selection. And in order to account for different rates of molecular evolution he allows that negative selection (selection against harmful mutations) will slow down the rate of molecular change in those parts of the protein which are crucial for the proper functioning of the protein. In those parts of the protein which are not important for proper functioning, the rates of evolution will be faster and will be selection neutral. Ridley's assessment of the evidence for this theory is that where there are synonymous changes in the bases of amino acids (changes which are selectively neutral), Kimura's hypothesis of there being a faster rate of change has been borne out. This indicates that some molecular evolutionary

---

[25] See M. Ridley, *The Problems of Evolution* (Oxford: Oxford University Press, 1985), esp. ch. 5.

change is neutral, but even this claim is fairly minimal; it allows that there is a lot of negative selection which takes place which shapes the features of the organism. Again, how much positive selection there is must be a matter for biologists to decide. Dawkins's opinion is that it is only selectionism which can explain the complexity of biological organisms:

large quantities of evolutionary change may be non-adaptive, in which case these alternative theories [neutralism and mutationism] may well be important in parts of evolution, but only in the boring parts of evolution, not the parts concerned with what is special about life as opposed to non-life.[26]

The case against biological reductionism must rest here. The opinions of Dawkins and Ridley can hardly be considered definitive (it may be that their views are just new orthodoxy); no doubt the debate between neutralists and their adaptationist opponents will continue. Our claim is simply that to the extent to which neutralism gains ground, the status of evolutionary biology as a non-reductive science is threatened. As Dawkins goes on to note,[27] neutral evolution is, by definition, random (more specifically, biologically random: it may be physically deterministic). Because it is it will be uninteresting from a biologically theoretical point of view. Any theoretical interest will lie in what physically produces the biologically random result. Adaptationism is, by definition, biologically non-random (even if the underlying processes are indeterministic). If we need to postulate adaptations to explain evolutionary change, then functional explanation will be appropriate and, as a consequence, evolutionary theory will be non-reducible.

5. UNSCIENTIFIC PSYCHOLOGICAL POSTSCRIPT

It has been argued above that it is selectionism which preserves the autonomy of the special sciences. In this postscript it is claimed that psychology does not quite fit this prescription, and as a consequence the task of respectably naturalizing the mental remains problematic. Psychology would be un-

[26] Dawkins, *The Blind Watchmaker*, 303.
[27] Ibid. 304.

problematic if psychological explanations were functional explanations. My (dogmatically asserted) claim is that they are not. One can accept that the mindedness of human beings is a product of evolution, so that our ability to form beliefs about our environment, for example, is an adaptation. This does not by itself license the conclusion that the intentional explanation of action is itself functional explanation. If what has gone before is correct, functional explanation is 'gappy': we are entitled to attribute functionality to an item even before we see how the item performs the function. It is because it is gappy that we can see how the causal mechanisms can fit into the functional scheme of things, and so there is no clash between functional and causal explanation. The attribution of intentional content to explain an action, however, does not share this feature. The *content* does not leave a space for the causal story to fill. As a consequence the causal explanation of action does not illuminate the intentional explanation in the way that the causal account can illuminate a functional explanation in biology.

Although this presents a problem for the naturalization of intentionality, I want to close by noting one aspect in which the attribution of mental properties chimes with the selectionist account which we have been suggesting is necessary for a supervenient special science. What the content does is to represent the world from the agent's point of view, and it explains actions as emanating from that point of view. An immediate tension arises between the point of view of the agent and the actions thereby explained: the agent has access to the intentional content, which nevertheless seems to perform its explanatory function in virtue of being *non-contingently* connected to the action explained. To use the old terminology, there appears to be a logical (in the broad sense of *rational*) connection between the mental explanans and the ensuing action. The tension results from the peculiarity of the agent having access to an introspectible content which nevertheless has its identity determined by the resulting action.[28] It is not

[28] This way of putting the point about the tension between first- and third-person perspectives on mental states is due to Crispin Wright, in his 'Critical Notice: *Wittgenstein on Meaning* (by Colin McGinn)', *Mind*, 97(390) (1989), 293–4.

this tension which is immediately relevant; what is essential to note is that it partly arises because the attribution of content is bound by the effects (actions) it produces. We are always prepared to revise our idea of the explanatory mental content if it does not result in the expected action. This produces a result analogous to a selection process. The selection process arranges causes so that they will produce the right effects; in the psychological case the cause (intentional content) is 'selected' by the effect it produces in the stronger sense of being (non-causally) determined by the effect.[29]

This analogy between the two kinds of selection is in keeping with our previous strictures on the possibility of an autonomous special science. Both types of selection ensure that causal harmony prevails. The second type of selection, however, has another aspect to it which causes further problems for the project of a scientific psychology, and that is that there is a strong tendency to view the selection as being 'only' epistemological. In the biological case the selection process is part of nature, and so there is no barrier to viewing the resultant functional properties realistically. In the psychological case the determination of content seems dependent upon us, answerable as it is to our own canons of rationality. As a consequence there is a far greater pull to viewing psychological explanation instrumentally, as being a convenient fiction replaceable when the causal story is available. In psychology it is eliminativism, not reduction, which is the threat.

---

[29] Although I have consistently talked in the singular about 'the effect' it will always be the case that there will be more than the single action to take into account in ascribing intentional content. The non-contingent link between action(s) and content(s) is not removed by this recognition of holism.

4

Structural Explanation in Social Theory*

Frank Jackson and Philip Pettit

Social theory pursues the relatively abstract explanation of social facts. Thus it is distinguished on two fronts: by its subject-matter, social facts, and by its method of explanation, one that is relatively abstract.

Social facts are easier to illustrate than define. They include facts, if they are facts, like the following: that the rich enjoy higher social status than the poor; that there has been a world-wide fall in the number of smokers; that the Soviet Union has withdrawn its troops from Afghanistan; that the crime-rate in Australia is lower than in the US; that every successful entrepreneur maximizes expected net revenue; and that the birth-rate in Western countries has fallen this century.

All such facts seem to have at least this in common, that they obtain or largely obtain in virtue of the intentional attitudes— the beliefs, desires, and the like—of a number of people, and/or the effects of such attitudes: the actions which the attitudes occasion and the consequences of those actions. The rich enjoying higher status than the poor is a matter of the attitudes that people take to rich and poor; the fall in the number of smokers is a matter of the actions of individuals in the past and the present. In such cases the social fact obtains in virtue of the attitudes and actions of the individuals and perhaps the contexts in which they occur. Rather than look for

* A draft of this paper was read on our behalf by Geoffrey Brennan at a conference in the Australian National University. We are grateful to him both for his own comments and for comments relayed from the conference discussion. We were also helped by remarks passed on by Greg Currie, Jon Elster, Barry Hindess, Behan McCullagh, Graham Macdonald, Peter Menzies, Elliott Sober, and Michael Taylor, and by comments made when the paper was presented at various locations

any more specific *differentia*, we shall assume that social facts can be identified as facts of such an intentionally supervenient character.[1] Given that definition, many social facts will be of no interest whatsoever; but some certainly will.

If a social fact obtains in virtue of a certain distribution of attitudes or actions, perhaps in a certain context, then the factors which would be invoked in our folk psychology as the sources of those attitudes and actions are also at the causal origin of the social fact. We might conceivably look to the detailed psychological antecedents of such facts in attempting to explain them. But if we are to do social theory then the explanation we seek must be relatively more abstract than this. It must prescind in some degree from that level of detail.[2] Or so at least we shall assume.

Understood in this way, social theory divides into two broad kinds, microtheory and macrotheory. Microtheory seeks to explain social facts by reference to psychological antecedents, macrotheory by reference to antecedents of other kinds: though those other antecedents are varied, we shall always describe the explanation provided as structural explanation. Suppose that a social fact obtains as a result of certain people, John, Mary . . . having certain attitudes and performing certain actions. If we can abstract from the identity of the individuals involved and explain the social fact simply by *some* people's displaying those attitudes and actions, then we have one sort of micro-explanation for the fact. But perhaps the best-known kind of social micro-explanation is that associated with the economic or rational-choice approach. This would have us abstract not just from the identity of the individuals involved, but also from the precise content of their motivations; it would have us argue that behaviour sufficient to generate the fact under explanation was probable or inevitable anyway, being in some sense rationally required. Both in this case and in the

[1] For an account of social properties which motivates this condition see P. Pettit, 'Social Holism without Collectivism', in E. Margalit (ed.), *The Israel Colloquium: Studies in the History, Philosophy and Sociology of Science*, v (Dordrecht: Reidel, forthcoming). For a rather different account of social properties see D.-H. Ruben, *The Metaphysics of the Social World* (London: Routledge & Kegan Paul, 1985), ch. 3.

[2] See R. Miller, 'Methodological Individualism and Social Explanation', *Philosophy of Science*, 45 (1978).

previous one we explain a social fact by its psychological origins, while doing so in the relatively abstract way distinctive of social theory.

Our prime concern in this paper is social macrotheory or structural explanation. This is a sort of explanation found in economics but it is associated particularly with other social sciences like anthropology, sociology, and political science. We shall assume, to start with, that structural explanation is often an interesting exercise. The question which we wish to raise is how such explanation can be useful. Social facts, by our definition, largely obtain in virtue of what happens at the psychological level. So how can they be usefully explained in abstraction from that level? Unless we can provide an answer to this question, we must cast doubt on the role of structural explanation in social theory.

In raising this question about structural or macro-explanation, we are going along with the common assumption that there is no comparable problem about micro-explanation. Towards the end of our discussion, however, we shall see that this is not so: that, surprisingly, micro-explanation raises a similar problem. At the point where we recognize the problem, however, we will already have a solution to hand: that which we derive for the macro-explanation case.[3]

The paper is in five sections. In the first section we try to articulate in greater detail the problem with which we are concerned. In the following three sections we deal with three different models of how structural explanation is possible; we dub these respectively the subversive, the pre-emptive, and the program models. We reject the subversive and pre-emptive models and endorse the program one. Finally, in the fifth section, we consider the significance of our resolution of the problem for issues in social ontology. We argue that the suggestion of collectivism involved in endorsing the program model ought not to worry an individualist.

---

[3] Notice the parallel with the position described in F. Jackson and P. Pettit, 'Functionalism and Broad Content', *Mind*, 97 (1988). There we try to solve a problem about broad functional explanation in psychology, as distinct, apparently, from narrow; but having found the solution—of a kind with that proposed here—we show that it is also needed to solve a problem raised by narrow functional explanation.

1. THE PROBLEM

In order to appreciate the problem raised by structural explanation, it is necessary to consider the sorts of case where such explanation is deployed. We will look at four. We will offer examples to illustrate each of these categories but it is important to note that we do not necessarily endorse any particular example as a good explanation.

Explanations which belong to the first of the four categories invoke aggregate-level correlates of the events explained. The following examples, however sketchy and impoverished, illustrate the category:

1. The increase in unemployment explains the rise in the level of crime.
2. Increased urbanization explains the decline in religious practice.
3. The advent of literacy explains the shift to a more secular society.[4]
4. The restructuring of manufacturing industry explains the decline of trade union power.

We describe such accounts as correlate explanations because in all of them an aggregate-level change is represented as correlated in an explanatory fashion with the social fact to be explained. Correlate explanations cover a variety of forms, ranging from those that invoke social statistics on inflation, divorce, mobility, and the like to explanations which call on less precisely defined antecedents like industrialization, urbanization, and literacy.

The second type of structural explanation has been the stock-in-trade of much anthropology and sociology this century. It is the kind of explanation associated with the functionalist paradigm, which invokes the beneficial effects of a certain type of fact to explain why that fact obtains or continues to obtain. We are familiar with the biological account which explains why the human heart beats by reference to the beneficial effect of that beating in circulating blood through the body. The idea

---

[4] See J. Goody, *The Domestication of the Savage Mind* (Cambridge: Cambridge University Press, 1977).

f'ism — one kind of
st'ist explanation.

here is that more or less exact analogues are available in the social world.

Function explanations are illustrated by the following accounts:

1. The fact that it produces a change in the feelings of the parties involved towards one another explains the nature and persistence of the peace-making ceremony.[5]
2. The fact that it is necessary for the survival of the local society explains why there is social stratification: that is, the unequal distribution of rewards.[6]
3. The fact that it is optimal for further development of productive power explains why the capitalist economic structure persists.[7]
4. The fact that at a given cost it maximizes the distances between phonemes explains the configuration of the vowel space.[8]

But explanations which invoke benefits are not restricted in social macrotheory to explanations of a functionalist character. It is common in macrotheory, as indeed in common sense—our folk sociology—to treat groups and organizations as agents and to explain certain happenings—the actions of the aggregate entity—by the fact that they promote interests imputed to the aggregate. Thus the following also count as structural explanations:

1. The fact that it was in their class interest explains why the bourgeoisie tolerated the introduction of universal suffrage.
2. The fact that it is in the country's interest explains why Great Britain has stayed in Nato.
3. The fact that doing so maximized expected returns explains why the company reduced its labour force.

[5] See A. R. Radcliffe-Brown, *The Andaman Islanders* (Glencoe, Ill.: Free Press, 1948), 238–9.

[6] See K. Davis and W. E. Moore, 'Some Principles of Stratification', *American Sociological Review*, 10 (1945).

[7] See G. A. Cohen, *Karl Marx's Theory of History* (Oxford: Oxford University Press, 1979), 175.

[8] See P. Van Parijs, *Evolutionary Explanation in the Social Sciences* (London: Tavistock, 1981), ch. 4.

Someone may feel that these examples are not truly structural explanations, since they seem to point us indirectly to psychological antecedents of the results explained. But we would urge that they do not refer us to such antecedents. For all that any of the explanations say, the individuals involved could have been in a variety of psychological states. Thus if we account for a group's doing something on the grounds that it is in their group interest, we do not imply that the members involved in the group action saw it explicitly that way. It may be that they acted according to a received formula and that the point of the explanation is to suggest that were such a formula not suitable for promoting the group interest then it would not prevail. At one level the group acted as it did because of the formula governing the case; at another it acted as it did because that response was indeed in the group interest.

Apart from explanations that invoke correlates, functions, and interests, social macrotheory often offers us examples of what we might describe as context explanations. These explain social facts by reference to cultural context. Some examples should make clear the sort of account that we are envisaging:

1. The contemporary Protestant ethic explains the rise of capitalism in modern Europe.[9]
2. The increasing dependence of the populace on publicly provided welfare explains the crisis of the capitalist state.[10]
3. The ethos of capitalism explains the breakdown of family and community values.
4. The nationalism which appeared in Britain during the Second World War explains much about the character of British films in the 1940s and early 1950s.

With these examples, as with those of explanation by aggregate-level interests, someone may again object that we are directed to psychological antecedents of the conditions explained and that they are not examples of structural explanation. But here we urge, as in the other case, that the factor

---

[9] See M. Weber, *The Protestant Ethic and the Spirit of Capitalism* (London: Unwin, 1930).

[10] See C. Offe, *Strukturprobleme des kapitalistischen Staates* (Frankfurt: Suhrkamp, 1972).

involved is meant to be explanatory under a variety of possible individual-level processes; its invocation does not point us to any particular psychological explanation. Thus when we are told that the Protestant ethic explains the rise of capitalism, we are not informed about how psychologically it did so. Perhaps the ethic condemned activities inimical to capitalism; perhaps it encouraged the relationships between people which capitalism requires; perhaps it gave people a goal which inspired capitalist activity as a means; perhaps it did all or a number of these things. Many psychological possibilities remain open and so the account on offer, if it is truly explanatory, explains in abstraction from the particular individual-level processes that are at work; it is not just another way of referring us to a micro-explanation of the result explained.[11]

These four varieties of explanation should suffice to illustrate the sort of thing we have in mind when we speak of structural explanation. In each case a social fact which obtains in virtue of people's dispositions and doings is explained other than by reference to psychological antecedents. In each case, therefore, we face the question how the factor invoked, be it a correlate, function, interest, or context, usefully serves to explain that fact.

In order to feel the force of this question, it is necessary to be absolutely clear about one point. This, and we have already laid some stress on it, is that structural explanations are not covert psychological accounts. They do not serve as ways of directing us to psychological antecedents which would furnish a micro-explanation of the social facts on which they bear. The sort of factor introduced in a structural explanation is consistent with a variety of psychological configurations and so its explanatory force does not come of identifying any one of them as the micro-explanans.

Suppose that an apparently structural explanation invokes a non-psychological factor X. It will direct us to a psychological

---

[11] If someone is unpersuaded that this fourth category is a kind of structural explanation, they need not worry: the main line of argument in the paper should still be of interest. Notice too that even if this fourth category is a sort of micro-explanation, it still raises a problem, as we shall see later, of much the same kind as we wish to focus on here: see the second last paragraph of the introduction.

antecedent, and not really be a structural explanation, if it is a matter of folk psychology that there is a suitably explanatory psychological antecedent associated with X. What is or is not a matter of folk psychology is going to be controversial sometimes and so there will be borderline cases where to some eyes an explanation belongs with macrotheory, to others with microtheory. We take a fairly austere view of the compass of folk psychology, identifying it with the thesis that human beings exhibit intentional states like beliefs and desires, that these states are more or less sensitive to the rational pressures of evidence and the like, and that they are responsible for people's actions, causing agents to do things that seem rational in the light of what they believe and desire.[12] Thus we are disposed to regard many borderline cases as macro- rather than micro-explanations. But even to our eyes there are many apparently structural explanations that are really psychological in character.

One is where the factor invoked, say X, represents an indirect way of identifying a particular psychological configuration. Suppose we are told that the image of an isolated Ireland explains why the Irish electorate voted massively for entry to the EEC. It ought to be clear that this account, on the face of it a macrostory, is actually a micro-explanation. The factor invoked, once it is spelled out, is just a psychological explanans: the fact that the Irish electorate generally saw the alternative to EEC entry as isolation.

A second way in which an apparently structural explanation may actually be a micro-account is less obvious. It is found where the explanation effectively invokes not the factor X that is explicitly mentioned, but the fact that certain people are aware of X. Imagine we are told that the volatility of the stock market explains why so many are investing in housing. On the most natural reading, this is not really a macro-explanation, for the factor invoked in explanation is not so much the volatility of the market as people's awareness of the volatility, and that is a psychological antecedent; it is not the stuff of which structural explanation is made.

---

[12] See our paper 'In Defence of Folk Psychology', *Philosophical Studies*, 57 (1990).

A third way in which a seeming structural explanation may be a micro-account is closely related to the second. It appears where the explanation effectively invokes, if not the fact that people are aware of the factor X that is explicitly mentioned, then the fact that they are aware of something that X is presumed to bring about. Suppose we are told that a certain central bank adjustment, which is understood between explainer and explainee to have caused rapid inflation, explains the unpopularity of the government. Clearly such a story may simply be a way of providing a micro-explanation of government unpopularity by reference to people's awareness of the inflation. The case is very similar to the one just considered.

The question which we face then is how a social fact that obtains in virtue of certain psychological antecedents can be usefully explained by something distinct from such antecedents. In the three sections following we consider different answers to that question. The first two answers are the responses which appear most articulately in the literature. The third is that which we ourselves endorse.

Before leaving this section it will be useful to see our problem in a more abstract way. Let factors of any kind *k* be said to be causal in the production of an event *e* if and only if they satisfy some loose, colloquial condition like the following: if an agent were in a position to manipulate those factors, then we can conceive of his doing so out of a desire to bring about *e*; the *k*-factors are instrumentally effective—they are potential controls—relative to *e*. If causality is defined in this loose but common way, then there is room for distinctions between factors of less or more basic causal kinds. The *k*-factors will be of a less basic causal kind than certain *j*-factors—for short, they will be less basic causes[13]—if and only if their causal relation to *e* is realized by a causal relation between the *j*-factors and *e*. Equally they will be more basic causes than any factors whose causal relation to *e* they in turn realize.

---

[13] This way of speaking will certainly not be misleading *if*, as in the social theory cases to be discussed, the *k*-factors are not contingently identical with the *j*-factors. Otherwise it may be, as there will be extra complexities to take into account. See our 'Program Explanation: A General Perspective', *Analysis*, 50(2) (1990), and C. Macdonald and G. Macdonald, 'Mental Causes and Explanation of Action', *Philosophical Quarterly*, 36 (1986).

It should be clear how this abstract picture fits the structural explanation case. For any social fact explained, the psychological antecedents certainly count as causal factors in its appearance. The structural antecedents may or may not always be thought of as causes but, since this will make our problem harder rather than easier, we will see them in that way: thus urbanization causes religious decline, the fact that stratification is functional causes it to persist, and so on. The point to stress, however, is that even if the structural factors are seen as causal, still it appears that they are less basic causes than the psychological antecedents. Their causal linkage to any fact they explain is apparently realized by the causal connection between the operative psychological antecedents and that fact. If urbanization causes religious decline, it does so through people's experience of city life leading them to form such attitudes as keep them from church. If the fact that stratification is functional causes it to persist, it does so through people having such attitudes in a stratified society as cause them to behave in a way that sustains the stratification. And so on.

Wherever the abstract pattern we have identified is to be found, there is a potential problem of the kind that we have raised for structural explanation. Suppose that there are at least two kinds of causal factor, j and k, which are relevant to certain events, and that j is a causally more basic kind than k. Suppose further, as is certainly true in the social theory cases, that the k-explanations are not useful pointers to causally more basic factors like the j-items; at more basic levels, the k-connections are realizable in any of an open variety of ways, so that the fact that a k-connection obtains tells us little or nothing about what factors are in play at a more basic level. Suppose finally, as in the social theory cases, that j-explanations and k-explanations both seem to represent interesting ways of accounting for the events in question. The problem is how the two sorts of explanation relate to one another, in particular how they relate to one another so as to remain independently interesting. If an event a causally influences an event b which causally influences something e, or if a and b combine to influence e causally, then we see no difficulty in how an a-explanation and a b-explanation of e can both be interesting. The problem on hand is how they can both be interesting if a third condition is realized: if they relate as more and less basic causal factors.

In any comparison of levels, it is natural to assume that the causally more basic kind of factor certainly does provide an interesting explanation, and we shall go along with that assumption. Thus our problem becomes that of showing how a higher-level explanation can be as interesting as a lower-level account of something: how the k-explanation of an event can be as interesting as the j-account. This problem will be particularly acute in cases where we are in a position, at least in principle, to develop j-explanations as well as k-explanations. The issue will be why we should maintain any interest in the k-explanations, rather than giving them up in favour of pursuing j-accounts.[14]

The social theory case raises the problem in its acute form, since we are in principle able to develop individual-level psychological explanations of social facts as well as aggregate-level structural accounts. Henceforth, therefore, we shall concentrate on the acute problem. The problem in its acute form is not restricted, however, to the social case. Given the growing potential of neurophysiology to describe the antecedents of any action, a similar problem arises of how even psychological explanations can retain an autonomous interest. After all, the connection between certain beliefs and desires and any action they explain is clearly realized neurophysiologically and, by all contemporary accounts, it is multiply realizable at the neurophysiological level. Thus it is not clear how belief–desire explanation can retain autonomous interest. But we shall not concern ourselves with that or any other non-social instance of the problem.[15] Our concern here is purely with the problem of structural explanation in social theory.

[14] The problem, particularly in its non-acute form, is discussed more fully in our 'Program Explanation: A General Perspective'.

[15] We deal with the psychological problem, among other issues, in Jackson and Pettit, 'Functionalism and Broad Content'. In that paper the sort of problem at issue is presented somewhat differently. See also our 'Program Explanation: A General Perspective'.

2. THE SUBVERSIVE MODEL

Faced with the problem presented by structural explanation, there are only three salient responses:

1. deny that structural explanation is interesting;
2. deny that structural causes are less basic;
3. deny that less basic causes make for less interesting explanation.

All three responses are to be found in the literature. The first response, associated with rank individualism—the sort described later as heuristic individualism—will say that any structural explanations that look interesting must turn out to be covertly psychological accounts; we shall not discuss it further here.[16] The other two responses dominate the literature. The second is associated with the subversive model described in this section, the third with the pre-emptive model described in the next and indeed with the program model which we ourselves endorse.

If we deny that structural causes are less basic, then we reject the claim that the abstract pattern identified in the last section applies to the social case. We deny that the causal linkage of every structural cause to the event it explains is realized by a linkage between the psychological antecedents and that event. We may then have any of the following pictures in mind of how macro-events relate to micro and serve to provide an explanation of the fact to be explained:

1. The macro- and the micro-causes are both parts of the total causal explanation but each explains on its own, on the assumption that the other occurs. An analogy: the striking of the match explains the fire, assuming the wood is dry; the wood's being dry explains the fire, assuming the match is struck.
2. The macrocause overdetermines the micro, so that if the micro had not occurred, it would have caused, and causally explained, the fact to be explained. An analogy:

[16] For an honest if unnuanced statement, see M. N. Rothbeard, *Individualism and the Philosophy of the Social Sciences* (San Francisco, Calif.: Cato Institute, 1979).

my poisoning the dog overdetermines its death, if the dog was shot before the poison took effect.

3. The macrofactor itself causes the realization of the micro and offers us an explanation by reference to a non-immediate cause. An analogy: if the slate falling from the roof causes the pedestrian to jump and the pedestrian jumping causes a car accident, then the falling of the slate can explain the accident.

Of these possibilities, however, only the third is really open. Neither of the first two is remotely plausible. The first fails because the micro-antecedents of a social fact are sufficient on their own to ensure that it obtains. The second fails because there is no possible causal route from the macrofactor to the social fact other than one which goes via the psychological antecedents. In any case the second possibility would not allow us to say that the macrofactor is explanatory. My poisoning the dog does not actually explain its death, if in fact it merely overdetermines it.

Thus, if we deny that structural causes are less basic, we must mean to assert the third possibility. We must mean to say that the macrofactor invoked in the structural explanation is itself a cause of the microfactor at work. That would be no problem, of course, if the macrofactor was said to cause the required psychological antecedents in the ordinary manner countenanced in folk psychology: that is, in the way in which the volatility of the stock market causes people to be aware of that volatility. But this route has already been ruled out: in distinguishing structural explanations from covert micro-accounts, we are supposing that the macrofactors invoked do not have that sort of psychologically familiar impact on people.

The only recourse for those approaching our problem on this tack is to brave the storm. They must say that, contrary to our own intuitive sense of these things, contrary to our folk psychology, structural explanations explain through pointing to factors which produce the psychological antecedents in virtue of which the fact explained obtains. They must say that, by whatever instrumentality, a relatively abstract feature like increased urbanization, the social benefit of stratification, the class benefit of tolerance, or the ethos of capitalism must be capable of eliciting in individuals the psychological profile which guarantees that the social explanandum obtains.

We believe that faced with this prospect most social theorists will try to cast interesting structural explanations as micro ones after all, or will want to explore one of our later models. There are two obvious objections to adopting this one and we think that they ought to be found persuasive, at least given the alternative model that we propose later. The first objection is that it is far from clear how most of the factors invoked in structural explanations are supposed to affect individual human beings, in particular to affect them other than by coming into their consciousness and constituting covertly micro-explanations. How is a high rate of urbanization meant, in itself, to transform the minds of people? After all, urbanization is an abstract statistic, not the sort of thing we expect to produce psychological effects other than by becoming an object of consciousness. How can the alleged fact, again something abstract, that stratification is socially beneficial cause people to transform psychologically so that they become disposed to group themselves in social strata? Again, how can something abstract like the Protestant ethic directly produce the psychological profiles of would-be capitalists?

The second objection is that, not only do most of the macro-factors invoked in structural explanation look unlikely candidates for having the alleged effects, it would undermine our folk psychology more radically than may at first appear to imagine that they act as influences of the kind required. It is part of the folk-psychological notion of belief that a belief is not formed or held in a manner that is entirely insensitive, at least under suitable exposure, to matters of evidence and consistency.[17] To count as a believer is to count, perhaps within certain limits, as someone who is sensitive in this way. Thus our image of ourselves, and more generally of human beings, as belief-driven agents is going to be put under strain by the view that structural factors have direct and unrecognized causal influences on our psychological make-up. That

---

[17] For a discussion of this view in the context of the social sciences see G. Macdonald and P. Pettit, *Semantics and Social Science* (London: Routledge & Kegan Paul, 1981).

theory will allege, at the least, that there are unfamiliar limits on our sensitivity to evidence and the like; it will subvert, in whatever measure, the manifest image of the human being as an intentional system.

Though we do not think that such a subversive model is attractive, there is no doubt that certain social scientists have been drawn to it. They have embraced the conclusion that social macrotheory offers us a view of human beings, and in particular of the forces to which they are subject, which is as subversive of everyday psychology as Freud was ever thought to be.

We see suggestions of such a subversive approach in some of Marx and Engels' discussion of false consciousness and ideology, and even in Durkheim's notion of the causal potency of the social fact. But it is probably only in the excesses of recent French structuralism that the theory achieves explicit formulation.[18] Louis Althusser proclaimed the abolition of the subject as the cost to be paid—in his case it appears to have been paid with some enthusiasm—for the insights of Marxist macrotheory, correctly understood. He writes:

The structure of the relations of production determines the *places* and *functions* occupied and adopted by the agents of production, who are never anything more than the occupants of these places, in so far as they are the supports (*Träger*) of these functions. The true 'subjects' (in the sense of constitutive subjects of the process) are therefore not these occupants or functionaries, are not, despite all the appearances, the 'obviousnesses' of the 'given' of naïve anthropology, 'concrete individuals', 'real men'—but *the definition and distribution of these places and functions. The true 'subjects' are these definers and distributors: the relations of production* (and political and ideological social relations).[19]

Under this subversive approach the human subject, as we understand him or her in everyday life, becomes in Levi-Strauss's words an 'intolerable spoiled child who for too long has held the philosophical scene and prevented any serious work, drawing exclusive attention to itself'.[20] We think the

---

[18] See P. Pettit, *The Concept of Structuralism* (Berkeley: University of California Press, 1975).

[19] L. Althusser, *Reading Capital* (London: New Left Books, 1970), 180.

[20] C. Levi-Strauss, *L'Homme nu* (Paris: Plon, 1971), 614–15; the translation is ours.

approach is extremely unattractive: it offers a very shaky foundation for structural explanation.

3. THE PRE-EMPTIVE MODEL

The subversive model of structural explanation suggests that macrofactors must directly produce those psychological antecedents in virtue of which the social facts explained obtain. Our second candidate, the pre-emptive model, suggests that the macrofactors must filter for, not actually produce, the psychological antecedents of the facts to be explained.[21] It presents a picture under which the structural factors may be less basic causes and still serve to provide autonomous and interesting explanations.

In order to understand this model, let us envisage that in the past there has been a certain sort of social selection. There will have been a social selection if at some stage in our history groups competed with one another in the struggle for survival, in such a way that the members of each group stood or fell together. We may imagine the selection working to the pattern of Darwinian biology, though it might also be based on genetically underdetermined behaviour; we shall see an example of this later. According to Darwinian biology it is genes that are selected in natural history and they are selected for the effects they have, given the contemporary environment, in the competition for survival. Such selection can work at the individual or social level, depending on whether the competition in question is between individual organisms or groups which such organisms form. Normally the competition envisaged is between individuals. It will be competition between groups if those groups each stood or fell together in the struggle for survival.

Suppose then that at a certain stage of human history there was a competition for survival among societies which differed in this respect: in some, given the genes at work, people were psychologically such that it became a fact that F; in others this

---

[21] See R. Nozick, *Anarchy, State and Utopia* (New York: Basic Books, 1974), 22.

was not the case. Suppose now that the realization of F was important in determining survival chances and that only the first sorts of society survived; F-societies might be cohesive ones or ones involving clear relations of power. Under these suppositions we might in a particular case claim that though the realization of F was of course due to the psychological configuration of the members of the society, still it can also be explained by the fact that F is functional for the society.

An example will make the possibility clearer and, happily, we can invoke one drawn from real-life social science; the example involves genetically underdetermined behaviour patterns but it appeals to social selection. Stuart Piddocke has argued that the potlatch system of the southern Kwakiutl, a system involving a ceremony in which individuals from different groups compete to confer valuable goods on one another, is a system which, however it emerged, accounted in the past for the survival of some populations rather than others; it assured the flow of food resources in time of need, since these could be given in return for wealth objects. Thus Piddocke argues that, although continuation of the potlatch is explained in microterms as the result of people's psychological dispositions, it can also be explained in structural terms by the fact that it is or has been functional for the survival of the Kwakiutl. 'The potlatch has adaptive value in allowing the Kwakiutl to preserve their entire population, even when some groups faced extinction through starvation. The potlatch was thus "selected" and retained because it facilitated, and now promotes, survival.'[22]

In such an example the fact that the potlatch is functional does not itself produce the behavioural dispositions in virtue of which the system persists but it does filter for the persistence of that system. It ensures, given the selectional story just told, that we can only expect to find, among the extant Kwakiutl, groups which maintain the potlatch. Any groups whose members were disposed to drop it would simply not have survived. The functional character of the potlatch pre-empts the psy-

---

[22] J. Turner and A. Maryanski, *Functionalism* (Menlo Park, Calif.: Benjamin-Cummings, 1979), 86. Turner and Maryanski note that Piddocke's empirical assumptions have been questioned, but that need not concern us here.

chology of individuals. It ensures that only a psychology that supports the maintenance of the system can have survived.

The potlatch example points us towards a general model of how structural explanation might be thought to be possible. On this model, a structural factor will be capable of explaining a given social fact so far as it pre-empts the actual psychological antecedents, ensuring for evolutionary reasons that there are only such antecedents around as go with realization of the social fact. This model is what we describe as the pre-emptive model of structural explanation.

The pre-emptive model is not much more attractive than the subversive one. There are at least two reasons why. The first is that, at most, it would vindicate only structural explanations in the functional category; a selectional story will not go through except for the sorts of factor invoked there.[23] The second is that with most function explanations, even those that are intuitively persuasive, a selectional story looks very implausible.

This second point may need elaboration. Note that a selectional story of the kind required in the pre-emptive model must postulate the following:

1. Over a suitable evolutionary period there emerged a number of distinct societies, the members of each of which were bound to fall or stand, disappear or survive together;
2. these differed in certain aggregate features, in virtue of their members differing, whether for genetic or other reasons, in behavioural dispositions and patterns; and
3. over the period in question there must have been a relatively unchanging environment such that a society's performance in the survival stakes would have consistently been favoured or jeopardized by the same sorts of aggregate feature.

---

[23] It is formally possible to represent the other sorts of structural explanation as explanations in the functional category. Thus we might represent the urbanization story as a function explanation by claiming that the decline of religious practice was explained by the fact that it was functional that urbanization should be attended by such a decline. That sort of claim has no plausibility. On related matters, however, see P. Pettit, 'Broad-Minded Explanation and Psychology', in P. Pettit and J. McDowell (eds.), *Subject, Thought, and Context* (Oxford: Clarendon Press, 1986).

Clearly these are demanding conditions and we have no evidence of their having been fulfilled in any widespread fashion. But even if they were fulfilled, we still could not be sanguine about the claim that the selectional story would vindicate many of our function explanations. Suppose that the question arises whether we can invoke the fact that a certain aggregate feature is functional in a contemporary society to explain its persistence. We can avail ourselves of the selectional story only if the feature involved is also likely to have been functional in the earlier, smaller societies on which selection operated. And that considerably restricts the sorts of feature to which the story can be applied. Thus since stratification in the sense in which we know it is unlikely to have had a suitably exact parallel in a small, primitive society, the selectional story would not serve to legitimize the explanation of stratification by the alleged fact that it is functional in current societies.

For those who think we are being excessively unimpressed by the possibility of selectionally vindicating function explanations, it may be worth mentioning one further complicating factor. This is that we will need to postulate a story of social selection, or take evidence of social selection seriously, only in the following event: that the behavioural dispositions which give rise to the socially functional feature are not themselves individually functional. If the dispositions are individually functional regardless of whether there is social selection—for example, to take the case of something genetically determined, if they maximize the chance of the individual's reproducing his or her genes—then we do not need any explanatory recourse to *social* selection. The persistence of the macrofeature will be explained as a by-product of the persistence of the dispositions which give rise to it, and the latter will be explained by the *individually* functional character of the dispositions. Thus, if it is argued that deference to the prior assumptions about how an interaction will go—in Goffman's phrase, the reluctance to break frame—is individually functional, and if that behavioural pattern gives rise to social hierarchies, that gives us no reason for claiming that such hierarchies persist because they are socially functional.[24]

---

[24] See S. Milgram, *Obedience to Authority* (London: Tavistock, 1974).

These considerations ought clearly to give us pause about resting the case for the interest of structural explanation, or at least resting it exclusively, on the pre-emptive model. It seems to us that there are probably only two sorts of case where the selectional story is likely to provide a legitimate function explanation. One is with primitive societies, as in Piddocke's account of the potlatch. The other is with commercial entities like firms which have survived the environment of a competitive market over a longish period and have done so in virtue of certain aggregate features: say, by following such decision procedures as mean that expected returns are maximized. If we assume that the decision-makers in such firms are not themselves intentionally focused on expected returns— say, they follow rules of thumb—and that the dispositions which produce the features are more or less faithfully reproduced across generations of the firm so that those rules of thumb become more or less sacred, then we may be able to explain the features by the benefit they confer on the firm.

But despite the limited attraction of the pre-emptive model, it should be clear that, at least in suppressed form, it has enjoyed great popularity in the social sciences. We see it in the background of most functionalist theorizing or at least of functionalist theorizing which seeks not just to analyse the social benefits of certain structures, but to explain the persistence— sometimes even the emergence—of those structures by appeal to the benefits. It is generally acknowledged that when functionalists explain a structure by its benefits, they deny that agents are or need be aware of the benefits it produces.[25] No explicit account is given of the mechanism whereby the functional character of a feature is supposed to explain its persistence.[26] But the account generally envisaged is that of social selection.[27]

---

[25] See J. Elster, *Explaining Technical Change* (Cambridge: Cambridge University Press, 1983). See also M. Douglas, *How Institutions Think* (New York: University of Syracuse Press, 1986).

[26] See Turner and Maryanski, *Functionalism*, ch. 5.

[27] This is conceded by Phillipe Van Parijs, *Evolutionary Explanation in the Social Sciences*, even though he himself investigates a different account of the mechanism. The account which he offers fits very nicely with the model which we describe in the next section.

4. THE PROGRAM MODEL

Our discussion so far teaches us two important lessons. First that structural explanations, as we understand them, do not invoke causes of what they explain, or at least not causes which are as basic as the psychological antecedents. And secondly that they do not generally invoke filtering factors either. The question then is whether there is any other way in which they can succeed in providing autonomous and interesting explanations. We believe there is and we want to introduce our answer in this section. The answer, in brief, is that structural explanations explain, when they explain, by introducing factors which program for the realization of the conditions explained. The fact that they have the programming feature means that, even if they are not suitably basic causes, still these factors can provide autonomous and interesting explanations. Programming factors include filtering factors but they also include much besides.

The best introduction to the program model may be to consider an analogy from the natural sciences. A closed flask contains water and the temperature of the water—the mean molecular motion—is raised. At a certain point the flask cracks. At that point the salient macroconsideration is that the temperature is boiling-point, the salient microconsideration—to simplify somewhat—is that a certain molecule or group of molecules collides with a molecular bond in the surface of the flask at a sufficient velocity to break it. (We are supposing that the case is one where the container breaks because of the internal pressure, not because of the temperature gradient between the water and the container.) The microfactor is apparently a more basic cause of the flask cracking than the fact that the water is at boiling-point: the causal connection at this level realizes the connection at the other. And yet we usefully invoke the macrofactor to explain the cracking. How is this?

Not, certainly, because an analogue of either of our first two models is relevant. Not because the mean molecular motion—an abstract statistic—causes the culpable group of molecules to strike and so is not really a less basic cause. And not because there has been a selection of substances like water which favours those in which the attainment of a certain rate of molecular motion is attended by the cracking of containers that are made of the same substance as our flask.

The answer is more straightforward than either analogue suggests. The rise in temperature explains the cracking of the flask simply because it makes it probable (to a point approaching certainty) that there will be a molecular collision of a kind sufficient to produce the cracking. It makes that probable, not because of any productive or selective mechanism, but simply because the rise in temperature means nothing more or less than that the rate of motion of the water molecules will increase, and if the rate of motion increases then it is more than likely that some molecule will have the effect explained.

In a case like this the fact that the temperature reaches boiling-point does not produce the effect explained in the more basic way that the molecular collision does. But the fact that the temperature reaches boiling-point programs for that effect in a manner in which the more basic cause does not. It means that there will almost certainly be this or that or any one of an indefinite number of molecular collisions and, since any such collision would crack the container, it means that the flask will indeed crack. The rise in temperature programs for the cracking in the intuitive sense that it arranges things non-causally so that there will almost certainly be a collision which will produce the breaking; alternatively, we may say that it programs for the occurrence of such a productive event.

The flask example forces us to recognize that relative to causal factors at a certain level causal explanation may assume either of two forms. It may be a process explanation which accounts for an event under a certain description by appealing to a property or properties in virtue of which such factors are causally operative at that level in producing the event. Or it may be a program explanation which appeals to a property or properties in virtue of which something—in our examples, something distinct from any of the factors in question[28]— ensures that there will be a process at that level which is suited

[28] As is clear in Jackson and Pettit, 'Functionalism and Broad Content', what is invoked may be individuated so that it is the same event as the cause. The important point then is that the property highlighted is not causally efficacious in the same way as the property invoked in the process account.

to produce the event. In the flask example, the process explanation of the breaking relative to causal factors at the level of molecular collisions is that which appeals to the momentum of certain water molecules at their point of impact with the surface of the container. The program explanation is that which appeals to the boiling temperature of the water as something ensuring that there will be a process of molecular collision— perhaps this, perhaps that—sufficient to produce the breaking of the flask.[29]

There has recently been a convergence of opinion on the view, in David Lewis's formulation, that to explain an event causally is to give information on its causal history.[30] Our distinction fits nicely with this view. The process explanation relative to any level identifies actual causes and relevant causal properties. The program explanation identifies a condition such that its realization is enough to ensure that there will be causes to produce the event explained: if not the actual causes, then some others. The process explanation provides information on the causal chain at work in the actual world, the program explanation provides information on the causal chains at work in different possible worlds: viz. the information that so long as the condition identified is realized in any world, or at least in any world more or less similar to ours, there is almost bound to be some causal chain in operation there which will produce an event of the appropriate type.

We believe that the program/process distinction is of great importance in the theory of explanation generally. Elsewhere we have argued that it enables us to make good sense of the relation between the neurophysiological explanation of behaviour and its psychological explanation in terms of beliefs and desires. Relative to the level at which we describe the neuro-

---

[29] Here we give a relativized sense to the phrase 'process explanation', so that a process explanation relative to one level may be a program explanation relative to another; this is convenient, given our concern with an acute form of the problem distinguished in Section 1. Notice, however, that the phrase can also be given an absolute sense, so that only an explanation which invokes causes from the most basic level counts as a process account. We follow this usage in 'Program Explanation: A General Perspective'.

[30] See D. Lewis, 'Causal Explanation', in *Philosophical Papers*, ii (Oxford: Oxford University Press, 1986). See also A. Ryan, *The Philosophy of the Social Sciences* (London: Macmillan, 1970), ch. 3.

physiological factors as the causes of the behaviour, and the neurophysiological features as the causally operative properties, certain configurations of belief and desire program for that type of behaviour: the realization of a configuration that rationally requires a certain type of action more or less ensures that there will be some neurophysiological process available to produce that behaviour.

But the program/process distinction is useful in other areas too. Just to rehearse some more or less obvious applications: if the impact of overlapping surfaces causally prevents a square peg from going through a hole of diameter equal to its side, the squareness of the peg programs for its failure to go through; if the light reflected off the surface of a rag evokes an aggression response in a bull, the red colour of the rag programs for that response; if the molecular bonding pattern of a glass causes it to shatter under a certain impact, the fragility of the glass programs for the shattering; and so on.

To return now to the problem in social theory, we maintain that the program/process distinction is also of use here, offering us a third model of structural explanation. Relative to the level at which the attitudes and actions of individuals are the causal factors which generate social facts, this model suggests that structural factors may program for the appearance of such facts. The idea is that a structural factor may explain a given social fact, not through producing it in the same basic way as individual factors, but through more or less ensuring that there will be some individual-level confluence of factors—perhaps this, perhaps that—sufficient to produce it. A case where the pre-emptive model applies will also be a case of program explanation, since if the fact that a structure is beneficial filters for dispositions which will produce that structure, then in our sense it programs for dispositions of that kind. The important point, however, is that, as our physical case suggests, a macrofactor may program for suitable microcauses even if it does not filter for them. Filtering is just a special case of programming.

In order to substantiate the program model of structural explanations we must turn to examples. Let us consider correlate explanations first: the increase in unemployment explains the rise in the level of crime; urbanization explains the decline in religious practice; and so on. The aggregate antecedent serves in these cases, just like the fact of the water rising to boiling-point, to make probable the occurrence of the sort of micro-event or -events in virtue of which the fact to be explained obtains: that crime increases or religious practice declines. Higher unemployment means more working-class youths free of work obligations, and more working-class youths short of money, so it makes it highly likely that events will occur which will increase the crime-rate. Similarly, urbanization means an increasing population in areas of new or no parishes, a break with traditional parish-centred life, the isolation of individuals from ties of family and village, and a host of other things any subset of which will tend to produce the microfactors in virtue of which there is a decline in religious practice. The program model fits.

It also fits many function explanations and this is perhaps the most encouraging fact of all, for it suggests that in the wake of the functionalist paradigm we can hold on to some of the social accounts—though certainly not all—which that paradigm inspired; in particular, we can hold on to them even if there is no appropriate selection story to be told. Consider, for example, the hypothesis that stratification is beneficial in the organization of society and that it persists for that reason. The benefit conferred by stratification—that is, the inequality of rewards—is usually held to reside in the fact that important positions which are generally difficult to fill in a society do still get filled. Now it ought to be clear that the fact, if it is a fact, that stratification is beneficial in this sense more or less ensures, at least if nothing else can do the trick of filling the positions in question, that it will persist in any society where it emerges. Imagine that we are in a stratified society where a consequence of the stratification is that the relevant positions get filled. If any initiative is adopted which reduces the given inequality of rewards then under the premises given that ought to mean that it will become more and more difficult to fill such positions. But if the positions really are important then short of collective action predicaments—and this is admittedly a substantive qualification—we must expect resistance to the troublesome initiative, resistance which in one way or another ought to restore the original level of stratification. Thus we may say, without invoking any story of selection, that the fact that the stratification is beneficial programs for its reliable persistence: absent collective action predicaments, it more or less ensures that whatever happens at the level of individual attitudes and actions will not cause at least a long-term reduction in the stratification.

This example is special in a way that requires remark. As we have described it, the causal factors whose presence the functionality of stratification ensures—factors associated with the resistance that any shift would elicit—are not actually effective in supporting the stratification; they are standby causes that will only provide support if the stratification comes under threat and support is needed. This means that the functionality does not strictly program for the persistence of the stratification, for the causal factors that actually produce that persistence are not ones whose presence it ensures. What the functionality does program for, however, is the resilience of the stratification—its reliable persistence, as we might put it. It ensures that there are such causal factors present—the standby causes—as suffice for such resilience, at least under the assumption that collective action predicaments and the like do not get in the way.

Still in the realm of function explanations, consider again the Marxist explanation that the capitalist structure persists because it is optimal for the further development of productive power. Suppose that we are in a capitalist society where the capitalist structure really is optimal in this way. Imagine now that an initiative is adopted which crucially alters that structure. Under the optimality assumption, that means that productive power will cease to develop, or at least to develop at the rate it would otherwise have done. But if this happens it is clear that certain individuals will be adversely affected and, more generally, that the society will begin to fall behind competitors in the economic stakes. Again, therefore, collective action predicaments aside, we must expect resistance to any such initiative, resistance which ought to undo the structural alteration. Thus we may say that the fact that the capitalist structure is optimal for the further development of productive power programs for the reliable persistence—the resilience—of that structure: it more or less ensures, collective action predicaments aside, that whatever happens at the level of individuals will not cause a permanent departure from capitalism.[31]

Interest explanations, to turn to our third category, invoke the interests of organizations and groups to explain events that get described as the actions of such aggregate entities. It is clear that with an organization like a firm or even a state our program model may save such explanations though it is not so clear that this is so for a group like a class.[32] The alleged fact that it is in the interest of Great Britain to stay in Nato, even if this is not recognized by those who act in the country's name, can explain why it may be relied on to do so because it can make it likely, for example, that any bureaucrats who proposed otherwise would meet with objections on the part of colleagues or superiors. On the other hand it is not so clear, especially since collective action problems abound in this area, that the fact that it is in the interests of their class explains why the bourgeoisie allowed universal franchise.[33]

Finally, the program model of structural explanation fits the sort of example we described as context explanations. That the ethic of Protestantism was abroad in seventeenth-century Europe means that many people believed things which encouraged them to condemn idleness, to seek out productive activities, to praise those who found such activities, and the like. And that people were led in any such directions would have ensured in the circumstances of the period that capitalist activity would flourish. That is a fair paraphrase of the Weberian line and it shows how that line readily makes sense on the program model of structural explanation. And such a paraphrase, it should be clear, is going to be available for most plausible context explanations.

Our survey of examples establishes that on the program

---

[31] Our analysis suggests a recasting of the argument identified by G. A. Cohen but a recasting he ought to find congenial. See G. A. Cohen and W. Kymlicka, 'Human Nature and Social Change in the Marxist Conception of History', *Journal of Philosophy*, 85 (1988), 171–91.

[32] See P. Pettit, 'Towards the Social Democratic Theory of the State', *Political Studies*, 35 (1987), and B. Hindess, *Politics and Class Analysis* (Oxford: Blackwell, 1987).

[33] See R. Hardin, *Collective Action* (Baltimore, Md.: Johns Hopkins University Press, 1982). See also P. Pettit, 'Free Riding and Foul Dealing', *Journal of Philosophy*, 83 (1986).

model the sorts of structural explanation at which we have been looking often make sense. That result is powerful support for the model, given that the same is not true of the alternatives we have considered. But there is a further point also to be made in its support and that is that structural explanation remains a significant and interesting sort of explanation on the program model.

Here's a test of significance for any program explanation. Suppose that we have a program explanation of an event E by reference to an antecedent P, and that P explains E because its realization effectively ensures that some factor of type F occurs. Imagine now that we identify the F-factor in operation. A useful test for the significance of the original program explanation is to ask whether it offers any information not available, at least under ordinary assumptions, to someone possessed of the F-explanation. Is the program explanation more than a proxy account which has no value in the presence of that for which it goes proxy?

By this test of significance at least some program explanations will certainly fail. Consider the explanation of why a jug breaks when tapped with a spoon: it is fragile. Relative to the molecular level of activity, this is a program explanation, for the disposition of fragility does not itself produce the breaking; its realization rather ensures that the jug is of a molecular bonding pattern which has that effect. Suppose now that we identify the molecular bonding of the jug and understand that it is this which accounts for the breaking. Does that account deprive the original program explanation of interest? We think it does, for under ordinary assumptions someone possessed of that account has information sufficient to know that the jug broke because it was fragile. The fragility explanation fails our significance test.

Other program explanations, however, certainly count as significant by this test. And among them, importantly for our purposes, is the physical analogue with which we have been working: the case where the rise in temperature of the water explains the cracking of the flask. We might know that the event which produced the cracking was the collision at a certain velocity of such-and-such molecules with this or that part of the flask surface and not know either that the water had reached boiling-point or, even if we knew that, that there is a constancy in the relationship between water boiling and events like the cracking of such a flask. Thus the program explanation is significant in its own right. It gives us explanatory information that is not necessarily available to someone possessed of the other account.

The lesson for social structural explanations should be clear. Since they generally go in parallel with the physical analogue just discussed, it seems that they must also count as potentially significant. The point is borne out by our examples. Logically you could have an explanation of the decline in religious practice which invokes changed values, changed parish structures, and the like without being in a position to see that urbanization programs for the availability of such an explanation. You might not advert to the fact of urbanization and, even if you did, you might miss the constancy in the relationship between urbanization and religious decline. A similar analysis clearly applies to all our cases and we conclude that, on the program model, structural explanation is not just generally a valid exercise; it is generally a significant one too.[34]

In conclusion, we return to a theme broached in the introduction. Now that we have seen how macro-explanation works in social theory, we can see that this also is how micro-explanation operates. We mentioned in the introduction that a micro-explanation abstracts from the identities of people, say explaining a particular result by the fact of *some* people's having certain attitudes or performing certain actions; or abstracts also from the content of their attitudes, perhaps explaining the result by the fact that it was in the rational interests of some people. It remains a form of micro-explanation, not through being less abstractive from psychological detail, but through keeping us focused on a single sort of psychological factor, however abstract: that some people think such and such, that some people have a rational interest in this or that. But if micro-explanation is abstractive in this way, it itself raises the sort of problem that has been troubling us with structural explanation. The linkage between *some* people's thinking such

---

[34] See D. Papineau, *For Science in the Social Sciences* (London: Macmillan, 1978), ch. 5, for congenial observations.

and such and a social result is realized by the linkage between John and Mary and . . . thinking such and such and the result. Similarly, the connection between a result's being in the interest of those people and the occurrence itself, or the reliability of the occurrence, is realized by the linkage between their thinking such and such and the result. The problem then is how such abstractive explanation can be of interest, given the possibility of access to the more concrete connections. Shouldn't microtheory, like macrotheory, give right of way to the detailed psychological aetiology of the results it aspires to explain?

The problem in the microcase lends itself, happily, to the same sort of resolution as the problem of structural explanation. That some people think such and such programs for the result explained in the sense that it ensures that whatever happens at the more detailed level—whether John and Mary are replaced, for example, by Jack and Jill—it will suffice for the occurrence of the result. And the fact that the result is in the rational interest of those people, so at least the explanation says, programs equally for the result or for the resilience of the result; alternatively, it programs for their thinking and doing, or reliably thinking or doing, such things as mean that the result materializes.[35] Thus we see that not only is the problem driving this paper a problem equally for micro- as well as macro-explanation. It is also a problem which is solved by the same feature in the two cases: the fact that the explanation is of the program rather than the process variety.

5. THE LESSON FOR SOCIAL ONTOLOGY

Our models of structural explanation bear not just on issues of methodology, but also on questions of ontology. There are two questions at the centre of social ontology, although they have not always been distinguished. We shall argue that making a choice between our three models, in particular going for the

---

[35] On this account, rational choice theory may have a role in explaining why behaviour that is itself explained in other terms is more or less robust or resilient: rational interest is a standby motive. See P. Pettit, '*Virtus Normativa*: Rational Choice Perspectives', *Ethics*, 100 (1990), for an illustration.

program model, determines the answer to one of these but not to the other.

The first question in social ontology has to do with how far the members of a society logically depend on their relationships with one another for the possession of those properties which distinguish them as rational agents. How far, for example, do I depend on the convergent responses of my fellows for being able to form concepts and think thoughts involving those concepts? The atomist tradition says that logically I do not depend in this way on the other members of my society. The non-atomist or holist tradition says that I do. Atomists have been in the ascendant in Western philosophy but holists abound too. The German Romantics who stress the social character of thinking, their Hegelian and other nineteenth-century successors, and those who follow Wittgenstein on the social nature of rule-following should probably all count as holists in this sense.[36]

The other significant question in social ontology is easily confused with the first. It has to do with how far the members of society, whether they are conceived of atomistically or holistically, retain their apparent autonomy in the presence of higher-order social constraints. Do I remain my own master, as it seems I do, even though I live in a society governed by aggregate-level regularities? The individualist tradition says that I do; the opposed collectivist tradition says that in some sense I do not.

Where the atomist/holist question bears on the 'horizontal' issue of the relations between individuals, the individualist collectivist question bears on the 'vertical' issue of the relation of individuals to higher-order social constraints. Although they are clearly distinct questions, they have been consistently run together in the philosophy of social science, and perhaps more broadly. One reason for this is that they are each often cast in the same procrustean mould, as the question of how far social matters can be reduced to matters that distinctively involve just the separate members of society.[37] Since holism and

---

[36] At least one of us finds such holism congenial. See P. Pettit, *The Common Mind* (New York: Oxford University Press, forthcoming).

[37] For other reasons why they have been confused see Pettit, 'Social Holism without Collectivism'. The reductionist model of the individualism/collectivism

collectivism equally argue against reductionism, they are easily taken for the same thing; and similarly for atomism and individualism.[38]

Our discussion of structural explanation does not bear on the issue between holism and atomism, and the program model which we prefer is compatible with either doctrine.[39] But the discussion clearly does bear on the issue that divides individualists and collectivists and we would now like to comment on where the program model would have us stand.

Let a person be said to exercise ordinary agent autonomy, just so far as it is generally true of the things she does that, as we say, she could have done otherwise. When we say that she could have done otherwise we do not mean that given exactly the beliefs and desires she had at the moment of action, still she might have done something other than what she did: that would be to deny that her beliefs and desires impose determinate requirements on her actions. We mean that fixing just the fact of her being susceptible to the influence of beliefs and desires, it is possible that she should have done another action: her beliefs and desires might have evolved or combined in a different way to produce action.

When we say that someone acted autonomously in this sense, we deny that anything undercuts the possibility that her beliefs and desires might have gone the other way. First we reject 'predestination': the claim that she would not have been there to do what she did but for the fact of her having the beliefs and desires that actually moved her. And secondly we reject 'predetermination': the thesis that she was compelled to

---

debate is rejected in favour of something like the model invoked here in Macdonald and Pettit, *Semantics and Social Science*; D. H. Mellor, 'The Reduction of Society', *Philosophy*, 57 (1982), 51–75; S. James, *The Content of Social Explanation* (Cambridge: Cambridge University Press, 1984); and B. Williams, 'Formal and Substantial Individualism', *Proceedings of the Aristotelian Society*, 85 (1984–5).

[38] It must be conceded, of course, that the exaggerated versions of holism which have thrived in the post-Hegelian tradition readily lead to collectivism. If you think that relationships with others are necessary for being able to think at least certain thoughts, then you may easily be led into reifying the collective mind or whatever; and in that case you have postulated a social entity sufficient to delight any collectivist.

[39] For a sketchy defence of this claim, see Pettit, *The Common Mind*.

have the beliefs and desires that she had in such a way that ordinary differences of evidence or whatever would not have changed them.

An example may help to make this notion of agent autonomy vivid. Imagine a schoolgirl at a hockey match who cheers for her school's team. We would say that such a girl could have done otherwise if certain pieces of evidence could rationally have caused different beliefs and desires, and thereby a different response: for example, if evidence that her side was cheating might have lessened her desire sufficiently for her not to cheer any longer; or if evidence that the goal-keeper on her side was unnerved by her cheering might have stopped her doing so; or something of the kind. There must be some such factors that would have been capable of making a difference.

We would hesitate to say that the girl could have done otherwise under at least two sorts of circumstance. One is where she is predestined to cheer, as in the case where her schoolmistress would remove her from the stadium if she failed to cheer. And the other is where she is predetermined to cheer in a manner that leaves her insensitive to the considerations mentioned in the last paragraph: say, if she was under a hypnotically or neurally induced compulsion to cheer.

When collectivists say that people's agent autonomy is compromised by the social macroworld, we shall take it that they mean that for at least some of the things that people do, the macroworld is such that they could not have done otherwise. There are structural factors which produce the behaviour in question, and do so without becoming objects of consciousness in the ordinary intentional way. Or there are structural considerations which filter for the presence only of people who are disposed to behave in that way.

Given this understanding of collectivism, it is clear that both the subversive and the pre-emptive answers to the problem of how macro-explanation is possible would commit us to collectivism. The subversive answer has macrofactors influence individuals in a way that directly subverts intentional processes and means that the agents could not have done otherwise. The pre-emptive answer has it that people are selected for the disposition to behave according to a certain pattern in some areas and that they would not be there to make their contribution if they were genuinely disposed to do otherwise. The first answer asserts predetermination, the second a sort of predestination.

The question then is whether the program model that we have endorsed involves a similar commitment to collectivism. The answer is that it does not. The model gives us no reason to think that in any areas of behaviour people cannot act otherwise than they actually do. The model does not explicitly invoke any predetermining or predestining device that would motivate such a belief.

We conclude then that the program model of macro-explanation ought to be found congenial by individualists. Still, there are things to say on the other side. We shall say three.

The first is that while the program model does not undermine individual agent autonomy, neither does it particularly flatter the individual. It suggests that for many of the things that happen in social life—specifically, those that are subject to structural explanation—the particular attitudes and actions of particular individuals which led to those things were not necessary prerequisites. If those people had not done those things, other people would have wittingly or unwittingly stepped into the breach. Thus, if our model does not undermine agent autonomy, it does suggest that the initiatives of individuals may not be as important as is often thought. There are constancies in social affairs which no individual is in a position to alter.[40]

The second thing that needs to be said on the collectivist side is that while the program model does not offend against individualism as a constraint on social explanation, it does break with the tradition which sees individualism as a heuristic for social explanation. The constraint approach insists that no social explanation ought to be acceptable, if it assumes that people behave otherwise than in an agent-autonomous way. The heuristic approach insists, much more strictly, that only micro-explanations—in the end, perhaps, only detailed psychological aetiologies—ought to be acceptable in social

---

[40] This theme is emphasized by Richard Miller in 'Methodological Individualism and Social Explanation' and Susan James, *The Content of Social Explanation*. See also Williams, 'Formal and Substantial Individualism' and Elster, *Explaining Technical Change*, 32–3.

theory. Thus, many proponents of the rational choice approach write as if the notion of structural explanation is intrinsically flawed. It is clear that if we endorse the program model of such explanation, then we break with heuristic individualism, even if we stick with the other variety.

The third thing to say on the side of collectivism is that the program model forces a break, not just with heuristic individualists, but also with those individualists who tolerate structural explanation but think that the micro-explanation of any social fact is always bound to be of more interest; such individualists may even think that the micro-explanation deprives the structural explanation of whatever interest it possesses.[41] On the program model, structural explanation serves a different sort of interest from micro-explanation, as micro-explanation serves a different interest from detailed psychological aetiology, since it gives a different kind of information on the causal history of the event explained. What is more, the information provided may not be available, as we saw in the last section, just through access to the micro-explanation. Thus the structural explanation may be just as interesting as the micro-account; indeed, depending on background assumptions, it may even have greater interest.

And so to our conclusion. The program model of structural explanation is not only a satisfactory account of how such explanation works.[42] It also gives us a nice perspective on the debate between individualists and collectivists. It means that we can embrace the persuasive individualist claim that individuals are agent-autonomous. But it also allows us to understand the collectivist thesis that individuals often make little difference in the course of history and that the best way to study society is often from the top down, not from the bottom up. Those claims constitute the true and attractive core of collectivism.

---

[41] Thus we reject the claim, in Michael Taylor's words, that 'good explanation should be, amongst other things, as *fine-grained* as possible', 'Rationality and Revolutionary Collective Action', in M. Taylor (ed.), *Rationality and Revolution* (Cambridge: Cambridge University Press, 1988), 96. Taylor follows Elster, *Explaining Technical Change*, 24 and 27–8. See our 'In defence of explanatory ecumenism', *Economics and Philosophy*, forthcoming.

[42] In our view social micro-explanation, being relatively abstract, also fits the program model. But that is another story.

5

Weak Externalism and Psychological Reduction*

Cynthia Macdonald

Arguments for and against the possibility of reducing intentional state types and tokens such as those of belief and desire to entities describable in purely physical (or in physical and topic-neutral) vocabulary have often proceeded on the assumption that any such reduction will require psychophysical correlation laws.[1] The argument against the possibility of such laws is a familiar one: beginning with the assumption that theories in general are governed by principles which constrain the ascription of properties to entities within their domains, it attempts to forge a distinction between intentional psychological state types or properties and physical ones on the basis of the fact that the principles which govern their attribution are not only different from, but ultimately incompatible with, one another. The attribution of psychological properties to persons, it is said, is governed by constraints of rational coherence and consistency characterized by the use of inductive and deductive principles of reasoning: absence of logical inconsistency, transitivity of preference, and so on. Such principles are normative in the sense that they license claims about how an agent ought rationally to behave or think conditionally upon the possession of other beliefs and desires. The principles which govern the attribution of physical properties, on the other hand, are non-normative: there is no place in physical

* I am grateful to Kathleen Lennon, David Charles, David Papineau, and Graham Macdonald for comments on various drafts of this paper

[1] See D. Davidson, 'Mental Events', in D. Davidson, *Essays on Actions and Events* (Oxford: Clarendon Press, 1980); J. Kim, 'Psychophysical Laws', in E. LePore and B. McLaughlin (eds.), *Actions and Events* (Oxford: Blackwell, 1985); and B. McLaughlin, 'Anomalous Monism and the Irreducibility of the Mental', in McLaughlin and LePore (eds.), *Actions and Events*.

theory for such notions as rational consistency and coherence. Psychophysical correlation laws would transmit the conditions of property ascription from one domain to the other, with the consequence that psychological properties would acquire non-rational conditions of ascription. This, however, is impossible: rationality lies at the very heart of what it is to be an intentional psychological type or property. Therefore there can be no psychophysical correlation laws.[2]

This reasoning has met with some resistance. It has been pointed out that the fact that psychological and physical pro-perties have different ascription conditions does not by itself show that there can be no lawlike connections between them.[3] Such a condition on theoretical reduction by way of correlation laws is plainly much too strong in general. For psychophysical laws to be prohibited, the different principles which constrain psychological and physical property attribution must be such as to conflict with one another. But again, it has been claimed, there is no obvious reason why a psychological property should not have logically necessary and sufficient rational conditions of ascription and *also* nomologically necessary and sufficient non-rational conditions of ascription. For conflict to occur, psychological properties must have not merely logically necessary and sufficient rational conditions of attribution, but also nomologically necessary and sufficient ones. But it is unclear why properties with logically necessary and sufficient rational conditions of ascription cannot have nomologically necessary and sufficient non-rational ones.[4]

I am sympathetic to the anti-reductionist argument sketched above. However, the doubts just expressed reveal a weakness in the strategy. Any two theories will be apt to differ in their constitutive principles, but this does not by itself prohibit the possibility of reduction by correlation laws. The fact that psychological property attribution must be logically con-strained by principles of rationality does not by itself show that

[2] The argument is Kim's. See 'Psychophysical Laws'.

[3] See e.g. T. Honderich, 'Psychophysical Lawlike Connections and their Problem', *Inquiry*, 24 (1981), 277–304 and *A Theory of Determinism* (Oxford: Oxford University Press, 1988), and C. McGinn, 'Philosophical Materialism', *Synthese*, 44 (1980), 173–206.

[4] See McLaughlin, 'Anomalous Monism and the Irreducibility of the Mental'.

those properties cannot also have nomologically necessary and sufficient non-rational conditions of ascription. Rather than address this problem directly, however, I would like to explore another anti-reductionist strategy which I believe might ultimately serve to explain why at least some psychological properties cannot have non-rational conditions of attribution and so to ground the argument against psychophysical correlation laws. This is to argue that common-sense psychological explanation, i.e. the explanation of action by way of beliefs and desires of agents, is externalist. A fundamental intuition governing such explanation is that the physical states upon which the psychological ones supervene both occur within, and are autonomous with respect to (i.e. are logically independent of) objects and phenomena that occur or exist beyond, the confines of agents' bodies.[5] If, however, common-sense psychological explanation is externalist in the sense that its explanans states have individuation conditions which require the existence of objects and/or phenomena beyond the confines of agents' bodies, and if, as seems likely, the physical states to which the psychological ones are thought reducible do not, then intentional psychological properties evidently are not reducible to physical ones. The physical states that are typically thought to be likely candidates for the reducing ones are either brain states or neurophysiological states, and it is reductionist theses of this kind that are the primary target of the strategy. However, the *normative* nature of the externalism argued for has consequences for other reductionist physicalist theses. In particular, the strategy, if correct, shows that *any* physicalism which seeks to reduce psychological types to physical ones, irrespective of whether

---

[5] See e.g. J. Fodor, 'Individualism and Supervenience', *Proceedings of the Aristotelian Society*, Supp. Vol. 60 (1986), 235–62, and *Psychosemantics* (Cambridge, Mass.: MIT Press, 1987). For externalism see T. Burge, 'Individualism and the Mental', in P. French, T. Uehling, and H. Wettstein (eds.), *Midwest Studies in Philosophy*, iv (Minneapolis, Minn.: University of Minnesota Press, 1979), 'Other Bodies', in A. Woodfield (ed.), *Thought and Object* (Oxford: Clarendon Press, 1982), 'Individualism and Psychology', *Philosophical Review*, 94(1) (Jan. 1986), 3–45, and 'Cartesian Error and the Objectivity of Perception', in R. Grimm and D. Merrill (eds.), *Contents of Thought* (Tucson, Ariz.: University of Arizona Press, 1988).

the latter have individuation conditions which require the existence of objects and/or phenomena outside the bodies of persons, is false.[6] This includes, for example, beyond-the-body type–type identity theses and constitution theses.

The claim that commonsensical psychological explanation is externalist is one, not specifically about the nature of token intentional psychological states, but about the nature of the types or properties that are typically referred to in the explanantia of psychological explanations. Two sorts of case are commonly brought to bear on its truth. The first concerns situations where the thoughts of two physically indiscernible individuals (or the same individual) in different physical (and/or social) environments are compared (the Twin Earth examples fall into this category). The second concerns situations where the thoughts of a single individual at different times, whose specification typically involves reference to the same object(s) in the physical environment of that individual, are compared. In Sections 1 and 2 below, I address the Twin Earth examples and argue against what I call weak internalism. Section 1 addresses the issue of whether and in what sense psychological explanation of both standard and non-standard cases of action is externalist. Section 2 applies the conclusions arrived at in the first section to the Twin Earth examples. The strategy invoked to deal with these cases is then employed in Section 3 to deal with examples of the second sort. The discussion throughout is restricted to examples of thoughts whose specification typically involves terms for natural kinds of substances, objects, or phenomena, where only the physical environment of the individual is imagined to vary. Finally, in Section 4, I briefly consider the question of how externalism in common-sense psychology might explain why intentional psychological types cannot have non-rational conditions of ascription.

1. WEAK EXTERNALISM AND PSYCHOLOGICAL EXPLANATION

There are a number of ways in which a defence of internalism might proceed. Much the most convincing case from the point

---

[6] See the final pages of the present paper.

of view of psychological reduction, however, is made out by some kind of dual component view of the nature of intentional types. According to this, intentional types have two components, a narrow (cognitive) one and a wide (referential) one. The former is independent of the latter and has to do, not with what is represented, but with how it is represented.[7] The latter is typically fixed by objects that exist beyond the confines of an individual agent's body. Total content supervenes on both components. However, only the cognitive component has an explanatory role to play in the intentional behaviour or actions of agents. The referential component is explanatorily idle.

The case for internalism based on a dual component view concerns, not whether narrow content can be *specified*, but whether, in explanations invoking intentional psychological types in which a referential component is clearly present, that component is *explanatorily idle*.[8] Two sorts of example are often cited in support of the view that it is. These examples are critical to the internalist's case. The first, familiar one concerns Twin Earth-type situations in which objects or phenomena beyond the confines of two individuals, say, Belle on Earth and Nell on Twin Earth, otherwise indiscernible with regard to their internal physical properties, differ (Earth containing water where Twin Earth contains *XYZ*), but where, weak internalists will argue, the content of the intentional psychological states involving such objects or phenomena had by these individuals remains invariant. Here the claim is that the actions of Belle and Nell are in an important sense type-identical (what Belle does with water—drink it, wash with it, etc.—Nell does with *XYZ*), and this can only be explained by reference to states that are at least partly type-identical. The second sort of case is one where objects or phenomena beyond the confines of an

---

[7] See Fodor, 'Individualism and Supervenience' and *Psychosemantics*, and C. McGinn, 'The Structure of Content', in Woodfield (ed.), *Thought and Object*.

[8] So it would be beside the point to argue that, since any commonsensical psychological explanation will typically make use of a description in the explanans which clearly contains a term referring to an object or phenomenon that exists beyond the confines of an agent's body, it is externalist. If McGinn is correct, the fact that intentional types associated with such descriptions have referential *components* does not show that those components have an explanatory role to play in the explanation of individual actions. And if Fodor is correct, since any sentence used to express a person's thought will have a determinate semantic value, the content of the thought expressed by means of it will be broad rather than narrow.

individual's body remain invariant from one time to another, but where, weak internalists will argue, that individual possesses distinct conceptions of those objects or phenomena and so has distinct types of thought about it. Take Loar's example of Pierre, a monolinguist living in Paris who acquires a belief which he expresses by saying 'Londres est jolie'.[9] Some time later he moves to London and, having learnt English, believes something which he expresses by saying 'London is pretty'. It is evident that Pierre doesn't realize that the city that he thought about in Paris is the city he now lives in. This failure is evidenced by certain inferential failures, which in turn are evidenced in his behaviour. For example, he fails to infer from his earlier belief that Oscar Wilde lived in London and his later belief that he now lives in London that he now lives in the city in which Oscar Wilde lived. This explains why, having intended while living in Paris to visit Wilde's London home, Pierre does nothing towards achieving that aim when he moves to London.

I believe that a proper reading of these examples in fact supports externalism. Consider the Twin Earth examples first. It is common for externalists to reply to this kind of argument by claiming that the actions of the relevant individuals are not in fact type-identical, and since they are not, there is no reason to think that the intentional types which explain them are even partly the same.[10] This is not a strategy that I intend to pursue, however. It is plausible to hold that, just as intentional psychological states are of types that have a broad and narrow component, so too are the actions that they typically cause.[11]

---

[9] See B. Loar, 'Subjective Intentionality', in *Philosophical Topics*, 15(1) (Spring 1987), 89–124. His is an adaptation of Saul Kripke's. See 'A Puzzle about Belief', in E. Margalit (ed.), *Meaning and Use* (Dordrecht: Reidel, 1979).

[10] See e.g. G. Evans, *The Varieties of Reference*, ed. J. McDowell (Oxford: Clarendon Press, 1982), 203. See also Fodor's second line of attack on the assumption that the mental states of Twins have the same causal powers in *Psychosemantics*, 36–7.

[11] So I fail to find this strategy convincing, but not for reasons that motivate Fodor (see *Psychosemantics*). He argues that the question of whether the relevant intentional types, narrowly construed, are the same is a matter of their causal potentialities, and that this is determined, not within contexts, but across them. The fact that Belle's beliefs on Earth cause her to drink water whereas Nell's on Twin Earth cause her to drink *XYZ* does not show that these beliefs have distinct causal potentialities. What's relevant is whether Nell's

The actions of Belle and Nell, narrowly construed, are type-identical: both are drinkings, both are washings. And it is these that might be thought to figure in the explananda of intentional psychological explanations. It is true that there are cases of common-sense psychological explanation where the act-type invoked in the explanandum evidently must be construed broadly. Thus, suppose that Sue, having decided to end her life, puts arsenic in her tea and drinks it. What needs explaining here is not why her act was of the type *drinks* but why it was a drinking of poison. However, there are other cases of common-sense psychological explanation, both standard and non-standard (e.g. cases of actions caused in part by mis-perceptions or hallucinations), where the act-types invoked in the explananda are narrowly construed. Sometimes, for example, we may simply wish to explain why a person washes or why she eats every day; or, in a case of an action caused in part by a hallucination, why a person moved in a particular way (so as to avoid an imagined obstacle, for instance). Examples like these seem clearly to be ones where the act-types invoked in the explananda are narrowly construed, i.e. are types whose individuation does not require the existence of objects or phenomena beyond the confines of an individual's body.

So the broad/narrow act-type distinction does seem to apply in certain cases of intentional psychological explanation, and the argument for externalism cannot rest on this. What externalists must argue is that, even in cases where the act-types invoked in the explanans of intentional psychological explanations are narrowly construed, the types of which their causes are tokens, to do their explanatory work, must be individuated

beliefs *would* cause her to drink water on Earth, and whether Belle's beliefs *would* cause her to drink XYZ on Twin Earth. By this criterion, the causal potentialities of Belle's and Nell's beliefs are the same and the beliefs are partly type-identical. A natural response to this is to say that the individuation of intentional types is not by way of their causal potentialities. Fodor assumes that it is because he thinks that the explanation of action by reasons (beliefs and desires) is causal explanation. But it isn't (see n. 13 below). In short, I think that the individuation of intentional psychological types does not proceed by way of their causal potentialities because such individuation is geared toward the explanatory purposes that those types are intended to serve, and I do not think that the explanation of individual actions by way of beliefs and desires is in general a species of causal explanation.

by reference to objects that exist beyond the confines of individuals' bodies.[12] The case for internalism has repeatedly focused on the issue of causes of actions, assuming that psychological explanation is a species of causal explanation. I think that this assumption is radically mistaken.[13] To see this, three types of psychological explanation need to be considered: standard ones, where the objects toward which individuals act are ones referred to by the referential components of the types invoked in the explanantia of explanations of those acts and are (roughly) as they are conceived to be, and non-standard ones of two sorts. First, explanations of actions based on misperceptions, where the objects toward which individuals act are those typically referred to in the referential components of the types

[12] Here I am talking about successful action, not about action as if there were objects of certain kinds beyond the confines of an individual's body. Explanations of actions of the latter sort seem to me to be parasitic on explanations of successful actions in just the way that explanations of successful actions based on misperceptions are parasitic on those based on veridical perceptions.
[13] Examples of those who think that psychological explanation is a species of causal explanation are Fodor ('Individualism and Supervenience', 242) and McGinn ('The Structure of Content'), where the view figures implicitly in his discussion of dual component theories of content. There are, of course, cases of psychological explanation which many would agree are not ones of causal explanation. I have in mind ones which attempt to provide answers to questions like 'What is it for a person to be in the state of believing (perceiving, etc.) that *p*?' This is a request for information regarding a certain capacity; and a natural way of responding to it is to give an analysis of the relevant intentional psychological property that explains an individual's possession of it by appealing to other properties of that (and other) individual(s) or their bodies and their mode of organization (for more on this, see R. Cummins, *The Nature of Psychological Explanation* (Cambridge, Mass.: MIT Press, 1983)). But these are not the controversial cases. The explanations that seem to many to be causal are ones which attempt to answer questions like 'Why did Betty pour herself a glass of water?'; questions which at least appear to be requests for information regarding the intentional mental causes of an individual's action. Despite the fact that such explanations are answers to 'why' questions and are cause-citing, I nevertheless think that they are non-causal. The reason is a familiar one: the explanantia of reasons explanations are logically connected to their explananda. Explanations by way of beliefs and desires make the actions they typically cause intelligible by virtue of being shown to possess contents, as expressed by 'that' clauses, which bear logical connections to their explananda. So, despite the fact that beliefs and desires cause actions, reasons explanations do their explanatory work not because they are belief-citing but because they invoke types which are content-specifying. Moreover, it is because beliefs and desires are of the contentful types they are that is it intelligible that they should cause the actions they do.

invoked in the explanans, but where the cognitive components either fail to represent such objects as they are or represent them as being as they are not. And second, explanations of actions based on hallucinations, where objects toward which individuals act (if any) are not ones referred to by the referential components of psychological types (viz. beliefs and desires) acquired on the basis of such experiences. These latter are particularly interesting, since they seem to be ones where only actions, narrowly construed, and intentional psychological states, narrowly construed, are required for the appropriate explanations.

Consider the standard cases first. Suppose that we set out to explain why a particular person washes or why she eats every day. Is it plausible to say that the psychological types invoked in the explanans of any such explanation are ones whose referential components are idle? I think not. Such acts, to be *intelligible*, require that the beliefs and desires concern, if not specific objects, kinds of objects and/or phenomena in the individual's environment. This is primarily because narrow-act taxonomy is itself possible only against the background of other acts, broadly construed, to which the narrow ones are similar and whose classification requires the notion of an *appropriate* object. This notion of appropriateness is normative and so cannot be captured in causal explanations. Whereas water is appropriate to wash with, ink is not. Accordingly, for Sue's act of washing to be intelligible, we need to suppose not only that she believes that washing gets things clean and that she wants something to be clean, but also that she believes that the stuff with which she washes is the appropriate stuff to get things clean. In other words, she needs not only to have beliefs and desires about the *activity* of washing, but also to have ones about the kind of substance that it is appropriate to wash *with*.

It is important to see that the same principles apply in cases of explanations of actions based on misperceptions and hallucinations, since the argument for internalism is often based on these.[14] Here it is tempting to say that the cognitive component of the intentional type invoked in any explanation of action based upon them is doing all of the explanatory work

---

[14] Loar is a good example of this. See 'Subjective Intentionality'.

when the act-type invoked in the explanandum is narrowly construed. For here the actions themselves are not typically of types that *are* appropriate to such objects as may exist beyond the confines of the individual's body and be involved in them, broadly construed. In cases of misperception, individuals act as though objects beyond the confines of their bodies either have properties that they in fact have not, or lack properties that they in fact have. This is in turn reflected in the type of act performed. If Sue mistakenly takes hydrochloric acid for water and as a result believes that it is the kind of substance that gets things clean, then her act of washing would seem to be explicable, not by the referential component of the type of psychological state she is in—what her belief is about—but by the cognitive component alone, how she conceives it. Similarly for explanations of actions based on hallucinations. Suppose that, as a result of a hallucinatory experience, Sue acquires the belief that there is water before her. Her subsequent action, narrowly construed as of the type *washes*, would seem to be explicable, not by the referential component of any intentional type invoked in the explanation, but by the cognitive component. The referential component here either fails to pick out any object at all, or picks out an object that is inappropriate to the type of action engaged in, narrowly construed.

Even in cases like these, however, the referential components of the relevant psychological types are not idle. The reason is that, in making such acts as washing intelligible *by* describing their mental antecedents as misperceptions or as hallucinations, one must bring to bear on these explanations all that is involved in standard reasons explanation and more. First, the relevant actions must be taxonomized so as to be seen as movements *as if* some object or phenomenon had (or lacked) certain properties, or *as if* some object or phenomena did exist beyond the confines of the agent's body. For the issue of what type of action is being performed, even when narrowly construed, is not independent of the issue of what kind of substance, phenomenon, or object is typically appropriate for that type of activity. One can wash with water or, perhaps, with sand; but one cannot wash with mud or with ink (though the same bodily movements may occur). The explanation of actions, narrowly construed, therefore requires classifying the types of which they are instances as similar to others, broadly construed, in which a person (and/or others) has or is apt to engage. This in turn requires the attribution of beliefs about objects which do exist beyond the confines of individuals' bodies and towards which those individuals have acted in similar types of way, beliefs whose referential components are crucial to the characterization of the *cognitive* components of the beliefs based on misperceptions and hallucinations themselves.

What emerges from all this is that the explanation of actions, narrowly construed, may be more *general* than the explanation of actions, broadly construed, but it is not for this reason internalistic. Even if one concedes that the referential components of psychological types invoked in explanations of actions, narrowly construed, based on misperceptions and/or hallucinations are explanatorily idle, the cognitive components are such that *its* explanatory efficacy requires the attribution of other intentional states of types whose referential components must be seen to be doing some explanatory work. The explananda of commonsensical psychological explanation can be of any number of types, and these may themselves be more or less general. So too can their intentional psychological causes. But just as narrow act taxonomy is subject to constraints imposed by the degree of similarity such acts bear to other types of acts, broadly construed, narrow content characterization is subject to constraints imposed by the relations such contents bear to other psychological types whose referential components are crucial in helping to specify the narrow content of others.[15]

2. WEAK EXTERNALISM AND THE TWIN EARTH EXAMPLES

If this is right, then the broad/narrow act distinction cannot obviate the need for a referential component in common-sense

---

[15] Cases of acts based on misperceptions seem in fact to be ones where the broad/narrow act distinction doesn't seem to work at all. What needs explaining when Sue's act of washing is caused by beliefs based on misperceptions is her act of washing *with hydrochloric acid*.

psychological explanations of actions, narrowly construed, even for explanations of actions based on misperceptions and hallucinations. However, more must be said to settle the issue at stake in the Twin Earth cases. Recall that the argument for weak internalism based on them was that, although water and XYZ are indeed distinct substances, the differences between them do not play an explanatory role *vis-à-vis* Belle's and Nell's actions, narrowly construed. What was said about standard cases of reasons explanations of actions, narrowly construed, does not appear to settle the issue in favour of externalism here, since XYZ in Nell's environment evidently plays the same role *vis-à-vis* the type of activity with which it is associated that water plays on Earth: both are used for washing, for drinking, and the like.

There are two ways of responding to this. The first is to argue that although Twin Earth cases are like standard cases of psychological explanation, the referential components of Belle's and Nell's psychological state types play different explanatory roles in the explanation of their actions, narrowly construed. This strategy might be developed by arguing that water on Earth and XYZ on Twin Earth could not, given their differing properties (specifically, their different chemical structures), play the same type of role *vis-à-vis* activities with which they are associated. Suppose, for instance, that the chemical constitution of XYZ is such as to make it highly inflammable at high temperatures and that this is common knowledge in Nell's community. Then, though Nell and others in her community wash with water and drink it, they refrain from washing on very hot days, never drink it hot, and in fact avoid warming it for any reason. It seems right to say here that, even though Belle's and Nell's acts of washing, narrowly construed, are type-identical, the role that XYZ plays with regard to other activities (such as drinking hot drinks made with it) justifies attributing an explanatory role to the referential component of psychological state types, broadly construed, involving XYZ, since it affects other activities which Nell would be apt to engage in with that substance and inferential connections between beliefs which cause washing acts and beliefs which cause drinking acts.

Suppose, alternatively, that the structural properties of

XYZ are causally responsible for that compound's behaving differently from water, but that those differences are manifested only in carefully controlled laboratory conditions and so are known only to the scientific specialists of the community. Despite the fact that such differences do not manifest themselves across the entire community, they affect the overall role that XYZ plays *vis-à-vis* the actions of people on Twin Earth. It is arguable that, in order to make sense of Nell's actions on Twin Earth (as well as to make sense of Belle's on Earth), the role played by XYZ (or water) in activities throughout the community must be taken into account. For this does affect the actions that the specialists in that community engage in with regard to that substance, and so also affects the attribution to Nell (and Belle) of dispositions to act conditionally upon the possession of such information.

A different response to the Twin Earth examples would be to argue that they should be assimilated, not to standard, but to non-standard cases of psychological explanation like those of acts based on misperceptions. The problem for externalists is to explain how the referential components of Belle's and Nell's psychological states could play an explanatory role *vis-à-vis* their actions, narrowly construed, given that these latter are type-identical and the referential components of their corresponding psychological states are not. The key to a solution is to see that the type identity of those actions is determined, not just by Belle's and Nell's actual behaviour in their actual environments, but also by their counterfactual behaviour across environments; by what Belle on Twin Earth *would* do with XYZ, and by what Nell *would* do with water on Earth. Consider Belle on Twin Earth. Her states are of types whose referential components refer to XYZ, not water. Still, we want to explain why her actions, narrowly construed, are type-identical with Nell's. It is plausible to say that Belle's actions on Twin Earth are the result of beliefs based on misperceptions; ones whose *cognitive* components can only be explanatorily efficacious by reference to the similar properties possessed by water (on Earth) and XYZ (on Twin Earth), and correspondingly, by beliefs with different referential components. In short, how Belle conceives things may not suffice to discriminate between water and XYZ, but for that to explain her washing and drinking actions in the absence of water on Twin Earth, her beliefs must be seen to be the result of misperceptions, where reference to both water and *XYZ* and to beliefs whose referential components differ is needed to make intelligible how she could be misperceiving.

Notice that both responses locate the source of narrow act explanation ultimately in differences in properties of objects in Belle's and Nell's respective environments. The first exploits these to argue that Belle's washing on Earth and Nell's washing on Twin Earth, though of the same narrow type, will ultimately require explanation by reference to psychological states whose referential components are not explanatorily idle, since other activities with which *XYZ* and water are associated will differ and this in turn will require the attribution of causally efficacious intentional states whose types differ in their referential components. Effectively, the suggestion is that, in standard cases of psychological explanation of actions, how an individual conceives is not independent of the properties of what is conceived; and that such differences in substances or phenomena that exist beyond the confines of individuals' bodies as are known by the specialists in a community alone will inevitably be manifested in the different activities with which they are associated and hence in the intentional psychological types that explain those activities. The second exploits these differences to explain the nature of misperception itself, since this requires the confusion of objects whose properties differ on the basis of properties they either share or appear to share. Both responses have at least some initial plausibility, but with regard to different versions of the Twin Earth thought experiments. Some formulations of the Twin Earth examples invite us to compare the intentional psychological states of two distinct but physiologically indiscernible organisms (Belle and her *doppelgänger*, Nell) in distinct physical (and/or social) environments. Others invite us to compare the intentional psychological states of the same individual as they occur before and after the transportation of that individual to another planet. The first response is intuitively more plausible with regard to the *doppelgänger* formulations whereas the second is more plausible for the transportation ones.

3. WEAK EXTERNALISM AND FINE-GRAINED BELIEFS

The claim to be defeated in the last section was that, because Belle's and Nell's actions, narrowly construed, are type-identical, so too are the psychological causes that explain them. This was defeated by showing that, in both standard and non-standard cases of psychological explanation, narrow act taxonomy requires reference to other act-types, broadly construed, in which individuals are apt to engage, and consequently to intentional psychological states of types whose referential components are doing explanatory work. In both cases, the explanation of individual actions requires reference to objects beyond the confines of individuals' bodies. But it is important to note that in neither case is the object–content connection a direct one. The connection is mediated by other psychological states whose attribution is externalistically constrained by virtue of their connections with actions of other types, broadly construed.[16]

Let us turn now to the second kind of case that is often cited in support of weak internalism, the Pierre-type case. This situation is exactly the reverse of the Twin Earth one: whereas there the internalist claim was that an individual's psychological state could remain partly type-invariant while objects in her environment differ, here the claim is that objects in an individual's environment could remain the same while the type of psychological state that he is in differs. It is tempting to think that examples of this second kind are more effective than the Twin Earth ones in proving the internalist case. Since externalists are committed to the view that intentional states are type-individuated by reference to objects that exist beyond the confines of individuals' bodies, so that different objects make for different types of intentional state, it is natural to assume that they are also committed to the view that if the objects referred to by the referential components of intentional psychological types are the same, so are the types themselves.

However, externalists need not be committed to this latter

---

[16] This point is also brought out clearly by Akeel Bilgrami in 'An Externalist Account of Psychological Content', *Philosophical Topics*, 15(1) (1987), 191–226.

view: they too can be dual component theorists. What matters
is whether, in types of state that are distinct *only* because their
cognitive components are distinct, the referential components
can be seen to be doing any explanatory work. Because psychological explanation is rationalistic rather than causal, what
needs explaining is why Pierre *fails* to make the inferential
connections that one would expect of him, and, more importantly, why he fails to engage in acts which would serve
as a basis for attributing those inferences and which those
inferences would rationalize. It is here where the need for
externalism in the characterization of the cognitive components
of Pierre's two beliefs arises. It is true that, for his behaviour to
be explicable, we must suppose him to have beliefs (about
London) whose cognitive components differ. Moreover, the
differences in those components must be explicable in terms of
information which is accessible to Pierre. As it happens, these
differences will be associated with perceptual states of different
types, Pierre's belief that London is pretty being based on
perceptions of the city itself. But in order to explain this mis-
match between Pierre's actions and beliefs, we need not only
to refer to the differences in cognitive components, but also
to represent those components as being traceable to a *single*
object. It's not just that Pierre's conceptions are different, but
that they are different conceptions *of the same city*, that explains
his wayward behaviour. The differences in other intentional
psychological states which ultimately explain the differences
in Pierre's conceptions of London therefore serve to make
explicable his behaviour only when *they* are seen as deriving
from descriptive or other information concerning one and the
same city.

   In short, the explanation of Pierre's actions is externalist
because it involves not one, but two, factors. First, Pierre's
conceptions must differ, i.e. the cognitive component of the
belief expressed by 'Londres est jolie' must differ from that
expressed by 'London is pretty'; and for this to be so, those
beliefs must relate to different sets of intentional psychological
states of Pierre. Second, in order for these cognitive differences
to explain Pierre's actions in London, these different conceptions must be represented as conceptions of the same city.
The intentional states which provide the basis for the cognitive

differences between Pierre's two beliefs must therefore be ones whose attribution requires reference to, not two cities, but one, beyond the confines of Pierre's body.

This strategy for dealing with the Pierre-type examples assimilates explanations of actions in cases where a single individual has beliefs whose referential components are identical but whose cognitive components differ to explanations of actions in non-standard cases, i.e. ones motivated by beliefs based on misperceptions and hallucinations. With regard to those, it was argued that the cognitive components of states whose types explain the relevant actions cannot do so independently of relations they bear to others whose referential components are not explanatorily idle; so that, even if it is true that the referential component of those types themselves fail to serve an explanatory purpose *vis-à-vis* the actions they explain, the referential components of others are required in order for those cognitive components to do their explanatory work. The argument here is that, although the explanation of Pierre's actions in London invokes intentional psychological types whose referential components may be explanatorily idle, the cognitive components, to do their explanatory work, must relate to other intentional psychological states whose referential components refer to one and the same city. In both cases, as well as in the Twin Earth ones, the intentional states which explain the relevant actions are distinct because they bear relations to others whose referential components are distinct. Without these relations, the *cognitive* component of the former would be explanatorily idle. So Belle's water thoughts are type-distinct from Nell's XYZ thoughts, and Pierre's London beliefs are type-distinct from Pierre's Londres beliefs. This poses no real problem for externalism, however. That view requires that explanations of actions invoke intentional types whose referential components are explanatorily efficacious, and this requirement is met in both the Twin Earth and the Pierre-type examples. Externalism is not threatened by the claim that intentional states whose referential components are the same but whose cognitive components differ are different types of state, since it is not committed to the view that sameness of referential components is sufficient for sameness of psychological types. It would be threatened by the claim that intentional psychological states whose referential components differ are nevertheless the same. But the best case for this rests on the claim that the referential components of these *and other* psychological state types are explanatorily idle in explanations of actions, and this claim has been discredited.

4. WEAK EXTERNALISM AND NORMATIVITY

I take it that this brand of externalism, however weak it may be, is incompatible with the thesis that intentional types are reducible to ones expressible only in physical or physical and topic-neutral vocabulary, where these latter are such that their attribution does not require the existence of objects and/or phenomena beyond the bodies of persons. But the consequences are much more global than this. If I am right, externalism is incompatible even with theses which seek to reduce psychological types to ones expressible in physical and topic-neutral vocabulary whose attribution *does* require the existence of objects and phenomena external to persons' bodies. This includes both beyond-the-body (type–type) identity theses and constitution theses, and so covers more or less *any* sort of physicalist psychological reductionism. The reason can be seen by exploring the connection between the arguments for externalism and the more familiar anti-reductionist strategy mentioned at the outset of this paper, whereby psychological types are held to be irreducibly distinct from physical ones because they have, whereas physical ones cannot have, rational conditions of ascription. It is unlikely that psychological types have rational conditions of ascription *because* the explanation of action is externalist. Nor is it likely that physical types cannot have rational conditions of ascription *because* physical explanation is in general internalist. There do not seem to be any a priori reasons for thinking that externalist constraints on explanatory types in general must result in their being governed by normative principles of the sort that govern the ascription of intentional psychological types. It is plausible, for instance, that the classification of types of movement by objects through space-time is externalistically constrained. Nor, as this example itself suggests, does it appear to be true that physical explanation is in general internalist. In short, normativity need not attach only to explanation which is externalist: though psychological explanation is both externalist and normative, at least some physical explanation is arguably both externalist and non-normative.

It seems, rather, that the individuation of intentional types is externalistically constrained because those types have rational conditions of ascription. The arguments for externalism given above bring this normativity to bear both on the classification of actions, narrowly construed, and on the characterization and explanatory efficacy of intentional content. Consider, first, narrow act classification. Earlier it was argued that what counts as a given type of act, say, a washing, depends in part on the types of object or substance that are appropriate to that type of activity, where the idea of appropriateness is normative. In one community it may be appropriate to wash with water, whereas in another it may be appropriate to wash with sand. Objects, substances, and phenomena are apt to differ from one physical environment to another, and this will inform and help to circumscribe the nature of the activities involving them. Since, however, the same substance or object may standardly figure in different communities in very different activities, there is no getting away from the normativity involved in the classification of activities themselves. Without some standard of appropriateness for objects involved in a given type of activity, it is difficult to see how individual actions can be taxonomized as of that type. And unless this can be done, explanations of actions cannot be effected. So the classification of actions into types for the purposes of explanation requires that there be standards or norms concerning the sorts of object typically involved in them. In the light of these norms, actions can be shown to be rational or irrational. Sue's act of washing with hydrochloric acid, for example, is intelligible—can be seen to be rational—given that the ordinary observable qualitative properties of that substance resemble those of water, that water *is* the appropriate stuff to wash with in Sue's community, and that Sue believes the stuff she is washing with is water.

Consider now the characterization of intentional content. Normativity enters into this in two ways. First, by way of the norms which govern the classification of actions into types. These indirectly constrain the characterization of content, since actions, to be intelligible, must be seen to issue from causes that are of types which bear logical connections to the types of which they are instances. Sue's act of drinking water is made intelligible by reference to her belief that water quenches thirst and her desire to quench her thirst. But second, normativity enters into the characterization of content by way of the inferential connections intentional state types bear to one another. Here the ascription of content to an intentional type is constrained by the role it plays in an agent's reasoning processes; that it conforms to principles of inductive and deductive reasoning, that it is logically consistent with the contents of other intentional psychological states, etc. Ultimately this too has consequences for externalism, since the inferential role that an intentional type plays with regard to others is not independent of its referential component. This is hardly surprising given that that role is not independent of the actions that that type of state would, in conjunction with others, dispose an agent to engage in; actions the explanation of which requires the ascription of states of types whose referential components are not explanatorily idle.

Familiar though this may be, I think that it sheds some light on the question of why intentional types cannot have non-rational conditions of ascription. It is not that the individuation of physical types is not holistically constrained, since this seems false in general.[17] Nor is it that the individuation of physical types is not externalistically constrained, since this too seems false in general. It is that the physical types referred to in the *explananda* of physical explanations, whether broadly or narrowly construed, are ones whose individuation requires no mention of an appropriate object or type of object, where what counts as appropriate is not fixed simply by the physical properties of the relevant object or type. The actions referred to in the explananda of intentional psychological explanations,

---

[17] See Davidson, 'Mental Events', Kim, 'Psychophysical Laws', and C. Peacocke, *Holistic Explanation* (Oxford: Clarendon Press, 1979).

on the other hand, are ones whose individuation ultimately requires reference to the notion of an appropriate object or type of object; and since intentional psychological states are type-individuated to serve the purposes of rendering intelligible such actions, this normativity constrains the individuation of intentional mental types themselves. It is not rational, for example, for Sue to wash her clothes with mud, given that she knows that mud is not the appropriate stuff to get things clean. And whether or not mud is the appropriate stuff to get things clean is not simply a matter of its physical properties. It is a matter, also, of the norms that govern types of action in a community. One can wash with water or with sand; figurines can be worshipped or used to scratch backs.

It follows, I think, that the ascription of intentional content is not only externalistically constrained but *socially* constrained, and that philosophers such as Burge are right in thinking so but for the wrong reasons.[18] Burge sees social norms as serving to fix the extensions of natural kind terms embedded in sentences used to ascribe content. But this is not where the social element enters into the individuation conditions of intentional types. Where it enters is in helping to fix the extensions of narrow act-type specifications which are in turn required for the specification of those intentional types that figure in rationalistic explanations of actions. Narrow act types are individuated by reference to the objects that are appropriate to them, where this is socially constrained; but that constraint does not thereby enter into the individuation conditions of the objects that are appropriate to those acts.

If this is right, then both the explanatory efficacy of referential components of intentional psychological states *vis-à-vis* actions and the fact that the states themselves have rational conditions of ascription are traceable to the fact that those actions, even when narrowly construed, cannot be type-individuated independently of types of object that are appropriate to them, where this is at least partly socially determined. Unless agents themselves are understood as having this information, they literally do not know what they are doing when they engage in acts of the relevant types. It is in this

---

[18] See 'Individualism and the Mental'.

way that externalist and normative constraints enter into the characterization of psychological content itself. These latter constraints have no counterpart in physical theory, since the appropriateness of a given type of object to a type of action is not capable of being fixed by the physical properties of that object alone, irrespective of whether these latter are internalistically or externalistically individuated.

6

Physics, Biology, and Common-Sense Psychology

Jennifer Hornsby

The attitude of philosophers to the physical sciences no doubt partly explains why the 'physical' has featured so prominently in their discussions of mind. If a subject-matter is shown to be reducible to physics, its metaphysical status is revealed, and, presumably (supposing that the reduction carries conviction), rendered unproblematic. A reduction of mentality to physics would, then, be satisfying if it were available. But suppose that we cannot be satisfied by such a reduction, because we are persuaded of its impossibility. Must we turn elsewhere for the satisfaction that reduction would (*per impossibile* now) have provided?

In recent philosophy of mind *biology* has come to feature more and more.[1] Not that biology has quite been cast in the role of candidate for a reducing science. But biology is thought to show us how we might better understand the mind's place in nature. This paper is part of an enquiry into where, how, and to what extent it helps, in providing the satisfaction that reduction to the physical might have been meant to yield, to appeal to our position as biological creatures. With what sort of optimism should we greet Darwin's aphoristic notebook entry: 'Origin of Man now proved—Metaphysics must flourish'?

[1] Three recent books that give biology prominence are R. Millikan, *Language, Thought, and Other Biological Categories* (Cambridge, Mass.: MIT Press, 1984), F. Dretske, *Explaining Behaviour* (Cambridge, Mass.: MIT Press, Bradford Books, 1988), and C. McGinn, *Mental Content* (Oxford: Blackwell, 1989). Their particular suggestions are not the subject of the present paper; but they have influenced me in raising the rather general questions broached in Sect. 3 here. Daniel Dennett, *Content and Consciousness* (London: Routledge & Kegan Paul, 1969) introduced a biological perspective; my attention to Dennett is confined largely to later work: see n. 2.

Daniel Dennett has recently made it clear how Darwin's theory is meant to provide support for his own view of the mind.[2] Dennett has always seemed to maintain that the claims we make when we see ourselves as rational beings and attribute intentional mental states are pieces of fiction—albeit parts of an extremely fruitful fiction. A recent argument of his would uphold this account by showing what we should think of ourselves when we take a biological view and see ourselves as the evolved products of natural selection. I shall criticize this argument in Section 2. In Section 3, I reflect more generally on how Darwinian theory may contribute to naturalism about the mental. But before I get on to any of this, I want to see where Dennett's biological thinking fits in with reductivist, physicalistic thinking about common-sense psychology.

1. REDUCTIONIST THINKING

By 'common-sense psychology' I mean the subject-matter that people use in understanding one another, that we all use all the time, usually quite unreflectively.[3] When its claims are made explicit, common-sense psychology employs terms like 'sees', 'thinks', 'wants', 'means to', 'says' (or when expressed by philosophers, more likely, 'perceives', 'believes', 'desires', 'intends', and 'asserts'); these are terms for so-called intentional mental states. Using these terms, we regard ourselves and others as rational beings, and can give explanations of what is said and done. Our explanations are not usually formulated: when we take people to think and to want and to say things, for the most part we do not actually enunciate

---

[2] All citations and page references in the text and notes below are to articles in D. Dennett, *The Intentional Stance* (Cambridge, Mass.: MIT Press, 1987): 'Setting off on the Right Foot', 1–11; 'Three Kinds of Intentional Psychology', 43–68; 'Reflections: Instrumentalism Reconsidered', 69–81; 'Making Sense of Ourselves', 83–101; 'Reflections: The Language of Thought Reconsidered', 227–35; 'Intentional Systems in Cognitive Ethology: The "Panglossian Paradigm" Defended', 237–68; 'Evolution, Error and Intentionality', 287–321.

[3] Dennett, along with others, speaks of *'folk* psychology'. If this is construed by analogy with 'folk physics' or 'folk linguistics', there is an implication that folk psychology is the perhaps defective version of a subject-matter that others (physicists, linguisticians . . .) study with more appropriate methods. I say 'common-sense psychology' in an attempt to nullify the implication.

what they think or want or say; but we nevertheless rely on people as being subjects of thoughts, wants, etc. In communicating with others, for instance, we rely continually on their being such as to be interpreted as purporting to say how things are.

A leading question in recent philosophy of mind has been how we should conceive of the relation of this pervasive subject-matter to the subject-matter of the physical sciences. It is rare these days to find the claim that the *laws* and *terms* of common-sense psychology reduce to the laws and terms of physics. But it is not at all rare to find it held that the relation between the two subjects is—or ought to be—*some sort* of reductive one. The idea, very roughly, is that common-sense psychological explanations ultimately do—or ought to—fall within the scope of natural physical scientific explanations. The 'ought to' comes in here because of the belief on the part of some philosophers that any real phenomenon, however we may actually understand it, is intelligible from the perspective of physical science. This belief may be thought to be essential to a physicalist world-view. Common-sense psychological phenomena, then, on this view, 'ought to' have physical scientific explanations ultimately, because it would count against them—against their 'reality' or against physicalism—if they did not. Once this view is taken, there is the possibility that common-sense psychology fails to live up to a standard which the metaphysician sets. If so, common-sense psychology might be refuted.

It would have massive repercussions if someone could show that common-sense psychology both required vindication of a certain sort and lacked vindication of that sort. For if we could not take seriously the notions that we apply to one another in putting it to work, then we could not take ourselves seriously—as perceivers, as cognizers, and as agents. But we have to take ourselves seriously to take, for instance, the project of science seriously:[4] it would be strange to allow that human beings have understood quite a bit about the world's workings if we also held that human beings have never

[4] See also A. Donagan, *Choice: The Essential Element in Human Action* (London: Routledge & Kegan Paul, 1987), 14–15.

been such as to communicate knowledge to one another. If common-sense psychology were false, then even if a world of objects did exist independently of us, that world would not be something of which we really had any conception of ourselves taking any view, nor something on which we could have a conception of ourselves as having any influence. We have to envisage a scepticism far more devastating than any with which we are familiar. In sceptical philosophy as we find it in recent history, psychological truths are taken as assured (even if they are truths about the mind of a solitary enquirer merely), and to entertain scepticism is to doubt the existence of further truths about the world (or the existence of other minds within it). But a sceptical position based upon suspicion of the psychological which overthrew common-sense psychology would leave nothing assured; it would be nihilism.

Some philosophers seem committed to this nihilism. There are eliminativist materialists who tell us that common-sense psychology is straightforwardly false.[5] But it is not only philosophers who hold such devastating views who are implicated in a potential threat to it. Many think that common-sense psychological explanations work through their connection with theories in physical science, without contemplating the possibility that the connections do not exist. Functionalists provide an example. Few actually speak of common-sense psychology as needing vindication; they take it for granted that there are projectible psychophysical correlations and that, through them, common-sense psychology is grounded in physical science. But presumably if there were no correlations of the sort that they assume, our use of common-sense psychology would, so far as they are concerned, be only 'fictionalizing and contrivance' (as Loar has put it[6]).

Some philosophers, though, are content to allow that our common faith in common-sense psychology is misplaced. They believe that it lacks the scientific vindication it requires, but take consolation in the thought that it is somehow invulnerable

---

[5] See e.g. P. M. Churchland, 'Eliminative Materialism and the Propositional Attitudes', *Journal of Philosophy*, 78 (1981).

[6] In his *Mind and Meaning* (Cambridge: Cambridge University Press, 1981), ch. 1. Brian Loar is more explicit than many functionalists are that functionalism places trust in science.

in the face of refutation. Quine held that we continue to use 'the intentional idiom' only because we cannot abandon it even on discovering it to be false. When we engage in science, we are on firm, true ground; but we must use a double standard to give credence also to what is said using the intentional idiom, and treat that as 'drama'.[7] Quine's 'intentional idiom' may suggest something narrower than common-sense psychology. In fact, though, if the idiom could be faulted, then so too could all the thoughts people have about one another as thinkers and agents, even if these thoughts are for the most part not expressed in the intentional idiom (because not expressed at all). And it is not easy to see how we could set ourselves a lower standard in interpreting ourselves than in understanding the rest of the world; for it surely cannot be taken to be the case that p while it is taken not to be the case that anyone (literally, really) believes that p. The same point that led us to think that we should be taken to nihilism if we convicted common-sense psychology of falsehood must lead us now to wonder how it could be afforded an inferior place in our world-view.

Dennett also accords it an inferior place. Where Quine speaks of the intentional idiom, Dennett speaks of 'adopting the intentional stance'; where Quine speaks of 'drama', Dennett speaks of 'fiction', and he tells us that statements made from the intentional stance are 'true only if we exempt them from a certain familiar standard of literality' (p. 72). Dennett's position is not presented as arising from questions about common-sense psychology's relationship to science; and he is reluctant to allow that common-sense psychology might suffer *refutation*. Perhaps that explains why he can be as sanguine as he always has been about its failure to be literally true. But it makes it harder to explain his non-realist tendencies in the first place.[8]

I think that Dennett's position has been clarified since he has been most explicit about the way in which evolutionary biology

---

[7] W. V. O. Quine, *Word and Object* (Cambridge, Mass.: MIT Press, 1960), 219–21.

[8] Non-realist tendencies revealed in his sympathies with eliminativism: Dennett represents his decision not to espouse eliminativism as a choice of *tactics* (p. 234). See also n. 9.

enters into it. His views about biology may be seen as the crux of a purported reconciliation of two apparently contradictory features of his thought: they are meant to underwrite both his irrealism as shown in his sympathy with eliminativism, and his optimism, his 'sort of realism' (p. 73). A satisfactory reconciliation would be a way of avoiding nihilism.[9]

In the days when Dennett was happy with the title 'instrumentalism' for his position, it sometimes appeared that he wanted to urge it as a reason for his view of common-sense psychology that the intentional stance provides us with a successful mode of understanding. It was tempting then to reply that this might seem to be at least as good a reason for an attitude of realism. But Dennett is clearer now what he takes to be involved in seeing common-sense psychology as the successful product of a useful stance. When we see ourselves commonsensically, he thinks, we adopt a perspective from which we see ourselves as biologically designed. It is to common-sense psychology's detriment that it is the product of a useful stance, because the stance is one we can adopt only if we engage in fiction, since (of course) we have not really been designed, and the fictional designer, Mother Nature, is only our invention. Dennett writes that 'we are still just coming to terms with [the] unsettling implications of Darwin's de-

---

[9] See G. McCulloch, 'Dennett's Little Grains of Salt', *Philosophical Quarterly*, 40 (1990), for an attempt (successful, I think) to demonstrate that there is a major incoherence in Dennett's position. An overall interpretation of Dennett is not the project of the present paper, and I confine to footnotes consideration of arguments bearing on, but independent of, that discussed in Sect. 2. See nn. 18 and 23. Also I pay little attention to the instrumentalist strands in Dennett. The following, from Loar (*Mind and Meaning*, n. 6, pp. 14–15), spells out a connection between eliminativist-style non-realism and instrumentalism: 'If it were to turn out that the physical mechanisms that completely explain human behaviour at no level exhibited the structure of beliefs and desires, then something that we had all along believed, viz. that beliefs and desires were among the causes of behaviour, would turn out to be false. Naturally we would continue to use the belief–desire framework to systematize behaviour, but that should then at the theoretical level have the air of fictionalizing and contrivance.' Dennett is confident that it will 'turn out that the physical mechanisms . . .'. His instrumentalism is, then, his endorsement of the claim about 'the air of fictionalizing'. Biology can now be seen as Dennett's device for showing why common-sense psychology should have the air which it should have ('at the theoretical level'). (Perhaps, then, Dennett no longer sees himself as instrumentalist, because he takes himself to have explained (away) the instrumentalist posture.)

struction of the Argument from Design' (p. 321). The implications Dennett believes in are unsettling because they disturb
our realism. But once we have come to terms with them, he
thinks, common-sense psychology will have been vindicated to
the extent that it can be: it will not have been shown to be true,
but to be such as to deliver what it is appropriate to expect
of it.

2. MOTHER NATURE'S ARTEFACTS

2.1

Dennett's evolutionary argument, which is meant to show that
our own intentionality is less than literal, is meant also to show
that any property that may be postulated from the design
stance is less than literal. The intentional stance, he tells us,
can be viewed as a 'limiting case of the Design stance' (p. 73);
and the design stance is adopted whenever something is seen
as possessing a function or an end or a purpose. Thus he
hopes to establish that anything said about anything organic
from an evolutionary point of view is metaphor.

This line of thought in Dennett appears to have no use for an
idea that at times seems absolutely crucial for him—the idea
of *being derived*. In 'Evolution, Error and Intentionality', he
suggests that the underlying disagreement between him and
his principal opponents is encapsulated in his thesis that our
intentionality is not the real, original sort; there common-sense
psychology's non-literalness is founded in our intentionality's
derivativeness. An example of derived intentionality is a heating
system with a thermostatic control: it behaves as if it had
properties that it does not really have, having been made
by its human designers to behave as if it had them. If we
were relevantly like heating systems, then it would be only
as if the statements of our everyday explanations of one
another were true.

It can seem as if our intentionality were meant to suffer a
double blow at Dennett's hands: like a wide range of other
phenomena, it is accessible only from the design stance, and
thus within a fiction; *and* it is of the derived kind, which

detracts again from its reality. The first blow is directed towards all biological phenomena, the second only to things that
we take to be subjects of common-sense psychology. Dennett
himself evidently intends to inflict the two together, saying, as
he does, that 'the problems of interpretation in psychology and
the problems of interpretation in biology are *the same problems*'
(p. 277). I shall question this. But I think that it must first be
clear that the two lines of thought can be separated. Then we
shall be in a position to consider the biological argument in
isolation and on its merits (Section 2.4). So I shall begin with
the idea of a derived property and the role that it might have
been supposed to play in Darwinian thinking (Section 2.2); but
this is in order to introduce Dennett's fiction of Mother Nature
as creator (Section 2.3), and to postpone consideration of the
argument which actually makes use of the idea of a derived
property (until Section 2.5).

2.2

The sense of 'derived' that matters to Dennett is evidently
meant to take off from the idea of artifice: artefacts derive
properties from their makers. And an artefact's seeming to
possess a property by derivation is evidently meant to count
against its really possessing it.[10]

Some properties conferred on artefacts by their makers
are surely not derived properties as Dennett intends this. If
someone makes a knife in order that she should cut with it, the
fact that she made it because she wanted to cut in no way
detracts from the knife itself's really being such as to cut. The
heating system with a thermostatic control is like the knife that

---

[10] I build it in that that which is derived tends not to be the real thing, in
order that there should be some use for Dennett's thought that what is derived
is not literally possessed. A notion of 'derivation' in connection with artefacts
could receive any number of definitions, and I am deliberately not precise. (If
someone's purpose stands to another purpose of that person as means to end,
the literalness of the ascription of the means is not cast in doubt. But it is
arguable that our understanding of *derivation* extends from our understanding
of means and end. So it is hard to contrive a definition of 'derived' which non-
stipulatively rules out the idea of something that is both derived and literally
possessed.)

cuts if we think of its property of keeping the room at a constant temperature: it is only when we think of it as sharing its maker's end, of its *wanting* to have the room a constant temperature, that we come to a derived property. We have a different sort of case of derivation where there is no specific practical end of the maker apparently inherited by the artefact. Cognitive psychologists who simulate intelligence or other faculties have a theoretical end, of understanding a process, which the artefact (the computer program or robot or what-ever) need give no appearance of possessing. What is inherited now is not an apparent purpose, but rather something like the property of purposiveness. But here again possession by its creator of an end gives the real explanation of the artefact's being as if it had some design stance property, and here again it may detract from the artefact's really possessing the property to see it as derived: so these cases of simulation presumably provide another kind of example of what Dennett had in mind.

Now neither of these two ideas of a derived property has a role in the Darwinian thinking that Dennett believes to have such unsettling implications. This is revealed when we see that they have no place in the argument that the Darwinian thinking displaces—the argument from design.

Advocates of the argument from design looked at the living world, and found it hard not to see organisms other than as systems composed in such a way as might have been expected if they were constructed by an intelligent, purposive being. If God exists, there is an excellent explanation: organisms seem to have been designed because they were—by God. This argument does not work by seeing particular ends of God reflected in the behaviour of his creatures. In connection with his aims in creation, theologians often speak of God's inscrutability; in their view, we cannot expect to say why we find what we do in the world he made. Their view reflects the fact that the argument from design says nothing of God's purposes or of his reasoning from means to end. Working in mysterious ways (though purposefully enough), he conferred properties on the things he created. Some of these properties are functional ones, and it is part of God's design, for example, that the heart should pump blood. But organisms do not exist to carry out some purpose of God's.[11] If derived properties serve that which confers them, they are out of place in the thinking of an advocate of the argument from design.

Human beings relate differently to God, of course: according to the traditional Judaeo-Christian story, God created 'mankind in his own image', 'to be like him, to imitate him and to resemble him'. If our properties were supposed to be derived from God's, then it would be on the model of simulation, rather than by the seeming inheritance of particular purposes. (I shall return to this.) But in any case human beings are not supposed to play any special role in the argument itself (albeit that they provide an ultimate point for God's creation). So we may say quite generally that the argument does not work by attributing particular purposes to God. His creatures are his artefacts, it is true; but they stand to him more as works of his art than as means to his ends.

2.3

Abandoning the argument from design, but continuing to take the design stance, we have to postulate a new designer. Dennett's name for her is Mother Nature. If we are to follow Dennett in thinking that Darwin's account of the natural world destroyed the argument from design, then she must be supposed to be a good Darwinian construct, and as such a new candidate for the role that God played.

What Darwin showed was that if natural selection had been at work, there would be an alternative explanation of the appearances that God was invoked to explain. The cumulative effect of many small changes brought about by natural selection would be productions which 'plainly bear the stamp of far higher workmanship'.[12] This is what the positing of Mother Nature records: it is as if she were the higher workperson and

---

[11] Aquinas: 'Vult ergo hoc esse propter hoc, sed non propter hoc vult hoc.' So it is contrary to theological wisdom to suppose that God in creating means to ends was creating those means as means to his ends.

[12] Far higher than *man's*, that is: 'Can we wonder, then, that nature's productions should be far "truer" in character than man's productions; that they should be infinitely better adapted to the most complex conditions of life, and should plainly bear the stamp . . .?' (*The Origin of Species*, in *The Essential Darwin*, ed. Mark Ridely (London: Allen and Unwin, 1987), 86–7).

producer of such accumulated effects. Where the conclusion used to be that God exists, now it may be that it is *as if* Mother Nature existed. The argument from design is destroyed because the unfoldings of a purposeless nature now account for the 'as if'. To the extent that natural selection works through the agency of death and extinction, it is as if a higher being had sought to achieve fitness for life and perpetuation. The features of Mother Nature's creations that are features of her design, then, are those that biologists call adaptations. Natural selection at once explains their presence, and the appearance of design.

We must wonder now why Dennett should think that the implications of Darwin's theory are unsettling. For Mother Nature surely cannot subvert such appearances as she is invoked to explain. When people thought that it was part of God's design that the heart should pump blood, it was never meant to have detracted from the reality of that function of the heart that it had been so designed.[13] Why should we think that our being able to speak as if biological things had been designed with functions makes it any the less literally true that they have those functions? A fictional story about Mother Nature is one that we may construct if we think it gives us a good myth—if things are as they would be if the myth were true. It is because of the way that biological things actually are that the argument from design was so compelling. And it is because of the way that things actually are that the Mother Nature story provides a good myth (to the extent that it does). But the fact that we can make a fiction does nothing to interfere with the way things actually are. (There is a fiction in which children are given toys by Father Christmas: no one who recognizes it as a fiction thinks that it undermines what we know about how the children really come by their toys.)

---

[13] Not that Dennett is the first to have thought that by taking the design stance we are compelled to see all teleology as only appearance. Arguably Kant thought something like this. In so far as I use considerations in the history of thought against Dennett, it is the history of English (-speakers') thought. Darwin, in his assumption that it was adaptation that needed explanation (n. 12), was following the tradition of natural theology. Dennett's arguments are firmly in the same tradition. See S. J. Gould, 'The Hardening of the Modern Synthesis', in M. Grene (ed.), *Dimensions of Darwinism* (Cambridge: Cambridge University Press, 1983), esp. p. 91.

2.4

Evidently this cannot be the end of the argument with Dennett. If Darwin's theory is to disturb our attitude of realism in biology, then Mother Nature must evidently do more than usurp God's role as explainer of the appearances. And indeed it is clear that she is meant to do a great deal more when she is used to bolster Dennett's claim that the intentional stance is 'inescapable' in biology (p. 314). Dennett is claiming now not only that there is a story we may tell in which we see properties as conferred by Mother Nature, but that we must postulate Mother Nature in order to see those properties as biologists do. His reason for thinking that we speak so often within a fiction is his claim that the inside of a fiction is the only place from which we can say what we do.

This claim seems plainly wrong in the light of our comparison of God with Mother Nature. If ascription of a design stance property presupposed a posited designer (as Dennett is now suggesting) then any doubt about God's existence would have been an obstacle to appreciation of the phenomena that, in the argument from design, he is introduced to explain: it becomes impossible to understand how that argument could ever have been given. (The argument 'from Design', one should notice, is in fact an argument from the appearance of design: the conclusion is simultaneously that God exists and that there really has been design.)

When Dennett offers support for the intentional stance's inevitability in biology, he says that evolutionists, in asking any question about why some feature is present, are 'seeking the rationale that explains why the feature was selected', and that the complete answer to the question 'will almost always, in at least some minimal way, allude to *better* design'. Now these points suggest at most that biologists have to be open to the idea of traits and states and organisms being as they would be if natural selection had introduced them, and as being as they would be if they had been designed. But features can be characterized as better or worse in meeting an environmental challenge without being thought of, even metaphorically, as designer products; and organisms may be said to be more or less fit according as their reproductive success is higher or lower than alternatives.[14] To take the perspective of as-if design towards an item is not to be committed to a hypothesis that its origin was in natural selection or that the appearance of design is (as Darwin would say) not to be wondered at. There are ways to explain how something can appear well designed without anyone's making believe that an Intentional Being has been at work.

The practices of twentieth-century biologists (not only the thinking of eighteenth-century theologians) expose Dennett's error. If the adoption of the design stance were all one with the postulation of Mother Nature, then there would be nothing more to recognizing a property as adaptive than being able to tell some story in which a designer introduced it. But a major controversy in evolutionary biology concerns the extent to which genuine adaptation is manifest in the biological world— the extent to which the actual fitness of organisms is correctly historically explained by the kind of (non-accidental) differential reproduction to which followers of Darwin give the name of selection.[15] If evolutionary biologists may respond

[14] For distinctions between concepts of adaptedness (of which only one is Darwinian adaptation), see R. M. Burian, 'Adaptation', in Grene (ed.), *Dimensions of Darwinism*, n. 13. (Note that even the two *non-selectional* notions of adaptedness I have gestured at (defined by reference (1) to meeting challenges, (2) to reproduction) need not correlate perfectly with one another.) Distinctions here are enough to show what is wrong with Dennett's idea that 'Function is in the eye of the beholder' (p. 314): whether something is correctly ascribed a function depends (not on what strikes a beholder, but) on whether it is an adaptation in a particular sense (so that a certain sort of historical account of its evolution can be given).

[15] Dennett of course is well aware of the controversy between adaptationists and others. He takes his opponents to be the anti-adaptationists, and his task to be that of showing that even then they are adaptationist enough for his purposes. But here I think he simply trades on ambiguities in the notion of 'adaptation' (see n. 14), and detracts from the specific commitments of the adaptationists by making a great deal of the fact that hypotheses about evolutionary history are hard to confirm or refute. Dennett's claim that even the anti-adaptationists regularly use the concept of adaptation is a claim about the scope of what is visible from the design stance. But what Dennett needed to persuade us of is the ubiquity of what is explicable by positing an as-if designer in Darwin's manner. It is no wonder then that Dennett thinks the anti-adaptationists will object: they will think that Dennett is encouraging us in empirically false beliefs. They reject, for example, the idea, described by Dennett as 'both compelling and familiar' (p. 300), that 'we are artifacts designed by natural selection': in their view, natural selection provides a partial account of our seeming to have been designed.

to a 'why' question about some feature by saying that its presence lacks any natural selectional explanation, it cannot be a compulsory assumption that there is a good myth in which Mother Nature has played a part.[16]

2.5

We should return to intentionality, and to Dennett's thesis in the philosophy of mind that common-sense psychology is fiction.

It is worth considering what the standing of common-sense psychology would be if the evolutionary argument we have just considered had succeeded. Presumably Dennett means us to treat the property of being common-sense psychologically interpretable as just one more biological property whose ascription should be viewed within the fiction and treated as metaphor. But how does this work? Questions about the interpretation of humans are now supposed to boil down to questions about the interpretation of Mother Nature—to the detriment of their answers because she isn't real. But how do we interpret Mother Nature? Presumably we model her on our (psychological) selves. But then we have to construct a fiction (Mother Nature) in order to tell a story (or the biological world's being designed), yet we have to construct the fiction out of material (common-sense psychology) that could only be available once the fiction had already been constructed and the story told.[17]

---

[16] I have over-simplified, and spoken as if a structure's apparent design was either a direct result of natural selection (i.e. originally shaped by natural selection for its current use), or straightforwardly not. But there must be room for ideas of (1) what originated as correlated characters of directly selected traits, and (2) what originated via selection for a use different from the current one. So if we were to tell a story about Mother Nature which corresponded to the biologist's vision of how things evolved, then we should have to recognize that she has different parts to play as the story unfolds. (This is not a concern of Dennett's, however, since the myth of Mother Nature that he would have us construct is not meant to recapitulate any of the historical facts (or 'etiological details' as he disparagingly calls them, at p. 28).)

[17] This objection is a version of a natural protest against Dennett, which has been put like this: 'Derivative intentionality, like an image in a photocopy, must derive eventually from something that is not similarly derivative' (see J. Haugeland, 'The Intentionality All-Stars', in J. Tomberlin (ed.), *Philosophical Perspectives*, iv (Ridgeview, Calif.: Atascadero, 1990), 385). A response to this

This suggests that we cannot really make sense of Dennett's biological argument unless we treat human beings as somehow removed from it. If we, but not other organisms, are like Mother Nature in being intentional beings, then our relation to Mother Nature is surely different from theirs. It is no wonder that man was separated from the rest of creation when the argument from design was given, and that God was attributed a particular, beneficent desire (that 'there be beings with intellectual power and free will over themselves'). If our intentionality springs, by design, from an Intentional Being, she (in the fiction) presumably has to set out with some purpose similar to God's. It is no wonder also, then, that we find a further strand in Dennett's argument when it is addressed to common-sense psychology: the idea of *derivation* was a red herring in the general biological argument; but if the fiction is elaborated to provide for our own manufacture, it seems bound to enter.

Mother Nature's simulating herself is thus the natural ending to Dennett's story. Or it would be natural if it were not utterly fantastic. Dennett intended us to remain faithful to neo-Darwinian natural science as we became convinced of the compulsory character of the Mother Nature fiction. But if it is to be part of the story that Mother Nature undertook the project of simulating herself, we shall surely find the fiction all too easy to resist.

In fact Dennett spares us. When he gets on to the idea of our intentionality as simulated, it is not Mother Nature at all, but our *genes*, from which our intentionality is supposed to be derived. He cites Richard Dawkins's vision of us (and all other biological species) as 'survival machines' designed to prolong the future of our selfish genes; and suggests that just as a robot that you might make to simulate yourself would possess only derived intentionality, so we all possess only derived intentionality because we stand to our genes as your robot does to you (pp. 298–9). Of course our intentionality might be supposed to 'derive' from our genes in some bland sense, not requiring that genes should be carrying out their own

from Dennett might use the arguments considered in n. 18 and at (1) in n. 23. I have tried to state the protest so that it bears on Dennett's evolutionary argument itself.

purposes. But if that is all Dennett means, he has worked fast and loose with the notion of derivation, and is appealing now to a sense in which something's being derived has nothing whatever to do with its not being the real thing. What his argument requires is a quite new fiction in which genes have the project of self-simulation. This is, as he admits, 'a bit outrageous'.

Perhaps there was a grain of plausibility in the idea that the design stance is essential to seeing things as having functions and that Mother Nature's postulation is essential to the design stance. It would have got a bit far-fetched if we had been asked to cast Mother Nature as simulator and still see her as playing an essential role. But it is hard to see how any plausibility could attach to the claim that we are compelled to enter a fiction in which we are designed by our genes.[18] Dennett and his readers are probably alone in participating in the fiction; many have treated one another as persons.

3. HUMAN BEINGS AS EVOLUTIONARY PRODUCTS

Many philosophers, even without reductionist aspirations, have thought that it cannot unproblematically be said that

---

[18] Dennett of course wants us to judge that, however perfect a replica of yourself a robot might be, it would not really possess intentionality. The effect of my claim that Dennett's far-fetched fiction has no particular bearing on reality is to allow us to suspend judgement on that. Although Dennett's biological argument certainly requires us to think that it is not an *option* for us to take the standpoint from which it is *as if* there were a designer, it may be that the particular story of genes as creators is meant to introduce an analogy, rather than the last act of a compulsory fiction. If so, we cannot suspend judgement on the robot, who comes into play now in another, superficially better argument. This other argument would have us believe that what we take to be a sufficient condition for real intentionality applies where we know that a sufficient condition for non-real intentionality applies; hence it is all unreal. More precisely: (1) the fact that something is an artefact shows that it does not really possess intentionality; (2) there is nothing more to x's possessing intentionality than its being fruitful to adopt the intentional stance towards x. (2) would be supposed to put human beings on all fours with the robot of Dennett's tale, and (1) would then ensure, given a judgement about the robot, that our own intentionality had the metaphysical status of the derivative variety. I should question this argument in the first instance by asking whether 'fruitful' and 'stance' are eliminable from (2). Suppose that (2) amounted to the claim that we may equate x's being a proper subject of common-sense

psychological beings obey only physical laws yet have properties irreducible to physical ones. In Dennett's account, though, common-sense psychology's irreducibility would not present an obstacle to any physicalist thesis; its fictional status was supposed to ensure that. Yet it is not just any old fiction for Dennett, but precisely that fiction that purports to be true to creatures in a physicalist world who have 'tried to make sense' both of nature and of themselves. Dennett's story, though not allowing us to treat common-sense psychology as telling us the truth, would have ensured at least that the error we call truth was an error that nature naturally gives rise to.

And there surely is a difficulty about viewing our own presence in the world as the upshot of blind forces. The question now must be whether we should seek an account to put in the place of Dennett's. At times his attempt to persuade us that we should not take the deliverances of the intentional stance literally appeared to rely on nothing more than the idea that we are evolved creatures—that our intentionality has a source simply. Perhaps, then, intentionality can be brought into line with other evolved properties without introducing the fiction of a designer. Is there an argument from biology whose consequence is that people really are interpretable in the way we think? Dennett would have had evolutionary biology protect us against nihilism; but should we expect it to vindicate common-sense psychology?

If intentionality were to have been swallowed up in Dennett's general argument for the metaphorical character of what the design stance makes visible, then 'being a subject of common-sense psychology' would have to be treated as an adaptive property that nature has selected for. How credible is this?

The suggestion has an initial plausibility. We believe that it helps us to get on in the world to be rational creatures: 'having a rational mind' surely is conducive to survival. But it is not clear that one can make very much of this in fact. Having a mind is harder to fathom than having an eye or having a

psychology with x's being intelligible in the way that we find (at least at present) only human beings intelligible—i.e. as a creature capable of the full range of cognitive attitudes, behaviours, human emotions, etc. Then we should have to doubt whether (1) can be judged a priori.

stomach. The property of being a subject of common-sense psychology, or being an intentional system, may strike us a property too broad and general to be explained in selectional terms. And we have seen that it is an error to suppose that all useful traits—let alone all properties on the scale of being interpretable common-sense psychologically—arise as direct results of natural selection.[19]

In fact there are actual difficulties about seeing rationality (and thus intentionality) under the head of adaptation. People often enough deviate from the norm of rationality which common-sense psychology works by. Psychologists suggest that many such deviations are systematic: adult humans can be demonstrated to adopt styles of inference that lead less to truth than the fully rational alternatives.[20] The important point here is not that we stray from pure rationality, but that explanations can be given of why we stray, and that the explanations themselves are cast in terms of usefulness. Malfunctions of reason can often be viewed as the operation of heuristics that tend to work; people give undue weight to evidence that is readily available, for instance, and in doing so they over-apply a strategy that otherwise serves them well. To make sense of this, we need a distinction between correctness, so far as rationality's canons are concerned, and what is suited to the actual world. There would be no such distinction if a style of reasoning's being correct amounted to no more than its serving well. If the design stance were all, we should have no place for a norm which might conflict with those it introduces.

Still, even if we cannot reduce rationality to properties that we may hope to account for in terms of selectional advantage, Dennett was surely right that our genes confer on us properties that contribute to our appearing to be intentional creatures.[21] Even if a trait's presence has no natural selectional explanation,

---

[19] See nn. 14 and 16 and related text.

[20] See e.g. R. Nisbett and L. Ross (eds.), *Human Inference: Strategies and Shortcomings of Social Judgement* (Englewood Cliffs, NJ: Prentice Hall, 1980), Introduction.

[21] Earlier we saw Dennett's argument exploiting (through equivocation on 'derived') the thought that our intentionality is derived from our genes. Even where 'derived' has its blandest sense, however, the thought is cast in doubt by theses about the social constitution of the cognitive subject. Hence my even weaker 'contribute to'.

it cannot be unintelligible relative to what we know about natural selection. So may we not at least see common-sense psychological subjects as coming to inhabit a world in which the processes of natural selection have operated?

Well, for Darwin, natural selection is contrasted with the artificial sort. The natural/artificial contrast has come to have many nuances at a time when we have to attend to whether colours, flavours, and vitamins are natural or artificial. But Darwin himself was clear. There is artificial selection when someone's purpose intervenes in the matter of whether a creature reproduces. If that is so, then it seems that the advent into the world of beings who can, in the relevant sense, *choose*, for example, their mates is the beginning of the end of natural selection.

In illustrating artificial selection, Darwin emphasized cases where a human breeder of plants or animals intervenes in reproduction with a particular end in view. But, as he recognized, for natural selection to be counteracted, it is not necessary that anyone should act with some particular selectional purpose in mind. Nowadays our attention is drawn particularly and often to cases where no individual human being did or would intend what are actually the cumulative effects of human intervention and which determine whether creatures reproduce. We have come to understand the thought that technological advance is rendering the world a less *natural* place to live in. And we surely understand this by reference to a conception of nature set against humankind—which seems to have been Darwin's conception. The metaphor of Mother Nature could be apt in making the point: whereas Mother Nature supposedly acted alone before beings with purposes came into the world, she has come now to face constant competition.

We might then associate the advent of minded creatures like ourselves with the introduction of a new force for evolutionary change.[22] But it is not evident that this has to be the right way

---

[22] The anti-adaptationists of course already allow that explanations of evolutionary change are not all natural selectional (see n. 15). In speaking of a 'new' force, I have in mind something without a basis in genetics. (Compare Richard Dawkins's idea of cultural evolution, operating, as he would say, through *memes*, in *The Selfish Gene* (Oxford: Oxford University Press, 1976).)

to tell the story. We might accept the 'new force', but think that if we have to depart from neo-Darwinian theory in an account of the last few million years of the earth's natural history, there is no particular pressure to see the arrival of *Homo sapiens* as itself making the first moment of departure. Perhaps the alteration came with the emergence of an ancestor who did not yet 'take the intentional stance'. We know that in accounting for the evolution of, say, mammalian vision, we need to be able to make sense of the idea of an organ which evolves into the eye, but which itself had far less visual acuity than the mature functioning eyes that mammals now have. Similarly, if we are to think of being common-sense psychologically interpretable as an evolved property, we need to be able to contemplate the possibility of something with (so to speak) less rational–social acuity than that which we find in people now. So there is a story we can tell in which it would be a mistake to assume that there could be a natural selectional explanation of the emergence of intentionality itself.

Evidently there are massive questions here, and these considerations are extremely superficial. But we may cast in doubt Dennett's idea that the design stance is the limiting case of the intentional stance, and that biological and intentional understanding are to be assimilated.[23] And we can see at least

---

[23] Dennett's assimilation of biology and common-sense psychology, of the design stance and the intentional stance, has many sources of support, of which I have considered only one—the treatment of intentionality as on a par with other biological traits in being the product of a fictional designer. (1) Dennett sometimes uses slippery slope arguments. He points out that we have a tendency to use teleological language outside the biological sphere and to use intentional language outside the human sphere, and in each case we are uncertain when we start to speak metaphorically. At times these points are taken to demonstrate the ubiquitously metaphorical character of each of teleological and of common-sense psychological language. If they did show that, then a similar argument could be used to show that vague predicates have no application: we are uncertain when they cease to apply. But sometimes these points are used to show that teleological and intentional interpretation are not really distinguishable. The argument here is no better, moving still from the presence of a shady border to the absence of any border. (2) Dennett sometimes appeals to the fact that teleological and common-sense psychological explanation are alike normative. This is no ground for their assimilation unless we cannot distinguish between different sets of norms. Different conceptions of adaptation (cp. Burian, n. 14) provide a corrective to the idea that there is only one source even of biology's normativity. And different conceptions of cognitive fitness (and ibid., n. 20) reveal that more

that whatever scope we give to Darwinian theory, it need not go the whole way in explaining what Dennett wanted Mother Nature and/or genes to explain as appearance.

I finish by saying why we should not have to find such a conclusion either surprising or threatening.

Dennett's evolutionary vision introduced a particular standard of literal truth. Viewing things from the lofty perspective from which we are supposed to appreciate the fiction in which intentionality presents itself, we are meant to see intentionality under the aspect of the inexorable and ubiquitous workings of physical nature on mere matter. Our inability to find, from this perspective, explanatory states that we can identify with states of belief and desire was what, for Dennett, counted against a straightforward realism. The perspective Dennett had us adopt was one from which our being sentient, and rational, and interpretable beings was to have been a brute and natural fact; mind was simply there in the world. Or, actually, as it turned out, for Dennett it was a fiction, not a fact: from the lofty perspective, it could be seen not that mind was there but that it would seem to be. Dennett declared his 'starting point to be the objective, materialistic, third person world of the physical sciences'; and he admits that this is a prejudice (p. 5).

What Dennett has prejudiced himself against is the view that things' appearing in certain ways to perceiving sentient creatures is a phenomenon, not an epiphenomenon, of mind. We saw the difficulty that arose for Dennett when his fiction required Mother Nature to be both an intentional being and the author of all intentionality—as if she had to be located from a perspective from which she could not yet be visible. There was no room in Dennett's story for the thought that those who use common-sense psychology to interpret (who 'take the Intentional Stance', who 'engage in common-sense psychology') coincide with those who can be interpreted using common-sense psychology. (If Dennett tried to make room for that, it would become plain that Mother Nature's own existence is presupposed by her inventions.) Once Dennett's

than one norm might be at issue when we ask, for example, 'What ought this person to believe?'

prejudice is abandoned, there is no reason to think that the standpoint either of physical science, or of evolutionary biology, is fitted for revealing what is distinctive about ourselves, the users and objects of common-sense psychology. Nor should we wonder at the fact that blind selectional forces on their own do not provide an intelligible account of our presence in the world.

To say this is not to give up on naturalism, or a natural physicalism. There is a sense of 'natural' in which the natural is not set against the artificial or the human: the natural world is the world of things composed out of matter and the interactions of those things. Provided we do not think that everything composed from matter should be completely intelligible in the terms of the science of matter, we may (of course) see ourselves as inhabitants of this natural world. And we do not have to think that anything magical has intervened to ensure our presence here. We know that the blind machinations of physical things threw up organisms with functional properties. The account we can offer of how this happened may help us to feel comfortable with functional biological explanations. But we should remember that such explanations were accepted, and not thought reducible to mechanistic ones, long before Darwin offered his account. Those who used the argument from design, or who embraced Darwin's theory, did not start by doubting whether the appearances of design are real. No more do we, except in philosophical moments, have any doubt that the appearance we give of being the subjects of common-sense psychology corresponds to reality. And we know that human beings were thrown up in the natural, physical world, even if we could never have an account of how this came about. The fact that we cannot give an account need not now make it perplexing that there is such a thing as common-sense psychological explanation, and that it is a sort of explanation which is irreducible in its turn.

Someone who rejects the physicalism that motivates eliminativism and instrumentalism (see Section 1) retains her faith in common-sense psychology without seeing it as leading to scientific theories and as founded in their truth: instead she may see it as standing with the beliefs about the world that fall without it. Common-sense psychology is then deemed irreducible, and its claims, unthreatened by their failure to be reduced, can (often enough) be (literally) true.

Much good recent work in philosophy has shown how salutary it can be to remind ourselves that we are biological creatures. To remember that we take our place in a biological world may help us to see why we should not expect physical science to answer all the questions we may raise about the basis of our understanding of ourselves. So I have not meant to oppose the introduction of biological thinking into philosophy of mind. The case I have tried to make is that biological thinking is to the point only if we have already forsworn the particular sort of metaphysical reassurance that a reductionist seeks.

7

The Limitations of Pluralism*

Adrian Cussins

1. SCIENCE AND EXPERIENCE

1.1. Elimination, Reduction, and Pluralism

Much of philosophy is motivated by an apparent conflict between the world as it is given in experience and the world as it is given in the physical sciences.[1] Experience presents the world as coloured but a physicist's atoms have no colour. We perceive the world as beautiful or ugly, sweet or salty, happy or sad, brave or cowardly, intelligent or stupid; yet none of these properties figure in the world of the physical sciences. In the scientific world-view, the universe is an arrangement of atoms in a four-dimensional void, where the properties of sentience have no place.

We might respond to this apparent conflict by thinking of experience as informed by outmoded theory; that contemporary science is the home of our best theory; and that our experience should, in time, alter to reflect our best theory. Where experience presents the world as propertied in a way which has no echo in the sciences, then we should eliminate those properties from our serious thought and talk. Talking of

* I would like to thank Justin Broackes, John Campbell, David Charles, Ron Chrisley, Michael Dummett, John McDowell, and Christopher Peacocke for help at different times and with different parts of the paper

[1] A different formulation might be: 'an apparent conflict between the folk, common-sense world-view and the world-view of the physical sciences', for might not experience be informed by the latter rather than the former? But this raises the question whether a folk 'proto-theory' can be extracted from the experience of the man in the street; something which is an *alternative* to the theory of the physical sciences. Perhaps the idea of such an extraction is a mistake, in which case the conflict should instead be thought of as being between the world in which experiencing persons have a place, and the world populated only by the entities of the physical sciences.

colour is only one animal's imperfect cognitive response to a complex physical reflectance property, concepts of which should supersede concepts of colour. (Perhaps talk of experience and cognition should themselves suffer the same fate, in which case a serious presentation of the thesis of eliminativism would have to take a different form from that which I have given it here.)

Or we might adopt a deflationary strategy and interpret the properties of experience in the light of our science. What we mean by the property of being coloured red is having the disposition to reflect light of a certain wavelength in certain conditions; what we mean by 'water' is H_2O and what we mean by 'heat' is kinetic energy of molecules. The properties of experience are reduced to the properties of science.

Both of these strategies give science the upper hand: the world of experience must reduce to the world of the physical sciences or else be eliminated. Both strategies take a priori positions on what counts as good explanation: if it's good it must be continuous with explanation in the physical sciences. But why give science the upper hand? Science deserves our respect but not our servitude, argues the pluralist. The structure of the scientific world-view is a more or less effective response to certain needs, both theoretical and technological; but these needs are not exhaustive of human life. The structure of the common-sense world-view is also a more or less effective response to certain (different) needs, both theoretical and practical. And as its concerns are quite different, so it is immune to scientific imperialism. Our talk of the world as coloured belongs to a different 'explanatory space' from that occupied by atomic physics.[2] When I experience pain or love, beauty or sadness, efficiency or idleness, I experience what cannot be threatened by the discoveries of science. Science has no authority over the attribution of these properties. That is, whatever happens in the development of the science,[3] over

---

[2] e.g. see John Campbell's use of the notion of an explanatory space in 'A Simple View of Colour', in J. Haldane and C. Wright (eds.), *Reality, Representation, and Projection* (Oxford: Oxford University Press, 1991).

[3] By 'science' and 'the sciences' I mean either the physical sciences or the sciences which are explanatorily continuous with the physical sciences in the kind of way in which chemistry is explanatorily continuous with physics. I

however long a period, should not alter our concepts of beauty, of what it is to think or experience, or of human history.

Of course there may well be border disputes about what does belong within the realm of science and what lies within the realm of the world-as-it-is-given-in-experience. For example, what are we to say about the action-like behaviour of a dog? Or the action-like behaviour of a subject who is mentally severely unwell? Are these cases in which science or experience is authoritative? But border disputes do not threaten the distinction itself, for there are always the paradigm cases: 'Is this gold?' 'Go ask the scientist.' And: 'Is this a chair?' and the scientist can have no special authority *qua* scientist.

Sensing a conflict between science and experience, the reductionist and the eliminativist resolve it in favour of science; whereas the 'tolerant pluralist', by multiplying explanatory spaces, denies that there is a conflict: there are both atoms and colours, and understanding talk about one does not rest on understanding talk about the other. But the price of the pluralist's intellectual tolerance is intellectual division. Colour and ugliness are beyond the explanatory reach of science:[4] the

don't a priori exclude the sciences of human behaviour from this claim of the pluralist. If it should turn out that there is a science of human behaviour which is explanatorily continuous with physics then the pluralist's claim would apply also to it. But if the only sense in which there is a science of human behaviour was the sense in which there is today a social science, then such a science would not be included in the pluralist's claim. For such a science is explanatorily dependent on the human conception of the world as it is given in experience. (And hence there would be no threat of the conflict with which I began the paper.) Of course I am making an assumption about the physical sciences: that they, unlike our present social science, are *not* explanatorily dependent on the human conception of the world as it is given in experience (i.e. they are such as to generate the threat of a conflict). One way to put this assumption is as follows: that the system of explanation of the physical sciences is, in principle (i.e. in its millennial form) capable of being operated by an automaton. (No doubt we *learn* physics in a way which is dependent on the world-as-it-is-given in human experience. In making the assumption, one is assuming that this is accidental with respect to the nature of the discourse levels themselves: i.e. with respect to *what* is learnt.) But pluralism is as dependent on this assumption as is my argument against pluralism: for the pluralist, all the major discourse levels are explanatorily independent of each other.

[4] See n. 3.

background concepts are not answerable to—because they are isolated from—the theoretical and technological concerns of the scientist. (And, similarly, the concepts of the scientist are not answerable to the concerns of the world-as-it-is-given-in-experience.) The intellectual world is inherently (by its concepts) divided; not just Two Cultures, but a plurality: as many as there are legitimate modes of discourse. (And legitimacy is determined internally to the discourse; for one level of talk can have no authority over another.)

1.2. *Levels of Discourse, Explanatory Spaces,* *and Conceptual Schemes*

Questions about the relative authority of science and experience cannot be raised without using the concepts expressed by the phrases 'level of discourse', 'explanatory space', and 'conceptual scheme'. My focus in the paper is on one of the questions about science and experience, not on the elucidation of the closely related concepts expressed by these phrases. But at least this much must be clear: The criteria of identity and difference for explanatory spaces, levels of discourse, and conceptual schemes have to do not with knowledge but with understanding. A person who is master of two levels of discourse may come to *know* truths at one level on the basis of knowing truths at another level, so the distinctness of levels cannot be drawn on the basis of knowledge. Instead, the levels are distinct if, and only if, there are no propositions at either level whose *understanding* requires a person to understand some propositions at the other level. That is to say, the distinctness of levels is drawn on the basis of understanding and explanation, not on the basis of knowledge and truth.[5]

It is for this reason that the pluralist—who is committed to the distinctness of the scientific level and the personal level of experience—may, without difficulty, accept ontological relations and relations of supervenience between these two levels. Thus a pluralist might agree that atoms mereologically compose coloured objects, or that colour properties supervene

---

[5] 'Level' is sometimes used in place of 'what is taken to be a level by a certain community at a certain time'. Much of the argument is about whether what are taken to be distinct levels of discourse are really distinct levels of discourse.

on atomic properties. Such relations of ontology and of super-venience are not explanatory relations which affect what it is to understand propositions at each level of discourse. They do not therefore affect the constitutive questions with which we are ultimately concerned.[6]

Elimination and reduction entail tight explanatory relations between the levels of science and the levels of personal ex-perience, in favour of scientific understanding ('scientism'[7]). Therefore, these positions entail that scientific and experiential levels of discourse are not really explanatorily distinct levels of understanding; and hence that constitutive questions about what it is to be an experiencing, thinking person cannot be pursued independently of scientific questions. There are other metaphysical positions, which I shall not characterize, which entail similarly tight explanatory relations, but in favour of person-based understanding ('humanism'?); whereas the third option, pluralism, rejects tight explanatory relations between these levels.

What other alternatives could there be? We need not accept that explanatory relations between levels of discourse are an all-or-nothing matter. Instead, a non-reductive, non-eliminative naturalism discerns different kinds of explanatory interlevel relations. Unlike pluralism, it entails that there are explanatory relations between levels, but unlike reduction and elimination it maintains a multiplicity of discourse levels. The explanatory relations are either relatively weak[8] or else[9] they

---

[6] This applies also to the relation(s) normally referred to by 'grounding', when one speaks of one level being grounded in another. Typically this means ontological or even causal grounding: 'Of course the mind must be grounded in the brain, but the legitimacy of our talk about mind cannot depend on facts about the brain.' What the pluralist denies is that our *understanding* of mind talk is (even partially) grounded in our understanding of talk at any scientific level.

[7] One might be a reductionist or eliminativist with respect to some propositions (or properties) but not with respect to others. 'Scientism', as a label, might best be reserved for the global position which maintained reductionism or eliminativism for all propositions (or properties) of the levels of personal experience. We might then speak of a partial scientism with respect to such and such.

[8] In the case where they belong to what I later call an 'implementation-construction'.

[9] In the case where the explanatory relations form what I later call a 'realization-construction'.

force a shift in understanding: a reconstrual of the purpose of at least one of the original discourse levels and the development of a new level which assimilates some of the functions of both the original levels of discourse. I look at some possibilities in Section 4.

(It would follow from the multiplicity of explanatory inter-level relations that the distinction between constitutive and causal questions is not a dichotomy.)

1.3. *Pluralism as the Null Hypothesis*

I think that it is a good strategy (at least initially) to take pluralism as the null hypothesis, the position about whose defects we must first be persuaded if we are to adopt a rival metaphysics. For pluralism is not discriminatory: it is neither scientistic nor humanistic. Pluralism denies very little at the primary level of discourse:[10] it does not reject a non-scientific level of discourse for being non-scientific; nor does it reject a non-person-based discourse level for being non-person-based. It rejects only those putative levels of discourse which are unable to maintain their internally established conditions of success.

Thus the astrological level of discourse might reasonably be rejected by the pluralist who believed that the following proposition is basic to that discourse level: that patterns of human behaviour are determined by the position of the heavenly bodies and therefore the behaviour of individuals can be predicted by knowledge of the relative history of the planetary motions. The astrological level could be rejected reasonably by the pluralist because it establishes internal conditions of success which the pluralist might reasonably believe are not satisfied. But the pluralist would not reject a level of discourse because its ontology diverges from the ontology of other levels; that the physical sciences operate with an ontology which does not include colours is no strike against our folk talk of colour. Nor would a pluralist reject, or

---

[10] Of course, it is less than tolerant at the meta-intellectual (philosophical) level: the philosophical positions considered in this paper are rivals.

modify, a level of discourse because of its explanatory relations (or lack of relations) to other levels of discourse. For the pluralist, the question should rather be whether our talk of colour provides a successful way of interpreting the world; success to be determined internally. For example, it would count against our colour talk if the apparent colours of objects were not relatively stable over time, but were merely ephemeral. Or if the rules of use for our colour words were inconsistent; as is demonstrated, perhaps, by the sorites paradox.[11]

The pluralist metaphysics, then, rules out no level of discourse which does not rule out itself. And so (as the null hypothesis) the pluralist metaphysics rules out all competing metaphysics, unless it first rules out itself. My aim, therefore, is to explore some difficulties with explanatory pluralism, difficulties which should push us towards a rival metaphysics. But examining what's wrong with the null hypothesis shows us how there can be a non-reductive, non-eliminative naturalism: a mid position between pluralism on the one hand and reduction and elimination on the other. If this is right, then this mid position forms the new null hypothesis, the new position about whose defects we must first be persuaded in order to adopt a rival theory. Reduction and elimination do not gain victory by pluralism's defeat.

I want, in short, to argue that there are external (metalevel) limits to intellectual tolerance. But the benefit of a little intellectual intolerance is intellectual continuity.

2. PLURALISM AND NATURALISM

2.1. The Argument and the Problem

The problem with pluralism is that it is incompatible with naturalism. Most of what I want to say is intended to clarify and defend this claim, but the basic form of the argument is this: Pluralism entails that how things are within a discourse level cannot be affected by how things are between discourse

---

[11] See M. Dummett, 'Wang's Paradox', in M. Dummett, *Truth and Other Enigmas* (London: Duckworth, 1978).

levels.[12] But naturalism requires that interlevel relations can have explanatory effects within a discourse level. Causal interaction between the ontologies of different discourse levels entail naturalism. Hence pluralism is false.

I shall examine the metaphysical need for explanatory constraints between levels of discourse in the case of the cognitive and the bodily levels of discourse. I focus on both synchronic behavioural prediction and the evolution over time of cognitive capacities, arguing the need for explanatory constraints in both of these areas. But it should be remembered that the general conflict between pluralism and naturalism goes well beyond these examples from the philosophy of mind, which I have chosen for the purposes of my argument.

The general problem has to do with the relations between concepts and systems of concepts in all areas of enquiry: between the concepts of physics and the concepts of history, between the concepts of biology and the concepts of sociology, between the concepts of the physical sciences and the concepts of architecture and design. For each of these (and many more) pairs we must ask whether the system of explanation of one member of the pair should be affected by its explanatory relations to the other member. In determining constitutive questions of understanding at a level ('What is it to be an *x*?' etc.) must one have regard to how that level of discourse fits into an overall world-view (how it is related to other levels of discourse)? Is metaphysics wholly posterior to intralevel explanation (a philosophical story added on top for the sake of narrative continuity)? Or is metaphysics—should it be—an essential, integrated part of each local piece of understanding? In examining what kind of object the brain is, should we ignore metaphysical questions about the relation of mind and brain? In examining how *Homo sapiens* has evolved, do we have to worry about the relation between chemistry and cognition?

2.2. What Is Naturalism?

A thoroughgoing naturalism takes every real phenomenon to be a part of, or an aspect of, nature. It must show how every-

---

[12] With respect to what is understood at a level, not with respect to what one may know. Remember Sect. 1.2.

thing we should recognize, everything about which we may think, belongs to The World (i.e. the same world). For the thoroughgoing naturalist, rainstorms, amoebas, geological strata, galaxies, chairs, electrons, persons, minds, societies, and God are all aspects of nature: parts of the one world.

When it was understood how the natural sciences which apply terrestrially also apply astronomically to the stars and (as it used to be thought) the heavenly bodies, that was an achievement of naturalism. The explanatory system for motions of terrestrial particles worked also for non-terrestrial bodies, so it was no longer necessary to say that the stars of the night sky belonged to a different (supernatural) order.

Exemplified here is a general form for naturalism: there are two quite distinct levels of discourse, with apparently no explanatory constraints between the two. In this example there is a level of discourse for terrestrial bodies and a level of discourse for 'heavenly' bodies. The distinctness of the two levels provides no bar to the view that there are two worlds: one earthly and one heavenly. But there is an apparent inconsistency: *the heavenly bodies can be seen from the earth*. Vision of one from the other requires interaction between the two worlds, an interaction which must itself be governed by causal laws. But the laws of which world? It seems that the laws must be from both worlds, and from neither.

The laws must be from both worlds, it seems, because the vision of heavenly bodies from earth involves processes in both worlds: The heavenly bodies must have some effect on the process for otherwise it would not be the heavenly bodies that we see. And certain earthly bodies must have some effect on the process for otherwise it would not be we who see the heavenly bodies. But the laws can be from neither world because they must govern an interaction between the earth and the heavens, yet the two systems of explanation to which the two sets of laws belong establish the heavens and the earth as explanatorily isolated domains. We cannot explain what happens in one domain in terms of what happens in the other. Is there then some third domain which subsumes both the earth and the heavens?

Such conundrums are avoided in this case because of the success of a form of eliminativism: heavenly phenomena are eliminated in favour of earthly phenomena by showing how *all* of the explanatory work can be performed by the laws which have hitherto been understood to govern only earthly phenomena. My purpose, however, is not to encourage the belief that naturalism requires eliminativism, but rather to provide examples of how interaction forces naturalism, and of how the successful defence of naturalism requires a good deal of explanatory work which alters our conception of how things are within at least one of the (original) discourse levels. A pluralistic understanding of the phenomena of motion gives rise to a conception of a multiplicity of worlds, which is revealed to be explanatorily inadequate because of the necessity for causal interaction between the worlds. To recognize the inadequacy, and to argue that therefore monism must be true in this case, is not sufficient. We have also to alter our conception of the nature of the heavenly bodies.

When it was understood how the natural sciences could apply to biological phenomena, that was an achievement of naturalism. It was no longer necessary to recognize two natures, animate and inanimate, with an obscure mediating force: the *élan vital*. Again, the special laws of an apparently distinct domain are eliminated in favour of the 'lower-level' domain, with the result that our conception of what it is to be a living thing is fundamentally altered.

What, then, of mind and body? Has it not been an achievement of naturalism to show why we do not require the Cartesian dualism of mind and body, mediated by an obscure pineal gland? For don't we now possess a scientific psychology which has, in outline at least, the explanatory resources for explaining human behaviour without recourse to a mysterious interaction between the mental and the bodily?

But so far our scientific psychology has not successfully sustained eliminativism or reductionism about the mind as biochemistry has eliminated the *élan vital*, or as physics has eliminated a heavenly cosmology. Why not instead adopt a pluralist metaphysics of mind and body? Haven't we got a scientific psychology which leaves the humanities' conception of mind essentially intact?[13]

---

[13] There are some oddball psychologies around. And mainstream cognitive psychology forces us to say some surprising things in unusual situations. The kind of threat that science poses to our ordinary conception of mind is of a

2.3. What is Required by the Justification of Naturalism

The *justification* of naturalism requires showing, for every element of the objective, that we may come to understand what it is, and how it came to be, in a way which *Coheres with* our natural science.[14]

'Coheres with' does not entail *reduces to*[15] or *is eliminated by*. It refers to a symmetrical relation, whereas 'reduces to' and 'is eliminated by' refer to asymmetric relations. Within physics, the theory of electromagnetic phenomena Coheres with the theory of mechanics, even though electromagnetics does not reduce to mechanics as thermodynamics reduces to statistical mechanics. Or within zoology, the anatomy and physiology of an organ Coheres with its biochemistry, even though the anatomical and physiological concepts do not reduce

different order from the threat posed by Freudian psychology, or cognitive psychology. These essentially 'humanistic' psychologies may change what we say in the language of mind, but they do not change the language itself. (Our understanding of the new words which they introduce is explanatorily dependent on our understanding of the old words.)

[14] I capitalize the initial letter of 'Cohere' in order to indicate that its sense is partly fixed by what I am saying about Coherence. For the pluralist, coherence must be an intralevel relation, whereas Coherence is an interlevel explanatory relation which is equivalent to the relations of neither reductionism nor eliminativism. Showing how every level of discourse Coheres with the physical sciences is part of the larger project of showing how every (legitimate) perspective on the objective Coheres with every other (legitimate) perspective. There is no materialistic myopia here. It is assumed in the statement of naturalism that the perspective of the natural sciences is a legitimate perspective; which is to say that it is a perspective on the world. It is not assumed that the perspective of the natural sciences is the only legitimate perspective.

[15] Thomas Nagel in *The View from Nowhere* (New York and Oxford: Oxford University Press, 1986), in the section on evolutionary epistemology, assimilates the naturalist's appeals to evolution to reductionism. Reductionist use of natural selection has often been made, but Nagel does not appreciate that natural selection may be an essential component of a non-reductive naturalism. He thinks that the view that the development of the human intellect is to be explained by natural selection is due to 'one of those powerful reductionist dogmas which seem to be part of the intellectual atmosphere which we breathe'. So Nagel is committed to the need for an alternative explanation of the development of thinking creatures: 'What, I will be asked, is my alternative? Creationism? The answer is that I don't have one . . .'. Escape from the 'reductionistic atmosphere' does not require the rejection of the scientific theories which have been employed by reductionists within their enterprise. Rather, the challenge is to reconstrue the science as part of a non-reductive naturalism.

to biochemical ones. Thus some of the anatomical and physiological concepts may be macrofunctional; the concept of
the heart, for example, for which there are no biochemical
counterparts. Instead, the key component in the idea of two
levels of discourse Cohering with each other is the idea of both
levels of discourse providing perspectives on a common world.
I want to spend a little space on this notion of Coherence (see
also Section 4), and then give my argument why pluralism
cannot do it justice.

InCoherence, as I am using the concept, refers to a relation
between two or more levels of discourse which entails that
they cannot all provide perspectives on the same world: the
objects referred to at each level cannot belong to the same
world. The modality is constitutive: inCohering discourse
levels are about different worlds because of what is involved in
understanding propositions at the different levels. When there
is causal interaction between the referents of inCohering
discourse levels, we can often generate a contradiction: for
example, the combination of (some forms of) the thesis of
mind–body dualism and the thesis of mind–body causal
interaction yield a conflict with the conservation principles of
the physical sciences.

InCohering mental and bodily discourse levels result in
conflicts not only with conservation principles, but also with
principles governing explanation and causation. Any one
of these conflicts can be used in an argument to show that
the two aspects must be aspects of a single phenomenon, a
common nature.

Causal interaction requires explanatory connection, and then
we may argue with Davidson that the events of both the bodily
and the mental kinds must be subsumed under a single level of
description which is capable of yielding genuine laws about the
behaviour which results from the interaction.[16] Once we have
subsumption under a single level of description, we have a
single world. Davidson wishes to go further and argue that the
single world is physical. For what but the physical level of
description is capable of yielding genuine laws? But this is a

---

[16] D. Davidson, 'Mental Events', in D. Davidson, *Essays on Actions and Events*
(Oxford: Clarendon Press, 1980).

further claim, which requires the premiss that there are no psychological or psychophysical laws, and which is therefore less certain than the claim that there is a nomological level of description which applies to both mental and physical events. The style of argument which Davidson has employed is that the dual substance theory has yielded a conflict with a principle (the principle of the nomological character of causality) which we do not wish to abandon. Therefore, only one nature could be involved; the mental and the bodily *must* both be aspects of a single world.

Peacocke has employed the same style of argument to demonstrate the token identity of mental events with physical events.[17] His argument does not yield a conflict between dualism and the nomological character of causality, but yields a conflict between dualism and the belief that behavioural events have a sufficient physiological cause and are not over-determined. His argument does not require the premiss that there are neither psychological nor psychophysical laws. There may be other arguments of the same style[18] which demonstrate that the two worlds theory is not compatible with entrenched beliefs that we hold about nature. So monism must be true.

None of this, by itself, will cut much ice with the pluralist of this paper. For, such a pluralist will deny that his position is incompatible with naturalism, claiming that what is held to be plural are explanatory systems, not ontological systems. What Davidson's and Peacocke's arguments show, if they are successful, is that we need to combine mind–body token identity with explanatory pluralism. To suppose that *explanatory* monism follows from the argument involves an equivocation on the two senses of monism.

This response seems to me to be superficial. For what is our right to ontological monism, to one world? If we operate with explanatorily isolated discourse levels, then we need to provide a justification for our claim that the distinct discourse levels nevertheless refer to the same world. We need to justify that

---

[17] C. Peacocke, *Holistic Explanation* (Oxford: Clarendon Press, 1979), ch. 3, §3.

[18] e.g. Stephen Schiffer's in *Remnants of Meaning* (Cambridge, Mass.: MIT Press, Bradford Books, 1987), 146–50.

the pluralist's distinct discourse levels *Cohere* with each other and with other legitimate levels of discourse. But the modality of Coherence is possibility, not necessity: To show that the mental and the bodily *must* both be aspects of a single world (for otherwise there would be intolerable conflict) is not to show how they *could* both be aspects of a single world. We may know that mind and body are dual aspects of a single nature, but not understand how it is possible for mind and body to be dual aspects of a single nature. The ontological problem of interaction between plural worlds has a mirror image in the explanatory realm, an equivalent problem whose solution imposes essentially the same explanatory burden as the problem of interaction. I call this problem 'the problem of miraculous Coincidences' and I develop it for the causation of human behaviour and for the evolution of cognitive capacities in Sections 3 and 5.

The cosmological and biological examples of the successful defence of naturalism depended on establishing the explanatory relations between levels necessary for eliminativism or reductionism. The establishment of these explanatory relations altered our conception of the constitutive nature of the objects referred to by at least one of the levels. The explanatory relations characteristic of eliminativism or reductionism are not entailed by a solution to the problem of miraculous Coincidences. But explanatory relations of some sort which are sufficient to alter our conception of the objects of at least one level *are* entailed by a solution to this problem. Explanatorily pluralistic discourse levels which yield a miraculous Coincidence problem *inCohere* with each other, in my sense of the term.

3. THE FIRST MIRACULOUS COINCIDENCE PROBLEM[19]

Consider a pluralist with respect to neurophysiology and what—following the now common use in the literature—I

---

[19] The material in this section is a modified and shortened form of some of the material in §4 of my 'Varieties of Psychologism', *Synthese*, 70 (1987), 123–54.

shall call 'folk psychology'. (Folk psychology is commonsense knowledge of that part of the world-as-it-is-given-in-experience which has to do with persons and minds.) For such a pluralist, the neurophysiological and folk-psychological discourse levels are explanatorily isolated: understanding physiological propositions does not require one to understand any folk-psychological propositions, and vice versa.[20] Hence the term 'human behaviour' refers ambivalently to what is explained at the neurophysiological level and to what is explained at the folk-psychological level. The constitutive nature of mind is independent of how things are in the brain, and vice versa. Of course, there may be various kinds of causal and ontological dependency between mind and brain, but our understanding of what the brain is is independent of our understanding of what the mind is, and our understanding of what the mind is is independent of our understanding of what the brain is. Each discourse level provides an adequate (albeit developing) conception of its referent (the brain for one, and the mind for the other). And our conception of a *person* is essentially conjunctive: that which has a body and a mind.[21]

According to the pluralist. But it can be shown that such a position is untenable:

Fact 1: Parts of folk psychology have, on some occasions, some predictive success and they have this success independently of any folk psychologist's knowledge of physiology.

If this seems contentious, think of a simple action: when I get up to leave this room you would, if you were here, be able to predict within fairly fine limits how I would move my arm in order to open the door. Yet you know nothing of my physiology. The argument needs only banal predictions such as these. It does *not* require the assumption that all or most

---

[20] This is not to disallow the folk psychologist from using expressions like 'his arm goes up' as well as 'he raises his arm'. The imagined physiologist is millennial: he talks of the transformation of the position in coordinate space of bones, muscles, and tendons.

[21] By 'essentially conjunctive', I mean that the conjunction cannot be eliminated by appeal to a deeper level at which the dual aspects of the conjuncts are revealed to be different manifestations of a common substance. The presence of the conjunction follows from the essence of persons and is not an artefact of a level of analysis. See Sect. 4.

actions are predictable. Nor does it require the assumption that the prediction of behaviour is the primary function of folk psychology.

(*Purported*) *Fact 2*: According to the pluralist, neurophysiology[22] could, in principle, predict successfully token sequences of behaviour characterized in neurophysiological terms, and could do so independently of any neurophysiologist's knowledge of folk psychology.

Imagine a sophisticated folk psychologist and an advanced neurophysiologist working independently on a subject, *S*. The folk psychologist knows the complete folk-psychological history of *S* and thus has comprehensive knowledge of *S*'s folk-psychological states.[23] He knows no physiology. The physiologist has operated a comprehensive brain scan and knows the state and interconnections of every neuron of *S*, plus all relevant biochemical details. He knows no folk psychology.

Given fact 1, we may choose 1,000 behaviours of the subject which may be folk psychologically predicted by our folk psychologist. The times of these behaviours will constitute 1,000 temporal intervals. Given (purported) fact 2, our advanced physiologist can predict the physiological behaviour during the 1,000 temporal intervals. Working totally independently, the physiologist and folk psychologist successfully predict *S*'s behaviour for 1,000 distinct temporally individuated behaviour sequences. (I am not assuming neutral characterizations of behaviour, except in the weak sense of, for example, 'the behaviour that occurs between time t_1 and time t_2'. Anything that is said about this behaviour will be said in either physiological or psychological terms, but for the purposes of the comparisons, the behaviours are individuated purely temporally.[24])

---

[22] By 'neurophysiology' I mean that part of the brain sciences which restricts itself to entirely non-representational notions. Its level of analysis is the nerve-cell and networks of nerve-cells.

[23] This needn't be more than the claim that the folk psychologist is in on all the gossip about *S*. (He overheard what *S* said to . . . and how his interlocutor reacted; etc.)

[24] There will be some arbitrariness about exactly which times we adopt for individuation. Since fine-grain psychological behavioural events usually occupy longer time intervals than fine-grain physiological behavioural events,

For each behavioural slice the folk psychologist and the physiologist will offer a distinct description. But given complete success for our two predictors, then, for every time, the physiological and psychological behaviours at that time must march in step: Suppose a token psychological behaviour is the behaviour characterized as 'S opens the door'. The simultaneous token physiological behaviour is now strongly constrained such that the bodily movement must be or realize the door's opening. It would be no good, for example, if the token physiological behaviour were such that S walked away from the door. And, equally, the psychological behaviour is strongly constrained by the physiological behaviour, predicted by the physiologist.[25]

How can it be that the two predictors, working in complete independence, with (as the pluralist assumes) explanatorily isolated discourse levels, nevertheless produce behavioural predictions which march in step? For the pluralist, there can be no theory which explains *why* the two sets of predictions march in step, because he assumes that the two discourse levels are explanatorily autonomous. Since interlevel relations do not affect intralevel explanation, the pluralist is stuck with the view that we can provide no explanatory theory to support our confidence in the continuing coherence or rationality of human behaviour. For the pluralist, that humans act as persons must be a miracle.

Let me try to make the problem a little more vivid. Consider 1,000 behaviour sequences in each of which the belief that *every action should be performed as if one were mimicking a robot* plays an essential role in the successful predictions made by the folk psychologist. That is, we are to suppose that were the belief to have been different, or not to have been active, each behaviour

we may reduce the arbitrariness by giving the folk psychologist the lead in temporal individuation. We will adopt time-scales based on signing cheques and answering questions rather than on polarity changes in the axon.

[25] I am assuming that the environmental context of the predictions is fixed (both with respect to descriptions that would be used by the physiologist and with respect to descriptions that would be used by the folk psychologist). For example, I am assuming that the door is located in a certain part of the room, that the handle of the door is at a certain height, that the handle must be turned in a certain way for the door to open. Thus the constraints are between token behaviours relative to an environment. (Alternatively: take the constraints to be between the predictions, rather than the behaviours.)

predicted by the psychologist would not involve robot-like, staccato motion. But then, if the belief is present, the physiologist—who knows nothing about the presence of the effective belief—has got to predict muscle movements which are compatible (march in step) with the halting, staccato motion predicted by the folk psychologist. For the pluralist it must be Coincidental that the physiologist succeeds on each of the 1,000 occasions.

Suppose there were a physiological commonality between each of the occasions on which the belief was effective. The pluralist could still provide no explanation for the apparent Coincidence. For why should the physiological commonality be expected in just those cases in which the folk psychologist will predict the effective presence of the robot-mimicking belief?[26] No doubt there will be a physiological answer to why the physiological commonality is present on each occasion; perhaps a different answer for each occasion. But unless there is an explanatory link-up between the facts to which the physiologist appeals in making predictions and the facts to which the folk psychologist appeals in making predictions, there will be no way to explain why the commonality is present in just the right *folk-psychological* situations. To adapt a type of example used elsewhere:[27] to explain why a person leaving Balliol at t_1 arrives at Carfax at t_3, and to explain why another person leaving New College at t_2 arrives at Carfax at t_3 is not to explain why they arrive at Carfax at the same time. For suppose it keeps on happening; that is, suppose they keep on meeting up at Carfax on every occasion in which one of them leaves for Carfax. Their encounter will appear increasingly like a miraculous Coincidence, however well satisfied we may be

---

[26] One might say that the physiological commonality is to be expected in just those folk-psychological cases because otherwise the organism would not be a person: its behaviour would not be rational when viewed as a person. But, again, this is superficial. If we put the problem like this, then the miracle is that there are persons. (See Cussins, 'Varieties of Psychologism', 150–1). Remember that, for the pluralist, the nature of persons is conjunctive: by talking of persons we can explain what we can explain by talking about both minds and bodies. There is no deeper level.

[27] D. Owens, 'Levels of Explanation', *Mind*, 98 (1989), 59–79, 72–5, who cites Sorabji's use of an Aristotelian example: R. Sorabji, *Necessity, Cause and Blame* (London: Duckworth, 1980), 9.

with the individual explanations of why S_1 arrives at t_n and of why S_2 arrives at t_n, for each occasion. We should come to expect some communication between S_1 and S_2, and appeal to this communication in order to explain the apparent Coincidence. But in the two-predictors thought experiment, communication between the predictors was ruled out. And *ex hypothesi*, there can be no explanatory link between the physiological explanation and the folk-psychological explanation. Hence for the pluralist, the concurrence is an unexplained (apparently miraculous) Coincidence.

It is a miraculous Coincidence that on 1,000 occasions our two predictors, working in independence of each other and appealing to utterly different facts and laws (or generalizations), should produce predictions which meet the mutual constraints on behaviour. Our physiologist concerns himself with the chemical changes in the axon and knows nothing about S having the crazy belief that all actions should be performed as if mimicking a robot. Yet he predicts just those physiological behaviour sequences which our folk psychologist will see as robot-mimicking behaviour. Or view the problem from the other side: Our folk psychologist concerns himself with the patterns of rationality and intentionality amongst the beliefs, desires, intentions, memories, perceptions, and imaginations of the subject and knows nothing about the build-up of a causally potent neurotransmitter in a certain cortical region. Yet he predicts just those folk-psychological behaviours which are compatible with the physiological behaviour which was caused by the cortical activity. And this miracle, given the ubiquity of our two predictors, happens in each person every day.

Every time you venture on to the road and obey the convention to drive on the left, think to yourselves: Isn't it a miracle that the events in the nervous system which control your arm on the steering-wheel cause the wheel to be in just the place required to satisfy your intention to drive on the left? Even worse, think about the miracle that the events in all the *other* drivers' brains cause their arms to move in just that way which satisfies their intentions and our expectations! Our folk psychologist and millennial neurophysiologist made these predictions too.

If we take the physiological and folk-psychological discourse levels *as providing pluralistic perspectives on the behaviour of human persons* (the conjunctive conception of persons) then we should just boggle at everyday human activities. Would a mother hold her child close to the edge of the canyon so the child could see the view? She could count (she thinks) on her intention to hold the child tight, but neither folk psychology nor neurophysiology provide any assurance whatever that her neurophysiology will march in step with her intention; nothing to guarantee (or, rather, provide any probability at all—except that of mere Humean induction) that she will not suddenly, and, from the perspective of folk psychology, *inexplicably*, drop her child.

Isn't it a miracle that the predictions march in step?

Of course not. *It is the nature of human cognition that that is how things are.* It is because humans have the cognitive nature that they have that their physiology meshes with folk psychology; that the two march in step. Indeed, this mesh is constitutive of an organism's being a human person. Therefore, a theory of human nature (of the behaviour of human persons) could be neither a folk-psychological theory, nor a neurophysiological theory.[28] For, as we have seen, from those perspectives we would have to treat human behaviour as miraculous. Rather, we must take account of the relations between the two discourse levels which give rise to a miraculous Coincidence problem, in order to generate a new discourse level whose terms refer Coherently to human persons.[29] The interlevel explanatory relations between physiology and folk psychology should cause us to alter our conception of the brain and of the mind, and therefore to change the nature of explanation within the scientific psychological discourse level. Thus, pluralism in this case is false.

This is not to say that neither neurophysiology of the type I have in mind, nor folk psychology, have any useful explanatory role to play. But it is to say that neither of these discourse levels, nor their conjunction, can provide an explanatory home

---

[28] Assuming that neither level should be eliminated.

[29] It is not that we will then have three discourse levels, all of which provide a perspective on human cognition, as the addition of a third belief does not remove a contradiction between two other beliefs. See below.

for the concept of a human person. For that purpose, a new discourse level must be created which does not give rise to a problem of miraculous Coincidences.

The neurophysiological level will be reinterpreted as providing explanations of the behaviour of cell assemblies rather than explanations of the behaviour of human persons. Likewise, folk psychology might be reinterpreted as providing social rationalizations of human behaviour (amongst many other purposes). But both levels of discourse point the way towards a new, scientific level of psychological explanation; a level which explains how the mechanistic bodily transitions preserve the intentional patterns required for the predictions of the folk psychologist, and vice versa. Only with such a level can we understand the common focus which constitutes human cognition. To do justice to the physiological basis of behaviour, the concepts of the new level will have to be scientific. And to do justice to the folk psychology, they must be concepts of content-involving representational states. A genuinely naturalistic scientific psychology requires a scientific theory of representational content. That is naturalism's challenge to explanation in this area.

In summary: as far as this argument goes, neither folk psychology nor neurophysiology need be eliminated or reduced. Both may be legitimate discourse levels. But what does follow is that, given that both are legitimate levels,[30] they cannot provide the primary levels of explanation for our notions of cognition and personhood: the conjunctive conception of cognition and persons cannot be correct. Thus folk psychology may employ a quite legitimate conception of the psychological for its folk-psychological purposes. But—and this is what the argument shows—one may be fully a master of the folk-psychological discourse level without fully understanding what it is to be in a psychological state. This is what I meant by saying that folk psychology cannot provide the primary level of explanation for our concepts of cognition and personhood. The psychological concepts of folk psychology are explanatorily dependent upon the scientific psychological

---

[30] i.e. not requiring elimination or reduction.

concepts of that level (whatever it may be like) which *does* Coherently present and refer to persons.

4. CONSTRUCTION

4.1. *Coherence, Intelligibility, and Coincidence*

The two-predictors thought experiment has provided an example of explanatory relations between discourse levels which result in a miraculous Coincidence (MC) problem, and which therefore reveal the discourse levels, as interpreted by the pluralist, to be incompatible with naturalism. Can we save naturalism without being reductionist or eliminativist? To answer the question we need to understand what the explanatory relations between levels must be like in order to avoid miraculous Coincidences. We can see the answer to this by looking at some very simple cases in which the MC problem is avoided.

Many reflective high-school students taking zoology classes have a remarkable experience of intellectual satisfaction. As they learn about the different organs of the body, they gain a sense of how the different levels of understanding give rise to a unified conception of each organ. In the terms which I introduced in Section 2: they gain satisfaction from sensing the *Coherence* of the multiple levels of discourse used in biology. That is to say, their grasp of what it is to be a liver, a heart, a stomach, a kidney, or the lungs in part consists in their understanding of why it is that each organ has the cellular biochemistry, the anatomy, the physiology, and the homeostatic function that it has. Knowing what it is to be a heart one understands something about why its anatomy and physiology are like they are.

For every two levels of discourse about an organ we can think of the lower level as a way of knowing about the structure of the organ, and the upper level as a way of knowing about the function of the organ. Then perceiving the Coherence of the two levels is perceiving why it is that an organ with a structure like that (discourse level 1) is an organ with a function like *that* (discourse level 2), and vice

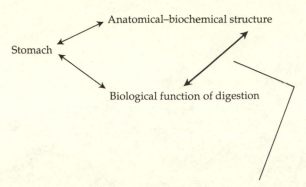

Stomach

Anatomical–biochemical structure

Biological function of digestion

Non-coincidental Intelligible connection

FIG. 7.1. *The structure–function relation in the stomach*

The structural and functional levels of description provide a Coherent conception of a stomach as something whose structure enables its function. In such a case, I say that the structural and functional levels are Intelligibly connected

versa. Where this relation is perceptible, I shall say that there is an *Intelligible* connection between the discourse levels. An Intelligible connection is the opposite of a Coincidental connection. Let's consider some examples:

Understanding the anatomy and the biochemistry of the membranes of the stomach enables an understanding of why it is that an organ with that anatomy and biochemistry has the function of digestion. There is an Intelligible connection between the structural anatomy and biochemistry of stomachs and the functional physiology of stomachs which yields a Coherent conception of a stomach. (See Fig. 7.1.) So the concept of a stomach is not conjunctive: it is not exhausted by the anatomical, biochemical, and physiological concepts. For in virtue of understanding these three discourse levels one understands also that the anatomy and the biochemistry are such as to support the physiology: given that this bit of the anatomy is like this, one understands why it has this physiology, and vice versa.

Knowing about the branching, bronchial structure of the lungs enables an understanding of why it is that an organ with that anatomy and biochemistry has the function of respiration.

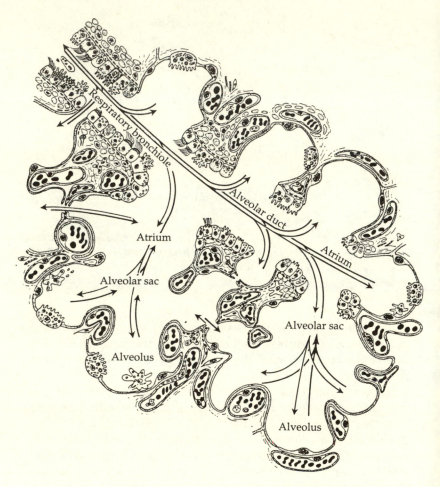

FIG. 7.2. *Diagram showing the respiratory portion of the lung. The arrows indicate the possible routes taken by air during inspiration and expiration*

The branching of the lungs' bronchial structures increases the surface area available for gaseous exchange, which is the essential component in the respiratory function of the lungs. There is, therefore, an Intelligible connection between the structural anatomy and biochemistry of lungs and the functional physiology of lungs, which yields a Coherent conception of a lung. For we understand not just the anatomy and the

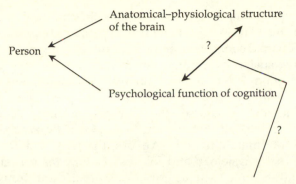

FIG. 7.3. *The structure–function relation in the person*

physiology, but why the anatomy *supports* the physiology. (See Fig. 7.2.) The high-school student has gained an understanding of the lung which goes beyond the conjunctive. The direction of explanation has been partially reversed: a lung is not explained merely as that which has a certain anatomy and a certain physiology. Rather, an understanding of what it is to be a lung (gained, of course, through learning the anatomy and physiology of lungs) can explain why a lung's anatomy and physiology are as they are: one can *move back and forth* between the anatomy and the physiology.

What an intellectual disappointment the student experiences when the zoology class comes finally to consider the brain! Not that there is any shortage of facts. Indeed, the student is submerged under the weight of anatomical and physiological data that the teacher provides. Although the teacher proceeds with classes on the brain in the same way as with classes on all the other organs, the student becomes increasingly puzzled that she does not gain the same sense of intellectual satisfaction, or a similarly Coherent grasp of the organ under study. The problem is not one of intralevel ignorance, but is a conceptual difficulty due to the relations between discourse levels: however much one learns (and, one has the sense that, however much one *were* to learn) it remains (and would remain) obscure why an organ with a structure like that (anatomical, biochemical, and neurophysiological discourse levels) should have the function of cognition. (See Fig. 7.3.) The only conception of a person which is available is the conjunctive conception: the concept of a person is explanatorily derivative upon the separate concepts of mind and brain.

It was just such a conception which was seen to be inadequate in Section 3: for the conjunctive conception entailed that the marching in step of the two sets of predictions was Coincidental. But, of course, the marching in step couldn't really be Coincidental; that, as we saw, would be an absurd conception of human nature. We are therefore led to the conclusion that physiology and folk psychology (as conceived by the pluralist) do not characterize the structure and function of persons. Given a commitment to the category of a person, the naturalist must show how to generate a new level of description of the behaviour of persons which does not generate an MC problem. Interlevel relations force intralevel change.

I have now provided examples of both the relation of Intelligibility, and of its opposite: Coincidence. The explanatory relation between the structure and function of the brain appears Coincidental, whereas the explanatory relation between the structure and function of the stomach and lungs was Intelligible. These relations are perceptual rather than inferential, in that our ability to tell whether or not they obtain is a perceptual *skill* rather than a matter of inferential calculation. Where there is an Intelligible connection between two levels of discourse there need be no laws governing the relation between the levels, but only this constraint: that a person who understands both levels of discourse understands why it is that having the structure given in the lower level is a way of having the function given in the upper level.[31] We may now define naturalism in terms of Coherence and Coherence in terms of Intelligibility.

4.2. The Construction Constraint

I propose that naturalism is successful if, and only if, the construction constraint is satisfied. The construction constraint

[31] This understanding can be manifested in different ways. For example, one may understand the lower-level conditions under which an upper-level breakdown will occur. Or how to go about constructing a successful prosthesis.

says that every two legitimate discourse levels must Cohere with each other.[32] The Coherence of two discourse levels can be captured recursively in terms of Intelligibility: Two discourse levels (*A* and *B*) Cohere with each other if either there is an Intelligible (non-Coincidental) connection between *A* and *B*, or *A* is Intelligibly connected to a level of discourse which Coheres with *B*.

4.3. Realization and Implementation

There are two kinds of construction connection between legitimate discourse levels: connections which are due to *realization-constructions* (R-constructions) and connections which are due to *implementation-constructions* (I-constructions). One discourse level is R-construction-related to another discourse level if, and only if, the two discourse levels are Coherent and it is not possible to fully understand the first discourse level without understanding the second discourse level.[33] Thus consider our grasp of what gold is. The everyday discourse level in terms of which we folk-identify gold and manifest our grasp of the use and role of gold in our community is R-construction-related to the scientific discourse level in terms of which the atomic structure of gold is identified. For we do not fully understand what gold is unless we understand about atomic numbers.

---

[32] An alternative formulation of the construction constraint is given in my 'The Connectionist Construction of Concepts', in M. Boden (ed.), *The Philosophy of Artificial Intelligence*, Oxford Readings in Philosophy (Oxford: Oxford University Press, 1989).

[33] I take this to entail that the legitimacy of the first discourse level cannot be determined properly without considering the second discourse level. For, if the two levels are R-construction related, one does not understand fully what it is to be an object at the first level without understanding second-level propositions. And, if one does not understand fully what it is to be an object at the first level without understanding second-level propositions, then the first-level world (of referents) cannot be properly assessed for legitimacy without taking into account the second discourse level.

If level *A* is R-constructed from an interposed level which is itself I-constructed from level *B*, it does not follow that level *A* is R-constructed from level *B*. Thus even though folk-psychology is R-constructed from the level of scientific psychology which is itself I-constructed from the level of neurophysiology, we may still want to say that folk-psychology is I-constructed from neurophysiology.

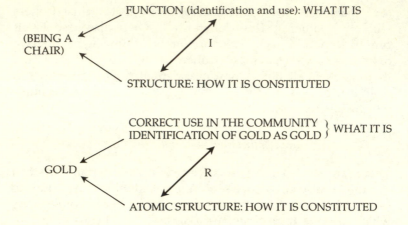

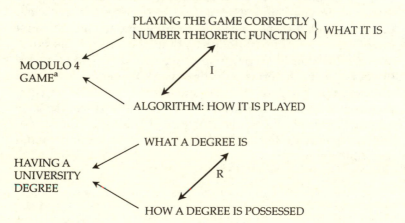

FIG. 7.4. *Implementation or Realization?*

[a] See A. Cussins, 'Varieties of Psychologism', Synthese, 70 (1987), 123–54. The modulo game has two players. One player mentions numbers in base 10, and the other player must answer with those numbers, modulo 4

Contrast our grasp of what a chair is. In this case the discourse level in terms of which we folk-identify chairs and manifest our grasp of the use and role of chairs in our community is I-construction-related to the scientific discourse levels which characterize the physical structure of chairs. For, we may fully understand what a chair is without knowing anything about the scientific mechanics of chair legs. One discourse level is I-construction-related to another discourse level if, and only if, the two discourse levels are Coherent and it *is* possible to understand the first discourse level fully without understanding the second discourse level. Fig. 7.4 shows some diagrams of I- and R-constructions.

There are two ways in which two discourse levels may fail to be Intelligibly connected. First, they may fail to be Intelligibly connected only because a third discourse level should be interposed between the two original discourse levels. This may account for a failure of Intelligibility because Intelligibility is a perceptual (rather than an inferential) relation and is therefore not transitive. Thus *A* may be Intelligibly connected to *B*, and *B* Intelligibly connected to *C*, but *A* not be Intelligibly connected to *C*. By contrast, Coherence *is* transitive. So this (first) way of failing to be Intelligibly connected is *not* a way of failing to Cohere. It therefore does not raise a problem for naturalism, and so does not require intralevel explanatory change to either of the original discourse levels. In these cases, the first discourse level is I-constructed from the interposed level, which is I-constructed from the bottom level.

Or, secondly, two discourse levels may fail to be Intelligibly connected because they generate a miraculous Coincidence problem. This second way of failing to be Intelligibly connected is a way of failing to Cohere, and so requires a different kind of resolution: it requires a change in the nature of at least one of the original two discourse levels. This is because inCoherence (like contradiction) is not removed by the addition of a supplementary discourse level (belief). As we saw in Section 3 above, the generation of a miraculous Coincidence problem indicates inCoherence which does require intralevel explanatory change. We may therefore adopt the following principle: Where two (putative) discourse levels (*A* and *B*) are so related as to generate an MC problem, then either *A* or *B* is R-constructed from an interposed discourse level, or both *A* and *B* are R-constructed from an interposed level.

Pluralism can only recognize failures of Intelligibility of the first kind. So where two levels of discourse generate an MC problem, pluralism is incompatible with naturalism. To preserve naturalism we must generate a new discourse level which is R-construction-related to one of the original levels. In the example which I called 'the first miraculous Coincidence problem' we saw the need to generate a scientific psychological level from which folk psychology is R-constructed. Similarly to the case of gold, we do not understand what a psychological state is without understanding the level of discourse from which our folk-psychological talk is R-constructed.

According to the simple account of discourse levels which I gave in Section 1.2, it would follow that the scientific psychological and folk-psychological levels would collapse into a single level of discourse. Would this not entail that folk psychology had been either reduced or eliminated?

The simple account of discourse levels recognized only a monolithic notion of understanding: either the understanding of propositions at one level required the understanding of propositions at the other level, in which case the levels collapsed into one level, or there were no explanatory relations between levels. Such an account is adequate where the possible explanatory relations between levels are only those envisaged by reductionism or eliminativism. But where we use a notion of *being R-constructed from*, we need a more complex account of discourse levels.

We may compatibly hold the following two beliefs: (1) We do not fully understand what gold is without knowing that gold is the element with atomic number 79, and (2) 'Gold' does not mean the element with atomic number 79. This is not the place to pursue a theory of the meaning of natural kind terms, but there are plausible theories which allow for a gap between meaning and understanding; for example, theories which hold that gold is a natural kind but which take the meaning of 'gold' to be indexical. On such a theory, our conception of gold would not be explanatorily isolated from the level of atomic chemistry, yet the meaning of 'gold' might be something like: 'the element of which *this* is (a probable example/a paradigmatic example/(probably) largely composed)'. We would then say that our folk concept of gold is R-constructed from the scientific level of atomic chemistry; that therefore our folk gold-practices are not autonomous of science as a pluralist about gold would require, but that it does not follow that our folk talk about gold should be eliminated or reduced because it is possible to grasp the meaning of 'gold' without understanding contemporary atomic chemistry.

As far as the first miraculous Coincidence thought experiment goes, we may hold the analogue of this for our folk-psychological concepts. There are psychological natural kinds; therefore the study of mind is not autonomous of science; but folk psychology need be neither reduced nor eliminated because it is possible to grasp folk-psychological meanings without being a master of the level of scientific psychology out of which folk psychology is R-constructed.

Such a story about natural kinds, including psychological kinds, would have to be supplemented with an account of the value of the indexical meanings for the community folk practices which involve the natural kind. That is, natural kinds can be specified both indexically and by means of abstract, theoretical descriptions. But the differences between the two kinds of specification ensure that only one kind of specification is suitable for the community's folk practice and that kind of specification is not suitable for scientific purposes (and conversely). To insist on the elimination or the reduction of the folk discourse level is to insist on the imperialism of scientific practice. The naturalist may agree with the pluralist that scientific imperialism is unwarranted.

In Section 3 I presented an argument for the parallel between chemical kinds and psychological kinds which exploited the relations between folk psychology and neurophysiology. In Section 5, I present an argument which exploits the relations between concepts and the embodiment of concepts. (The argument is neutral on how concepts may be embodied (in neurophysiology, in computational states, in the possession of internalist abilities or dispositions, or in the possession of abilities or dispositions to find one's way in the environment).) Whereas the first argument was concerned with the prediction of behaviour at a time, the second argument is concerned with the evolution of cognitive capacities over time.

5. THE SECOND MIRACULOUS
COINCIDENCE PROBLEM[34]

5.1. *Pluralism and the Embodiment of Concepts*

Consider pluralism about the discourse level for concepts and
the discourse level for the embodiment of concepts (whatever
level or levels that turns out to be). Given the motivation
of pluralism to establish the explanatory autonomy of the
humanities from the sciences, pluralism about concepts and
their embodiment is popular. This is so because explanation
and understanding in the humanities will constantly appeal to
or depend on the nature of belief and thought, and the nature
of belief and thought is explained in terms of the nature of
concepts. But the embodiment of concepts (whether neurophysiological, computational, or relating to ability) is something which we would expect the scientist to be authoritative
about. Hence the pluralist's preservation of the autonomy
of the humanities from the sciences rests on the explanatory
autonomy of concepts from the embodiment of concepts.
As they say, my thinking about home may be causally dependent on information-processing going on in my brain, but
it does not constitutively depend on information-processing in
the brain.

However, I think it is possible to show that the explanation
of what a concept is cannot be independent of the explanation
of the embodiment of concepts. For suppose it were independent. Then concepts would have to be characterized in
what I have called a *conceptualist* fashion.[35] For the conceptualist, concepts are canonically characterized in terms of
concepts that the subject must possess. That is to say, a concept is constitutively characterized internally to the conceptual
scheme to which the concept belongs, either by means of the
use of that concept itself or by means of other concepts out of
which the target concept can be defined.[36]

---

[34] This is a modification of some material in ch. 3 of my doctoral thesis: 'A
Representational Theory of Mind', Oxford University, 1986.

[35] See Cussins, 'The Connectionist Construction of Concepts', 380–401. In
this article I outline and defend a non-conceptualist theory of cognition.

[36] I am assuming that the cognition of a subject is characterized by a single
conceptual scheme.

The alternative to conceptualism about content is non-conceptualism. Non-conceptualist content is content which is canonically characterized by means of concepts that a subject of the content *need not* possess. The possibility of non-conceptualism about content rests on the possibility of explaining the *content* of a representation partly in terms of the nature of the *vehicle* of the representation.[37] For the subject of a content need not possess any of the concepts which are required to characterize the representational vehicle which carries the content: thinking about home requires the subject of the thought to possess neither computational concepts nor concepts of syntactic form. Therefore, non-conceptualism depends on the theory of content being (at least partially) explanatorily dependent on the theory of the embodiment of content. But, we saw above that it was just this possibility which the pluralist was forced to rule out. Hence the pluralist's commitment to conceptualism about content.

Conceptual schemes are partially holistic. That is to say, one cannot grasp one concept of a conceptual scheme without grasping a substantial part of the conceptual scheme. This affects both acquisition and evolution: it does not make sense to suppose that an organism could gain conceptual abilities one by one; rather 'light dawns gradually over the whole'.[38] And: 'the intrinsically holistic character of the propositional attitudes makes the distinction between having any and having none dramatic'.[39]

Since for the conceptualist, the canonical characterization of content is internal to the conceptual scheme to which the content belongs, and since conceptual schemes are holistic, holism is an essential property of content. If holism is essential to content then holism is essential to cognition: nothing could be a cognitive system unless it were capable of grasping a good deal of the whole conceptual system. But cognitive holism is incompatible with the evolution by natural selection

---

[37] 'Vehicle' is interpreted broadly to include any representational medium. The arrangement of silver bromide particles on paper is the vehicle for a photographic representation; there is no requirement that vehicles be syntactic.

[38] Wittgenstein, *On Certainty*, §141.

[39] D. Davidson, 'Rational Animals', *Dialectica*, 36 (1982); repr. in E. LePore and B. McLaughlin (eds.), *Actions and Events: Perspectives on the Philosophy of Donald Davidson* (Oxford: Blackwell, 1985), 318–27.

of cognitive capacities (Sections 5.2–5.6). Hence pluralism about content and the embodiment of content is false.

5.2. *The Explanatory Mechanism of Natural Selection*

Natural selection will occur if the organisms in a given population differ in their ability to survive and reproduce (their fitness), and if the features of the organisms which affect their fitness are transmitted from parents to offspring, and if no outside force intervenes. Species or organ-types or ability-types evolve, and genes are selected for.

The evolution of a species or of an organ-type or of an ability-type may be explained by means of natural selection if a linear temporal sequence (which I shall call 'the Sequence') of the following type may be constructed:

At each stage of the sequence is a genotype and a phenotype and an associated fitness (which may be represented by a real value)[40] which are such that:

1. the genotype differs by one gene from the genotype beneath it; and,
2. the phenotype has an associated fitness which is greater than the fitness associated with the phenotype beneath it; and,
3. the phenotype at the bottom of the sequence is not that of the species or organ-type or ability-type in question, whereas the phenotype at the top of the sequence is that of the species or organ-type or ability-type in question.

This formal characterization of evolution by natural selection requires a number of clarifying comments. First, the notion of fitness is relative to an environmental niche. This means that given environmental changes the fitness value associated with an unaltered phenotype may change. So it is quite possible that, given the current environmental niche, fitness values associated with later stages of the temporal sequence will be less than fitness values associated with earlier stages. Strictly speaking, instead of thinking of fitness as a real number associated with a phenotype, we should think of fitness as a function

---

[40] More strictly, fitness should be represented by a function from environments to values. See below.

from environmental niches to values. But, in general, I shall assume that the environmental niche is constant throughout the temporal sequence.

A phenotype will have a fitness in a niche in virtue of sustaining one or a number of organismal functions. For example, a phenotype which includes a heart will have a fitness in part in virtue of the fact that the structure of a heart sustains the biologically important function of pumping blood. A phenotype contributes to the fitness only in so far as the phenotype sustains a biologically useful function. We may speak, then, of the fitness being due to a biological function. Thus we should note, secondly, that the fitness at one stage of the sequence may be due to a quite different biological function from the fitness at a different stage of the sequence. For example, an explanation of the required kind of the capacity for flight may involve stages of the sequence where the possession of feathers contributes to fitness in virtue of sustaining the function of thermoregulation, and only later in the sequence contributes to fitness in virtue of sustaining the function of flight.

We may note, thirdly, that the sequence need not be one-dimensional, but rather may branch due to symbiotic combinations of genomes which have the effect of linking distinct sequences.

Fourthly, we should note that the explanation of the evolution of a capacity in terms of the Sequence is an ideal to which all natural selection explanations should aim at approximating. The better the approximation to the ideal, the better the explanation. The reason for this is that explanation of evolution by natural selection requires a variety of genotypes, and gene change occurs by random mutation. It is possible that a single mutating event, such as some cosmic radiation, will alter more than one gene in a reproductive gamete cell, or that several mutations may accumulate within a gamete during a single reproductive cycle. Likewise it is possible that a mutation alters one gene in a genotype which does not affect the fitness of the resulting phenotype, which does not therefore yield a reproductive disadvantage for the organism. Subsequent mutations may produce a genotype which combines a number of fitness-neutral genes of this kind. Both of these possibilities might figure in an evolutionary history of an organ or ability which would result in a departure from the kind of sequence which I have outlined. This we should expect since in many domains change is accounted for by appeal to a combination of explanatory mechanisms and chance factors. But as the appeal to chance increases and the appeal to explanatory mechanisms decreases, the overall success of naturalistic explanation decreases. In the limit, only chance factors are appealed to and no explanation is gained. Thus the Sequence is the paradigm of explanation of change by natural selection. The greater our need to depart from the paradigm, the less is our success in producing a naturalistic explanation of the change.

Where a number of gene changes are required for an adaptive phylogenetic change, but where the gene changes do not conform to the Sequence which I have described, the chances against the appearance of the required gene changes increase exponentially with the number of gene changes required. Thus if the probability of a single given gene mutation in a population is one in a hundred thousand, the probability of random changes which do not conform to the sequence producing a group of ten given genes will be the ludicrously improbable 10^{-50}. Precise conformity to the sequence may not be required in every case, but without general conformity we would lose the possibility of any evolutionary explanation.

Fifthly, I should note that adoption of the Sequence as an ideal of explanation of evolution by natural selection involves taking quite a strong stand on neo-Darwinian theory, and it is quite possible that this stand is mistaken for reasons that are not philosophical. If so, there is a fall-back position: it is *possible* that this is how explanation by natural selection works. I am going to argue, by using the Sequence, that pluralism about cognition and body yields a conflict with naturalism. If that argument is right, then the truth of pluralism (*pace* earlier arguments) would have to depend on the contingencies of explanation by natural selection.

5.3. *The Application of the Mechanism to the Function of Seeing*

In *The Origin of Species*, Darwin wrote about the evolution of the eye as follows:

To suppose that the eye with all its inimitable contrivances for adjusting the focus to different distances, for admitting different amounts of light, and for the correction of spherical and chromatic aberration, could have been formed by natural selection, seems, I freely confess, absurd in the highest possible degree. Yet reason tells me that if numerous gradations from a perfect and complex eye to one very imperfect and simple, each grade being useful to its possessor, can be shown to exist; if further, the eye does vary ever so slightly, and the variations be inherited, which is certainly the case; and if any variation or modification in the organ be very useful to an animal under changing conditions of life, then the difficulty of believing that a perfect and complex eye could be formed by natural selection, though insuperable by our imagination, can hardly be considered real . . . If it could be demonstrated that any complex organ existed, which could not possibly have been formed by numerous, successive, slight modifications, my theory would absolutely break down. But I can find out no such case.

The evolution of the eye may be traced through a sequence of small structural, heritable changes, each of which, in the context of the whole structure, makes available an increased functional capacity or a new functional capacity which confers selective advantage. Thus a possible (though not actual) evolutionary lineage might be traced from the leeches and flatworms with arrangements of light-sensitive cells dependent on a single pigment, through the pin-hole camera eye of the mollusc *Nautilus*, to the jelly-filled eye of some worms which provides a simple but poor lens, to the eyes of vertebrates.

What are the explanatory resources which are required in order to be able to represent (approximately) the evolution of the eye in terms of the Sequence? A representation would be possible only if we understand the correlation between three levels of description which are employed in the representation. *Gene changes*, on which the process of natural selection depends, may alter the amino acids which are produced in the organism, and thereby the proteins which make up the organism. Gene changes can, therefore, explain *structural and physiological changes* in the whole organism. But what we have been required to trace is the *evolution of a functionally defined organ*, where the functional concepts such as *lens* or *focus* may be variably instantiated by a range of quite distinct physiological structures.

As we shift from one stage of the Sequence to the next higher stage, the increase in fitness has been explained in terms of the possession of a new or increased functional capacity. The explanation is, therefore, dependent on being able to find Intelligible the connections between the structure of the geno-type and the physiological structures at each stage, on the one hand, and on being able to find Intelligible the connection between these physiological structures and imaging function at each stage of the Sequence, on the other hand.

One way in which our understanding of the structure–function relation for imaging is manifested is in our ability to engineer artificial eyes. Thus our ability to find Intelligible the evolution of the eye is correlated with our ability to find Intel-ligible the connections between physical structure and camera (or imaging) function. Let us assume that at each stage of the evolution of the eye, the structures of the eye evolved for the function of seeing or imaging (as seems likely). Thus other functions were not involved in the evolution of the structures of the eye, nor are these structures the causal consequence of the evolution of some other structures, as the evolution of the chin may be a causal (architectural) consequence of the evolution of the jaw-bones (again, as seems likely). Then, given that the model of natural selection applies successfully to the eye, each stage of the Sequence will involve a single gene change which causes a phylogenetic change which in turn contributes to a greater fitness value in virtue of its enabling some function or increased function of the imaging type.

Hence, the Sequence depends on our mastery of a set of functional concepts which allow us to make sense of an ordering of devices according to how successful at imaging they are. It must be possible to put the ordering into isomorphism with the temporal ordering of the physiological structures, which are the physical basis of the function at each stage of the Sequence. For example, without our understanding of the concepts of focus and resolution, we would not be able to represent one camera (or animalian 'eye') as better than another. For 'better' must mean 'better adapted for the function of imaging'. What was required was mastery of a set of concepts which allows us to represent a set of physical devices as ordered in a series of devices better and better adapted for the function of imaging.

5.4. The Extension of the Argument from Imaging to Thinking

Suppose, for a moment, that evolutionary biology had to make Intelligible the capacity for thinking in the way in which it has managed to make Intelligible the capacity for imaging. If the evolutionary explanation were to work in the same way, we would have to have mastery of a set of concepts which allowed us to represent a set of physical devices as ordered in a series of devices better and better adapted for the function of thinking. Two intimately interconnected features are required for a set of concepts of this type. First, the set of concepts must provide a conception of the relation *more-primitive-thinker-than* which is well defined for a large set of thinkers, as another set of concepts provided a conception of the relation *more-primitive-imager-than* which was well defined for a large set of imagers. Secondly, mastery of this set of concepts must allow us to understand how a set of physical devices may be ordered by the more-primitive-thinker-than relation. The first feature relates to our understanding of the function in question, whereas the second feature relates to our understanding of the structure–function relation.

But folk psychology does not provide such concepts. We are very poor at comparing a range of animals for their ability to think and cognize, and we have no idea how we could generate such a comparison on the basis of the structures of the animals. We cannot rectify this problem just by extending the concepts of folk psychology within the folk-psychological discourse level, for, if we are pluralists, we must suppose that cognitive systems are essentially holistic. And hence that we cannot—as a consequence of the nature of cognition—provide the kind of ordering of cognitive systems that would be required by the more-primitive-thinker-than relation; a relation which coherently applies to relata which are not concept-exercisers as well as to relata which are. But, the pluralist's conceptualism and the holism of concepts entails that if a system is a thinker at all it must already grasp much of the conceptual scheme in terms of which its cognitive states are characterized: the function of thinking or cognizing cannot stand to being a concept-exerciser as the function of imaging stands to having the sight of a higher primate. Thus pluralism entails that the concepts required in order to explain the evolution by natural selection of cognition cannot exist. For the pluralist, the evolution of cognition is a miraculous coincidence.

Any evaluation of the cognitive capacities of animals must rest on a theory of their ability to represent their world. So we require a scientific theory of representation which will allow us to order animals according to their varying representational abilities, and where our assessment of their representational abilities will rest in part on our knowledge of the animals' physiological or computational structure. Since conceptualism about content is incompatible with such a theory of representation, we will require a non-conceptualist theory of content which canonically characterizes the nature of content from outside the conceptual scheme to which the content belongs. The provision of such a theory will alter the psychological discourse level: understanding how it can be that changes at the genetic level and changes at the level of cognitive function can march in step must alter our understanding of the nature of cognition. Since the pluralist disallows intralevel change on the basis of interlevel relations, this result is incompatible with pluralism in this area. Moreover, it is incompatible with the pluralist's characteristic insistence on the autonomy of the scientific and human realms.

Without the concepts required by the Sequence, the persistent correlation between genetic changes, phylogenetic changes, and increased fitness will appear as a miraculous Coincidence. Unless we have some way of explanatorily connecting (finding Coherent) changes at the discourse level which characterizes the genes to changes at the discourse level which characterizes the cognitive phylogeny of organisms, we will have no way of understanding how the two sets of changes march in step. And continue to march in step through evolutionary time.

5.5. *Some Ways of Avoiding the Argument?*

Let us proceed more cautiously with the extension of the discussion from the realm of imaging to the realm of thinking. Some organisms think. Therefore the evolutionary biologist is committed to explaining the evolution of organisms which think by means of the mechanism of natural selection. To what does this commit him? Some organisms have eyes. So the evolutionary biologist is committed to explaining the evolution of organisms with eyes. This commits him to explaining the evolution of the function of imaging (or gaining visual information), only because the possession of eyes contributes to fitness in virtue of enabling the function of imaging, and such a fitness contribution is essential to the evolution of organisms with eyes. That is, organisms with eyes would not have evolved had the possession of eyes not enabled the function of gaining visual information. This seems reasonable, but is the parallel claim about the structural basis of cognition and the cognitive function of thinking also reasonable: that is, that the structural basis of thinking would not have evolved had the possession of it by an organism not enabled the function of thinking and thereby contributed to the fitness of the organism? To say that thinking organisms have evolved is not the same as to say that thinking has evolved.

How could it have been otherwise? The brain of the higher primates, under some description of it, is the phylogenetic structure correlated with the function of thinking. Nevertheless, the brain may have evolved because of some function other than thinking, in virtue of which it contributed to the increasing fitness of those genes causally responsible for the brain. As, perhaps, feathers evolved for thermoregulation rather than flight. Or, indeed, the brain may not have evolved *for any function at all*. This would be so if the development of the brain were like that of the chin in being the inevitable causal consequence of some quite different change to which the theory of natural selection did apply. For example, suppose there were selective pressure for the evolution of a larger and larger cranium. The quantity of nerve-cells would increase but only because there was a greater volume to be filled. Once a threshold of neural complexity was crossed, thinking would result. If either of these cases obtained, the biologist would not have to explain the evolution of thinking organisms in a way which parallels his explanation of the evolution of organisms with eyes.

The second objection to the claim that it is thinking, not just thinking organisms, which has evolved is not very forceful. It would be implausible to explain the increase in nerve-cells in terms of selective pressure for an increase in the size of the cranium, rather than to explain the increase in the size of the cranium in terms of selective pressure for an increase in the number of nerve-cells. For example, increasing cranial size has the effect of making parturition more and more hazardous. This would lead directly to a selective pressure against increasing cranial size, which would have to be overcome by some other selective force.

It is sometimes suggested that it would be absurd to try to apply natural selection to higher cognitive abilities, such as knowledge of calculus or musical appreciation, and then inferred that it would be absurd to apply natural selection to cognition. According to Stephen Gould, Alfred Wallace, the co-discoverer of the theory of natural selection, reasoned in this way. His conclusion, if correct, would be disastrous for naturalism, for it was at this final stage of evolution that God must have miraculously intervened. But Wallace differed from Darwin in holding a rigid form of natural selection (hyperselectionism) according to which no feature of a phenotype or difference between phenotypes could have been produced by selection unless it was now, or once had been, useful to (contributed to the fitness of) the individuals or races that possessed them. But natural selection should not be construed so rigidly. The chin is a causal consequence of selective processes, even though the chin has not itself been selected for, has not contributed to fitness. Likewise, the ability to do higher mathematics or appreciate music is a causal consequence of more general reasoning, thinking, and perceiving abilities which have been selected for. The inference from particular 'higher cognitive abilities' to cognition in general is not a good one.

So we should not argue that cognition has not evolved because our knowledge of calculus has not evolved. But what is the level of ability which is the cause of our higher cognitive abilities? Might not our higher cognitive abilities be the causal consequence of representational abilities which are not thinking abilities? It could be argued that thinking has not evolved, because thinking is a causal consequence of more basic representational capacities which are modular[41] or bound to specific situations: representation in the 'primal sketch', for example.[42] Instead of thinking of the evolution of cognition in terms of the relation more-primitive-thinker-than, we should employ relations like more-primitive-representer-of-spatial-relations-than, or more-primitive-sensory-motor-co-ordinator-than. Certainly, if there is some function other than thinking which explains the evolution of cognizing creatures, then such functions as these are the best candidates.

This objection is difficult to assess because it is not easy to see how the possibility helps the pluralist. For the case is not directly analogous to the evolution of flight or the evolution of the chin. Modular situation-bound representation does not stand to cognition as thermoregulation stands to flight, because the manipulation of modular, situation-bound representation is a process of the same generic kind as cognition: both essentially involve the manipulation of representations. A pluralist who makes this objection has to maintain two things: that a Sequence of the kind required for the explanation of the evolution of thinking organisms is constructed on the basis of notions of representation and representational content, but that we cannot explain the nature of higher (cognitive) representational capacities partly by means of these notions of representation which apply to other animals as well as to humans. Perhaps such a case could be made out, but it seems implausible, for there can be at most only a minimal behavioural gap between behaviours which could be explained on the basis of animal (non-conceptualist) representation, and behaviours which are the result of concepts. (For, otherwise, the pluralist would not have an evolutionary explanation, which conformed to the Sequence, of the higher concept-exercising behaviour of humans.) Could it be that we can explain cognitive behaviour by means of non-conceptualist representation, but that we cannot explain cognition by means of non-conceptualist representation?

It seems more plausible to suppose that if the explanation of

[41] J. A. Fodor, *The Modularity of Mind* (Cambridge, Mass.: MIT Press, 1983).
[42] D. Marr, *Vision* (New York: Freeman, 1982).

the evolution of cognizing organisms requires us to appeal to this form of basic representation, and we must be able to explain thereby how humans are able to perform cognitively in all the ways in which humans are able to perform, then our understanding of the nature of cognition is a matter (partly) for science. Modular, situation-bound representation carries what I call 'non-conceptual content'[43] whose elucidation is a theoretical, scientific matter. It is not experience but the brain and information scientist who is authoritative with respect to the primal sketch.

5.6. *The Evolution of Thinking Entails a Non-conceptual Theory of Cognition*

Both ways of denying that cognition has evolved are unattractive. The attractive option is to suppose that the higher cortical reaches of the brain have evolved for the function of thinking or cognition. But now it *is* obligatory to make intelligible the capacity for thought or cognition in the way in which we managed to make intelligible the capacity for imaging. We require an explanation of cognition which makes room for the relation more-primitive-thinker-than[44] which is well defined for a large set of thinkers (having at least as many types of member as there are stages in the canonical sequence, less one), and which may be used to order a set of physical systems. We must be able to employ the relation in constructing a linear sequence of the kind which we saw that canonical explanation by means of natural selection requires. At the top of the sequence will be a phylogeny which includes conceptual capacity for thought and at the bottom will be a phylogeny which lacks any such capacity.

If we have to portray the evolution of thinking in terms of

[43] See Cussins, 'The Connectionist Construction of Concepts'.
[44] A commitment to a theory of cognition which can sustain the more-primitive-thinker-than relation does not involve the rejection of the explanation of the evolution of cognition in terms of relations such as is-a-more-primitive-representer-of-spatial-relations-than. Indeed, the best explanation of how to make room for the more-primitive-thinker-than relation is to explain the phenomena of cognition in terms of a theory of non-conceptual content. That is, in terms of a theory of precisely the kind of content employed in situation- or purpose-bound representational tasks.

the Sequence, then we have to understand concept-exercising as a capacity which is more complex than, but *of the same functional kind as*, some capacities which are possessed by animals which are not concept-exercisers. For by condition 3 of the Sequence, and by holism, animals at all rungs of the Sequence except the top rung have a phylogeny that excludes concept-exercising abilities, and animals at the top rung have a phylogeny which includes such abilities. Moreover, we could find no function available to the conceptualist which stands to thinking as thermoregulation stands to flight. Given this, it follows from condition 2 of the sequence that each stage (except the lowest stage) in the Sequence must be represented as having a fitness advantage over the stage below, which is due to its being better at some particular function than the stage below; the same function for all stages. Hence the ability of concept-exercising must belong to the same functional kind of ability as an ability possessed by non-concept-exercising animals.

Conceptual content is a complex kind of non-conceptual content, just as a super-sophisticated Nikon (or the human eye) is a complex kind of imager. As we should not explain the imaging capacity of *Nautilus* in terms of the imaging capacity of a Nikon, rather than vice versa, so we should not try to explain non-conceptual content in terms of conceptual content, rather than vice versa. As in Section 3, we find that the avoidance of a miraculous Coincidence problem requires a scientific theory of content. The world-as-it-is-given-in-experience and the world of the sciences are not autonomous.

8

Reduction, Causality, and Normativity

Kathleen Lennon

1. ONE ANTI-REDUCTIONIST POSITION

Is it possible to maintain a causal explanatory view of intentional explanation, hold some strong(ish) version of anti-reductionism with regard to intentional states and intentional laws, and be respectably materialist enough not to be accused of closet Cartesianism?

The causal explanatory view I shall be considering is one in which the causal relation between our intentional states and intentional acts is supported by lawlike generalizations employing *intentional* vocabulary. The causal relations are predicated on the backs of the rationalizing links between intentional states. The intentional causal generalizations characterize empirical regularities between states as a consequence of these states having contents which bear rationalizing links to each other.[1]

To attempt to combine this claim with both materialism and physicalism is to provide an immediate motivation for reduction. If we regard psychological events/states as in some sense constituted out of physical events/states (materialism?) and accept that such physical events can be causally explicable from within the confines of physical theory (physicalism?) then we seem to need some account of how the explanations at each level of description interconnect. We need a framework which allows the validity of explanation at both levels of description, but avoids both overdetermination of particular events/states, and a miraculous coincidence of prediction from the distinct causal explanatory schemes. For some theorists, moreover, we need to accommodate the claim that all causal connections are

---

© Kathleen Lennon 1992

[1] For a defence of this view see K. Lennon, *Explaining Human Action* (London: Duckworth, 1990).

constituted out of, or mediated by, interaction of forces at the microlevel.[2]

The reductionism which would meet these needs is that envisaged in classical discussions of the unity of science. Intentional kinds featuring in intentional laws will be paired with physical kinds, occurring in physical laws. Consequently, the causal generalizations linking such intentional kinds will be derivable from such physical laws. All the causal explanatory work done by our intentional generalizations will be captured at the physical level. This is the picture that the anti-reductionist wishes to resist.

The first move initially made by functionalists was to challenge the possibility of one to one pairings between intentional kinds and the kinds of any physical theory. What functionalists emphasized was the 'multiple realization' of psychological kinds. This is not sufficient to rebut the reductionist project, however, for the distinct realizations might be formed into a *disjunction*, which would then constitute the reduction of the higher-level kind. From the laws governing these disjuncts we could then derive the intentional laws. What is important for anti-reductionist arguments is the kind of *unity* such a disjunctive set can be taken to possess. Characteristic of classical reduction was the reduction of higher-level properties to properties which formed a *natural kind* at the reducing level. If the reducing properties consist of a disjunct which we required the higher-level classification to unify, then no genuine reduction has been effected.[3] An anti-reductionist defending the autonomy of intentional causal explanation makes this claim. The distinct physical groundings of a given intentional kind will be *shapeless* from the viewpoint of physical theory. (The reasons she might have for claiming this will be considered in the next section.) Our classifications into intentional kinds provides a pattern of conceptualization which yields empirical generalizations and conditional dependencies. These patterns of dependency are at the heart of causal explanation, and could not be captured without the employment of intentional notions.

How is a theorist who adopts such an anti-reductionist position to respond to the motivations which prompted reduction-

[2] See the Introduction to this volume.
[3] Ibid.

ism? One suggestion would be that if we accept that mental states *supervene* on physical states, then we can accommodate as much of the reductionist motivation as is compelling. To do so the claim of supervenience must be interpreted in a robust way. The causal role we attribute to intentional states requires us to adopt a realist stance towards them. A link of supervenience between them and physical properties will then have to be viewed as a real relationship between properties, not simply a constraint on our assignment of predicates.[4] Such a relation is one in which the base properties necessitate the higher-level properties, and on occasion, in the absence of alternative base properties, are necessary for them.[5] These relations would need to be localized, for we are attempting to characterize a relation which can hold between the intentional causal antecedents of action and the physical causal antecedents of movements. A mere global dependency of intentional kinds on physical ones will not be adequate.[6]

Where such localized strong supervenience holds, it is suggested, conditional links between intentional and physical causes are maintained which rule out problems of overdetermination. Moreover, each *token* intentional causal interaction is grounded in/mediated by a physical one. There is no mental effecting without a physical effecting. What is resisted, due to the shapelessness of the multiple bases, is any general vindication of the higher-level causal regularities in terms of physical theory.

This then is one version of an anti-reductionist package with regard to the mental. One which defends an *independent causal* explanatory role for the intentional. Is it defensible?

2. ANTI-REDUCTIONIST ARGUMENTS

What reasons does the anti-reductionist have for the claim that the distinct physical bases grounding our intentional kinds will be shapeless from the standpoint of physical theory, and,

---

[4] See J. Klagge, 'Supervenience, Ontological and Ascriptive', *Australasian Journal of Philosophy*, 66 (1988).

[5] See Introduction, Sect. 4.

[6] *Contra* G. Currie, 'Individualism and Global Supervenience', *British Journal for the Philosophy of Science*, 35 (1984).

therefore, that there will be no nomological correlation of predicates linking physical and intentional theory? The most famous anti-reductionist arguments in recent years have derived from the work of Donald Davidson.[7]

Davidson's argument rests on the *constitutive role of rationality* in the assignment of intentional descriptions. He has recently put the matter thus:

Beliefs, intentions and desires are identified by their objects, and these are identified by their logical and semantic properties. If attitudes can be identified at all, then, they must be found to be largely consistent with one another (because of their logical properties), and in line with the real world (because of their semantic properties) . . . if a creature has propositional attitudes then that creature is approximately rational.[8]

If we are to assign propositional attitudes at all then we must assign them in such a way that the creature conforms to certain standards of rationality. Beliefs, for example, tend to produce other beliefs, for which they provide reasons, that is, beliefs which they deductively or inductively support. They are not causally stable in the presence of environmental conditions which count as evidence against them. In combination with desires they tend to produce actions which are ways of satisfying those desires. Desires produce other desires which they are regarded as needed to promote their satisfaction. Davidson claims that the reason-giving relations which serve to define our intentional kinds 'have no echo in physical theory'.[9] Without the use of intentional vocabulary such links could not be expressed. This seems right. It is difficult to see how we could capture our relations of providing evidence for, inductively or deductively supporting etc. without the use of intentional or semantic vocabulary; for such relations are relations between intentional contents.

These arguments of Davidson have been utilized in a number of ways. One is straightforward. In pointing to the constraints

[7] D. Davidson, *Essays on Actions and Events* (Oxford: Clarendon Press, 1980).

[8] In B. Vermazen and M. Hintikka (eds.), *Essays on Davidson* (Oxford: Oxford University Press, 1985), 245.

[9] *Essays on Actions and Events*, 231.

governing our classification into intentional kinds we render it highly implausible to suppose that any classification in extensional terms could be nomologically coextensive with a classification anchored by a network of rationalizing links, or yield the pattern of conditional dependencies which are generated by consideration of such links. Given the very disparate anchorages of the two conceptual frameworks it would seem *simply coincidental* if at any places they should appear isomorphic. Such a use of Davidson's arguments takes the distinctive features of our intentional schema to provide very good grounds for the speculation that, in practice,[10] there will be no nomological isomorphism between intentional and physical theory. This speculation fuels the causal anti-reductionists' belief in an autonomous causal role for the intentional.

For Davidson himself, however, and many writers influenced by his work, attention to the constitutive role of rationality with regard to our intentional states yields conclusions which are stronger than this. The anti-reductionist position emerges from these conclusions as a matter of principle. What is problematic, however, is that such principled arguments seems to rule out more than reductionism. They also cast doubt on essential components of the causalist position. If they are vindicated the coherence of that position is cast in doubt.

One version of the principled argument is as follows. Our intentional characteristics are holistic. The validity of one depends on the validity of others. Such interdependence works intertemporally, and is constrained by the overriding principle of making the agent as rational as possible. What happens later, therefore, has a constitutive bearing on my present intentional states. Here the picture is one in which the addition of new pieces can change the overall pattern; so where there is a chance of new pieces the overall pattern cannot be regarded as determinate. (For example, when he said 'she should look out for herself more' I took it as an indication of friendly

---

[10] I'm not happy with the 'in practice/in principle' division, though I use it here. The rationality constraints give us *good reasons* not to expect isomorphism. For a discussion of the in practice/in principle issue in this area see H. Putnam, 'Why Functionalism didn't Work', in H. Putnam, *Representation and Reality* (Cambridge, Mass.: MIT Press, 1988).

concern. In the light of his future lack of support for her, it takes on the aspect of a warning.) If we accept this picture then our intentional states are not determinate at a time prior to the items they are invoked to explain; which undermines the possibility of their playing a causal explanatory role. Neither can localized supervenience hold, for if it did the physical states causing movement would fix our intentional descriptions without leaving them open to future modification.

To be moved by this argument, however, we need to accept that the future pieces play a constitutive and not an epistemic role in fixing the pattern necessary for intentionality. What happens later fixes the nature of the earlier utterance and does not just reveal to us its already present potentialities. But why should we interpret the operation of the constraints of rationality in this way? Indeed, at first sight, it seems very implausible that whether I want tea now should be answerable to behaviour tomorrow in any but an evidential way. To assume otherwise undermines not only the explanatory claims of the causal theorist but the coherence of our positions as agents engaged in making decisions about our own actions.

Such a version of the Davidsonian arguments is compatible with taking the structure of rationality as an objective feature of a system, though not one which could be fixed at any point in time, and may be compatible with some global form of robust supervenience. Such realism, however, runs contrary to arguments developed out of other strands of Davidson's thought. Here intentional concepts have their home within a project of *interpretation*.[11] The constraints of rationality become methodological constraints on the assignment of predicates by interpreters. The intentional states of others become constructions from within *our* interpretive projects. This framework is embroidered in various ways. The rationality constraints are open-ended. They constrain their applications but do not uniquely fix them. This indeterminacy is resolved by interpreters who attempt to interpret others as *like themselves*. What emerges is a view of psychological hypotheses as 'artefacts reflective of our current stage of self-interpretation'.[12]

[11] See L. Antony, 'Anomalous Monism and the Problem of Explanatory Force', *Philosophical Review*, 98 (1989).
[12] Ibid. 179.

This view of our psychological properties has certain analogies with the non-realism adopted by some[13] with regard to moral properties, viewed as projections or constructions, whose source is projects of agents. In both cases any appeal to supervenience has the status of an additional methodological constraint of consistency, rather than a claim that physical–naturalistic features of reality can fix psychological–moral ones.

Whatever the merits of such non-realism in the case of moral properties, there seem disanalogies with the psychological case, which tell against regarding intentional descriptions as a matter of construction. Firstly, unlike the moral case, intentional descriptions play an explanatory role in relation to the behaviour of the objects of description themselves, and not just with regard to the behaviour of the interpreters. Secondly, the projects of the interpreters which play the role of grounding the interpretations are themselves intentional projects. Within the framework of the moral–non-realist, the states which ground our moral projections are given a realist construal. Our judgements are real—they lead to the projection of moral properties which are not. In the intentional case, however, our own states grounding our construction of others' also must be constructions. This either threatens regress or adopting a radically different account of intentionality in the first and third persons.

If we reject the claim that intentional descriptions are constructions out of the projects of interpreters, then we can reject other components of the non-realist picture. This includes the view that the *goals* and *rules* we are given to perform the construction leave an openness which can only be resolved by decision or an act of identification. It may be the case that the a priori principles of rationality which serve to anchor our intentional kinds do not yield necessary and sufficient conditions for the assignment of intentional descriptions. They can be viewed, however, as providing the framework of an empirical

[13] See S. Blackburn, 'Moral Realism', in J. Casey (ed.), *Morality and Moral Reasoning* (London: Methuen, 1971) and 'Rule-Following and Moral Realism', in S. Holtzman and C. Leich (eds.), *Wittgenstein: To Follow a Rule* (London: Routledge & Kegan Paul, 1981).

theory.[14] The indeterminateness is to be resolved by investigation not fiat.

None of this is to deny that we will, of course, assign intentional descriptions to ourselves and others in a way that reflects our own beliefs about the world and our position in it. But this does not put intentional descriptions in a special position. It is true of all our theories of the world.

3. THE CHALLENGES OF NORMATIVITY

There is a third development of the Davidsonian anti-reductionist arguments which I regard as much more problematic than those outlined above. I shall concentrate on its exposition by John McDowell in 'Functionalism and Anomalous Monism',[15] though it can be found in much post-Wittgensteinian writing on the explanation of behaviour. Here anti-reductionism is a consequence of certain distinctive explanatory projects within which our intentional notions are located. These projects are ones which cannot be captured within physical vocabulary. The problem, however, for a causal theorist is that the pattern of intelligibility which our intentional notions reveal is also claimed to be incompatible with their use in a causal explanatory theory.

For McDowell the explanatory use to which our intentional notions are put requires the interconnected features of *normativity* and *perspectivity*. Thus:

concepts of the propositional attitudes have their proper home in explanations of a special sort: explanations in which things are made intelligible by being revealed to be, or to approximate to being, as they rationally ought to be. This is to be contrasted with a style of explanation in which one makes things intelligible by representing their coming into being as a particular instance of how things generally tend to happen.[16]

---

[14] For more here, see my *Explaining Human Action*, ch. 3.
[15] J. McDowell, 'Functionalism and Anomalous Monism', in E. LePore and B. McLaughlin (eds.), *Actions and Events: Perspectives on the Philosophy of Donald Davidson* (Oxford: Blackwell, 1985).
[16] Ibid.

This mode of explanation is tied up with the essential subjectivity of the mental. There is

a connection between the ideal-involving kind of explanation and the
irreducible subjectivity of propositional attitudes. Achieving the kind
of understanding for which rationality plays its constitutive role requires a sensitivity to the specific detail of the subjective stance of
others.[17]

The subjectivity involved here is not necessarily 'first-
personal'. The kind of identification with myself required by
some interpretational accounts is not the issue. When we
provide rationalizing explanations we make, for example, an
action intelligible by adopting the *agent's perspective* on it. It is
from that perspective that goals are detected as desirable and
the courses of action appropriate to the situation. These features
are not objective in the sense of being 'fully describable from
no particular point of view'.[18] The standpoint of an agent
deciding how to act is not that of a detached observer simply
predicting the next move. When I find something desirable and
judge an act an appropriate route for achieving it, I conclude
that a certain course of action should be taken. This is different
from my reflecting on my past behaviour and concluding that I
will do X in the future. Anyone understanding my action must
appreciate it from my position as an agent deciding how to act.
Appreciating the rationality of an action, therefore, requires
engagement. We need to appreciate the normativity 'from the
inside', as it were (although that terminology can be misleading: it is more like 'from a given position, in a given
mode').

For McDowell our intentional notions have their home in
this form of explanation. Their role in structures of normativity
are constitutive of them. To understand what it is to desire is to
appreciate what is involved in finding something desirable and
thereby to appreciate the appropriateness of pursuing it.
Normativity cannot be grasped without engagement. We can,
therefore, only grasp our intentional concepts by taking up the
perspective of agents engaged in making decisions.

Such a development of the Davidsonian account carries no

---

[17] Ibid.
[18] Ibid.

necessary anti-realism. Indeed theorists such as McDowell insist on the *reality* of properties which are subjective, in the sense of capturing a particular perspective on the world. Therefore, neither the desirability of the action, nor the fact that a certain agent desires to perform it, are states of affairs which we must regard as non-determinate, or mere projections from our projects. It may even be possible to accept the supervenience of such subjective properties on objective characteristics of the world. (This depends on the intelligibility demanded of the supervenience relation—of which more below.) The anti-reductionist thrust of this argument rests on the normativity and perspectivity of our intentional descriptions. These features cannot be captured at the physical level, because physical descriptions are regarded as non-normative and non-perspectival.[19] But the argument has further consequences. It is regarded as excluding intentional notions from featuring in causal explanations, for such explanations are cast in an objective mode, and to use intentional concepts within them is like making a radical category mistake.

There are two kinds of response which a causal explanatory theorist can make to these points. One is much braver than the other. I'd like to make the brave one, but may be forced back on the more modest one. To be less brave is to accept the objectivity of causal regularities, and of the properties which they conjoin. Indeed just such an objectivist conception motivates the demand to integrate the regularities of distinct sciences, which leads to reductionist claims or at least to the conditional interdependencies of robust supervenience. From within this framework any perspectivity which attaches to our intentional states is purely *epistemic*. We may gain access to them perspectivally, but there is no principled reason why they could not be accessed in other ways. The rationalizing links between intentional states have the status of an objective schema of description. (Which is not to suggest that it is a schema which can be captured in non-intentional language.) Judging the rationality of an action is analogous to judging

---

[19] But see T. Nagel, *The View from Nowhere* (New York and Oxford: Oxford University Press, 1986), Introduction, for doubts about eliminating all perspectivity.

whether a line is straight, judged by reference to an ideal, but an objective process none the less.

Those emphasizing the normativity of our intentional notions have challenged causal theorists with the lack of contingency of the generalizations governing our states of desire and belief. That beliefs are sensitive to evidence, and desires lead to be-haviour designed to promote their satisfaction, are a priori not empirical, claims. They are, it is suggested, *normative* principles, the appropriateness of which is grasped perspectivally. The modest causal explanatory theorist, however, views the *con-stitutive* link between belief and truth and desire and satisfac-tion differently. It is explained by their position within a causal explanatory theory implicitly defining its core notions. The principles reflect the individuating functional roles of those states.[20] The normativity of rationality becomes a reflection of the causal role such constitutive principles play in the activities of forming beliefs or deciding how to act. It is an objectively accessible fact that where agents take such rationalizing links to hold they tend to form their beliefs and intentions in accord with them. Any additional insight we gain by being participants in such processes is simply insight into what it is like to engage in reasoning of a certain kind. It contributes nothing essential to our understanding of intentionality.

The brave response is willing to accept much more from the perspectivalist. It accepts that the modest account of inten-tional notions fails to capture their genuine normativity. What is graspable from the agent's perspective is not only that we tend to form our decisions according to a certain formula, but that we should do so. From this perspective the link between the recognition of rationalizing links and the adoption of beliefs and intentions loses the contingency it has within the objectivist account. Recognizing appropriateness requires engagement with motivational or evidential force.

On the other hand the brave response emphasizes, unlike McDowell, that as well as engaging with the normative face of rationality when deciding what we should do or believe, we also step back from ourselves and others and make predictions about what we *will* do or believe (which is not always what we

---

[20] This is the position I adopted in *Explaining Human Action*: see ch. 1.

should!). We have not provided a sufficient explanation of an action in showing that it should be done. For we often fail to do what we should. The normative stance therefore needs to be supplemented by a causal one. Such a causal stance, however, would make reference to intentional states constitutively anchored in a normative framework, which reflects an agent's perspective on to the world. In this sense the features invoked in our causal explanation are subjective.

What we gain from an objectivist causal position is a recognition that beliefs and intentions are commonly formed when certain relations hold between their contents. What we gain from the agent's perspective is a recognition of the appropriateness of forming beliefs and intentions in this way. The brave move is to try and integrate these two aspects of intentionality. For without the agent's perspective we cannot properly grasp what properties it is that are causally related. This approach would have consequences for the metaphysics of causation. Some causal relations would not be purely objective in the sense of relating properties which reflect no particular perspective.[21] Moreover, a purely regularist account would not be applicable to the causal relations here. Our engagement in the normativity of intentional notions gives us an insight into why the regularities hold which undermines the contingency of the relation (although it does not undermine the distinctness of cause and effect). The coherence of such a metaphysic is beyond the scope of this paper to explore.

4. SUPERVENIENCE AND INTELLIGIBILITY

In recent years arguments against reductive correlations between psychological and categorical physical properties were brought to the fore by functionalists, who took the accommodation of multiple realization as one of the advantages of their theory. However, in most of its forms functionalism does require a reduction of its own—of intentional states to functional states whose causal characteristics can be captured in

---

[21] This conclusion could also be drawn from the essential role of indexical thought in the explanation of action.

extensional language. This is, however, a problematic position. The arguments against psychophysical reduction seem equally telling against *any* attempt to capture our intentional distinctions in non-intentional vocabulary.[22] This seems to be the case whether appreciation of the constraints of rationality simply make us sceptical of the feasibility of cross-categorical coincidences or whether we accept the strong normativity of our intentional concepts.

The virtue of functionalism was the support which it provided for claims of supervenience. Where supervenience holds there are relations of upward determination from the base properties to the supervening kinds. Functionalism rendered such relations intelligible, for the functional equivalences of our intentional descriptions would be derivable from the physical bases and their accompanying theory.

If supervenience needs to be rendered intelligible in this very strong way, and anti-reductionist arguments rule out such intelligibility by ruling out functionalism, then their materialist and physicalist credentials seem put in doubt. It is not clear, however, that we need to accept the intelligibility demand in a way that yields supervenience conditionals as the output of systematic theory. If we accept supervenience then we need reasons to believe it is true. These might derive from our general metaphysical commitments. We might also need reasons to believe that it is *possible*. This latter demand requires that we have some insight into how a physical system can become susceptible to intentional characterization. Even with an objectivist framework, this requirement falls short of the systematic derivability envisaged by functionalists. An often used example is the relation between micro- and macro-descriptions of objects. There is no reason to suppose that we can derive our descriptions of a room in terms of tables and chairs from its descriptions in terms of micro-objects. Once that latter description is instantiated, however, we can *see how* certain macrodescriptions are also made true, without anything else needing to be done. The same may hold for the link between the extensional and the intentional.

If we accept the *perspectivity* of intentional characterizations

---

[22] I argue this in 'Anti-reductionist Materialism', *Inquiry*, 27 (1984).

while maintaining their causal role, we retain a motivation for supervenience. But the demand that supervenient properties should be systematically derivable from their base looks quite misplaced. If we wish to adopt such perspectivalist positions and retain our materialist credentials then we will need to reject strong intelligibility constraints on the relation of super-venience. It is less clear, however, that *any* attempt at making intelligible the link between perspectival and non-perspectival properties is ruled out.[23] But much work remains to be done, both in clarifying what kind of perspicuousness is possible here—and in providing it.

[23] In *The View from Nowhere*, Nagel suggests that the supervenience of the mental on the physical might only be intelligible if we can come to see them as essential components of a more fundamental essence. But maybe Nagel is operating with too strong an intelligibility demand.

9

Elimination versus
Non-reductive Physicalism*

Brian Loar

There is reason to be pessimistic about the physicalist reduction of the mental, especially as regards propositional attitudes. But the straightforward alternatives are unappealing, namely, dualism and the eliminativist proposition that mental ascriptions are never strictly true. The question is whether some form of non-reductive physicalism is a more promising alternative, that is, commitment both to the comprehensively physical nature of things and despite non-reduction to the reality of mental facts. I am going to argue that current versions do not stand up. But the point is not that reduction or elimination must then hold (putting aside dualism as incredible). It is quite consistent with my argument here that we reach an impasse, that standard presuppositions permit no viable position. At least there is no easy non-reductive way out, despite the claims of two distinctive theses: Stephen Schiffer's to the effect that nominalism about mental properties permits physicalism without reduction; and the widely prevalent doctrine of non-reductive supervenience. Non-reductive physicalist views reject an atomist picture of how physical facts make mental ascriptions true, namely by correspondence: the mental ascription must correspond to a physical fact in such a way that the ascribed mental predicate stands for a physical-property constituent of the truth-making fact. Schiffer rejects this by rejecting properties, and supervenience views reject it by making the relation between ascription and the physical facts more oblique. The argument of this paper is in effect that the correspondence picture is not so easy to get rid of.

* I would like to thank Kent Bach, David Charles, and Stephen Schiffer for helpful discussion of the issues raised in this paper

1. NOMINALISM AND ONTOLOGICAL PHYSICALISM

In *Remnants of Meaning* and in a recent paper[1] Schiffer denies
that rejecting reduction forces a choice between a non-natural
view of thoughts and their elimination. His argument is direct
and ingenious. Mental properties are irreducible. On the face
of it, however, mental properties are causes of behaviour. But
if mental properties are not reducible to physical or functional
properties, then we have an unbelievable causal overdetermination of behaviour by mental properties and physical properties. So mental properties must be reducible, and hence,
given the failure of reduction, both reducible and irreducible.
Now that implies that there are no such properties as mental
properties. But this does not mean that there are no true
ascriptions of mental states. For Schiffer denies that the
truth of statements of any sort, mental or physical, requires
the existence of properties; he subscribes to thoroughgoing
nominalism. Schiffer calls his anti-reductionism sentential
dualism: there are true mental ascriptions and true physical
statements, and the former are not reducible to the latter. But
this dualism is innocuous. For it is quite compatible with (what
he calls) ontological physicalism: all actual entities—particulars,
properties, relations—are physical. Given nominalism, ontological physicalism is true because all particulars are physical.

Schiffer allows that we may *speak* of mental properties and
facts, in what he calls a pleonastic sense of property and fact.
Why deny the trivial inference from 'Alfredo believes in ghosts'
to 'Alfredo has the property of believing in ghosts'? What
makes this ontologically neutral is that, on one understanding,
that property is a sort of ghost itself, not introduced by ontologically committed objectual quantification. Schiffer speaks of
pleonastic properties as not language-independent, as though
they are introduced by merely substitutional quantification.
He hesitates about this, however, and so let us say merely
that pleonastic properties are introduced by non-objectual
quantification. The important point is that, according to Schiffer,

---

[1] *Remnants of Meaning* (Cambridge, Mass.: MIT Press, Bradford Books, 1987),
ch. 6; and 'Physicalism', in J. Tomberlin (ed.), *Philosophical Perspectives*, iv
(Atascadero, Calif.: Ridgeview, 1990).

no awkward causal overdetermination arises from merely pleonastic mental properties (a central point, to which we will return). Nominalism then makes sentential dualism, anti-reductionism, harmless by making it compatible with onto-logical physicalism.

Schiffer's reason for rejecting ontological dualism—in par-ticular, the existence of non-physical non-pleonastic mental properties—is that it implies an unbelievable overdetermination of behaviour by both physical and non-physical causes. As to why his own sentential dualism does not imply such an over-determination, he says roughly this. We may suppose that the *conceptual roles* of my mental ascriptions to *x* are related non-accidentally to *x*'s underlying physical workings in such a way that predictions of *x*'s behaviour based on my mental ascriptions mesh with the output of *x*'s physical workings. Given this, he says, there is nothing like causal overdetermination, but rather a nice fit between a predictive technique and a system of physical causation. Nothing in that picture, even with the failure of reduction, warrants overturning our entrenched view that mental ascriptions are or can be literally true.

Before we examine Schiffer's proposal it will be useful to have in mind some conditions that any interesting non-reductionist physicalism ought to meet. I take the following to be fair.

1. Mental truths should be *not second string*, not assigned, for example, an instrumentalist status while physical truths are taken more substantively. It is a kind of eliminativism to assign mental ascriptions an etiolated truth basis, making them true in a way secondary to the truth of physical ascriptions. A risk for non-reductive physicalism is that the non-competing or non-dualist role it assigns to mental ascriptions is so thin that we have a sort of genteel eliminativism.

2. If a non-reductionist physicalism is to be interesting, both mental and physical truths should be counted as true in a *realist* sense, that is, independently of ascribers' verifications, and not consisting just in successful systematizing. Evidently if physical truths are taken in a realist sense and mental truths some other way, the latter are second string; and the reverse asymmetry would not be physicalist. Suppose we have across-the-board anti-realism. Then, faced with the failure of

reduction, but given the ideal instrumental success of mental explanation, we might simply acknowledge two instrumentally successful systems—the physical sciences and ordinary psychological explanation—with each constituting facts at its own level of description. Naturally anti-realism does not rule out motivations for seeking unified science, and if the mental does not fit in with the rest of science that would count as a significant discovery. But suppose the mental does not fit in, that there is no reduction. Given anti-realism it is difficult to see this as threatening a problematic metaphysical dualism that requires metaphysical countermeasures, say nominalism or non-reductive supervenience. Across-the-board anti-realism could even be seen as a non-reductive dissolution of the mind–body problem, removing a picture that is problematically dualist only given realism. But it would not be a physicalist solution, and it would make physicalist proposals such as nominalist ontological physicalism and non-reductive supervenience beside the point. So a realist sense of both mental and physical truths is essential to motivating non-reductive physicalism.

3. A non-reductive position is genuinely physicalist only if mental properties are allowed *no independent causal powers*; otherwise we have a kind of causal dualism. A sort of minimal physicalism may be characterized in a non-arbitrary, non-question-begging sense thus: no non-physical properties or resemblances make a causal difference. The matter is complicated by epiphenomenalism: epiphenomenalist mental resemblances are intuitively as incompatible with a well-motivated physicalism as causally potent irreducible mental resemblances. (Why should impotence make you metaphysically unobjectionable?) Of course the condition of no independent causal powers is intended merely as a necessary condition of a successful non-reductionist physicalism. But it can be strengthened. Count a property or resemblance as epiphenomenal in an objectionable sense if, while it does not make a causal difference, there is nothing incoherent in the idea of its doing so, or, a somewhat different idea, it could (does in another possible world) make a causal difference. So unreduced mental resemblances meet our strengthened condition only if it makes no sense to regard them as having independent causal powers. The delicate question then is how and whether nominalism, or

non-reductive supervenience, permits this condition to be met without making mental resemblances second-string affairs.

4. Objective mental resemblances—the realist satisfaction conditions of mental predicates—must be *naturalized*, that is, shown to belong to the natural order, and a non-reductive sense must be given to this. For the conjunction of non-reduction with realism about those satisfaction conditions is prima facie tantamount to classical property dualism, and the burden apparently lies with the non-reductive physicalist to counter this perception and to naturalize the mental.

Condition (4) may well seem necessary and sufficient for blocking problematic dualism, so that (3) need not be mentioned as a distinct constraint, on the grounds that if the satisfaction conditions of mental predicates are part of the natural order their causal powers are natural and hence not independent. But it is worth stating (3) separately, for these reasons. (*a*) There may be a temptation to assert supervenience, thus purporting to meet condition (4), but then to tell a story about the explanatory role of the mental (see below on autonomous explanation) that despite the assertion of supervenience seems to endow mental properties with independent causal explanatory powers. (*b*) Suppose one is sceptical of supervenience because of its reliance on modal notions. Then denying problematic dualism may consist in denying that mental properties have or could have independent causal powers. (*c*) Schiffer addresses what is in effect condition (3) as the main issue, putting the naturalizing of mental predicates somewhat on the margin of discussion (its most salient form being non-reductive supervenience).

As we noted earlier, the principal motivation for Schiffer's nominalist ontological physicalist position is that unreduced mental properties, in the Platonistic sense, generate an unbelievable causal overdetermination of behaviour. These properties 'are objects . . . that have causal powers, but ones that are utterly superfluous, adding nothing to the causal powers of physical properties that suffice to govern physical events'.[2] The first question I wish to pose about Schiffer's position is whether nominalism—the elimination of Platonistic mental

<hr />

[2] 'Physicalism', p. 158.

properties—blocks causal overdetermination in the sense that violates condition (3), *given* that there is causal overdetermination without nominalism.

Objective resemblances, or realist satisfaction conditions, apparently are easily generated from Schiffer's pleonastic properties. For any pleonastic mental property M and any person x, we can say that it is verification-independent whether x is M, that is, that x's being M is not constituted by its verifiability by us. And if M is univocally true of x and of y, we then ought to be able to speak, again in pleonastic mode, of its being verification-independent that a certain objective mental resemblance, being M, holds between x and y. So if we have pleonastic properties for the taking, we also have a non-Platonistic sense of objective or realist resemblances. There are then two senses of 'realism about properties': (*a*) quantification into predicate positions makes sense 'objectually'; and (*b*) the question whether a given object has a certain perhaps pleonastic property is verification-independently true or false. In denying realism about properties in the Platonistic sense Schiffer is not on the surface of his words denying realism in the latter sense.

Now it could be said that realism about properties in the second sense amounts to Platonism. But if nominalism is not compatible with objective mental resemblances a non-reductive physicalist position that depends on it fails to meet condition (1). If on the other hand they are compatible, overdetermination looms. Do irreducible objective mental resemblances (pleonastic sense) make an independent causal difference? It can hardly be said that it is only on a Platonistic view of properties that the question of making an independent causal difference arises. For what does that leave intact of the causal role of *physical* resemblances? If we say the difference is that in the case of the physical there are non-pleonastic physical properties that do the causing, then we not only depart from Schiffer's fully nominalist account, but also give mental ascriptions a second-string status, with the noted obliquely eliminative upshot.

If mental resemblances are there independent of our ascriptions and verifications, then, however 'pleonastic' our conception of them, they are out there, they are not physical, and they causally matter. Prima facie this looks like overdetermination in the problematic sense. This is not to deny that the appearance can be deflected, perhaps by some account of supervenient causation, on which more below. The point is simply that if there is a prima-facie problem of overdetermination without nominalism, then there is one with it, provided of course that nominalism is compatible with a realist view of mental resemblances and does not cast them in a second-string role.

But there is another way in which nominalism may be intended by Schiffer to block overdetermination. At points he adopts somewhat deflationary language about mental explanation, that is by comparison with physical explanation, and he takes nominalism to motivate that deflationary language. In a nominalistic world, Schiffer writes, 'there are no nonpleonastic propositional-attitude properties but only our cognitive and linguistic propositional-attitude *practices*'. He goes on to say 'and they [those practices] are anything but superfluous. Just think of all the ways we'd be worse off without them.'[3] To repeat my earlier characterization of his view, the *conceptual roles* of my mental ascriptions to x are related non-accidentally to x's underlying physical workings in such a way that predictions of x's behaviour based on my mental ascriptions mesh with the output of x's physical workings. Nominalism motivates this, it seems, because if mental predicates do not stand for Platonistic properties then all that remains is their conceptual role. But that strongly suggests that mental causal explanation is entirely a matter of the conceptual role of the ascriber's predications, which on the face of it is not compatible with realism about the mental.

We have on our hands not just the conceptual roles of mental predicates, but also verification-independent mental resemblances (pleonastic sense). Even if the required quantification is merely non-objectual, the verification-independence of mental resemblances gives them a solid standing in fact apart from the conceptual roles of their ascriptions. And the question is why that does not mean: (*a*) verification-independent mental resemblances (satisfaction conditions, pleonastic properties); (*b*) verification-independent physical resemblances; (*c*) given common sense, causal roles for each;

---

[3] Ibid.

and (*d*) given non-reduction, independent causal roles for mental resemblances, that is, short of some adjustment apart from nominalism. This is the prima-facie situation.

2. NON-REDUCTIVE SUPERVENIENCE

A non-reductionist physicalist view cannot avoid endorsing the *supervenience* of the mental on the physical, even ·given nominalism. This is physicalism at its minimum: with or without reduction, mental resemblances cannot vary independently of physical facts. But ontological physicalism and nominalism do not entail supervenience, and so it must be an added component of Schiffer's non-reductive physicalism. How else to naturalize the mental? The question then is whether nominalism is essential, why non-reductive supervenience is not all the physicalism anyone needs. A possible answer, constructed from separate things Schiffer says, is this. He endorses supervenience but he rejects as obscurantist non-reductive supervenience between non-pleonastic properties. He accepts supervenience for *pleonastic* mental facts (somewhat tentatively): in every world in which the physical facts are as they actually are, so are the pleonastic mental facts. This avoids obscurantism because on a pleonastic view supervenience involves just the *conceptual roles* of mental ascriptions (the very move that was intended to deflect problematic causal over-determination). Given nominalism, supervenience is not a relation between language-independent properties, but is a conceptual relation. So, on this construction, the function of nominalism in non-reductive physicalism is to make sense of supervenience.

Now I do not think nominalism succeeds in this, nor, more generally, that non-reductive supervenience is a promising account of the mental. Let us begin with supervenience between full-blooded non-pleonastic properties and then extend the point to pleonastic properties. Suppose it is held that *x* and *y* cannot differ in their aesthetic properties without differing in their natural properties, even though aesthetic properties are not natural properties. This of course is silent about how narrowly individuated are the subvening natural properties: if

x and y differ in their aesthetic properties must they differ in their *sensible* properties? Or, at the opposite extreme, might any Cambridge property of x and y be relevant? No matter. If x has aesthetic property F it has some natural property or set of natural properties G such that whatever is G in any possible world is also F. This is not a determinable–determinate relation, for determinables of natural properties are themselves natural properties. Supervening properties ride on the backs of natural properties; and one straightforward picture is that supervening properties are higher-order properties.[4] The aesthetic property F of individuals is the having of some natural property G that, in every possible world, has the non-natural aesthetic property of properties F^*. Elegance is non-reductively supervenient if it consists in having natural properties that are (essentially and non-naturally) elegant*, for then a thing's elegance is metaphysically determined by, but not identical with, its natural properties.

Let this serve as the official model. In its terms we can see that non-reductive supervenience purports to combine factors that drive in opposite directions; intuitions swing from one unacceptable extreme to another. Here is one. Invoking supervenience is meant intuitively to *naturalize* mental properties, that is, to show that non-reduction fits a naturalistic view of the world. But if the higher-order property picture is apt, supervenience no more intuitively brings mental properties into the natural order than it does Moore's ethical properties. 'The physical determines the mental' is misleading. This sense of 'determines' is weak enough that even on Moore's account the natural determines the ethical; for if elegance* is an essential property of a natural property, then necessarily whatever has that natural property is elegant. But Moore's view of aesthetic or ethical properties is determinedly not naturalistic, and does not purport to bring them into the natural order. Why should intuition be different regarding the mental? Now to the other extreme. In reaction it may be said that Moore's diagnosis was confused. A relevant higher-order ethical or mental property is *of the essence of* the subvening natural or physical property, for the latter has the former in all possible worlds, and thus the

---

[4] As Hilary Putnam suggested to me in conversation.

ethical or mental property is naturalized, indeed is a natural or physical property. Now this seems both correct and self-defeating. Correct, for how to make sense of a property's being of the essence of physical properties and yet not physical—that is, not even in the broad sense in which temporal, causal, and numerical properties are physical? Self-defeating, because the non-reductive point is that an ethical or mental property is not a natural or physical property. (No doubt some diehard will distinguish physical₁ and physical₂ properties.) The upshot as it appears to me is this: to the extent that non-reduction—'mental properties are not physical properties'—is the leading idea, the non-naturalizing Moore picture dominates, and to the extent that mental properties are seen to flow from the essence of the physical, non-reduction is contradicted.

The difficulty is compounded. A straight thesis of non-reductive supervenience leaves it open that mental properties supervene also on non-physical properties (first-order non-physical properties, unrealized in the actual world). Now, that is quite different from *functional* properties' being realized by non-physical states. For functional properties involve (in addition to physical input or output) only topic-neutral categorical factors—time, causation, number—that are counted as physical, and if mental properties involve merely such factors the question of non-reductive supervenience does not arise. So we have this choice: either accept that mental states are of the essence both of some physical and of some non-physical states and yet are not topic-neutral in any way we understand; or impose the constraint that mental states supervene only on physical states. The former I take not only to be mystifying but also to reinforce considerably the difficulty of seeing how supervenience naturalizes the mental; and the latter reinforces the puzzle how mental properties can be of the essence of physical properties without being physical properties.

The question is whether nominalism helps with these problems. Does the trouble stem from taking properties too seriously? As earlier noted, a realist perspective on pleonastic properties makes them language-independent in the sense that their realization is verification- or theory-independent. A light construal of predicate quantification should not undercut a realist commitment to what predicates ascribe, for otherwise we have reason to reject nominalism.[5] Nor should pleonastic properties resist higher-order predication; that would again be reason to reject nominalism, for we want to make sense of 'He practises the third oldest profession' and the like, not to speak of higher-order functional properties. So nominalism does not block those puzzling consequences of non-reductive meta-physical supervenience. And they are not an artefact of the critic's arbitrarily imposing modal formulations; non-reductive supervenience is a modal thesis without which there is no apparent distinction of non-reductive realism from dualism, no way for non-reduction to leave mental properties part of the natural order.

Schiffer's proposal to make supervenience just a matter of conceptual role then goes beyond nominalism. Indeed it can be seen as inconsistent with realism about mental properties even if nominalism is not. If a mental property M (pleonastic sense) consists in having a physical property that verification-independently is M^*, that is not just a matter of conceptual roles. On the other hand, an anti-realist or eliminative position can of course accommodate mere conceptual supervenience: if mental ascriptions have only a systematizing role, super-venience could well be just a constraint on assertability. Counting supervenience as merely conceptual does demystify it, but at the cost of anti-realism.

3. SUPERVENIENT EXPLANATION

On a non-reductionist physicalist theory mental properties ought not to be 'independent causal powers'. Nominalism does not secure that this is so, and presumably we have to look to supervenience. But the matter is delicate. It would be a poor defence of the mental against elimination that implied that mental properties do not explain behaviour. If they are to be counted as real they must presumably be capable of making a real difference: if they made no difference to behaviour and were not even the causes of apparent introspections of mental

---

[5] Or we have across-the-board anti-realism, which as I noted earlier seems to preclude interesting worries about dualism.

properties, our devotion to them would seem more theology than common sense. We had better not go too far in insisting on 'no independent causal powers'. On the other hand, if they are supervenient on the physical properties that completely causally account for behaviour but they are not identical with such properties, in what sense do they make a difference?

I assume that explanation by functional properties is, in its way, genuine explanation, and that if mental properties were functional properties the problem would be solved. Failing functional reduction, it may still be true that our best ascriptions of mental predicates are correlated *person-specifically* with physical properties, different properties for different people. Now, the idea may be, unreduced mental predicates can be taken to explain a person's behaviour in the sense of indicating that in that person there are corresponding physical (say) properties that explain his behaviour, properties that are structurally and causally related to each other and to behaviour in ways parallel to the structural and explanatory relations among mental predicates and behavioural descriptions. If mental predicates express supervenient properties, the idea then is that they explain by *pointing to* the existence of such underlying explanations.[6]

A systematic development of the idea might have the effect simply of relativizing the reference of mental predicates to individuals: M refers to physical property P in x, to Q in y, etc. But that on its own would not apparently imply objective respects in which the physical states of different people resemble each other. And so this sort of 'explanation' would not show that mental predicates stand for real unreduced supervenient properties. Suppose it is said 'We have to suppose that there are such common properties in order to capture objective psychological generalizations among people'. This is fair. But these common properties must not only generalize; they must in each person's case explain behaviour, and the current proposal is that they do so *just* by indicating physical properties that explain. I suggest that this conjunction—mental

---

[6] This perhaps bears some resemblance to Frank Jackson and Philip Pettit's proposal, although some of their examples suggest explanation in terms of functional properties (see 'Program Explanation: A General Perspective', *Analysis*, 50(2) (1990)).

predicates express properties that generalize across people and they point person-specifically to physical explanations—makes sense only if mental predicates express specific functional properties.

It is somewhat perplexing that one would care enough about the reality of mental properties to find the disjunction of reduction and elimination unacceptable, and on that account accept the not overly clear notion of unreduced supervenient properties, and yet go on to propose that the 'explanatory' role of mental properties is the foregoing totally passive one. If mental properties explain merely by pointing to what really explains, why resist the eliminativist idea that they are just manners of speaking—that what points are the predicates without the properties? Puzzling. It seems that mental properties must have some more substantive role if allegiance to them as objective resemblances is rational given the failure of reduction.

The question of the explanatory role of supervenient properties overlaps a related question about propositional attitude explanation. Consider a thought about a distant object, say Genghis Khan. And suppose that the thought itself, the current event (token), is a physical event in the brain, which causes a certain action. How is the wide content of the thought (= that brain state) related to this causal fact? Presumably the content does not explain the action in a way to which the brain state's causal relations are irrelevant; the thought's content does not, say, merely rationalize the action. If the content explains the action it explains why this thought caused this action; that is, it is an explanatorily or causally relevant property of the thought. But how can this be? How can a historical property of an event explain its current causal role?[7] One expects its causally active properties to be its current non-historical properties.

The question arises regardless of whether wide content is reducible, and it is not specifically about non-reductive super-

---

[7] It is worth noting that the 'pointing' account of supervenient explanation does not answer this question, not if the supervenient property explains by pointing to a physical property on which it supervenes. For if a mental property is wide, it supervenes on a physical property only if that property is itself wide, and the question remains how the latter explains. But if wide content 'explains' by pointing to narrow properties, then the wide content's supervenience on the physical apparently plays no explanatory role at all.

venience. But a certain current answer to the question, proposed by several writers, seems also relevant to supervenience
and is worth looking at in that connection.

The idea is to explain explanation counterfactually. The
wide, or supervenient, properties of our current brain states
make a counterfactual difference to what their effects are, and
this is said to amount to an explanatory difference.[8] Half of
the analysis is this: if the thought had not had that wide
content, had it not been about Genghis Khan, it would not
have caused that action, say the utterance of 'Genghis Khan
was a great horseman'. The other half introduces counterfactual
sufficiency: if a thought with that wide property were in
those circumstances to occur, it would cause that action. This
roughly is LePore and Loewer's suggestion.[9] (The truth of the
antecedent and the consequent should not conjointly entail this
latter counterfactual, as happens on some accounts.) Schiffer
puts a different second condition on the explanatory role of
wide contents, to secure sufficiency: their ascriptions should
systematically predict actions.[10]

The relation between counterfactuals and causal explanation
is notoriously controversial, but I do not see these conditions
as yielding explanation of any sort. They may imply that wide
contents make a difference, but, as Kent Bach put it to me, the
difference they make may be merely a correlational difference.
Now, it will be conceded on all sides that a thought causes
what it causes primarily because of its internal physical features. Suppose there are person-specific systematic compositional associations of wide content with neural features, and
that, in a given case, if no state with certain neural features had
occurred no other state whose neural features were correlated
with the same wide content would have occurred. It appears
obvious that this mere correlational fact does not imply that
either the state's neural features or its causal consequences are
explained by its wide content. But the correlational fact does
imply in a sense that if that state had not had that wide

---

[8] See E. LePore and B. Loewer, 'More on Making Mind Matter', *Philosophical
Topics*, 1 (Spring 1989); S. Schiffer, 'Ceteris Paribus Laws', *Mind* (Jan. 1991);
T. Horgan, 'Mental Quasation', in Tomberlin (ed.), *Philosophical Perspectives*, 3.
[9] 'More on Making Mind Matter'.
[10] 'Ceteris Paribus Laws'.

content, it would not have been true that it had those neural features, perhaps not even true that it occurred, and thus not true that it had those behavioural effects. This resembles 'back-tracking' counterfactuals. If proponents of a counterfactual account of explanation required counterfactuals that are not merely correlational or backtracking, why would that not exclude the counterfactuals that relate wide content and be-haviour? At the very least it begs the question. The point applies also to the counterfactual sufficiency of wide content for behaviour, and also to its predictive role. Mere counter-factuals do not explain, unless one stipulates that they are not merely correlational, which begs the question.

If these counterfactuals do not mean that wide content ex-plains a thought's behavioural effects, then presumably similar counterfactuals, for similar reasons, do not show that unreduced supervenient intentional properties are explanatory, even if the putative supervenient properties involve, say, only some sort of non-wide content. We appear to have seen that if counter-factuals connect content (wide or narrow) or other supervenient properties to behaviour, merely by virtue of some projectible mapping of contents or other supervenient properties to neural states that causally explain the behaviour, then those counter-factuals do not thereby yield an explanation of behaviour in terms of the correlated content or supervenient properties. We might note that it would not in itself be fatal to wide properties' reality that they do not explain behaviour, for that is compatible with their being reduced in some other connec-tion. But one may well wonder about unreduced supervenient properties, how real they can be if they do not in some real way explain.

It may seem that the argument proves too much. Surely we want statements such as 'He said it because he thinks that Genghis Khan was a great horseman' to be assertable. Granted. But this does not mean that we thereby assert that wide con-tents in some sense explain actions. In general, the property an explanation explicitly mentions may be extrinsic to the implied explanation: 'The man became ill because he drank some green stuff'. Ascriptions of such extrinsic properties can be explana-tory because they implicitly indicate (in varying degrees of definiteness depending on contextual background information) further properties that are intrinsically causally explanatory. And we can in fact see propositional attitude explanation as extrinsic, as purporting to point contextually to internal intentional mental factors of the belief—aspects of how a thought conceives things, modes of presentation—that are straightforwardly causally explanatory. There is no guarantee of course that such internal properties are reducible to physical or functional properties. But reasons for being sceptical that they are reducible appear to me far less impressive than reasons to be sceptical of the reduction of wide content properties.[11]

Suppose then that internal intentional properties are reducible, and that propositional attitude properties have only an extrinsic role in explanation. We may then take a relaxed view of the status of 'that' clause ascriptions if they resist physicalist reduction. If they explain extrinsically by pointing to real internal intentional mental factors, it does not matter to the reality of intentional explanation whether propositional attitude ascriptions themselves are literally true or are second string,[12] for the internal intentional factors do the real explaining and their prospects for reduction have (in my view) not seriously been challenged.[13] So an argument for non-reductive supervenience would then fail, if it holds that unless propositional attitude ascriptions are literally true there are no correct commonsense mental explanations. On the other hand, suppose that internal content cannot be made sense of, or that if it can it is not reducible. Whether we then would have reason to regard wide or narrow intentional properties as really out there, supervening on the physical, is the next topic.

4. A PRIORI REASONS FOR SUPERVENIENCE

There are subject-matters in which supervenience without reduction appears well motivated. Consider the totality of *social*

---

[11] For the latter, see Schiffer's *Remnants of Meaning*.

[12] Though of course it will matter to the reality of truth conditions and reference, not to be lightly abandoned.

[13] A bold remark. But the objection to the reduction of propositional attitude ascriptions that I find most compelling is simply that all promising proposals appear refutable. I do not think the same is true of (see below) demonstrative–introspective reductions of internal mental factors. And I do not find

facts, about language, conventions, law, money. Let the non-social facts include facts about individual psychology, physiology, and causal relations that are specifiable independently of social facts. Conceiving pairs of situations in which the social facts but no non-social facts differ is not easy. Apparently it is not conceivable that 'dog' means something other than dog even though our society is in all non-social respects as it actually is, with people saying 'dog' in response to dogs in the same non-socially described circumstances as we do, with sensory and functional internal states associated with 'dog' the same as ours, and so on. Then apparently it is a priori that social facts supervene on non-social facts. And it would be brave to assert that there exists a reduction of social facts to non-social facts, that socially constituted resemblances are identical with physical or physical–functional resemblances.

The moral is not that metaphysical supervenience without reduction makes sense. For that ignores the live philosophical option of taking social facts to be second-string facts. One interpretation of the case is that here again we have mere conceptual supervenience, the sort of thing a non-cognitivist about moral properties might hold, that there is a supervenience of *acceptable ascriptions* of moral or social predicates on the natural or non-social facts.[14] Metaphysical questions about supervenience and findings of obscurantism are avoided because that proposal would be deflationary about moral or social facts. Granted that it is counter-intuitive to relegate social facts to second-string status. Still, we have not seen reason to suppose that supervenience rescues the social from this fate, for we have not seen reason to suppose that there is a coherent notion of metaphysical supervenience without reduction. It is hardly obvious that one saves common sense by appeal to such a relation.

The point can be made independently of the coherence of non-reductive metaphysical supervenience. Consider a latter-day behaviourist position, one that is non-reductive, that is, does not count each mental predicate as standing for a distinct

compelling a priori objections to the reduction of intentionality that are based say on the alleged normative status of content.

[14] Of course the *point* of moral discourse and of systematizing social discourse is substantially different.

behavioural–environmental property. It holds merely that the totality of the behavioural–environmental facts determine all mental facts, and in familiar behaviourist style holds this a priori. This means rejecting the conceivability of inverted spectra, of radically dissimulable thoughts and feelings, etc. The question is the resultant status of mental facts, whether they survive with a first-string status. Is the a priori supervenience of mental facts on the behavioural–environmental facts more than notionally different from an anti-realist position on which mental ascriptions merely conceptually supervene on the physical facts and have no claim to truth beyond their systematizing the behavioural–environmental facts? It is hard to see how there can be a real difference. And if the a priori supervenience of the social on the non-social is parallel, if that is the strongest assertable dependence of the social on the non-social, then we ought to regard the truth of statements ascribing social properties as consisting in their systematizing the non-social facts.

It might appear that this is all to the good, that not only does it elucidate a *reason* for holding certain statements to supervene non-reductively on a certain totality of facts (it being the point of mental and social concepts to organize those facts), but it also makes metaphysical supervenience unmysterious. If the social facts are constituted by their successfully systematizing the non-social facts, we then have supervenience without reduction. And this is not anti-realist in a verificationist sense; for the fact that certain statements systematize certain verification-independent facts may itself be verification-independent.

There are two sorts of systematizing. If statements of a certain class have non-systematizing truth conditions (say statements about conscious thoughts and feelings), an eliminativist or sceptical attitude toward them is compatible with acknowledging their systematizing capabilities, in an instrumentalist spirit. Successful systematizing in this case does not secure truth, and so the position is eliminativist, assigning a straightforwardly second-string status to the 'truth' of such statements. But as regards statements whose *semantic point* is systematizing, things are not so clear. Given their marked contrast, though, with statements that have non-systematizing truth conditions (say from chemistry), regarding their truth as second string, in this case constitutionally so, appears reasonable. If asked whether a social or mental predicate (given a priori supervenience) stands for an objective resemblance, I would not know what to say, except perhaps that the question is idle: social and mental ascriptions would supervene conceptually on the non-social and the behavioural–environmental and nothing seems to be gained by saying that that is anything more than mere conceptual supervenience.

5. A POSTERIORI REASONS FOR SUPERVENIENCE

But is it a priori that mental facts supervene on physical facts? It takes a large dose of either functionalism or Wittgensteinianism to accept that for sensations. Nothing seems easier than to conceive the phenomenal facts varying while the physical– functional facts are the same. (Not that this epistemic point implies anything interesting about the nature of sensations.) But the concern of many proponents of non-reductive supervenience is with propositional attitudes, with content-bearing states, and not sensations. A possible view is that there is an a priori supervenience of propositional-attitude ascriptions on behaviour and external relations. But should we ignore *conscious thoughts*? These are content-bearing states with prima facie intentional properties that can be conceived in the Cartesian way as varying even while the physical facts stay the same. This is bound to be conceptually coherent if internal conscious factors play an essential role at some level of thought individuation. Dualism could not have been so successfully entertained if the intentional in general supervenes a priori on behaviour and external relations.

If that is granted, then there have to be a posteriori reasons for holding that there are mental properties that non-reductively supervene on the physical. It is instructive to compare a posteriori reasons for reduction. Simplify for the moment, by supposing that non-reductive supervenience is an incoherent idea, so that physicalism is necessarily reductive. Now a distaste for dualism and eliminativism would provide merely a reason to seek reduction and not a reason to hold it can be found. There are, of course, indirect empirical reasons

for physicalism and against dualism. But given physicalism
(and the provisionally assumed incoherence of non-reductive
supervenience) the only empirical reasons for rejecting elimination would be empirical reasons for reduction. If you dig
your feet in and say there could be no good empirical reason
for the eliminative position, then presumably you will allow
that there could be empirical reasons to give up physicalism.
But if you say there could be no empirical reason to give up
either, and assert reduction despite the non-existence of empirical reasons, then (given that supervenience is not a priori) I
doubt you hold a rational position.

Reverse the roles of non-reductive supervenience and reduction. Suppose we reject both reduction and a priori supervenience. If there is no empirical reason to assert that there are
unreduced supervenient mental properties, then continuing
both to accept physicalism and to reject elimination is not
rational. If the reason for denying that there could be empirical
evidence for elimination is that normal human behaviour
makes it inconceivable that humans lack mental states, the
position reverts to a priori supervenience. If on the other hand
one rejects elimination on introspective grounds, then the
absence of further empirical grounds for taking the introspected
properties to be supervenient is a reason to entertain dualism.

Thus asserting non-reductive mental–physical supervenience requires non-trivial a posteriori reasons, this by
contrast with the usual reliance on right thinking; you cannot
simply assert that non-a priori supervenience holds because
you want to endorse physicalism and to reject elimination.
Now it is useful to consider what those reasons might be in the
light of potential empirical reasons for asserting reduction.
Speaking very roughly, there are two kinds of a posteriori
reason for which one might assert reduction—as we might call
them *demonstrative–introspective* and *functional–explanatory*. Regarding the first, suppose we accept introspective phenomenal
concepts as legitimate despite Wittgensteinian objections,
and take them to be recognitional concepts, so that conceptions of toothache have the form 'feeling of that sort'—type-
demonstratives, as we might say. If it is discovered that our
ascriptions of such concepts correspond projectibly to properties
of the brain, then we may regard them as discriminating those

properties, as pointing demonstratively, and hence as referring to them.[15] Would there be empirical reason to take them to discriminate physical properties directly, rather than indirectly via the discrimination of non-physical phenomenal qualities with which those physical properties are correlated? The answer is yes, in this sense: there would be no empirical reason to think there are any such non-physical qualities and plenty of empirical reason to regard all our properties as physical (putting aside dubious conceptual arguments for dualism).

Suppose instead that phenomenal concepts do not discriminate physical–functional properties. Then they discriminate unreduced supervenient properties, or non-supervenient (dualist) properties, or no objective repeatables at all. Might there be empirical reasons to assert supervenience? In the reductive case we envisaged that phenomenal concepts discriminate physical properties to which we have *independent* scientific access. But there is no independent access to unreduced supervenient properties, and so the epistemological situation would be importantly different, presumably requiring a blind inference-to-the-best-explanation to unreduced supervenient properties, perhaps along the following lines. 'Something must explain our inclination to use a given range of concepts as if in discrimination of a real repeatable; the best explanation is that there are genuine repeatables there. And independent empirical reasons for physicalism warrant holding that this something is supervenient rather than non-supervenient (i.e. dualist), namely precisely those independent reasons that the reductionist relies on in the above argument against mediating dualist properties.'

Consider another possible empirical reason for reduction, *functional–explanatory* we can call it, and then its non-reductive-supervenience counterpart. Suppose the systematic success of causal explanations in terms of mental states is explained by a system of physical properties that yield explanations of the same behaviour, systematically parallel to the mental explanations—that is, some one-to-one assignment of mental to physical properties (or to small sets thereof) preserves causal explanatory adequacy. Mental properties are then identified with the corresponding physical properties, and we have physical reduction. This matching of explanatory structures does not appear to me to require laws, even *ceteris paribus* laws, and so would differ from classical reduction.[16] What is essential is a systematic matching of causal explanations (which do not presuppose laws couched in mental terms). Think of good mental causal explanations as systematically *reflecting* underlying physical causal explanations.[17] In confirming this reductive situation we again have independent scientific access to the physical properties with which we identify the mental properties that systematically reflect them.

But suppose instead that no such systematic matching of mental and physical properties turns up. To justify unreduced supervenient properties we are again led to a blind inference to the best explanation, this time an inference from the success of these explanatory patterns to the causal role of properties to which we have no independent access. This, let us suppose, is preferred to the hypothesis of dualist properties on the same grounds as above, namely, 'independent empirical reasons for physicalism'.

Thus we have two very similar arguments, each offering itself as an a posteriori reason for non-reductive supervenience, corresponding to the two a posteriori reasons that could exist (but that we are supposing do not exist) for physical-reduction. They assume that either our inclinations to make phenomenal discriminations, or the success of third-person mental explanation, constitutes a prima-facie reason to infer, as their best explanation, the reality of mental properties. That proposition is then coupled with independently empirically established non-

[16] For a version that invokes laws, see H. Field, 'Physicalism', in J. Earman (ed.), *Empiricism, Explanation and Philosophy of Science* (Berkeley, Calif.: University of California Press, 1991). For a telling attack on *ceteris paribus* laws see Schiffer, *'Ceteris Paribus* Laws'.

[17] If you think of mental explanations in terms of 'that' clauses, this conception of reduction may appear implausible. But if you think of mental explanations in terms of projectively ascribed modes of presentation or ways of conceiving things, then it is not at all implausible in my view. I know of no current good objections to the idea that introspective ways of individuating thoughts systematically capture physical–functional properties of the brain. On this way of conceiving our conceptions of mental content, the two styles of reduction may well converge.

reduction and physicalism to give us a complex a posteriori argument for unreduced supervenient mental properties. But there is an obvious soft spot in the argument, for adding physicalism and non-reduction to the prima-facie assumption of best explanation may well undercut its prima-facie plausibility. Granted that explanatory success, and inclinations to make phenomenal discriminations, each provide prima facie abductive reason to suppose that mental properties are real. Unless, however, we have an independent reason to take unreduced supervenient properties seriously, physicalism conjoined with non-reduction could instead give us strong reason to suppose that the success of mental explanation can be *explained away* in physical terms.

It may be suggested that there is independent reason to take unreduced supervenient properties seriously in the success of special sciences, say biology, thus strengthening the above argument. But there is a well-known, and indeed quite reasonable, alternative attitude to biology: if no physical–functional properties correspond reductively to biological predicates, the latter lack reference and are of instrumental import only, and we can expect biology to revise itself accordingly. Of course this makes sense only if those biological predicates have a revisable role. But suppose they are so persuasively projectible that no one who both has a feel for science and is not a village eliminativist would regard them as not standing for real properties and relations. This is how Jerry Fodor sees the special sciences—they contain *ceteris paribus* laws that any non-extremist must see as both unreducible and true.[18]

But is this an argument for unreduced supervenient properties? Let us divide the discussion into two cases, assuming with the argument that reduction fails: there is an explanation of the projectible systematizing success of those laws in physical terms, or there is no such explanation. In the former case, we have then explained the apparent truth of those laws without the hypothesis that they refer to unreduced objective properties. Fodor says that without special science laws we 'lose generalizations', that is, over creatures that physically

[18] See e.g. 'More on Making Mind Matter', *Philosophical Topics*, 17(1) (Spring 1989).

differ but of whom the laws apparently hold. This could suggest that the laws' predicates stand for functional properties that are multiply realized, but that would mean functional reduction. If the general application of special science laws has a physical explanation that does not yield physical or functional reduction, then there is no inference-to-the-best-explanation to unreduced supervening properties: the best explanation of the systematizing and generalizing success of those laws lies in the straight physical facts.

Suppose that the physical facts imply the projectibility of special science laws, but that they do not explain them in some pragmatic or epistemic sense of 'explain'—they don't explain them for us. That a computer could derive the projectibility of those laws from physical fact and theory, it may be said, does not mean that there is a physical *explanation* of those laws' success. The underlying physical facts may be too unwieldy, too diffusely related to special science laws to explain, for us, what the latter explain. If anything is to explain what they purport to explain, the special sciences themselves then have to be counted true. Now this appears a somewhat anti-realist understanding of 'inference to the best explanation'. It is hard to see how, on a realist view, the limitations of our knowledge and intelligence could be an empirical reason to hold that there are, out there, certain biological or other properties. And, as I earlier suggested, an anti-realist understanding of these matters considerably lessens the interest of non-reductive supervenience.

The remaining possibility is this: the special science's success is not explained by the physical facts even in the objective non-pragmatic sense. Now evidently this is not the situation proponents of non-reductive supervenience suppose we are in. For how are we to make sense of the special science predicates' supervening on the physical facts if the physical facts do not imply the projectible success of special science predictions? We have then, presumably, either unexplained success or a dualist explanation of it. With or without a physical explanation, one is left thinking, there cannot be a 'special science' vindication of unreduced supervenient properties.

The eliminative alternative to unreduced supervenient properties means that very fundamental common sense could be overthrown. But surely we cannot bring ourselves to doubt that our fellows have thoughts, feelings, and experiences! Now this rhetorical point ought not to be just another way of asserting the a priori supervenience of mental states on behaviour and external relations, for here we are assuming that supervenient mental properties need an inductive explanatory inference from the straight physical facts. But what then is the point? If common sense is not behaviourist, it is not easy to see how it can have an unrevisable commitment to supervenient mental properties. It might appear that unrevisability derives from introspective certainty that there are mental properties, and that this leaves it open whether they are supervenient or dualist properties. But it is difficult to see how this makes sense. If the physical facts explain (without vindicating) our introspective property-identifying tendencies, there is no empirical reason then to suppose we are discriminating unreduced supervenient properties. On the other hand if the physical facts do not explain (in the non-pragmatic sense) those tendencies, it seems that what we introspect cannot be properties that supervene on the physical facts. So if introspection were unrevisable, and if we accepted that the physical facts do not explain our introspective inclinations, we would be committed to dualist properties. Again unreduced supervenient properties lack empirical support on any supposition. They appear to be irrelevant.

10

Supervenience, Composition, and Physicalism*

David Charles

1

Physical reality is fundamental and all genuine mental states and properties are grounded in physical states and properties. The mental is dependent on the physical, but the physical is not dependent on the mental. In this way, the physical determines the mental.

These ideas are a commonplace in a central contemporary tradition in the philosophy of mind. They express (at least part of) the 'physicalist' preference for the *physical* as (in some sense) more basic than the *mental*. For physicalists, the major difficulty has been to make this set of ideas precise without undermining their initial plausibility. In the recent past, philosophers beginning from this starting-point have been led to propose accounts of mental phenomena which have proved difficult to defend in detail. One such account is the type identity thesis of the mental and the physical; another is analytical functionalism.

Donald Davidson gave these ideas new significance and distinctive content within his account of psychological explanation and its physical basis. In his writings he sought to support the conviction that the mental is dependent on the physical, while

* An earlier version of this paper was read at the Bradford Workshop on Reductionism in September 1988. I am very much indebted to helpful discussions with participants at that conference, and also with Justin Broackes, Bill Brewer, John Campbell, Quassim Cassam, Bill Child, Adrian Cussins, Kathleen Lennon, Brian Loar, Michael Martin, Helen Steward, and especially Timothy Williamson. Several of the ideas in this paper derive from reflecting on Aristotle's strategy in *de Anima*; but many classical scholars would be reluctant to regard the results as Aristotelian

at the same time holding that the mental need not, and indeed should not, be reductively defined in terms of the physical or the functional. He wrote concerning this type of dependency:

mental characteristics are supervenient on physical characteristics. Such supervenience might be taken to mean that there cannot be two events alike in all physical respects but differing in some mental respect, or that an object cannot alter in some mental respect without altering in some physical respect. Supervenience of this kind does not entail reducibility through law or definition.[1]

Davidson's proposal generated much interest in, and enthusiasm for, the notion of supervenience. In discussions of the mind, value, colour, social facts, and personal identity, it was employed to capture a way in which a set of facts could be grounded in another without being reduced to them. It promised to safeguard what was worth while in physicalism while rejecting its otherwise objectionable excesses.

In the first part of this paper, I shall examine some of the developments of Davidson's initial proposal and try to indicate why I think they are not a finally satisfactory account of the dependence of the mental on the physical. In the second part I shall sketch an alternative approach which attempts to follow the same general approach. Finally, from the vantage point secured by this sketch, I shall look briefly at some recent discussions of the required dependency relation.

2

As Davidson introduced it, supervenience is a relation between mental and physical characteristics. Davidson follows Quine in preferring to talk of predicates rather than properties. But in what follows I shall employ the latter, more robustly realist, idiom, and construe the relevant characteristics as properties. Davidson, in his formulation, spoke of events, but noted that the account could also be applied to semantic or evaluative predicates true of objects. Thus one might understand Davidson's formulation thus: if two entities are indiscernible with respect to their physical properties, then they

---

[1] D. Davidson, *Essays on Actions and Events* (Oxford: Clarendon Press, 1980), 214.

are indiscernible with respect to their mental properties. And this permits a generalization. A property P supervenes on a set of a properties B if and only if when two entities are indiscernible with respect to their possession of B-properties, they are indiscernible with respect to their possession of P. This entails the further claim that Davidson also makes: a property P supervenes on a set of properties B if for every pair of objects such that P belongs to one and not the other, there is a property in B which belongs to one and not the other. For this states that if two objects are discernible with respect to their possession of P, they are discernible with respect to the set of properties B.

Both formulations exclude the possibility of two objects being indiscernible in their physical properties, but differing in their mental properties. They do not, however, require that *all* mental properties supervene on *some* physical properties. It follows from these formulations that if Cartesian souls lack all physical properties (and so are physically indistinguishable), they must all possess the same mental properties.[2] Thus, neither formulation excludes the possible existence of Cartesian souls, God, angels, or other beings with no physical properties; but each does require that they all have precisely the same thoughts, intentions, and beliefs. These claims could only generate the thesis that all our mental properties are enmattered if one added the further (no doubt, plausible) supposition that all our mental properties are properties of beings with distinguishable mental lives. By themselves, they do not sustain the standard physicalist thesis that all mental states and properties are enmattered. This is one physicalist thesis that supervenience alone cannot capture.[3]

---

[2] I assume that if objects lack all physical properties, they are indiscernible with respect to physical properties. It is noteworthy that Davidson's formulations are stronger than the claim that the occurrence of certain specific physical properties is sufficient for the occurrence of certain specific mental properties. For this latter claim would allow that there could be distinct mental properties in differing organisms without any physical properties being present.

[3] Davidson seeks to secure this further thesis by his argument for the token identity of mental and physical events. But this argument only shows that mental events are physical provided that they are causes of physical events. As such, it leaves open the possibility of certain of our mental events which are causally inert not being physical events.

This formulation is distinguishable from a further claim that Davidson also makes: 'an object cannot alter in some mental respect without altering in some physical respect'. This latter claim appears weaker. It allows that two distinct objects at the same time could possess the same physical properties but differ in mental properties. It also allows that the same object at different times could possess the same physical properties while differing in its mental properties. It does not imply that indiscernibility with respect to physical properties of two objects at a time requires indiscernibility with respect to their mental properties at that time.[4] The initial, more general, formulation appears to be the basis for the relevant *supervenience* claims used to express physicalist claims; so I will focus on this in what follows.

Davidson's formulations are clear in outline, and will provide our starting-point. Other non-equivalent formulations have been proposed, and some will be mentioned in footnotes. Davidson exercises his customary caution and restraint in employing modal notions. So, perhaps predictably, his own formulations allow several modal variants.

In one version, the relevant claim of indiscernibility holds across all possible worlds. In this version, if two entities in any distinct possible worlds are indiscernible in physical (or *B*-) properties at any time they are indiscernible in their mental (or *P*-) properties. This might be formulated for an unrestricted domain:

$$\forall x \forall y \forall w_1 \forall w_2 \forall t_1 \forall t_2 \{\forall B[B(x,w_1,t_1) \leftrightarrow B(y,w_2,t_2)]$$
$$\rightarrow \forall P[P(x,w_1,t_1) \leftrightarrow P(y,w_2,t_2)]\}$$

This formulation is designed to cover all entities, all worlds, and all times.

It stands at the opposite end of a spectrum from a far weaker claim that applies to a more restricted domain of objects, worlds, and times. One version of this might be: for some restricted domain of objects:

---

[4] These permissions could be revoked if one defined 'physical property' somewhat differently so that (1) they were indexed to times, and (2) they were indexed to objects, so that *A*'s being red at t_2 was *A*'s instantiation of a different property from *A*'s being red at t_1 or *B*'s being red at t_2. But this proposal cannot be Davidson's since it does not allow that there could be two distinct objects with indiscernible physical properties.

$$\forall x \, \forall y \, \forall w_1 \, \forall t_1 \{ \forall B[B(x,w_1,t_1) \leftrightarrow B(y,w_1,t_2)]$$
$$\rightarrow \forall P[P(x,w_1,t_1) \leftrightarrow P(y,w_1,t_2)] \}$$

This version applies to one world, one time, and a restricted domain of objects. A somewhat stronger alternative might apply to all entities in a world at any time:

$$\forall x \, \forall y \, \forall w_1 \, \forall t_1 \{ \forall B[B(x,w_1,t_1) \leftrightarrow B(y,w_1,t_1)]$$
$$\rightarrow \forall P[P(x,w_1,t_1) \leftrightarrow P(y,w_1,t_1)] \}$$

There is clearly a dense spectrum of supervenience relations between these two poles. Some are restricted to accessible possible worlds, others to a certain set of close accessible possible worlds, or to this world, or to the nearest-possible world. Others again will be more or less restricted with reference to times and domains of object. Still others might be differentiated by areas within worlds. Davidson's formulation is a 'broad church' one with very many possibilities left open.

This diversity is compounded when one considers the range of possible interpretations of the terms 'physical predicate' or 'physical property'. Quite apart from general difficulties over the notion of 'physical', the range of relevant physical properties might be restricted to non-relational physical properties, or expanded to include relational properties also. It might be limited to categorical physical properties, or to those which figure in causal regularities, or widened to admit dispositional or non-causally active properties. Equally, it might be restricted to some specific set of physical properties—for example, non-external-world-involving properties of the brain and central nervous system, or a certain narrow subset of such properties—or involve all physical properties of any type in the relevant worlds at given times.

Recognition of the wide variety of available options should lead to care and caution on the part of both proponents and critics of the 'supervenience option'. Since the proponent has many alternatives to choose from, she cannot claim to have characterized her favoured vision of 'physicalism' merely by adverting to *the* supervenience of the mental on the physical. She is required to specify which of the alternative possible formulations is most suited to the physicalist intuitions she wishes to capture. Correspondingly, the critic cannot claim to have overthrown *the* supervenience claim solely by raising difficulties for one variant of it. Without philosophical clarification of the relevant intuitions, critic and proponent are unlikely even to join in *one* debate, let alone successfully to resolve the issues at stake.

Two examples show the consequences of lack of clarity on these points. Friends of supervenience have sometimes argued that supervenience claims relativized to our world are too weak to satisfy physicalist intuitions, because they permit the possibility of there being a world like this in all physical respects but discernible in mental respects. And this seems to leave physicalist claims about our world mysterious and unbelievable. So they have concluded that one should adopt a very strong form of supervenience with no relativization at all to worlds, natural kinds, times, places, etc.[5] But this is to ignore the variety of intermediate positions available to the physicalist. She might wish to confine her claims to accessible or causally possible or near-possible worlds, or to worlds which contain natural kinds which have evolved in the way the kinds of this world have. It is a non-trivial task to determine the precise strength of the supervenience relation which best captures physicalist intuitions.

Critics of supervenience have argued that strong, non-relativized supervenience entails reduction, because it is possible to form a disjunctive property of the sum of base properties on which a mental property supervenes.[6] The disjunction may be infinite and unstructured, but there will still be a physical property (being a member of this disjunction) which will stand in a nomological biconditional with the mental property. But this objection has force only if one accepts a weak notion of 'physical property'. The property invoked may play no role in laws or causal interaction at the physical level, and hence (on one view) will not be a genuine physical property. Care over the specification of the 'physical properties' permitted pays dividends at this point. Strong supervenience does not entail reduction if one holds to a conservative, scientifically useful

    [5] See e.g. R. M. Hare, 'Supervenience', *Proceedings of the Aristotelian Society*, Supp. Vol. 58 (1984).

    [6] See J. Kim, 'Supervenience and Nomological Incommensurables', *American Philosophical Quarterly*, 15 (1978).

notion of property.[7] And even if it had done, there would have been many other forms of supervenience thesis left open once one had rejected the strongest and the weakest forms of such claims. There may be several acceptable physicalist theses which limit supervenience claims to causally possible or near-possible worlds, and so run no risk of collapsing into reductive claims.

A further example illustrates the same point. It has been claimed that Twin Earth thought experiments undermine *the* supervenience of the mental on states of the brain and central nervous system. In these thought experiments, two denizens of different possible worlds are held to have different beliefs while being in the same brain states. If such thought experiments are legitimate, they may tell against some form of supervenience claims. But not against all. They are clearly consistent with weak supervenience claims relativized to specific worlds. But they are also consistent with world-unrestricted claims in which the relevant physical states of the brain include their relational properties (e.g. being in an environment with H_2O, being in an environment with XYZ), or in some other way manifest environmental sensitivity. It is a matter of considerable philosophical difficulty to see whether these thought experiments tell against the type of supervenience relation which should be important for the defender of the claim that mental properties supervene on the physical properties of the brain.[8] It is by no means clear that the latter should maintain an unrestricted supervenience relation between mental properties and non-relational physical properties of the brain.

[7] 'Reduction' is itself said in many ways. Scientific reduction requires the presence of a scientifically useful property at the base level. Metaphysical reduction—the claim that there is nothing 'over and above' the physical—may be achieved if one has an infinite and unstructured disjunction of genuine scientific physical properties on which the mental property supervenes. On this see the Introduction, Sect. 4.

[8] Environment-dependent or world-relative supervenience relations might be justified in these cases by noting the importance of the *causally necessary* conditions for the brain being in specific conditions in, for example, W_1 or W_2. These conditions would be part of the closed physical system required to describe W_1, for example, and would be important in a full description of the causal conditions in W_1. This point need not require that in all causally possible (let alone metaphysically possible) worlds the relevant brain state is produced by this physical state.

Physicalist defenders of brain supervenience claims have to ensure that they select the specific modalized version of supervenience theses and the specific set of properties of the brain which accurately reflect their physicalist intuitions.[9]

Despite this plethora of possible positions within the supervenience family, there are grounds for believing that none of them alone adequately captures our physicalist intuitions. According to the physicalist, the mental is dependent on the physical, but the physical is not dependent on the mental. The physical underlies the mental, and is the basis for it. The indiscernibility relation which we have introduced does not capture this intuition. It states that there will be no relevant case with indiscernible physical properties and discernible mental properties. But this does not require that the mental properties be based on the physical ones. For it is consistent with this that the converse claim is also true: that for certain mental properties their indiscernibility requires indiscernibility in their subject's physical properties. This is because the proposed indiscernibility relation is, in its logic, *non-symmetric*, while the relation required to capture the thought that the physical is the basis for the mental must be *asymmetric*. And

---

[9] The indiscernibility relation sketched above is distinct from several other relations which have been invoked to characterize supervenience. Thus, for instance, supervenience is sometimes said to involve one of the following claims: (1) $\forall w \, \forall x \, [B^* \, (x,w) \rightarrow A \, (y,w)]$, where B^* is the *property* formed from the maximal set of properties involved in the indiscernibility relation. But this only follows from a strong supervenience claim if one's view of properties is so relaxed as to allow one to form properties by infinite disjunction when the property plays no role in laws at its own level. Indeed, from a more conservative viewpoint there would be reason to reject (1). (2) $\forall w \, \{\forall x [B^*(x,w) \land A \, (x,w)] \rightarrow \forall y \, (B^*y \rightarrow Ay)\}$. Again this presupposes that there is some such B^* property. (3) $\forall w \, \forall x \, [P(x,w) \rightarrow A \, (x,w)]$. In (3), P is a named specific scientific property. But this in no way follows from the indiscernibility claim. It is consistent with the truth of the indiscernibility claims given in the main text that there is no determination of named mental properties by named physical properties. There may be limited sets of such properties which determine given mental properties, but there is no requirement that this be so. For these reasons there is no direct connection between the truth of supervenience claims and the existence of physico-psychical laws linking specific mental and physical properties. Nor need there be upwards laws between total physical states and total mental properties, if supervenience is true. For there may be conditions on laws which are not met by such claims. Thus, for instance, if one thought that laws linked genuine properties, or that laws had to be graspable by us, one might accept that there were true modal claims linking the physical and the mental but deny that they were lawlike.

this the indiscernibility notion so far introduced cannot capture. The idea of the physical underlying the mental is absent
from the relations so far mentioned, as is the idea of the mental
being above (super) the physical.

One immediate response to this objection runs as follows.
To capture the relevant asymmetry we should merely add an
additional clause. The initial indiscernibility relation stated that
if two objects were indiscernible with respect to their physical
properties, they were indiscernible with respect to their mental
properties. One might add to this: and not necessarily vice
versa. This would allow the possibility of there being two objects indiscernible with respect to their mental properties, but
not indiscernible with respect to their physical properties. In
effect this would guarantee a logically one-way indiscernibility
relation: if physically indiscernible, mentally indiscernible, and
not necessarily vice versa.

This certainly states an asymmetry between the physical
and the mental, but does not adequately capture the core
physicalist idea of the mental being based on the physical. The
latter requires some form of *primacy* for the physical over the
mental. But this primacy could still be found where distinct
properties modally required the existence of each other. Thus,
if a modal biconditional were established between pain and C-
fibre stimulation, for example, this would be consistent with
the physicalist claim that pain was dependent on, or composed
of, C-fibre stimulation, and not vice versa. Indeed, physicalists
have often aimed to establish precisely these biconditional
relations to capture their intuitions. It would be paradoxical if
success here would have undermined the intuitions it was
intended to support.[10]

There seem to be at least two physicalist claims at work here.
The first is that physical properties are explanatorily prior or

---

[10] I found after developing this line of thought in the Bradford Workshop on
Reductionism (September 1988) that J. Kim has independently deployed a
similar argument against attempts to capture the relevant dependency in terms
of supervenience in 'Supervenience as a Philosophical Concept', *Metaphilosophy*,
21 (1990), 13–15. While I have retained my own earlier formulations, I am in
agreement with Kim on this point. However, I do not accept his further
conclusion that there is no way to capture the dependency without embracing
some form of reductionism. See his 'The Myth of Non-reductive Materialism',
Proceedings of the American Philosophical Association, 3 (1989).

primary, and that mental properties are explanatorily dependent or secondary. The relation of explanatory priority appears to be stronger than the modal notions so far introduced. As Aristotle noted long ago, certain properties of the triangle necessarily require and are required by properties of the line; but the latter are primary, as it is because the line is thus and so that the triangle is thus and so and not vice versa. Thus, he held that triangles are equiangular because they are equilateral even though these two properties require each other.[11] In these cases, one set of properties can be *explanatorily* prior to another; but this priority has not been captured by invoking the modal notions so far employed.[12]

The second physicalist intuition is expressed by a certain ontological thesis: the physical is what the mental is *composed of*. The physical constitutes the basic building blocks of the universe, and everything else is *made up from* these. This intuition is distinguishable from the former. The first is more general and abstract, and is not tied to the composition relation. Further it is a major claim that what is compositionally basic is also explanatorily prior. It is one thing to claim that houses are made from bricks and mortar; it is another to claim that houses have all their relevant properties *because* of the properties of bricks and mortar. Atomists have typically taken what is compositionally prior to be explanatorily prior. But other physicalists have separated these claims, and emphasized that the principles of composition which combine the physical elements need not be derivable from basic physical science, but may be based on higher-level activities (e.g. the art of house-building).[13] Compositional priority is stronger than the rela-

---

[11] Aristotle, *Physics* 200ᵃ15–19. He held that angle properties of triangles were necessary but not essential because they were not explanatorily basic (*Metaphysics* 1025ᵃ31–3). One of Aristotle's other cases of this type of phenomenon is an appealing one. The stars twinkle because they are near rather than vice versa, even though all and only near stars twinkle (*Post. Analytics* 78ᵃ36 ff.).

[12] Classically reductionists have emphasized explanatory basicness, taking lower-level laws or properties as the basis for the derivation of higher-level laws. See the discussion of E. Nagel's view in the Introduction.

[13] Here I would include Aristotle, but this claim is controversial. For one view of Aristotle's project see my 'Aristotle on Hypothetical Necessity and Irreducibility', *Pacific Philosophical Quarterly*, 69 (1988). For an opposing interpretation, see Aryeh Kosman's 'Animals and Other Beings in Aristotle', in

tions introduced by the modal notions above. Mental states and properties (such as pain) could be composed from physical states and properties (C-fibre stimulations) even if all and only pain states were (necessarily) C-fibre stimulations. But this intuition is not captured by any supervenience claim. Nor is this asymmetry regained if one adds to the supervenience claim the view that each mental event is token-identical with some physical event. Identity by itself clearly cannot capture any asymmetry. Further, the intuition of a compositional priority would survive even if all and only mental events were token-identical with physical events, and there was no physical event which was not token-identical with some mental event. For even in such a case, for a physicalist, who accepts the compositional priority of the physical, the physical would be what the mental was composed of.

Both these sets of intuitions need refinement. It is an important task to determine which is essential for the most defensible physicalist account. However, supervenience (even as amended above) fails to capture either of them. The relations of *being explanatorily prior* and *being the ontological basis of* are stronger than the one expressed by any member of the supervenience family.

There is another way to bring this out. The supervenience option is not very discriminating in selecting the appropriate basis for the occurrence of a given mental property. Two physical situations might be indiscernible in all nomologically possible worlds because the only relevant possible way for a given base-state S (with its properties P_1, P_2) to occur is because certain specific causal antecedents (Q, R, etc.) occur. Clearly there could be situations of this type in *close* possible worlds. There would be examples in *all* possible worlds if certain necessity of origin claims could be sustained about the relevant physical states. But in each of these cases, the properties of psychological state M would be grounded in those of state S, and not also in those of the set of states (Q, R, etc.) which cause S to obtain. Similarly, state S with its properties would be the correct basis from which to explain the properties of M, and not the set of states (T, U, etc.) which S causes to obtain.

A. Gotthelf and J. Lennox (eds.), *Philosophical Issues in Aristotle's Biology* (Cambridge: Cambridge University Press, 1987).

In the same way, being H_2O would be the explanatory basis for the properties of water rather than the causes and effects of H_2O's existence. In these cases there would be a wide range of *true* supervenience claims, but only one true composition or explanatory basis claim (or at least a more restricted set of them). This is not to say, of course, that the *set* of supervenience claims (including ones which specify the properties of causes and effects) is false. But supervenience is not a sufficiently discriminating relation to select precisely those physical properties which, on the relevant occasion, underlie, either ontologically or explanatorily, the relevant psychological properties. For within the supervenience account these properties are not distinguished from others which necessarily produce them or are produced by them.

Both these points raise essentially the same problem. The reasons which lead physicalists to believe that certain supervenience claims are true appear to be more demanding and more precise than the relation they articulate through such claims. They accept that the mental supervenes on the physical because they wish to capture the *priority* of the physical in either an explanatory or ontological mode. But supervenience does not do their intuitions justice.[14] And there are reasons to doubt whether they could be captured using modal notions alone.

These arguments do not depend on the assumption that one must be able to analyse the type of necessitation involved in supervenience claims in other terms (e.g. efficient causation, logical necessity). It is consistent with these considerations that the necessitation in question be taken as a brute modal fact, provided that we have reasons to believe that the relevant necessitation claims are true. The objection is that supervenience, as we have formulated it, does not capture physi-

---

[14] There may be physicalists who would wish to reject the two physicalist intuitions I have sketched, while retaining their physicalism. For these physicalists, supervenience might appear to be the correct relation. But what grounds will they offer for believing that physicalism is true? The slogan 'the physical *determines* the mental (and not vice versa)' does not by itself either clarify the nature of the determination or command automatic assent. The difficulty for the physicalist who wishes to rely on supervenience alone is to support this slogan without using the richer notions of composition or explanatory priority.

calists' reasons for believing in the primacy of the physical over the mental.[15]

There is a second, separate reason to reject supervenience accounts as inadequate to capture physicalist intuitions. If one holds that mental states and properties are causally explanatory, one will wish to hold true a series of counterfactual and subjunctive conditional claims. For example, if one believes that John's judgement that *A is best* caused him to φ, one will wish to accept also:

(1) If John had not judged that *A is best*, John would not have φed, in cases where there is no overdetermination

and

(2) In roughly similar conditions, if John were to judge that *A is best*, John would φ.

If one accepts a weak supervenience thesis which is restricted to this world, it is clear that neither (1) nor (2) can be supported. Weak supervenience makes a claim about our actual world to the effect that in it there are no two cases indiscernible at the physical level but discernible at the psychological. Since it says nothing about near-possible worlds, it cannot support either (1) or (2). But stronger notions of supervenience are equally flawed. The most that follows from a strong supervenience claim is that if the mental properties differ from those in the actual world, there is some difference in the relevant physical properties. But it does not follow that the relevant physical properties present in nearby worlds where John does not judge that *A is best* will fail to produce the bodily movement of φing. Since this issue is left completely open, (1) is not supported.

[15] One might reply to this as follows. 'In certain cases, our reasons for believing the supervenience conditionals to be true are of a physicalist type, and these reasons allow us to select one of the set of true supervenience conditionals as the one which captures the basic physicalist intuition. If one distinguishes our grounds for believing in supervenience claims and the claims believed in, one can formulate the physicalist claim using supervenience alone.' But this reply seems unsatisfying. Why, if our physicalist intuition is stronger than the supervenience claim, formulate it in terms of supervenience? It appears that the supervenience claim is not the heart of the physicalist case, but (rather) a consequence of certain other, more demanding, physicalist intuitions.

(2) is an equally bad state. For (2) requires that if John in a near-possible world judges that *A is best*, he will be in some physical state which produces the relevant bodily movement. This demands that he cannot be in that psychological state without being in a physical token-state of a type which possesses given causal powers. But it is clear that no such claim follows from the supervenience conditionals. For they say nothing about what types of physical state John must be in, if he is in a given psychological state. This latter claim is essential to support (2); but it is not captured by any version of the supervenience claims we have considered.[16]

If this is so, no member of the supervenience family is by itself sufficient to sustain the claim that psychological properties are causally explanatory, if one also holds that there are no psychological causal powers independent of underlying physical ones. Supervenience alone cannot provide the basis to sustain the claims which are essential for the causal explanatory view of the psychological.

This second argument has a more limited target than the first. That spoke to any physicalist who accepted the existence of psychological and physical properties, and also held that the psychological was *based* on the physical. The latter is addressed only to physicalists who further maintain that psychological states and properties are causally explanatory, and that there is a complete physical account of every physical event or state.[17] There can be no physicalist position which

---

[16] This would be so if one characterized supervenience in one of the other ways mentioned above. Even if it were required that $\forall x \: \forall w \: [P(x,w) \rightarrow A \: (x,w)]$ obtained, this would not give one the material to support the subjunctive conditional (2). For this requires that one be able to sustain the claim that $\forall x \: \forall w \: [A(x,w) \rightarrow P(x,w) \lor Q(x,w) \ldots]$, where P, Q, ... are unified by their ability to sustain the causal explanatory claim embedded in (2).

[17] Some physicalists would deny that there are causally efficacious psychological properties. On one reading, Davidson takes such a view, and would not accept (1) or (2) in the version in which they demand that psychological properties are causally explanatory. However, on an alternative reading, Davidson would accept (1) and (2), allow that psychological predicates figure in genuine explanations, but deny that the relevant explanation is *lawlike*. On this latter view, Davidson would need to find a way of supporting (1) and (2) consistent with his acceptance of the completeness of the physical domain. The difficulty with Davidson's position appears to be this. The first alternative involves a high price, as (1) and (2) look plausible claims, which one would not wish to deny. But the second seems to raise just the problems which it

fails to accommodate the basic role of the physical. But there may be physicalists prepared to give up the idea that there are psychophysical causal explanations underwritten by truths at the physical level. However, for many (myself included) this concession would be too high a cost to pay to defend a version of physicalism.

If these arguments are correct, supervenience is not sufficient to capture some of our basic physicalist intuitions. Supervenience has been the ontological flagship of a substantial fleet which has wished to retain a belief in physicalism without embracing reductionism. If their destination is to be reached there must be an alternative and better route to capture the required type of dependency of the mental on the physical.

3

These reflections on supervenience serve to crystallize certain physicalist intuitions. An acceptable physicalism should capture the thought that (at least) *our* mental states are necessarily enmattered. It should also express the idea that the mental is grounded in the physical, and therefore must formulate a relevant asymmetry between the mental and the physical. Further, the physicalist should make it plausible that the truth of

(1) If John had not judged that *A is best*, he would not have φed

and

(2) In roughly similar conditions, if John were to judge that *A is best*, he would φ,

rest on the presence of certain physical states and properties (in this and relevant possible worlds).

In meeting these demands, the physicalist should offer a proper characterization of the *physical*, of the way in which the

appeared that his strategy had avoided. This dilemma is somewhat obscured in Davidson's writings by his reluctance to invoke modal notions in discussing supervenience, and his subsequent refusal to embrace either stronger or weaker versions of this relation.

mental is *grounded* in the physical, and of the *modal* strength of this grounding relation. In the previous section, we uncovered two physicalist reasons for believing that the mental is grounded in the physical. The mental is composed out of the physical. The mental is explanatorily dependent on the physical. My primary focus will be on the first of these intuitions, as this seems the weaker and more defensible of the two. My aim is to attempt to capture a grounding relation which is sufficient to capture the physicalist intuition of the compositional priority of the physical.

A first attempt at such position might run as follows. Let us focus on members of the human species. The argument proceeds as follows: all members of the human species necessarily are physical organisms, composed from physical elements. If something is physical, it is necessarily physical. So all members of the human species are necessarily physical. (In this argument and what follows, I use 'necessarily' with narrow scope.) Further it seems clear that (paradigm) members of the human species must necessarily be able to act, think, and perceive in certain ways. Thus, paradigm members of the human species must necessarily be composed from physical elements in such a way as to be able to function in these ways. Paradigm members of the human species must necessarily be composed from physical elements in such a way as to sustain (1) and (2). If this were not so, they would not be able to act appropriately as human beings.

What then is the 'physical'? Surely this cannot be defined as what is studied in present-day physics. For that will almost certainly be false or inadequate (or both). But what constrains the physics of the future? Typically, physical systems are held to be complete. But what type of complete system is a physical one? One suggestion runs as follows: physical objects are necessarily spatial. They must themselves have spatial location and magnitude. The existence of something in time which is not necessarily spatial (in this sense) would be an affront to physicalist intuition. Not everything needs to exist in time. Perhaps numbers or God do not. But, according to my physicalist, if anything exists in time, it exists necessarily in space. At the base level (if there is one) there are spatial objects without further components which necessarily have spatial magnitude. Above that, there are spatial objects necessarily made from components which have spatial magnitudes. If an object is a physical spatial object, there can be no other spatial object which occupies exactly the same spatial location at a given time, unless they both share all the same spatial parts (at that time).[18] Thus physical spatial objects exclude other physical spatial objects from occupying their location at a given time, unless they then share all spatial parts.[19] The relevant principle allows that there could be two physical objects in the same place at a given time (e.g. this statue, this quantity of bronze) providing that they share all spatial parts at that time, and exclude all spatial objects with which they do not share spatial parts.

This will be the basic notion of the 'physical' in what follows. Members of the human species are necessarily physical if they are necessarily spatial in this sense. Let us assume that individual states and processes of necessarily physical organisms are themselves necessarily physical. So, individual psychological states and processes of members of the human species are necessarily physical. Given our present characterization of the physical, this amounts to the claim that individual psychological states of members of the human species are necessarily spatial (in the way indicated).

This conception of the physical gives rise to a weak, but persuasive, form of physicalism, which rules out the metaphysical possibility that we, members of the human species (or terrestrial persons), should be in time but not be necessarily spatial. It serves to capture the necessary dependence of our psychological states on the physical, construed as the spatial. There can be no individual states of ours that are not themselves necessarily spatial. Further, the notion of the physical as the necessarily spatial underwrites the thought that the phys-

[18] On this view there can be differing conceptions of the physical as physical theories change. Thus, for example, Aristotle's potentiality-based theory would still be a theory of the physical, even though his physical theory differs from our own.

[19] On this view, ghosts would not be physical *spatial* objects if they could pass through other spatial objects (e.g. walls) without sharing any of their parts. Similarly, rainbows are not physical if spatial objects (e.g. aircraft) can pass through them without sharing their spatial parts. (The ghost in the machine would not be a physical object either!)

ical system is complete. For so understood it rests on the idea that there is *one* spatio-temporal system which can be completely characterized in spatio-temporal terms. If this is so, physical causes must have physical effects (and vice versa).[20] For if they did not, the world would not be *one* spatio-temporal system, completely characterizable in spatio-temporal terms.

This undemanding form of physicalism succeeds, where supervenience theories did not, in capturing the necessary dependence of our psychological states on the physical, and ensures that all our individual psychological states and processes are necessarily physical. Further, if terrestrial persons form a natural kind, their psychological states will be, of metaphysical necessity, physical. However, it does not capture the relevant asymmetry noted above between mental and physical properties. Nor does it ground the two explanatory claims (1) and (2) mentioned in the previous section. However, this form of physicalism is not empty. If true, it rules out substance dualism about human persons and their psychological states. And it suggests a way of making it comprehensible how individual psychological states can be physical and be related to other (non-psychological) physical states in a unified spatial system (see below).

To strengthen this physicalist claim we need to add to the characterization of the physical. For many, the physical is not merely the necessarily spatial. It is also the locus of the causal forces which operate in our unified spatio-temporal world. 'Cause' itself may be a natural kind term which picks out certain types of interaction involving energy transfer or conservation between certain spatially located phenomena. On this view, states and properties of states will be physical only if they are essentially involved in causal interactions of this type. Physical matter is necessarily spatial matter which possesses this type of property essentially. The physical (thus understood) is a closed system if all physical effects (of this type) have physical causes. And it is a complete system if physical states of this type possess all the causal powers there are.

This picture of the physical as the locus of a closed and

---

[20] This is sometimes called the principle of causal closure: every physical effect has a physical cause and every physical cause has a physical effect.

complete set of causal powers exercises a powerful grip on much contemporary physicalist thought. In what follows, I will understand by the term *core-physical* that subset of physical states and properties which figure essentially in causal laws of this type. The core-physical, so understood, is not confined to ultimate constituents or the most fundamental physical laws. It may also include higher-order physical laws, such as those relating rigid round holes and square pegs, which cut across varying basic constituents, provided that they involve the same general types of causal power as are found at the fundamental level.[21] And this will be so if, for example, they meet certain conditions on lawlikeness, or involve the same basic concepts (e.g. mass, velocity, magnitude), or are surveyable from an objective standpoint, or are true of objects made up of parts which are fundamental constituents.

If we accept this conception of the core-physical as a *closed* and *complete* system, it is natural to argue as follows. If psychological states are causally explanatory, they possess causal powers. But since all causal powers are core-physical ones, a psychological property can only be causally explanatory if it is identified with some core-physical property. If this were not so, it would be causally powerless. The relevant core-physical properties cannot be categorical, non-causal, properties of core-physical states (if psychological properties can be variably realized). So psychological properties which are causally explanatory must be identified with specific (and probably higher-order) properties of core-physical states.

Further, a psychological property can only be causally explanatory if the token-states to which it belongs possess non-accidentally the relevant core-physical causal property. If this were not so, the psychological property would not be genuinely realized, as the token-states to which it belongs would not themselves possess a relevant core-physical property. Indeed, if one further assumes that *all* physical states are states with core-physical properties, the token-state to which this psychological property belongs would not be a physical state at all. If so, either the psychological property is always

---

[21] Examples of this kind are offered by H. Putnam in *Philosophical Papers*, ii: *Mind, Language, and Reality* (Cambridge: Cambridge University Press, 1975), 29 ff.

realized by core-physical token-states, or we are committed (at least) to an unacceptable form of epiphenomenalism, if not to dualism, concerning psychological token-states.

There are two separate strands in this line of argument. It is suggested that any satisfactory physicalist view must accept that:

(3) the token-states to which causally explanatory psychological properties belong are of a type which possesses non-accidentally core-physical causal properties which figure in the core-physical causal laws;

(4) genuine psychological causal properties are to be identified with core-physical causal properties of core-physical states.

(3) requires that whenever one has a genuine causal relation at the psychological level, there is a mental state token identical with one of a type which possesses (non-accidentally) certain core-physical causal properties. This is a condition for the *genuine realization* of the relevant psychological property. (4) completes the picture, yielding extremely tight connections between causally explanatory psychological and core-physical causal properties. The only alternative to this picture (it is claimed) is some version of epiphenomenalism.

This viewpoint certainly sustains an asymmetry between core-physical properties and the rest. It also underwrites (1) and (2), the explanatory claims noted above. If humans desire to φ, this will be because desiring is being in a state which essentially possesses a given core-physical causal role. If so, the relevant psychological properties will be identified with basic causal ones. If this were not so, they could not be causally explanatory.

This viewpoint might be characterized as a weak, or sober, version of functionalism. It is weaker than classical versions of functionalism in several ways. It does not require that *all* psychological properties be identified with core-physical causal properties; only that all causally efficacious ones are. As a consequence, it does not require that all properties of pain, for example, be identified with core-physical causal ones— provided that all its causal properties are. There may be other properties (e.g. involving *qualia*) which are not identified with core-physical ones, provided that they are not causal ones. Such additional properties may be essential to pain, and hence preclude the possibility of a full functionalist definition of pain. But a sober functionalist will give up the latter more ambitious programme and hold only to (3) and (4).[22]

The immediate task is to investigate whether there is any acceptable form of physicalism which is still weaker than this. Indeed, this was precisely the goal which the supervenience theorists set themselves. If their approach is flawed (as argued in the last section) the issue is clear: can their aim be achieved by any other route? Or must all physicalists accept (at least) a weak and sober version of functionalism?

Let us begin at the token level. The psychological token-state is physical, *qua* necessarily spatial. It is still physical even if it is not identical with a token of a type which possesses certain core-physical causal properties. There may be several distinct core-physical token-states with their own causal interactions present when one psychological state occurs. Further, while each of these may be modally required (in the circumstances) if the psychological token-state is to obtain, only one (or some of them) may be needed for it to play its causal role. Token core-physical states of this type will also be necessarily spatial. There seems to be no problem in principle in understanding how a psychological token-state can be grounded in these by principles which involve only spatial organization and location. Indeed the idea of there being one spatio-temporal scheme appears to ensure that these relations at the token level are intelligible to us, without requiring that the psychological token be, for example, a whole made up of core-physical parts.

These claims do not require that the set of core-physical token-states be identical with token psychological ones. There

---

[22] Sober functionalism does not require that psychological properties be defined a priori solely in terms of their causal role. Nor does it take a view on the issue of whether causally explanatory psychological properties are to be found in common-sense or scientific psychology. Sober functionalism may be fairly described as *weak functionalism*. However, it is to be distinguished from still weaker versions of functionalism in which the functional properties with which psychological ones are identified are not core-physical causal ones, but rather those that play a role in 'a given rational architecture', for example. This latter view does not fulfil the sober functionalist's goal of making it intelligible how psychological properties are causally explanatory.

may be cases where the set has the same persistence conditions but different identity conditions from the relevant psychological token.[23] Nor do they by themselves require that the set of token core-physical states forms a unity which is itself a core-physical state instantiating a core-physical causal property.[24] The principle which collects the relevant core-physical token-states need not be a core-physical law. If (*pace* (4)) higher-order principles can be causally explanatory without being grounded in core-physical laws, one of the former could itself explain the relevant unity at the core-physical level. In this case, the relevant set of core-physical tokens would be shapeless if viewed from the perspective of core-physical theory. However, they will not be shapeless within (weak) physical theory if they form a describable spatio-temporal unity.

To reject token identity between core-physical states and psychological ones does not force us to adopt an epiphenomenalist perspective. Introducing the richer notion of the core-physical is compatible with retaining the basic notion of the physical as the necessarily spatial. There is no need to disqualify the psychological token from being physical merely because it does not itself instantiate a basic core-physical causal power. To insist on this is to impose an extremely strong, and apparently unwarranted, demand on genuine realization.

This gives the outline of a non-functionalist route to meet the first functionalist challenge (3). But it does not address the second (4). How can psychological properties be causally explanatory if they are not systematically identified with certain core-causal properties from which they derive their causal efficacy? How can one sustain the two causal explanatory claims (1) and (2) without accepting that causally explanatory psychological properties must turn out to be lower-level causal properties? If this is unavoidable, the principles and properties at the higher level must be grounded in lower-level laws and

---

[23] If, for example, they admit of different modal possibilities. Thus, a set of core-physical token-states might have sustained a different higher-order computer token-state if the former had been differently programmed.

[24] This is argued by Jennifer Hornsby in 'Physicalism, Events and Part–Whole Relations', in E. LePore and B. McLaughlin (eds.), *Actions and Events: Perspectives on the Philosophy of Donald Davidson* (Oxford: Blackwell, 1985).

properties. There will be no possibility of the relevant token unity at the core-physical level arising from the operation of a higher-level principle without there being a matching lower-level one. If so, it appears that the relevant set of core-physical states must itself be a core-physical state which is token identical with the psychological state.

One could, of course, give up these two causally explanatory claims. But an alternative runs as follows: on each occasion that psychological properties are instantiated, the relevant psychological token is a physical one in some way grounded in a set of core-physical tokens with core-physical causal powers. But this is not because the individual psychological properties turn out to be specific functional ones. It is rather because—if the terrestrial person is to succeed—the psychological properties must be instantiated *token by token* in physical states appropriately grounded in ones with the relevant core-causal powers. This, however, does not require that at the level of types and properties there be a specific set of core-physical causal properties, unified at their own level, which realize this psychological property. Terrestrial persons are physical organisms. If we are to succeed in our environment, we must be organisms sufficiently unified and robust (in the standard case) for the relevant conditionals and counterfactuals to be true. But this does not, by itself, demand that there be specific core-physical causal properties with which specific psychological properties are identified. It requires only that on *each* relevant occasion the instantiation of the psychological property be appropriately (and unproblematically) grounded in some core-physical state or states.

This suggests a way of making (1) and (2) believable without giving even the weak functionalist account of our relevant psychological properties. The route has two features. It focuses on the requirements for our being successful organisms of a given kind, rather than on the explanatory role of psychological properties considered in isolation from their respective subjects. If one follows the latter course, it will be natural to try to vindicate (1) and (2) by considering only the core-physical causal properties with which they are identified. But, on the first alternative, given that there are successful examples of these types of organism, we have good reason to believe that their core-physical properties are sufficiently integrated with relevant psychological ones for (1) and (2) to be true. This does not demand that the core-physical properties form a core-physical unity in basic-causal terms as is required in functionalist theory. In some cases no doubt there will be just this type of core-physical unity at the underlying level. But it is not required in all. There may be variable realization of the same psychological property in functional states of different types which can achieve the same psychological result by differing causal routes. Indeed this appears to occur in certain empirical examples where some parts of the brain are damaged, and the same psychological activities are grounded in other, compensating, areas involving different types of functional state.[25]

The second feature of this proposal is that it refuses to accept the functionalist demand that there be general or intelligible connections between core-physical and psychological state-types or properties. It is enough that in each token-case there is an appropriate connection between token core-physical and psychological states and properties. And this will be guaranteed (in general) because it is required for the general success of the organism in question. This could not be achieved unless the token-states which instantiate psychological properties were themselves physical, and appropriately related (in the token-case) to a set of core-physical token-states with the relevant core-physical causal powers. But this does not require that the psychological properties be *in general* identified with an ordered grouping of core-physical ones. On this view, one can exclude 'miraculous coincidences' at the token level without requiring even the weak functionalist account identifying causally explanatory psychological properties with core-physical causal ones.[26] From this perspective, the demand for a

[25] For discussion of such cases of plasticity, see R. McCarthy and E. Warrington, *Cognitive Neuropsychology* (San Diego, Calif.: Academic Press, 1990), 8–10.

[26] But doesn't this make the very existence of integrated terrestrial persons a miracle? There are, of course, evolutionary accounts of the emergence of the human species from more basic organisms, and perhaps from those which lack sentience. These accounts (if successful) will make the existence of such persons non-miraculous. But they do not require that specific psychological properties be identifiable with core-physical causal properties (as in the functionalist theory).

functionalist account of these properties appears exaggerated and misplaced.

This account faces two major challenges. Some will question whether it succeeds in vindicating the claim that the psychological is causally explanatory, if it allows that psychological properties need not be identified with core-physical causal ones. However, the psychological story gives additional causal information. (1) and (2) make true claims about what will happen in close possible worlds where there are (let us assume) differences in the core-physical properties. Further, the psychological properties make a difference to the physical state to which they belong, allowing it causally to explain a bodily movement which composes an *action*. Actions will themselves be physical events, *qua* spatial ones, but may be distinct from the bodily movements from which they are composed. In this case, the sum of actual causal powers of the antecedent state (although not their core-physical ones) appears to be increased by the presence of these psychological properties.

In these ways, the psychological appears to be genuinely causally explanatory. Its properties certainly do more than signal the presence of causal factors in the way that the ignition light on a car indicates that its electric current is operational. For in the latter case the operation of the light does not add to the effects of the electrical current on the motor. Further, in close possible worlds, the electrical current may start the engine without the ignition light functioning, and this light may work without the electrical system starting the motor. It is not a necessary condition of this being a successful car ignition system that there be true conditional and counterfactual claims linking the operation of the ignition indicator with the starting of the motor. The causal powers of the electrical system in its dealings with the motor are not increased by the presence of the ignition indicator. By contrast, the causal powers of the agent are increased by his possession of the relevant psychological properties.

If this is correct, psychological properties are causally explanatory—adding causal information to that which is given in core-physical terms. They are (we are assuming) causally explanatory only because they are grounded (token by token) in states (at least parts of) which instantiate core-physical properties. The psychological would lack all causal powers were it not for this token-grounding. The core-physical is (let us assume) a closed system, and there are no causal powers which operate independently of core-physical ones. But it does not follow from this that *all* causal powers are confined to the core-physical level. There may be higher-order causal powers of (for example) human agents which are not isomorphic with or identifiable with core-physical causal properties or groupings of such properties. Such causal powers may reflect our natures and interests as human agents (our point of view), and not be discernible from within core-physical theory or indeed from any perspective which abstracts from our point of view. But in terrestrial persons, it is no accident that on each token-occasion the relevant psychological property is appropriately grounded in some relevant core-physical property. If it were not so, the creature would not succeed. But there can be autonomous causal explanation at the psychological level which is not underwritten by a well-ordered isomorphic set of core-physical laws. The latter may be a closed system, not requiring the addition of higher-order causal powers, to explain its effects; but core-physics will not include *all* the causal powers there are.

The second challenge is to make more precise the kind of intelligibility required in the token-case. What is it for a particular psychological property to be appropriately grounded in some set of core-physical token-states? One proposal runs as follows: a psychological property is grounded in a core-physical property at a time only if the token psychological state to which it belongs has the same identity or persistence conditions as a set of token core-physical states (at least some of) which possess the core-physical property. This will be so only if the tokens occur at the same time, belong to the same subject (or part of the subject) and are spatially connectable. But it will also require that these tokens (both psychological and core-physical) are produced by a set of organizing principles or mechanisms which operate on core-physical properties and matter. In this case, the psychological token will be composed out of core-physical properties and matter of the type possessed by the co-present core-physical tokens. This is because there is a compositional principle which operates on core-physical matter to produce both core-physical and psychological tokens. In this case, the relevant psychological property will be grounded in the core-physical properties of the core-physical tokens. Compositional asymmetry is maintained because psychological tokens and properties are made from core-physical properties and matter, whereas core-physical tokens are not made from psychological properties or psychic stuff.

In some cases, the relevant compositional principles will be core-physical causal laws. In some of these, the resulting psychological states and properties will be grounded in core-physical states and properties in the way required by functionalist theory. But in others, the compositional principles may be more radically autonomous, and not even be isomorphic with core-physical laws. This will be so if, for example, the relevant compositional principles reflect our interests, goals, and perspectives as human agents, and thus introduce groupings and explanatory connections of a type different in kind from those found in core-physical theory. In these cases, the relevant compositional principles will reflect the operation of higher-order causal properties which are not susceptible to a functionalist account.

Two non-psychological examples may help to make the general view clearer. First, table construction. The principles which collect pieces of wood or core-physical molecules to create tables belong to the art of carpentry and are not (presumably) to be found in core-physical theory. The types of molecule or wood which the carpenter can use need not form a ready-made natural unity at the core-physical level. Even if each act of the carpenter were token identical with a core-physical process, the general principles governing his actions would not be core-physical laws. Rather, they will reflect our interests and goals as producers and consumers, which would be absent from, or have no significance in, core-physical laws. Similarly with the principles of programming, which collect electrical chips to form computer tables. In neither case need we assume that there must be laws governing basic particles which group them in general in the way required for table construction of a type which benefits us or is appropriate to our interests.

Secondly, colour composition. The colour of a particular pigment mixture (e.g. red) is determined by the colours and quantities of its components and by their spectral reflectance characteristics (the relative energy they emit). But (let us assume) what leads us to group pigments or spectral reflectance characteristics in the way we do is their importance for us, to whom only certain objects or surfaces look red. A given pattern of light reflectance or the relative energy emission of a surface is significant for us because of its impact on our perceptual mechanisms. There is no reason to believe that, for example, the particular energy distributions which we select must have a distinctive role or form a significant grouping in core-physical science. Rather the principles through which we classify the colours of surfaces are constituted by our perspective as human observers, and need not reflect the laws of core-science (or any grouping of such laws independent of our perspective).

In a similar way, the principles of organization which govern the operation of our perceptual processes may be capturable only within information-processing theory, and not even be isomorphic with basic laws governing their 'hardware implementation'.[27] If so, the kind of information theory true of creatures like us will be a consequence of our natures as rational agents, and will not require that the informational properties or laws governing our behaviour map on to core-physical causal properties and laws (in the way demanded in the functionalist account). For the distinctions marked out at the higher level need have no significance within more basic causal theory. No doubt, higher-level principles of organization can only operate on hardware properties of certain types if the organism is to perceive and survive. This naturally limits the range of cases where these principles of organization can function successfully. But there is no need to assume that the hardware properties capable of being thus organized must form a unity which can be specified in terms of their role in core-physical causal laws. From the perspective of the relevant higher-order organizing principles, a variety of causal core-

[27] For this viewpoint, see D. Marr, *Vision* (New York: Freeman, 1982), 23–31.

properties which cut across causal differentiations at the core-physical level may be suitable as the basis for the compositional task. In certain cases, these may only be unified as 'the material or properties appropriate for composing psychological tokens with given properties'. In a similar way, the range of causally differentiated properties suitable for the construction of tables or computer tables need not fit into a unified set in terms of core-causal laws (or a conservative extension of them). But in all these cases the higher-order token-states will be composed out of a range of core-physical properties and particles in a way which is, in its logic, asymmetric.

When there are true composition claims of this kind, there will be true specific supervenience claims linking certain core-physical properties of the set of core-token-states, and specific psychological properties of the token psychological state. Further, these claims will be true in all possible worlds where terrestrial persons exist. But they derive from the compositional principles and are not its basis. It is composition and not supervenience which captures the relevant form of physicalist priority.

4

The present proposal is to be distinguished in several ways from the earlier supervenience account. It captures the necessary dependence of the psychological states of humans on the physical, and the way in which the psychological is based in the physical (and not vice versa). Further, it provides a way of sustaining the explanatory claims ((1) and (2)) without requiring a functionalist account of psychological properties. The intelligibility it offers is at the level of particular instantiations of properties and not at the level of the properties themselves.

If it is successful, it avoids the following dilemma: if psychological properties are causally explanatory they must be grounded in the functionalist mode in core-physical properties; alternatively, if they cannot be so grounded, they cannot be causally explanatory and should be treated in an instrumentalist or eliminativist mode. Either one can offer a general reductive account of psychological properties in functionalist terms, or one should regard their attribution as a convenient 'manner of speaking' which we choose to adopt for our convenience in interpretation without any underpinning in physical reality. This dilemma exercises a powerful grip on much contemporary thought. For some, failure to meet the functionalist requirement leads to an anti-realist account of the relevant semantic and psychological properties.[28] For others (more cautiously), it motivates to the search for alternative and non-causal explanatory models at the psychological level.[29] Still others, in the grip of this dilemma, are led to defend theories which map semantic on to syntactic (language of thought) properties in the favoured functionalist mode in the face of powerful empirical challenges from alternative (e.g. connectionist) models.[30] But this dilemma can be avoided if—as in the previous section—one can allow psychological properties to be causally explanatory without requiring even a weak functionalist account of their realization.

But is it successful? Is it sufficient to make it intelligible how psychological properties can be instantiated in token physical states to note that these are essentially spatial and thus intelligibly connected to core-physical processes whose properties ground the psychological ones in the way specified? Surely, the psychological essentially involves properties (such as subjectivity) which cannot be intelligibly based in any objective physical properties. If so, how can they be grounded, even in this token-by-token way, in core-physical properties? Perhaps we need proto-mental properties to provide the basis for these psychological properties? For how can a token mental unit have physical parts, without a radical change in our concept of the physical?[31]

[28] See e.g. S. Schiffer, *Remnants of Meaning* (Cambridge, Mass.: MIT Press, Bradford Books, 1987), 139–73.

[29] From this viewpoint, the psychological has to be causally *anomalous*. If there were psychological or psychophysical laws, psychological properties would have to be identified with functional ones. If this is accepted, the only way to avoid sober functionalism is to deny that there can be lawlike causal explanation involving the psychological. If so, the only possible form of psychological explanation must be of a different type: e.g. rational or holistic. The desire to avoid a functionalist account of psychological properties explains some of the attraction of Davidson's *anomalous monism*.

[30] See e.g. J. A. Fodor and Z. Pylyshyn, 'Connectionism and Cognitive Architecture: A Critical Analysis', *Cognition*, 21 (1988).

[31] See T. Nagel, *The View from Nowhere* (New York and Oxford: Oxford University Press, 1986), 49–51.

In the present proposal, the relevant psychological property need not have physical parts. Nor need the psychological token state be a whole composed of core-physical spatial states as parts. All that is required is that there be a *principle of organization* governing the core-physical which yields psychological tokens. But this need not involve the part–whole relation as understood in mereological theory. The first is composed from the hand, when clenched. But neither clenching nor the hand are parts of the fist, nor is the hand the mereological sum of clenching and the hand. Similarly, white light is composed from a mixture of all other coloured lights mixed according to the principles of colour science. But this does not prevent us from thinking of white light as simple (at least phenomenologically) or require us to conceive of bits of blue and red light as separate atomic parts present in white light.

The notion of composition invoked in the previous section does not depend on mereological part–whole relations. The latter seem in any case inadequate to capture the relevant sense of composition, even when they do apply. A brick has two half bricks as parts, but is not composed (in the relevant sense) from two half bricks (except when they are glued together in the process of its creation). The part–whole relation, although frequently used in contemporary physicalist discussions, seems incapable of capturing the way in which the mental is composed from the physical. It is no objection to the present proposal that it fails to show how a mental unit can have physical parts.

But has enough been done to dispel the mystery of how a principle of organization can operate on core-physical properties to generate subjective token-psychological states? Is the composition account likely to be more successful than ones based on supervenience or the part–whole relation?

Colour may again provide a helpful analogy. Let us assume that in the case of particular red surfaces the relevant principles for organizing coloured light, energy transfer and pigmentation, advert essentially to visual experience of our type. In this case, the general organizational principles will refer essentially to us. But the input to these principles will be properties and states which are thoroughly objective and describable in terms of wavelength and energy transfer etc. In any token-case, the relevant properties will be core-physical ones organized in the way required for us to perceive this red surface. But these relevant ways, in general, need have no special significance at the core-physical level, nor be invoked in any core-physical laws. It will no doubt be possible in any particular case to describe the relevant basic states in core-physical terms. But in general the type of dependency may only be captured in a way that adverts to us and our capacities. In this event, redness will be a *subjective* property because it is only in virtue of its connection to us that certain types of energy dependency, for example, are marked out as relevant for its presence. There need be no objective essence of redness to be found in core-physics which is significant independently of its relation to us, and for this reason there need be no core-physical laws isomorphic with colour laws. But this does not mean that the components of the redness of particular surfaces need be anything other than, for example, particular energy transfers and pigmentations. We do not need proto-colour elements to bridge the explanatory gap.

Subjective experiences of redness may, by analogy, be composed from the effects of certain types of energy transfer on physical receptors of a given type. In general, it will not be possible to state outside of autonomous human psychology (involving perhaps informational theory) the principles which select certain types of energy transfer as significant for us. In token-cases, there may be ways of stating in objective terms what grounds the particular instantiation of a given psychological property. But this will not generate objective type generalizations statable in core-physics independently of any reference to our natures and particular mode of sensitivity. Rather the relevant principles will fall within an autonomous psychology, unsupported by objective essences in core-physics or by the types of law and property which the functionalist required. A full recognition of the degree of subjectivity in colour science and human psychology should not lead us to despair of finding causal laws in either case. It shows only that their support is to be found in what is required for the continued existence of successful human organisms and not in the causal principles of basic physics.

11

Values: Reduction, Supervenience, and Explanation by Ascent

James Griffin

1. TWO PRELIMINARIES

I doubt that there is one metaphysical status for values. To take just ethics, the status of prudential values is different, I suspect, from that of most moral values, and moral values are not uniform among themselves. For that reason, we should, at the start, choose one sort of value to concentrate on. I shall choose prudential values. I use 'prudence' in the philosopher's broad sense, in which it has to do with everything that makes an individual life, seen on its own, good. I concentrate on the prudential case for two reasons. First, it seems to me a bit easier than the moral one, while raising all the central meta-ethical questions. It is easier, I think, even though it is impossible to make a sharp cut between prudence and morals. And secondly, human interests hold a particularly basic place among values generally. They get us into the subject not only more easily but also at a deeper point.

Also, I do not myself find it fruitful to separate meta-ethics and normative ethics for long. I think that their best hope for advance is to advance together. It is hard to decide on the reducibility, or supervenience, or reality of values without a fairly full idea of what is valuable and what arguments are actually available to us in deciding this. So my way into this meta-ethical subject is through some normative ethics.

2. PRUDENTIAL DELIBERATION

Suppose that one is struck by the thought that someone else's life is worth while in a way that one's own is not.[1] You are

[1] In this section, I offer a very summary treatment of the complex issues of

accomplishing things with your life, let us say, that strike me as giving it a point or a weight that mine lacks. But precisely what is it, I should have to ask myself, that makes your life better? And when I can see it clearly, will it still seem valuable? I have a definitional problem on my hands. Clearly, not any achievement will count: flag-pole sitting, even of Guinness-Book-of-Records duration, will not. If it is to be the sort of accomplishment I am looking for, it must be more than bare, even rare, achievement; it has to be the achievement of something that is itself valuable. But that is not quite enough either. The flag-pole sitter might give some people mild, momentary amusement, and such amusement, though not nothing on the value scale, lacks the sort of importance to give life point or weight. And 'accomplishment' (if I may take over that word for what I am after) should not be confused with public admiration for one's achievements; the public often admires worthless things, and if accomplishment has a value it is different from the pleasure of being admired. And so on.

The fairly lengthy definitional exercise I would have embarked upon seems to me to consist of two parts. First, I should have to focus on the candidate for value status, largely by distinguishing it from other values and from the valueless. Then, I should have to decide whether accomplishment, finally seen plainly, is indeed valuable. This exercise looks like, and in some sense is, a process of discovery and it looks as if the value discovered is valuable quite apart from my personal desires and inclinations, indeed is valuable for humans generally. And accomplishment is not in this respect a special case. The same seems true of many central prudential values: deep personal relations, contact with important features of reality, living autonomously.

Admittedly, other cases look rather different. They seem to rest far less on our understanding, and more on our individual desires and inclinations. Enjoyment is an obvious prudential value, and what each of us enjoys is closely connected to what each spontaneously wants or is motivated to get. And what one of us enjoys is often very different from what another enjoys.

prudential deliberation. For fuller discussion, see my *Well-Being* (Oxford: Clarendon Press, 1986), pt. I.

We might see these two cases as extremes, the first in which understanding is important and desire is not and the second in which the reverse is true. And there are many cases in between, in which the mix of the two elements, understanding and desire, is more even.

There are various ways of bringing these different cases under a single explanation. Hume, for instance, thinks that, in the end, things are valuable because desired. Given the sort of biological and psychological creatures we are, our desires fix on certain things, which thereby become valuable. It is not that everything that we desire is thereby valuable; our desires can be faulty. They can be based on false belief or on incomplete acquaintance. For instance, one might be happy-go-lucky and not want to accomplish anything with one's life. Then one might embark on the train of thought I have just sketched, in the course of which one might spend much time bringing accomplishment into focus. But once the object is in focus it will owe its status as a value to its then being desired. This explains the appearance of discovery that this case often presents; in a sense the value is discovered, but understanding comes in merely to bring the natural world into clearer focus for oneself, while desire, if it follows, is what transforms the object focused upon into a value. In general, what is valuable to a person is what the person desires when sufficiently informed about the natural world. Hume offers a simple picture: a natural world, including humans and their responses, exhausting reality; values not being a further element of reality but, rather, what humans react approvingly to, when they are aware of the relevant features of reality.

Hume's picture must be too simple. There are three considerations, not independent of one another, that complicate it. First, the picture does not make the standards for a desire's being 'informed' strong enough to explain value. If value can be explained in terms of desire at all, it can be in terms of only informed, not actual, desire. But 'informed' in what sense? Suppose we say that a desire is informed if it arises when I am aware of the relevant natural facts and in the absence of logical error.[2] I might have wanted always to be the centre of attention

---

[2] This is Richard Brandt's proposal in *A Theory of the Good and the Right* (Oxford: Clarendon Press, 1979), 10.

and have learned from experience, perhaps even learned
deeply from years of psychoanalysis, how this harms my life.
But I might, none the less, go on wanting to be the centre of
attention, because I do not react appropriately, or strongly
enough, to what I have learned. To get a plausible account of
value, the desires would have to be 'informed' in some such
sense as 'formed in proper appreciation of the nature of their
object'. But this shifts emphasis away from the mere occurrence of desire on to a sufficient understanding of its object.
And the Humean picture has no ready answer to the question
'When is a response appropriate?' One cannot answer that
the appropriate response is the 'natural' or 'normal' one. If
'normal' here means 'most common', then we sometimes find
that most of us, even when informed, go on wanting certain
things—say, self-assertion—too much. If 'normal' is taken
to mean something closer to 'correct', then that is just the
stronger standard we are trying to explain. In any case, there is
something more than a majority response to appeal to: certain
responses just are appropriate to certain things, such as living
a life of point or weight. Another way of putting this is that the
Humean picture supplies no adequate account of progress in
prudential deliberation. Hume's own account in his essay 'On
the Standard of Taste' does not do it.[3] The better moral or
aesthetic sensibility, Hume suggests there, is one more open to
reality. But moving from a narrower to a wider sensibility
is, on this account, a matter of responding to more in the
natural world; it turns limited perspectives into fuller ones. But
an account of improvement in response cannot stop there.
Widening our sensibility, in this weak sense, might end up in
any of several different places. It might, for instance, find two
objects to be of equal merit, or one better than the other by a
lot or a little, or of such different merits that no ranking is
possible. What determines that the 'improved' sensibility ends
up at one of these points rather than another? When we widen
our sensibility, do our responses just change, as a matter
of brute psychological fact, and so become better? But why
should we regard this as improvement, and not as mere

---

[3] I go into this more fully in 'Against the Taste Model', esp. §6, in J. Elster
and J. Roemer (eds.), *Interpersonal Comparisons of Well-Being* (Cambridge:
Cambridge University Press, 1991).

change? And what if they do not change, or do not change enough, or change differently for different persons? The questions need answers and it is not clear what Hume's would be.[4]

Secondly, it is not that no one has answers; there are the makings of an answer in the sort of prudential deliberation that seems possible for us. According to Hume, for a desire to improve is for it to change in content as a result of greater knowledge of the natural world. Desires are then fully improved when knowledge of the relevant natural facts is as full as possible; there is then no further scope for criticizing each person's subjective set of desires.[5] But there seems to be further scope. If certain desires happen not to be present in a final subjective set of improved desires, they ought to be. And there are forms of deliberation that seem to lead to their introduction. The subjective set that is supposed on the Humean picture to be final is not really final. We ask more searching questions about our aims, and resort to more radical criticism to answer them, than the Humean picture allows. If I am a Fool-like person living for day-to-day pleasures and meet a Socratic sort who strikes me as making something of his life, I might start on the radical reflection I outlined earlier. Does accomplishing something with one's life make it prudentially better? What is accomplishment? I should then be embarked on the search for the definition of the possible value. I should have to use value-rich vocabulary to focus on it: accomplish-

---

[4] Nor, I think, what Simon Blackburn's would be either. He adopts and embellishes Hume's account in his book *Spreading the Word* (Oxford: Clarendon Press, 1984), ch. 6 esp. §3. See also his article 'Rule-Following and Moral Realism', in S. Holtzman and C. Leich (eds.), *Wittgenstein: To Follow a Rule* (London: Routledge & Kegan Paul, 1981), 186: 'Morally I think that we profit from the sentimentalist position by realising that a training of the feelings rather than a cultivation of a mysterious ability to spot the immutable fittingness of things is the foundation of knowing how to live.' This seems to me the unreal contrast between understanding and desire once again. Quite aside from his unsympathetic description of the realist position, Blackburn says nothing in this paper above how one 'trains' one's feelings. To explain this is to explain what prudential, moral, and aesthetic deliberation is like. Another explanation has the potential—realized, I think—to undercut the sentimentalist tradition.

[5] Bernard Williams, in his paper 'Internal and External Reasons', also claims that there is no further scope, so the criticisms below apply to him as well. See his *Moral Luck* (Cambridge: Cambridge University Press, 1981), esp. 101–6. For a more adequate discussion of Williams's position, see my *Well-Being*, 134–9.

ment is roughly the achievement of the sort of value that gives life weight and point. But, then, having isolated it, I should have to decide whether the apparent value is really a value, or, rather, since the search for a definition already brings in value-rich language, these two processes—definition of the putative value and decision about its value—go hand in hand. And one decides whether it is a value not by appeal to one's final subjective set of desires. There is nothing there to appeal to, except the vacuous desire to have a good life, which will not do the job, because the present job is to decide whether accomplishment, so defined, makes a life good. So the final subjective set of desires that you or I happen to end up with plays no real role here, while understanding what accomplishment is plays a large role. This sort of understanding, which has its own standards for success, can introduce a new item into one's set of desires in a way that the Humean picture does not explain.

Finally, the Humean picture assumes that we can isolate valued objects in purely natural terms and then, independently, react to them with approval or disapproval. But can we? Prudential deliberation about accomplishment is not a case of first perceiving facts neutrally and then desire's entering and happening to fix on one object or other. The act of isolating the objects we value is far from neutral: we bring accomplishment into focus only by resorting to such terms as 'giving life weight or point'. Such language already organizes our experience by selecting what we see favourably. Desire is not left free to happen to fix on one object or another; its direction is already fixed in and manifested by what we see favourably. It is not that understanding is now dominant and desire subordinate; it is not that the Humean order (valued because desired) is reversed. It is doubtful that we can fully explain the sort of understanding at work in this case—that is, the sort that involves fixing on certain objects and seeing them in a favourable light—without introducing certain volitional elements. There is no adequate explanation of their being desirability features without appeal to certain natural human motivations. To see something as an accomplishment leaves no space for desire to follow along in a separate, subordinate position.

There is a parallel semantic point that John McDowell has

made.[6] We regard accomplishment as a genuine concept—that is, as a term that marks a kind, that is not shapeless, that does not merely give vent to our feelings. How could we come to master its use? On the Humean picture, we learn the range of things to apply it to through their natural attributes. So even if you value different things from me, I can understand what you are saying: I know what in the natural world you are speaking of and that you have the approval-response to them. Mastery of the word consists of those two parts: natural description and evaluative reaction. Now, some prudential value terms may be like this, but many are not. And those that are not undermine the assumption in the Humean picture that natural properties alone are capable of giving the concept—say, accomplishment— its shape. We must accept either that something more is needed to give it its shape than purely natural attributes and human reactions to them, or that the term has no shape and that we are not reacting to anything that constitutes a kind on its own but merely reacting from time to time as we happen to be moved.

The Humean picture gives clear priority to desire over value. But when one looks at the details of prudential deliberation, it is hard to find a priority to either. This leaves the relation of desire and understanding in need of a lot of explanation. But whatever the final explanation, it seems doubtful to me that it could be anything as simple as the Humean picture.

The final explanation will have to give a smaller role to personal reaction and feeling. For me to see anything as valuable, I must see it against a background of characteristic human aims. We tend to overlook how central certain prudential values are to our conception of a human person or of human agency. For me to see you as a fellow human being I must see you as having certain common sentiments, likings, aversions; I must see you sharing many prudential values with me. Both Wittgenstein and Davidson make this point in connection with language. One cannot understand the rules for the use of a word, Wittgenstein says, apart from social practices, which are

[6] He makes it in various papers. See esp. 'Non-cognitivism and Rule-Following', in Holtzman and Leich (eds.), *Wittgenstein: To Follow a Rule*; and Simon Blackburn's reply in the same volume, 'Rule-Following and Moral Realism'.

possible only through shared aims, interests, and dispositions. We cannot, Davidson thinks, interpret the language that others are using without assuming that we have many aims, concerns, and interests in common with them. What seems to me true is not only that a basic set of prudential values is involved in the intelligibility of human persons, but also that the notion of a prudential value is: to see anything as prudentially valuable is to see it as enhancing life in a generally intelligible way, in a way that pertains to *human* life. This seems to me true of all prudential values, even enjoyment. What persons enjoy, it is true, varies enormously and often in individual, even idiosyncratic, ways. But these various instances are valuable because they are enjoyments, and as subsumable under that heading can be seen as enhancing *human* life.

The final explanation will also have to work with a less sharp contrast between reason and desire. There are many kinds of desire. Some desires are, in effect, afflictions: cravings, obsessions, compulsions, addictions, habits. We passively observe their occurrence in us. But the desires which have a close connection to values are a different sort: they are the desires that are part of ordinary voluntary action. We have options; we consider, choose, and act. Desire, in this sense, aims at the good: an agent's typical procedure is to recognize and to act to meet interests. This sort of desire fails in its own terms if it does not aim at something that will meet an interest. So this sort of desire cannot be sharply separated from recognition of prudential values; its role essentially involves what is involved in judgements of good. Similarly, reasons for action cannot be understood independently of normal human motivation. In some sense, 'ought' implies 'can'. 'Practical reason' also implies 'can'. That is, we should not say that someone has a 'reason' to do what clearly is beyond human capacity. If I see a young girl teetering on a cliff far above me, I might wish that I could fly, Superman-like, and snatch her from death. It would be desirable for me to do it, but I should resist saying that I had a 'reason' to do it. And there are psychological as well as physical limits. There are limits to normal human motivation—difficult to discover but clearly somewhere—which impose boundaries on practical reasons in general and morality in particular. My point is not about the location of these boundaries, but about their existence. Practical reason is not independent of the shape of the will.

3. REDUCTION

3.1. *Strong Naturalism*

Our simplest meta-ethical option is to reduce values to facts. But what is a reduction? And what is its point? To describe a particular reductive programme tolerably fully one needs to know its aim or point. One aim is ontological soundness. Suspect entities or properties can either be eliminated by dissolution into others or legitimized by composition from others, hard though it can sometimes be to distinguish elimination from legitimization. A second aim is epistemological satisfactoriness. Puzzling explanations can either be replaced by explanations on a different, clearer level or be legitimized by finding bridges between the two levels. Reduction therefore has a built-in bias towards the unpuzzling, which is generally a bias towards physicalism or naturalism. This may seem to be an unchallengeable bias. But we are not always puzzled by what we should be. And there is another strategy for dealing with the puzzling besides reduction to the unpuzzling: namely, managing to make it unpuzzling on its own level of explanation.

Reduction requires two levels of explanation—for instance, the level of values and the level of natural facts. One thing we should be puzzled by are the boundaries of 'natural fact'. The question of the reduction of values to natural facts is not like that of mental states to brain states. We know fairly well what a physiological explanation is, but we do not know at all well what falls under a category as grossly defined as the 'natural'. We can define the natural as, roughly, what is explained by the natural sciences,[7] but that merely puts the puzzle back one step to the boundaries of 'natural science'. Do natural sciences include social sciences, themselves the subject of reductivist

---

[7] This is Moore's first suggestion in *Principia Ethica* (Cambridge: Cambridge University Press, 1903), 40; he there explains the 'natural' as 'that which is the subject-matter of the natural sciences and also psychology'.

ambitions? The best prospects for reducing values to natural fact is to make the category of the natural wide: a natural science is any systematic set of empirical regularities. This throws all the burden on to the hardly sharp-edged notion of the 'empirical', and it is there that it seems to me best to leave it. Naturalism can be distinguished from materialism, which is the view that everything is reducible to matter in motion, since the empirical is, at least potentially, wider than the material. G. E. Moore, who struggled for many years to clarify the term 'natural', at an early stage suggested that 'natural' might be understood as 'exists by itself in time'.[8] But this account destroys the distinction between natural and non-natural attributes, because a natural attribute, such as yellow, cannot be found on its own in time either. *Attributes* in general cannot; Moore thought that some could, such as yellow, because he thought that natural attributes were actual, substantive constituents of, parts of, the wholes that they are the attributes of. But this conception of properties as ingredients that, when they coincide in space and time, constitute the substance of an object, is to my mind implausible. At a later stage, Moore seems to have preferred explaining natural attributes as 'independent' and non-natural ones as 'dependent':[9] that is, a natural property, such as yellow, may be present in an object independently of what other properties it has, whereas a non-natural property, such as good, may not. This shifts the natural/non-natural distinction, as we shall shortly see, very close to the supervenient/non-supervenient distinction. But a property like large, even a property like yellow, does not seem to be independent of other properties of the object. So I think it best to keep to the explanation of 'natural' in terms of 'empirical'. The empirical/non-empirical distinction is, though not sharp, better than the alternatives. Any thought about reduction or supervenience will, at the start, have to put up with rough, intuitive meanings for terms such as 'natural' and

[8] Ibid. 41.

[9] See his 'Reply to my Critics', in P. A. Schilpp (ed.), *The Philosophy of G. E. Moore* (La Salle, Ill.: Open Court, 1942), 588. Thomas Baldwin thinks that this interpretation of the distinction is already present, in a confused way, in the *Principia Ethica* discussion; see Baldwin's 'Ethical Non-naturalism', in I. Hacking (ed.), *Exercises in Analysis* (Cambridge: Cambridge University Press, 1985), 30.

'empirical', because much of what is at issue is where those lines are best drawn. I shall come back to this later.

If one uses the term broadly, one could call the reduction of value to natural facts 'naturalism'. As successful as many reductionist programmes seem to me to be elsewhere in philosophy, I know of no persuasive form of naturalism. There is the strong form that claims that value terms are definable by natural terms.[10] I do not want to spend much time on this strong form, because I do not think that it is promising. It is not that G. E. Moore's famous argument finishes it off; on the contrary, I do not think that his argument works. As you know, he argues indirectly. If 'good' were definable in the sense that matters (namely, analysable), we could say something of the form: 'good' means '*x* plus *y* plus *z*'. However, then the claim 'whatever is *x* plus *y* plus *z* is good' would be a tautology. But it never is. Moore offers, of course, less an argument than a challenge: try it and you will fail.

In 1960 Paul Ziff published a book *Semantic Analysis* in which he tried and largely succeeded. Ziff suggests that 'good' has associated with it 'the conditions of answering certain interests, which interests are in question being indicated either by the element modifying or the element modified by "good" or by certain features of the context of utterance'.[11] In short 'good' means 'answers to certain interests'. And this semantic analysis seems to be an analysis in just Moore's prohibited sense. What is more, it looks promisingly naturalist. We should say that a tree had good roots, because roots anchor and feed and these roots do just that. Such judgements seem to be well within the bounds of the natural world. Now, I think that most nouns that can be modified by 'good' apply to things with a function or role, and that the modifier 'good' applies when they fulfil the function or play the role; that is true not just of 'good roots' but also of 'good parent', and even of the very general moral assessment 'good person'. That semantic setting of interests to be met is, I think, seldom missing.

---

[10] For it to be reductivist, it must also claim that the terms in the definiens are more basic than those in the definiendum; equivalence (in sense) is two-way reduction, and we want one-way.

[11] P. Ziff, *Semantic Analysis* (Ithaca, NY: Cornell University Press, 1960), ch. 6, see esp. p. 218.

But two things seem to me to stop a naturalist from claiming Ziff's definition as vindication. First, the semantic analysis does not entirely succeed. A few nouns modifiable by 'good' apply to things without a function or role, and there is no interest being served. A good Roman nose is merely one that has the defining characteristics to a high degree. More damagingly, a prudentially good life is good in a way not analysable in terms of satisfying interests, at any rate not analysable in Ziff's canonical form. Even if one can set some of these cases aside as falling outside the scope of the thesis (good Roman noses?) and others as connected with interests in some more remote way still to be explained (prudentially good lives?), strong naturalism would still not be saved. While what the relevant interest is in the case of good roots may be a fact about the natural world, in the case of a good parent or a good person (in the morally weighted sense of that term) the notion of interest becomes so rich as no longer to be purely natural. At least, if it were still purely natural, then the distinction between the natural and the non-natural would not be what is usually meant. This seems to me the fate of all naturalist definitions: either they fall short of establishing full criteria for the use of the term, or they occasionally establish something close to full criteria by going beyond the resources of what we ordinarily think of as the natural world.

3.2. Weak Naturalism

Much the most interesting forms of naturalism are weaker ones. They do not make the strong claim that value terms are definable in natural terms but claim merely that certain matters of value in effect come down to certain matters about the natural world. It looks on the surface, they say, as if ethics has its own autonomous subject-matter, but, when we dig deeper, all that it really turns out to be about is facts about the human psyche, say, or about social needs and organization. Values, they say, can be derived from natural facts, but not vice versa; perhaps not all that we now say about values is derivable but all that does any genuine explanatory work is.

Weak naturalism can, of course, take many different forms.

Let me consider just two. It might take the form of a reforming definition. For the question 'What is the best for someone to do from his own point of view?' Richard Brandt substitutes what he wishes to be understood as a purely empirical question: 'What would a person want for himself, if his desires were put through maximal criticism by facts and logic?'[12] So he turns the question 'What would make my life prudentially better?' into the psychological question 'What would I end up wanting after being subjected to this sort of maximal criticism?' Since this is meant as a way for me to discover what traditionally are referred to as prudential values, I cannot assume these values in the process: I must confine myself to psychological facts, or, at any rate, to certain contrary-to-fact conditional judgements about my mind. But it is a consequence of this reductionist view, as Brandt admits, that the man who wants always to be the centre of attention, though it often harms him, may well go on wanting to do it after maximal criticism. As we saw earlier with Hume's picture, Brandt's stipulation would move the notion of prudential value so far from our intuitive conception of what is in our interest as no longer to be an acceptable stipulation. And we can hardly conclude that we are forced to swallow the unpalatable consequences of this reductive account for lack of better. We are in the middle of trying to find the best account, so cannot help ourselves yet to any conclusions about it.

Still, can we not loosen Brandt's definition a bit to accommodate this objection while still keeping it empirical? An informed-desire account of prudential values readily lends itself to a naturalist interpretation. It needs, it is true, a rather rich account of 'informed', but could we not retain a lot of the richness without sacrificing the empirical standing?[13] Thus, for the question 'What is prudentially best for a person?' we might ask 'What would a person want for himself, if he had all the facts, his imagination was in good working order, and so on?' This differs from Brandt's account by making the antecedent of the counterfactual more ideal: if the man who wants to be the

---

[12] See *A Theory of the Good and the Right*, ch. 1, §2.

[13] This is Peter Railton's aim in his paper 'Moral Realism', *Philosophical Review*, 95 (1986), in which he adopts an informed-desire account but regards the result as a kind of naturalism. See esp. §3.

centre of attention had not only all the facts and correct logic, but also the sensitivity to appreciate the import of some of those facts, then he would not want always to demand attention. But what we crucially need is to have the exercise of that sensitivity spelt out in some detail. I suggested earlier that it involves recognizing a reason for action grounded in one's well-being, that it requires bringing a situation under some concept—enjoyment, accomplishment, and so on—that is generally intelligible as something life-enhancing. Without those elements, one's account would not be rich enough. But, with them, would it any longer be naturalist? This brings us up against the fuzziness of the notion of the natural. But recognizing something as a reason for action or reason for belief, though it is an event in the natural world, clearly also has a strong normative element to it, and I doubt that what is commonly understood as a naturalist or an empirical account of the world includes the normative recognition of reasons. What we need to focus on is the difference between a person's regarding something as a reason for belief or for action and its really being one. The former would appear in empirical explanations of behaviour. The latter, however, involving as it does a normative sort of assessment or judgement, probably would not. I put that conclusion cautiously, both because of the fuzziness of the boundary of the natural and because the natural/non-natural distinction, as it stands now, may be an untenable dualism. In any case, there are important claims that cannot easily be parcelled into either class. So all that I want to conclude is that, as the term is now generally used, the sensitivity that we have to explain involves events that are not fully describable in natural terms.[14]

---

[14] Railton would, I think, regard my account of this sensitivity as being too rich; he keeps his account spare enough to pass as a form of naturalism. But that it is too spare shows itself, it seems to me, in various ways. He explains prudential value as, roughly, what a person would want to want when fully informed (see 'Moral Realism', §3, esp. pp. 174–8). But this does not solve the problem of excessive breadth: we want things when fully informed (e.g. the success of the stranger we meet on the train, or the well-being of our twenty-second century successors) that, if realized, do not enhance our personal lives at all. Furthermore, Railton's account, being restricted to a certain sort of causal interaction (namely, such-and-such features of objects produce, in a state of full knowledge etc., a reaction of desire), leaves out the reason-giving side of what is going on: that certain features are life-enhancing, that they constitute

The second sort of weak naturalism that I said that I wanted to mention does not take the form of a definition at all. Our evaluations are themselves events in the natural world, and it is always illuminating to consider empirical explanations of their origin and growth. Freud suggested that 'ethics is . . . to be regarded as a therapeutic attempt—as an endeavour to achieve, by means of the command of the super-ego, something which has not been achieved by means of any other cultural activities', namely control of the constitutional inclination of humans to be aggressive towards one another.[15] And it is likely that some ethical standards originally arose as solutions, not always conscious, to co-operation problems—for instance, problems with the form of the Prisoner's Dilemma. Ethical constraints serve the useful social function of making things go better than they would if natural human failings ran on unchecked. One might think—some philosophers do[16]— that these psychological or sociological explanations become wide-ranging and deep enough to leave nothing more to ex-

reasons for action rooted in a person's good. Certain features of objects are desirability features, features generally recognizable as human aims—such as enjoyment, accomplishment, and so on. Railton's relational account concentrates exclusively on the fact that, in certain circumstances (e.g. full knowledge), one's desires become such and such. Well, what is so special about *that* pattern of desires? Why should those desires have any authority over action? The explanation has to be in terms of reasons for action of a special sort, namely, that fulfilment of these desires makes one's life better. The facts that Railton stresses about causal interaction resulting in desire are indeed objective in the sense that Railton wants, but they do not go far enough to explain prudential value. We need mention of desirability features and an explanation of their status. And once they enter the picture we have a solution to the first difficulty: the success of the stranger on the train and people's flourishing in the twenty-second century, though both qualifying as what we should want to want, are not subsumable under one or other of the right sort of value headings. But once this complication does enter the picture, the issue of realism about values becomes more difficult, I think, than Railton makes it.

[15] S. Freud, *Civilization and its Discontents*, ch. 8, p. 89. See the interesting discussion of Freudian explanations of value and obligation in R. Wollheim, *The Thread of Life* (Cambridge: Cambridge University Press, 1984), esp. 204–5, 215–16; much of its interest is how extraordinarily thin this psychological explanation is, even in Wollheim's sensitive hands.

[16] e.g. G. Harman, 'Is There a Single True Morality?', in D. Copp and D. Zimmerman (eds.), *Morality, Reason and Truth* (Totowa, NJ: Rowman and Allanheld, 1985) and also in *The Nature of Morality* (New York: Oxford University Press, 1977), ch. 1. J. L. Mackie approaches this position; see his *Ethics* (Harmondsworth: Penguin, 1977), ch. 5.

plain. Just as psychological or sociological explanations of religion might explain it so cogently as to convince us that religion is no more than the natural phenomenon just explained, whatever we thought of it before, the same fate, these philosophers think, befalls ethics. The causal explanation of ethics has a corrosive effect, leaving no non-natural subject in need of separate understanding.

Reductive arguments are strong only if they start with a sufficient appreciation of what it is they have to reduce. And the arguments I have just sketched—and all weak reductionist arguments, I think—fail that test. It seems to me right that one central and important function of ethical standards is to control our instinctive aggression towards one another. But that and other possible psychological explanations cover only part of the ground. We also want to make our life both reasonable and fulfilled. We naturally ask 'What would make my life prudentially better?', and the deliberation that we should find ourselves necessarily involved in cannot plausibly be exhaustively explained in terms of controlling aggression or in any other depth psychological terms that would keep it a reductive explanation. Enough, I hope, was said about this earlier. Similarly, some value judgements clearly have their origins in solutions to co-operation problems; they arise and they survive because they make social life go better than it otherwise would. But this sort of sociological explanation could not begin to explain all evaluation. If we reflect a moment on the nature of prudential deliberation—on the resources available to us to decide whether accomplishment, say, or deep personal relations are life-enhancing—the reductive explanation looks superficial, very little in accord with the details of what actually goes on. Most of the issues that concern us in prudential deliberation could not check aggression or solve co-operation problems. They are less psyche-directed or society-directed, more reflective and detached, than these reductive accounts make them. It is true that explanations in terms of controlling aggression or solving co-operation problems are intended primarily for moral judgements, and I oppose them by citing prudential judgements. But this does not matter. We are looking for reductions for values generally, including prudential values, and what is difficult is to find any extension of the psychological or sociological proposals that will fit prudential values. And if one cannot reduce prudential values to natural facts, the project of reducing moral values itself becomes altogether more problematic. It runs into the difficulty of the close connections between prudential values (for example, the disvalue of pain) and judgements well on the way to moral judgements (for example, that everyone's pain is a disvalue). This, I think, is a point at which some normative ethics—say, an interest in substantive prudential deliberation—would help meta-ethics: one would not advance these reductive explanations if one had a keener appreciation of just how much needed explaining.

These forms of weak naturalism, in trying to reduce what we explain with values to psychological or sociological explanations, raise the old problem of the boundaries of the natural. These explanations employ intentionality, and the intentional may fall outside the bounds of the natural, on some important conceptions of the 'natural'. But even if it does not, these lower-level explanations fail to do all of the genuine explanatory work done on the higher level of values. An essential part of saying that accomplishment is prudentially valuable is to say that we have reason to aim at it, and not merely that we do aim at it in certain naturally described circumstances.

Despite the failure of naturalism, one of the deep motive-forces propelling it seems to me admirable. Values do not need any world except the ordinary world around us—the world of humans and animals and happenings in their lives. An other-worldly realm of values just produces unnecessary problems about what it could possibly be and how we could learn about it. All of that seems to me right. But to defend it one does not have to adopt a reductive form of naturalism. I shall come back to this later too.

4. THE SUPERVENIENCE RELATION

Values cannot be reduced to natural properties. All the same, there is clearly some very intimate connection between the two. Put vaguely, the relation seems to be one of dependence without reducibility. The most common way nowadays of making that statement less vague is to say that values 'supervene' upon natural properties: that is, if objects are the same in all natural properties, they must be the same in value.[17] Supervenience allows the dependence of the higher level of explanation upon the lower without reduction, and the autonomy of the higher level without dualism. That middle course seems to me right for values. Still, I doubt that values supervene upon natural facts.

On the common definition I have just given, supervenience is a weak relation. It concerns only indiscernibility: if one has indiscernibility on the natural level, then of necessity one has it on the value level. But the chances are that any difference in value will go along with some difference in natural fact, if only in trivial properties such as when and where it occurs. The relation needs to be tightened.

But how much? It is part of the definition of supervenience, as it stands, that the properties supervened upon are specified according to kind, and are of a different kind from the supervening properties. And the specification makes the relation non-tautological: the properties supervened upon are not defined as 'any properties, regardless of type, relevant to something's having the supervening property' (e.g. in the present case, relevant to being valuable) but as being of one independently specified kind (e.g. in the present case, natural properties). But I think that something yet stronger is intended. We do not, in the present case, mean any natural property at all, but only ones that appear in explanatory regularities at the natural level, and those explanatory regularities mention kinds of spatial and temporal relations but do not mention such particulars as, say, occurring today and in Parks Road, Oxford. But I think that we have to go somewhat further and add a relevance requirement. When we consider the supervenience of, say, mental states on physical states, a relevance requirement is implicit. We would not accept that mental states supervene (trivially) upon physical states, if it happened to

---

[17] For an early version of the proposal, see R. M. Hare, *The Language of Morals* (Oxford: Clarendon Press, 1952), 80 ff., 131. See also W. D. Ross, *The Right and the Good* (Oxford: Clarendon Press, 1930), 116–23. For more recent statements of the proposal, see R. M. Hare, 'Supervenience', *Proceedings of the Aristotelian Society*, Supp. Vol. 58 (1984).

turn out that there are always likely to be differences at some deep subatomic level that are irrelevant to differences at the physiological level. Nor would we, if it turned out that there are likely to be physiological differences in the epidermis unconnected with what is happening in the brain. In the case of mental states, we consider whether they supervene upon a particular kind of physiological state—namely, brain states. Similarly, we consider whether evolutionary biological explanations supervene not upon any lower-level natural explanation but upon microbiological ones. We specify the level supervened upon in the way we do because we believe that there are certain sorts of connection between it and the supervening level. That is why, in expressing our intuitive notion of supervenience, we use words such as 'dependence', 'underlying', 'consequential property';[18] they express, in rough terms, the sort of connection we have in mind. But this creates a problem for us. How do we specify the level supervened upon in the present case? It is the problem alluded to earlier, of the grossness of the class of 'the natural'. What we are interested in is whether values supervene upon not any natural properties but some subclass of the natural, a subclass relevant to something's being valuable. Though it is not easy to specify the subclass, I think that we should accept the relevance limitation that it represents. Most moral philosophers do.[19] Accepting this relevance restriction moves supervenience towards, though it does not make it quite as strong as, the 'true in virtue of' relation. The latter relation holds only if truth at the higher level is a function just of truth at the lower level, whereas

[18] 'Dependence': see e.g. D. Davidson, *Essays on Actions and Events* (Oxford: Clarendon Press, 1980), 214: 'mental characteristics are in some sense dependent, or supervenient, on physical characteristics'. 'Underlying': see Blackburn, *Spreading the Word*, 182: 'The idea is that some properties, the *A*-properties, are consequential upon some other base properties, the underlying *B*-properties.' 'Consequential': see the quotation from Blackburn, and also R. M. Hare, *Freedom and Reason* (Oxford: Clarendon Press, 1963), 19: 'moral properties do *not* vary quite independently of non-moral properties, but are in some sense consequential or supervenient on them'. See also *The Language of Morals*, 80.

[19] See e.g. A. H. Goldman, *Moral Knowledge* (London: Routledge, 1988), 134, where he defines supervenience as 'the requirement that we not make different moral judgements when we cannot find differences in non-moral judgements (and furthermore, that we take the latter differences to be generally morally relevant)'.

supervenience claims no more than that there is some function or other.[20]

5. ARE VALUES SUPERVENIENT?

Supervenience is often regarded as an indisputable fact about value that we must come to terms with.[21] I doubt, though, that values are supervenient. I put it inconclusively because I think that, for reasons that I shall come to, it is not easy to say.

The restriction of lower-level properties to relevant natural ones and of upper-level properties to values, which gives supervenience its interest, also, to my mind, makes it doubtful. Supervenience about values accepts a sharp and hardly un-contentious division between the natural world and the world of values. So the supervenience relation is itself far from meta-ethically neutral. It shares the assumption of the sharp division with the Humean picture and is open to similar objections. As we saw earlier, there is no sharp separation of a natural from an evaluative component in a concept such as 'accomplish-ment'. And purely natural description is not enough to give the concept a shape, to pick out its extension.

That earlier argument, though, does not yet upset super-venience. It shows only that the content of prudential concepts does not respect boundaries between natural fact and value. To deny supervenience is to make a stronger claim. We have certain firm intuitions in favour of supervenience. How valu-able a thing is *must* depend upon what it is like. If there is a difference in supervening property, how could it *not* show up in a difference in base properties? But this is where the dubiousness of the separation of fact and value, or reason and desire, matters. To regard some properties as 'base' suggests that *they* are where it all happens and that valuing is some-

---

[20] However, 'true in virtue of' does not have to take a truth-bearer as its second term: e.g. an analytic proposition is true in virtue of the meaning of its terms. This dependence of truth upon meaning is different from the sort of dependence, with potential ontological implications, that we usually have in mind with values and natural facts, mental states and brain states, etc. So 'true in virtue of' can be used of different kinds of relation.

[21] e.g. by Simon Blackburn, *Spreading the Word*, 182, but by many others.

thing entirely different—a human response, say, or a rather mysterious epiphenomenon. To contrast a thing's 'value' with 'what it is like' suggests that values have no hand in what it is like. Then, of course, our strong pro-supervenience intuition is easily explainable: things are valuable because, and only because, of what goes on in the (natural) world. But this picture begs the central question: what are the boundaries of the *world* or *reality* or *fact*? Once one has reason to doubt that those boundaries simply coincide with those of the natural world, and once one sees how much goes into a value concept besides the natural (indeed how relatively unimportant the natural component is compared to the rest), then our pro-supervenience intuition starts to weaken.

But the acid test is: can we supply difference in prudential value without any difference in relevant natural properties? I think that the answer is unclear. If we could mention *any* natural property to establish a difference, then we could always, though uninterestingly, come up with one. Smith's poetry is a genuine accomplishment; Jones's poetry, just as long, varied, innovative, and so on, is not. But Smith and Jones must at least have written in different-coloured ink or in different places. But these differences will not do; we need properties that are 'relevant' in the sense explained earlier. It is the relevance requirement in particular that seems to me to introduce a measure of doubt. A lot that is natural is not relevant, and a lot that is relevant is not natural.

Smith's poetry, let us say, is full of understanding of important matters: that is why it is an accomplishment, and that is the particular sort of accomplishment it is. It would be an accomplishment, I suppose, even if, like Emily Dickinson, he put his poems away in a bureau which, unlike Dickinson's, was never opened. Jones's poetry is not an accomplishment precisely because it lacks that complex quality: understanding of important matters. The crucial base properties in these cases are *understanding* and *importance*. Yet neither of them fits at all comfortably inside the class of the 'natural', so in our present sense they cannot be 'base' properties. Must there be some relevant natural differences between the cases none the less? The particular words Smith and Jones will have used will have been different. But is this any more relevant than the colour of their ink? Admittedly, there is a much closer relation between words and sense than between ink and sense, and a poem's sense connects with its being full of understanding. But the particular words Smith chose were not essential; the sense could have been, and in other drafts may have been, conveyed in different words. So is that, after all, a relevant difference? There is a question, I think, not only about the relevant/non-relevant distinction but also about the natural/non-natural one. On which side of the boundary should epistemological states, such as understanding, come? There is understanding in Smith's case but not in Jones's. But will understanding, with its requirement that norms be met, fall inside the class of the 'natural'? And will the understanding's being important, with that further norm to be met, fall inside it?

To my mind, the answers to those questions are not clear, and not clear for a reason: the various key distinctions on which the questions turn themselves run out of the sharpness that the answers need. We could certainly make them sharper and thereby defend the supervenience of values. We could drop the relevance requirement and allow base properties to be 'base' in a much weaker sense of the word. But then super-venience would be a much less interesting relation.

I am inclined to draw the following moral from these doubts about supervenience. To put it at its most general, prudential values have to do with the world's import for humans. We cannot get at the sort of thing that a prudential value is merely by assembling sets of facts about the natural world, in the fairly narrow sense of 'natural' common in philosophy, because this falls well short of capturing their 'import for humans'. It leaves out what prudential values are about: human interests. That, for instance, is why the person who wanted always to be the centre of attention failed to have the informed desires (in the strong sense of 'informed') that were needed to support values. That, too, is why the *focusing* that, on the Humean picture, is meant to precede the *reacting* cannot employ only natural facts; it will not succeed in delineating the appropriate object of the reaction. That is why we need the right value concepts in order to be fully informed. This is connected with my earlier claim that understanding and desire cannot be kept distinct. To understand *import for humans* is to understand what *matters to them* and so *what is worth their going for*. One of the ways in which the concepts in that set are complex is that they apply to points at which understanding and desire merge: what is to be understood *is* how humans, as beings with interests, fare in the world. That is the new subject that the vocabulary of prudential values addresses. It constitutes an ascent from that level of explanation concerned with description of events in the non-human world and of their effect on, say, human bodies. 'Ascended from' is not the same relation as 'supervenient upon'. It is wider and looser; it probably varies in form from one kind of case to another. It is worth looking at further.

6. EXPLANATION BY ASCENT

What I have in mind is a familiar notion of an ascent through the dimension of levels of organization of things—and the parallel levels of explanation. Things at a higher level are in some sense composed of things at a lower, but it is natural to talk of these new things standing in new relations and having new powers, often causal powers. What I mean by this phrase 'explanation by assent' is the sort of explanation one gets by shift to a higher level when the higher level cannot be reduced to the lower. To get an explanation of certain things we are forced to go higher. Supervenience is compatible with explanation by ascent. In the case of value, though, the relation between it and lower levels is not one of 'reduces to', nor even perhaps of 'supervenient upon'. With values, supervenience may still keep the relation between the levels too close.

Of course, the relation of lower to next higher level of explanation is not the same in every case, except in the abstract sense that each move to a higher level seeks to understand something by seeing it inside a larger frame. The rise to a higher level of organization opens up places for the appearance of new entities, new phenomena, and new concepts with which to describe them. That is why the tabulation of these different levels and of the kinds of relation between them is hardly just a taxonomic exercise. If we want to understand what there is, we have to understand what this move from lower to higher level in each case amounts to. It is not that this is the only ontological concern. It is not that the entities that appear on the most basic level are particularly unproblematic; in physics and chemistry they are often theoretical entities that are challengeable, and have often been successfully challenged. The point is, instead, that the entities that appear in the process of this ascent, and their relation to the entities on the level below, prompt ontological questions. It is unlikely that there is any general test for whether the entities that emerge on the higher level must be allowed really to exist; not even reducibility settles the question.

Now, what problems or puzzles are we dealing with in trying to understand the relation between levels of explanation? With the mental and the physical we have the problem of understanding the interaction between the two, and of how the patterns of explanation on one level relate to those on the other. What are the problems in ethics? There is the large problem of understanding how (I shall put it in a way that plays up the mystery) the world of fact could possibly be related to the world of value. And there is the ontological strain of talking about a *realm* of value, when the world seems to be simply the world of fact (not to mention the epistemological puzzle of how one would ever gain knowledge of the inhabitants of this 'value realm').

Let me end with a sketch of one way of solving those problems. I myself think that arguments will eventually take us to some form of realism about *prudential* values. But it does not involve us in anything remotely like a value realm. That is what seems to me right about naturalism. In talking about prudential values we are not talking about entities in such an other-worldly realm—detectable, say, by intuition—but, rather, about certain things that happen in the only realm that values need: mainly, what goes on in human lives, that *this* or *that* makes a life go better. It makes sense to ask how these sorts of happening relate to other, fairly well-defined levels of explanation: say, the psychological. But I doubt that, in the end, there is point in asking how such happenings relate to a level so grossly defined as the 'natural' or the 'empirical' world, because the boundaries that we use to delineate the natural or the empirical are not just fuzzy but so central to what we are now trying to settle as to make assumptions about where they come question-begging.

We do not start our investigations with the boundaries of 'reality', of 'what there is in the world', of the 'empirical', or of the 'natural' already satisfactorily drawn. We have only a common fuzzy intuition about the natural or empirical world that is itself full of contentious ontological assumptions. So we should not start by asking how values connect with the natural or empirical world, as if one really knew the territories in question and wondered only about their foreign relations. That procedure makes their relation more puzzling than it need be. If our notion of reality, or of fact, or of the empirical is wide enough to include events of meeting or failing to meet interests, then what seems to me the right position is a kind of naturalism. What I spoke against earlier was the familiar sort of reductive naturalism, in which one keeps the boundaries of the natural relatively tight: one keeps them roughly in the position that they have long had in the traditional fact/value split, for instance in Hume's belief that values cannot be derived from fact. What seems to be right, however, is an expansive naturalism in which the boundaries of the natural are pushed outwards a bit, in a duly motivated way, so that they now encompass prudential values.

12

Valuing: Desiring or Believing?*

Michael Smith

1. THE INTENTIONAL AND THE DELIBERATIVE

In general, we can explain intentional action from two quite different perspectives: the *intentional* and the *deliberative*.[1] Though at first sight the difference between these two perspectives is both intuitive and clear, on reflection the fact that intentional action can be explained from these two perspectives provides us with a puzzle. Let me begin by explaining the two perspectives.

From the intentional perspective, we explain an intentional action by fitting it into a pattern of teleological, and perhaps causal, explanation: in other words, we explain by citing the complex of psychological states that produced the action. Consider my typing these words. We explain this action from the intentional perspective when we cite my desire to produce a paper and my belief that I can do so by typing these words, for this is the desire–belief pair that teleologically, and perhaps causally, explains my typing these words.

From the deliberative perspective, by contrast, we explain an intentional action in terms of the pattern of deliberation that either did, or could have, produced it. Consider again my typing these words. In deciding whether or not to type these words I reflected on certain facts: that it would be desirable to

* An earlier version of this paper was read at Oriel College, Oxford University, and at the Research School of Social Sciences, Australian National University. In addition to Philip Pettit, I would like to thank Will Barrett, Geoff Brennan, David Charles, David Gauthier, Brad Hooker, Lloyd Humberstone, Julie Jack, Jeanette Kennett, Peter Menzies, Paul Snowdon, Michael Tooley, and J. David Velleman for their many helpful comments

[1] This terminology is introduced in P. Pettit and M. Smith, 'Backgrounding Desire', *Philosophical Review*, 99 (1990). The present paper attempts to answer some of the questions on which we remained deliberately neutral in that paper. I am grateful to Philip Pettit for helpful comments and conversations.

write a paper and that I can do so by typing these words. These are amongst the considerations I actually took into account in deciding what to do before I did it; they give my reasons. Of course, it would be wrong to suppose that we consciously go through such a process of reasoning each time we act. However, even when we don't, we can often reconstruct the pattern of reasoning that could have been explicit in our deciding to do what we did. In this case, *ex post facto* justification takes the form of constructing an 'as if' story, a story that may be more or less close to the truth.

At first sight, then, the distinction between the intentional and the deliberative may seem to involve a difference in *category*. For whereas, from the intentional perspective, we are interested in which *psychological states* of the agent *explain* his actions, from the deliberative perspective we seem to be interested in which *propositions*, from the agent's point of view, *justify* his actions. However, on closer examination, we see that both perspectives commit us to claims about explanation and that they are therefore potentially in conflict.

In order to see that the deliberative perspective is indeed a perspective on explanation, it suffices to note that to imagine otherwise is tantamount to supposing that the connection between what we decide to do, on the basis of deliberation, and what we do do, is altogether contingent and fortuitous. And that is patently absurd. But if deliberation is practical not just in its *content*, but also in its *issue*, then we must suppose that our attitudes towards the propositions that figure in our deliberations also figure in the explanation of what we do. And now the potential for conflict arises.

Consider again our example. If I accept that it is desirable that I write a paper and that I can write a paper by typing these words, then it seems uncontroversial to say that I *value* writing a paper and *believe* that I can write a paper by typing these words. We might say, then, that the attitudes in question are valuing and believing. But now we must ask how this deliberative explanation in terms of *valuing* and believing relates to the intentional explanation of the very same action in terms of *desiring* and believing.

The problematic attitude is valuing. What is valuing? And how does valuing relate to desiring?

2. DEVIANT CASES

An answer to the question 'What is valuing?' must remain faithful to ordinary thought. In this section I describe part of our ordinary thought about the relations between valuing and desiring. I discuss the proper interpretation of ordinary thought in the next section.

Consider the following passage from Ayer's paper 'Freedom and Necessity':

The kleptomaniac does not go through any process of deciding whether or not to steal. Or rather, if he does go through such a process, it is irrelevant to his behaviour. Whatever he resolved to do, he would steal all the same. And it is this that distinguishes him from the ordinary thief.[2]

Ayer rightly takes it as given that the kleptomaniac steals intentionally; that is, that what he does is explicable in terms of what he wants to do. The problem he highlights is that, though the kleptomaniac's action is therefore explicable from the intentional perspective, it need not be explicable from the deliberative. For there is, he notes, the potential for a gap between what the kleptomaniac 'resolves' to do as a result of deliberating and what he wants to do. This is important, for it suggests a distinction between valuing and desiring. In particular, it suggests that an agent may desire to act in a certain way without valuing acting in that way.

Harry Frankfurt makes a similar point. He has us imagine a heroin addict who:

hates his addiction and always struggles desperately, although to no avail, against its thrust. He tries everything that he thinks might enable him to overcome his desires for the drug. But these desires are too powerful for him to withstand, and invariably, in the end, they conquer him. He is an unwilling addict, helplessly violated by his own desires.[3]

The heroin addict certainly wants to take the drug. However, as Frankfurt notes, we can imagine him saying that he 'does

---

[2] A. J. Ayer, 'Freedom and Necessity', in G. Watson (ed.), *Free Will* (Oxford: Oxford University Press, 1982), 20.

[3] H. Frankfurt, 'Freedom of the Will and the Concept of a Person', in Watson (ed.), *Free Will*, 87.

not "really" want to' take the drug; or even that he 'would rather die than' take it.[4] Here, as elsewhere, talk of what we 'really want' is a surrogate for talk about what we value. Frankfurt's point, like Ayer's, is thus that we may desire to act in a certain way without valuing acting in that way.

Gary Watson makes a related point:

Consider the case of a woman who has a sudden urge to drown her bawling child in the bath; or the case of a squash player who, while suffering an ignominious defeat, desires to smash his opponent in the face with the racquet. It is just false that the mother values her child's being drowned or that the player values the injury and suffering of his opponent. But they desire these things none the less. They desire them in spite of themselves. It is not that they assign to these actions an initial value which is then outweighed by other considerations. These activities are not even represented by a positive entry, however small, on the initial 'desirability matrix'.[5]

Watson's woman may want to drown her bawling baby, and even do so intentionally. But if she does, she does something that she does not value at all.

The Ayer–Frankfurt–Watson cases all remind us that we may desire something without valuing it. These cases are deviant, to be sure: cases of psychological compulsion, physical addiction, and emotional disturbance. But ordinary thought tells us that these cases exist and are therefore not to be ignored. If we deliberate on the basis of our values, then, to the extent that we may act on the basis of such desires, our actions may fail to reflect our deliberations.

Consider a split of a different kind between what we value and what we desire. In 'Desiring the Bad: An Essay in Moral Psychology' Michael Stocker observes:

Through spiritual or physical tiredness, through accidie, through weakness of body, through illness, through general apathy, through despair, through inability to concentrate, through a feeling of uselessness or futility, and so on, one may feel less and less motivated to seek what is good. One's lessened desire need not signal, much less be the product of, the fact that, or one's belief that, there is less good to be obtained or produced, as in the case of a universal *Weltshmertz*.

---

[4] Ibid. 83.
[5] G. Watson, 'Free Agency', in Watson (ed.), *Free Will*, 101.

Indeed, a frequent added defect of being in such 'depressions' is that one sees all the good to be won or saved and one lacks the will, interest, desire or strength.[6]

Where the Ayer–Frankfurt–Watson cases remind us that we may desire something without valuing it, Stocker reminds us that we may value something without desiring it. Again, these cases are deviant: cases of severe 'depression'. But, again, ordinary thought tells us that these cases exist and are not to be ignored. If we deliberate on the basis of our values, then, to the extent that we may act on the basis of desires which do not adequately reflect our values, our actions may fail adequately to reflect our deliberations.

3. VALUES AND NORMATIVE REASONS

It is one thing to describe cases in which ordinary thought tells us there is a gap between deliberation and action, quite another to have a philosophically plausible interpretation of that gap. I attempt to provide such an interpretation in this section.

Note that we ordinarily distinguish two senses in which we can be said to have a reason for action.[7] The first is the sense in which we are happy to acknowledge that to do something intentionally is simply to do that thing for a reason. Here our talk of reasons is talk about the psychological states that motivate what we do, the complex of psychological states that teleologically, and perhaps causally, explain our actions. Or rather, and more accurately since we need not act on our reasons, such talk of reasons is talk about psychological states with the *potential* to motivate or explain behaviour. Let's call these our 'motivating' reasons.

In the second sense, however, we say we have a reason to do all and only those things for which we can construct a certain sort of *justification*. Justifications may, of course, be of quite different kinds. An action may be judged according to

---

[6] M. Stocker, 'Desiring the Bad: An Essay in Moral Psychology', *Journal of Philosophy*, 76 (1979), 744.

[7] M. Smith, 'The Humean Theory of Motivation', *Mind*, 96 (1987), §2. Note that what follows constitutes a correction of some of what I say there.

standards of rationality, morality, the law, etiquette, and perhaps according to other standards as well. If we are not to beg any questions, we should therefore be prepared to admit that each of these may give rise to reason claims, though such claims may not, of course, be autonomous—one kind of reason may reduce to another.[8] Let's call all these our 'normative' reasons.

When we explain an action from the intentional perspective we are clearly concerned with our motivating reasons, for we are concerned with the psychological states that teleologically, and perhaps causally, explain our actions. And when we explain an action from the deliberative perspective we are clearly concerned with our normative reasons, for we are concerned with our justifications for acting in the different ways in which we might act. But what *kinds* of justification concern us in so far as we occupy the deliberative perspective?

Certainly, we may appeal to quite different kinds of justificatory consideration when we deliberate. We may measure the alternatives against standards of morality, etiquette, the law, and perhaps against other standards as well. But, at bottom, when we have to decide how to act, we must weigh these different considerations against each other. And when we do that we seem to be trying to decide what the most reasonable or rational thing to do is. Deliberation thus seems to give a privileged place to our normative reasons where justification is judged according to standards of rationality. For the fact that some alternative is required by morality, the law, or etiquette matters in deliberation only to the extent that it is reasonable or rational to act on these requirements.

Indeed, we might now say that normative reasons, where justification is judged according to standards of rationality (and from here on I will omit this qualification), *are* the values to which we appeal when we deliberate. When we talk about

[8] I discuss the relationship between what is rationally required and what is morally required in 'Reason and Desire', *Proceedings of the Aristotelian Society*, 88 (1988); 'Dispositional Theories of Value', *Proceedings of the Aristotelian Society*, Supp. Vol. 63 (1989); 'Realism', in P. Singer (ed.), *Companion to Ethics* (Oxford: Blackwell, 1991); 'Objectivity and Moral Realism: On the Significance of the Phenomenology of Moral Experience', in C. Wright and J. Haldane (eds.), *Reality, Representation and Projection* (Oxford: Oxford University Press, forthcoming).

deliberating on the basis of our values, all we mean is that we take account of the different ways in which it would be reasonable or rational to act. And here we must emphasize the 'different', for one course of action may, of course, be *more* or *less* reasonable than another. Our concern from the deliberative perspective is with *pro tanto* reasons; with values that may be weighed one against the other; with finding out what is the most reasonable or rational way to act.

If this is right, and if, as seems plausible, motivating reasons are constituted by desires, then we have the following rough equivalences:

(1) *A* has a normative reason to φ iff *A*'s φing is valuable;
(2) *A* accepts that he has a normative reason to φ iff *A* values φing;

and

(3) *A* has a motivating reason to φ iff *A* desires to φ.

And, given these rough equivalences, we are now in a position to offer a philosophically plausible interpretation of the deviant cases served up by ordinary thought.

What is the significance of these deviant cases? The answer seems evident. They simply chart the different ways in which normative reasons and motivating reasons may *come apart*. Thus the Ayer–Frankfurt–Watson cases remind us that we may have a motivating reason to do something we have no normative reason to do; something for which we cannot, and even accept that we cannot, provide a rational justification. And the Stocker cases remind us that we may accept that we have a normative reason to do something, and perhaps even have such a reason, without having a corresponding motivating reason: that is, that we may accept that we have a rational justification for acting in a certain way and yet be entirely unmoved by that fact.

Psychological compulsions, physical addictions, and various emotional disturbances can cause us to desire to do what we cannot rationally justify and fail to desire to do what we can rationally justify. So says ordinary thought. In giving an account of the relationship between valuing and desiring we must respect ordinary thought on this score.

4. THE PUZZLE

I said at the outset that the fact that intentional action can
be explained from both the intentional and the deliberative
perspectives provides us with a puzzle. We are now in a position to explain that puzzle more fully.

To the extent that reflection on our normative reasons
moves us to act—that is, to the extent that we are effective
deliberators—accepting that we have certain normative reasons
must be bound up with having corresponding motivating
reasons. But the deviant cases remind us that our desires may
come apart from the normative reason claims we accept—that
is, that we may be ineffective deliberators. The puzzle, then, is
to explain how it can be that accepting normative reasons can
both be *bound up* with having desires and yet *come apart* from
having desires. In other words, the problem is to explain how
deliberation on the basis of our values can be practical in its
issue *to just the extent that it is*.

The puzzle here is a deep one, traceable to the view of
human psychology we have inherited from Hume.[9] For,
according to Hume, there are two main kinds of psychological
state, beliefs and desires, utterly distinct and different from
each other. Unfortunately, however, Hume's account of belief
and desire seems to leave no room for the idea that deliberation on the basis of our values is practical in its issue to just
the extent that it is. Let me explain why.

On the one hand, Hume held that there are *beliefs*, states that
purport to represent the way the world is. Since our beliefs
purport to represent the world, they are subject to rational
criticism: specifically, they are assessable in terms of truth
and falsehood according to whether or not they succeed in
representing the world to be the way it really is.

On the other hand, however, there are also *desires*, states
that represent how the world is to be. Desires are unlike beliefs
in that they do not even purport to represent the way the
world is. They are, in Hume's terms, 'original existences'.[10]
Desires are therefore not assessable in terms of truth and

[9] See esp. David Hume, *A Treatise of Human Nature* (Oxford: Clarendon
Press, 1978), esp. II. iii. 3.
[10] *A Treatise of Human Nature*, 415.

falsehood. Indeed, according to the Hume, and contrary to what we have just seen, our desires are, at bottom, not subject to any sort of rational criticism at all.[11] (We will return to this point later.)

The Humean view of human psychology is important because it provides us with a model for understanding human action: indeed, it underwrites the intentional perspective. Human action is, according to this view, produced by a combination of the two kinds of psychological state. Crudely, our beliefs tell us how the world is, and thus how it has to be changed, so as to make it the way our desires tell us it is to be. A desire without a belief would be ignorant of what change has to be made in the world so as to realize its content. A belief without a desire is simply an inert representation of how things are. An action is thus the product of these two forces: a desire representing the way the world is to be and a belief telling us how the world has to be changed so as to make it that way.

The puzzle the deliberative perspective presents should now be clear. We are to suppose that deliberating is practical in its issue to the extent that we act in the ways we do because we value what we value, and that deliberating fails to be practical in its issue to the extent that our values are irrelevant to the determination of what we do. But what is it to *value* something? That is, equivalently, what is it to accept a normative reason to do something? Is it a matter of *believing* or *desiring*? We face a dilemma.

If valuing is a matter of believing, then, given the Humean view of human psychology, it is difficult to see how anything we do intentionally could be done because we value what we value. For our beliefs cannot produce actions; they are simply inert representations of how things are. And if valuing is a matter of desiring then though it is now clear how we can act because of our values, given the Humean view, it is difficult to see how there could be the requisite *gap* between what we value and what we desire.

What is at issue is thus the very coherence of the idea that

---

[11] I discuss Hume's account of the ways in which we may rationally criticize desires in 'Reason and Desire'.

deliberation on the basis of our values is practical in its issue to just the extent that it is. In the remainder of this paper I therefore consider the two alternatives: that valuing is desiring and that valuing is believing.

5. DAVIDSON ON VALUING AS DESIRING

A reduction of valuing to desiring is proposed by Donald Davidson:

> The natural expression of . . . [an agent's] desire [say, the desire to improve the taste of the stew] . . . is . . . evaluative in form; for example, 'It is desirable to improve the taste of the stew'. We may suppose that different pro attitudes are expressed with other evaluative words in place of 'desirable'.
>
> There is no short proof that evaluative sentences express desires and other pro attitudes in the way that the sentence 'Snow is white' expresses the belief that snow is white. But the following considerations will perhaps help show what is involved. If someone who knows English says honestly 'Snow is white', then he believes snow is white. If my thesis is correct, someone who says honestly 'It is desirable that I stop smoking' has some pro attitude towards his stopping smoking. He feels some inclination to do it; in fact he will do it if nothing stands in the way, he knows how, and he has no contrary values or desires. Given this assumption, it is reasonable to generalize: if explicit value judgements represent pro attitudes, all pro attitudes may be expressed by value judgements that are at least implicit.[12]

Davidson succeeds in making it clear how we get ourselves to act by deliberating. But the cost of his doing so is a distortion in the extent to which deliberation on the basis of our values is practical in its issue. For, according to Davidson, it is impossible for an agent to act on a desire without acting on a normative reason claim he accepts. This is impossible because a desire is appropriately expressed *in* a normative reason claim. The question is therefore whether we are obliged to accept his reduction.

In so far as Davidson offers us an argument for his reduction

---

[12] D. Davidson, 'Intending', in D. Davidson, *Essays on Actions and Events* (Oxford: Clarendon Press, 1980), 86.

of valuing to desiring, it seems to me easy to see where he goes wrong. In short, he incorrectly assumes that a feature of *rational* evaluators is a feature of *all* evaluators. To be sure, a rational evaluator who says honestly 'It is desirable that I stop smoking' has some pro attitude towards stopping. But it does not follow that someone may not honestly say 'It is desirable that I stop smoking' and have no inclination to stop, and nor does it follow that someone who has some inclination to smoke may none the less be unable honestly to say 'It is desirable that I smoke'. All that follows is that, if either of these is possible, the agents in question are not *rational* evaluators. Davidson needs to rule out these forms of irrationality if his reduction is to secure conviction. And that seems no ordinary task.

In fact, however, in his earlier work on the relationship between reasons and actions, Davidson does offer us an explicit argument for the claim that motivating reasons bring with them the acceptance of corresponding normative reason claims. In 'Actions, Reasons, and Causes', for example, he tells us:

In the light of a primary reason . . . the agent is shown in his role of Rational Animal. Corresponding to the belief and attitude of a primary reason for an action [i.e. its cause] . . . we can always construct (with a little ingenuity) the premises of a syllogism from which it follows that the action has some (as Anscombe calls it) 'desirability characteristic'. Thus there is a certain irreducible—though somewhat anaemic—sense in which every rationalization justifies: from the agent's point of view there was, when he acted, something to be said for the action.[13]

The idea that a rationalization reveals the agent in his role of rational animal is a central theme in Davidson's work. For elsewhere, expanding on the theme of 'Actions, Reasons, and Causes', he notes that a rationalization must do more than merely provide us with a causal explanation of an action in terms of a desire–belief pair, for the 'problem of wayward causal chains' shows us that it must causally explain the action

---

[13] D. Davidson, 'Actions, Reasons, and Causes', in Davidson, *Essays on Actions and Events*, 9. The sense is 'anaemic' because the agent need not think that his action is desirable *all things considered*; the justification in question may be merely *pro tanto*. And this is precisely the claim to which I object. For ordinary thought tells us that even this 'anaemic' claim is too strong.

in the right way.[14] And, seeing no way in which this idea can be analysed in terms that do not take as primitive the idea that rationalizations render actions rationally intelligible, Davidson concludes that rationalizations must provide us with justifications. Why? Because, for Davidson, rational intelligibility amounts to seeing an action as having been done for a reason. And seeing an action as having been done for a reason amounts to seeing a rational justification for doing it.

The idea that rational intelligibility entails rational justifiability in some such way is in fact a common one. Thus, for example, Michael Woods has suggested: 'the concept of a reason for an action stands at the point of intersection, so to speak, between the theory of the explanation of actions and the theory of their justification'.[15] Leave out the explanatory dimension and you don't have a reason; for our appreciation of our reasons for action makes a difference to what we do. But leave out the justificatory dimension and you don't have a reason either; that's the lesson of the problem of wayward causal chains, for it teaches us that the idea of an act's having been done for a reason is primitive. Our reasons aren't mere causes, they make our actions rationally intelligible; that is, they show what we do to be rationally justifiable.

Davidson's reduction of valuing to desiring is thus a crucial element in his account of rationalization. For his reduction is supposed to show how it is possible for our desires both to explain and to justify what we do: desires, the psychological states that *causally explain* our actions, are to be thought of as appropriately expressed in evaluations, claims that permit us to *justify* our actions. How are we to reply?

Davidson is, I think, right to insist that rationalization

[14] D. Davidson, 'Freedom to Act', in Davidson, *Essays on Actions and Events*, 77–81. Here is Davidson's example of a 'wayward causal chain': 'A climber might want to rid himself of the weight and danger of holding another man on a rope, and he might know that by loosening his hold on the rope he could rid himself of the weight and danger. This belief and want might so unnerve him as to cause him to loosen his hold, and yet it might be the case that he never *chose* to loosen his hold, nor did he do it intentionally. It will not help, I think, to add that the belief and the want must combine to cause him to want to loosen his hold, for there will remain the *two* questions *how* the belief and the want caused the second want, and *how* wanting to loosen his hold caused him to loosen his hold' (p. 79).

[15] M. Woods, 'Reasons for Action and Desire', *Proceedings of the Aristotelian Society*, Supp. Vol. 46 (1972), 189.

reveals the agent in his role of rational animal; right that a rationalization must do more than merely provide us with a causal explanation of an action in terms of a desire–belief pair; right that, for it to count as a rationalization, the desire–belief pair cited must causally explain the action in the right way; right that a desire–belief pair causally explains an action in the right way only if it renders the action rationally intelligible, and thus as having been done for a reason, where this idea is not further reducible. The only question is whether he is right that, if a desire–belief pair can do all of this, it must be possible to show that the action in question is rationally justifiable. And the answer is that he is not right.

If irrational action of the kind we have been discussing here is at all possible, then it follows that rational intelligibility can be had *without* rational justifiability. And such actions certainly seem to be possible. Watson's woman who drowns her bawling baby in the bathwater, for example, certainly does something that is rationally intelligible. We do not have here an instance of a wayward causal chain; she acted for a reason. But, as we have seen, what she does is not rationally justifiable, not even by her own lights.

Nor is it difficult to see how such intelligibility can be had in the absence of a justification. For wherever we have an explanation of an intentional action in terms of a desire–belief pair we have an explanation that renders the action intelligible as one that serves a goal had by the agent. Such a teleological explanation, and thus such rational intelligibility, is not available when the action is not intentional; that is, in cases in which a desire–belief pair causally explains an action but not in the right way. The availability of a teleological explanation thus suffices for rational intelligibility, for it suffices to provide us with the motivating reason for which the act was done. However, it does not suffice for rational justifiability. For that we require a normative reason. The woman who drowns her bawling baby in the bathwater acts in a way that serves her goals, and thus her action is teleologically explicable. But what she does is not rationally justifiable, for the goal that she serves is itself unreasonable even by her own lights. She acts on a motivating reason, but she cannot provide herself with a normative reason for acting in that way.

In attempting to reduce valuing to desiring, then, Davidson

ignores this distinction between two ways in which an action can be rendered rationally intelligible. And the fact that he ignores this distinction infects his whole account of rationalization. It makes his claim that rationalizations reveal the agent in his role of 'rational animal' too strong to be credible. We therefore have every reason to reject Davidson's reduction of valuing to desiring in favour of an account that preserves the distinction between teleological explicability and rational justifiability.

6. GAUTHIER ON VALUING AS A MODE OF DESIRING

David Gauthier suggests that valuing is not desiring *simpliciter*, but rather a *mode* of desiring:

Practical rationality in the most general sense is identified with maximization . . . An objector might agree to identify practical rationality with maximization, but insist that a measure of individual preference is not the appropriate quantity to maximize. It is rational to maximize *value*; the theory of rational choice implicitly identifies value with [a precise measure of preference: i.e. with] . . . utility, but the objector challenges this identification . . . [He might] agree that value is a measure, but insist that it does not measure brute preferences, which may be misinformed, inexperienced, or ill-considered. We shall accept this view in so far as it concerns the manner in which preferences are held.[16]

Though on the surface Gauthier's view is preferable to Davidson's, on examination it is plain that his view too is in conflict with ordinary thought.

According to Gauthier, an agent values a certain outcome only if he desires that outcome *in a certain way*: that is, only if his desires pass certain tests of reflection and experience.[17] Suppose I prefer white wine to red, but without ever having had either a sip or a sniff of red wine. This preference may not pass the test of experience, for, tasting red wine, I might find that I prefer red wine to white. Or suppose I have to decide

---

[16] D. Gauthier, *Morals by Agreement* (Oxford: Clarendon Press, 1986), 22–3.
[17] Gauthier, *Morals by Agreement*, 29–32.

whether to have white wine or red, and that I choose white, so revealing my preference, but without having given the matter any thought whatsoever. This preference may not pass the test of reflection. For, on reflection, I might have found that I prefer red wine to white.

Though these constraints on the mode of desiring appropriate for valuing are not, as they stand, sufficient to rule out the deviant cases we have described, Gauthier could quite evidently enrich his conception of the appropriate mode. Thus, he might add, valuing is desiring where the desire in question requires no support from a psychological compulsion, a physical addiction, or a state of emotional distress. In this way he could agree with ordinary thought that we may desire an outcome without valuing it.

However, while these amendments would suffice to do that, they would fail altogether to show how we may value an outcome without desiring it. Indeed, if valuing is a mode of desiring at all, as Gauthier suggests, then valuing without desiring becomes a conceptual impossibility. But ordinary thought tells us that valuing without desiring isn't just possible, it is actual. The 'depressions' Michael Stocker describes sap our desires while leaving our evaluative outlooks intact.

The problem with any view according to which valuing is a mode of desiring, then, is that it will only account for the ways in which a desire we have may fail to be rational. It will ignore altogether the ways in which we may fail to be rational in virtue of lacking certain desires. Given that we may accept rational justifications for acting in certain ways and yet, due to depressions, remain unmoved, such cases certainly seem to exist. It therefore follows that we should reject the view that valuing is a mode of desiring.

7. LEWIS ON VALUING AS DESIRING TO DESIRE

It might be thought that a reduction of valuing to desiring is still on the cards. We need simply to reconceive the desire in question in a more radical way. Consider, therefore, David Lewis's reduction of valuing to desiring to desire:

So we turn to desires. But we'd better not say that valuing something is just the same as desiring it. That may do for some of us: those who manage, by strength of will or by good luck, to desire exactly as they desire to desire. But not all of us are so fortunate. The thoughtful addict may desire his euphoric daze, but not value it. Even apart from all the costs and risks, he may hate himself for desiring something he values not at all. It is a desire he wants very much to be rid of. He desires his high, but he does not desire to desire it. He does not desire an unaltered, mundane state of consciousness, but he does desire to desire it. We conclude that he does not value what he desires, but rather he values what he desires to desire.[18]

Lewis's reduction of valuing to desiring to desire avoids the problem facing Davidson's. For an agent may certainly first-order desire other than he second-order desires. And his reduction avoids the problem facing Gauthier's as well. For an agent may certainly second-order desire other than he first-order desires.

In this way, then, it might therefore be thought that Lewis's reduction promises us just the distinction we want between teleological explicability and rational justifiability. An action is teleologically explicable if it is first-order explainable. But in order to be rationally justifiable, an action must be second-order explainable. Let's consider this view in more detail.[19]

The point that emerged in our discussion of Davidson's and Gauthier's reductions of valuing to desiring was that though a *rational* agent desires in accordance with the normative reason claims he accepts, an *irrational* agent may desire other-

---

[18] D. Lewis, 'Dispositional Theories of Value', *Proceedings of the Aristotelian Society*, Supp. Vol. 63 (1989), 115. In 'Freedom of the Will and the Concept of a Person', Harry Frankfurt also defends the idea that valuing is desiring to desire.

[19] Let's be clear about the question we are asking. Since we have seen no alternative but to identify valuing with accepting a normative reason claim, the question is whether Lewis's reduction of valuing to desiring to desire makes that identification seem plausible. It must be said at the outset, however, that Lewis says nothing to suggest that he would accept such an identification himself. Thus we must not suppose that the discussion that follows constitutes a criticism of Lewis. Rather, his reduction provides us with a useful focus for discussing a view that naturally suggests itself given the failure of Davidson's and Gauthier's reductions. Our criticism of Lewis, at this point, is rather implicit in the argument given earlier for identifying valuing something with taking it to be a reasonable or rational thing to do. Mark Johnston develops this criticism of Lewis at some length in his 'Dispositional Theories of Value', *Proceedings of the Aristotelian Society*, Supp. Vol. 63 (1989), 149–61.

wise. This suggests that normative reasons are subject to the following constraint:

> (C1) If an agent accepts that he has a normative reason to φ, he rationally should desire to φ.

If accepting a normative reason claim is the same as valuing, and valuing is desiring to desire, then it follows that an agent who desires to desire to φ rationally should desire to φ. But is this right?

It might be thought that it is. Consider once again the Humean picture of the difference between beliefs and desires. The role of a belief is, you will recall, to represent the world. Thus a belief that arises independently of the way the world is is defective, a belief we can rationally criticize. But now consider desires by analogy.

The role of a desire is to make the world be the way it says it is to be. Thus a desire that persists without changing the world in the requisite way is, by parity of reasoning, a desire that we can rationally criticize. This form of rational criticism may be defeasible. For example, we may not rationally criticize a desire that fails to realize its content if it was outweighed by stronger desires. But, in the absence of appropriate defeaters, the criticism stands. If this is right, then it might be thought that an agent who desires to desire to φ but who does not desire to φ may be rationally criticized after all. Thus (C1).

Does this provide an adequate defence of (C1)? Even if it captures the letter of (C1), it does not capture its spirit. For our earlier discussions suggest that values rationally constrain desires in the following stronger sense. Suppose someone values φing, but desires not to φ. Such an agent rationally should get rid of the desire not to φ and acquire the desire to φ *instead*. However, for all we have said so far, he should merely acquire the desire to φ *as well*. Can we derive the stronger conclusion that he should get rid of his desire not to φ from the reduction of valuing to desiring to desire, plus further plausible assumptions? At this point we need to complicate our discussion. We need to ask what further principles rationally constrain desire formation and retention.

So far we have seen how an agent who desires to desire to φ, and who desires not to φ, may find himself rationally constrained to end up desiring to φ as well. But now consider his new set of desires. Is he irrational for having this combination? He may certainly seem to be. But why?

The obvious suggestion is that he is irrational because his desires are not co-satisfiable.[20] However, unco-satisfiability all by itself doesn't seem to be enough. For suppose I desire to be a musician and desire to be a philosopher. I do not seem to be irrational if I do not get rid of one desire or the other once I realize that I cannot satisfy both these desires in the world as it is. I may well end up being disappointed, but that is quite another matter.

It might be thought that this response helps focus on what is at issue. The crucial difference between this case and the other is that in this case it is at least logically possible for my desires to be co-satisfied. Where desiring to be both a musician and a philosopher maps out a coherent life, albeit one that is not empirically realizable, desiring both to φ and not to φ maps out nothing whatsoever. Co-satisfiability *simpliciter* may not be a constraint on rational desire formation and retention, but, the objector might say, the *logical possibility* of co-satisfiability does seem to be such a constraint.

Let's grant this line of thought for the sake of argument. Does it help? With the logical possibility of co-satisfiability under our belt can we show that the reduction of valuing to desiring to desire yields the stronger conclusion that someone who values φing, but who also desires not to φ, rationally should get rid of the desire not to φ and acquire the desire to φ instead?

Certainly we can now see that someone who desires to desire to φ, and who therefore ends up desiring to φ, and yet who desires not to φ as well, ends up having a set of desires that is irrational. However, and importantly, nothing said so far tells us why the rational thing for such an agent to do is to give up desiring not to φ, as opposed, say, to giving up his desire to φ, and, perhaps, his desire to desire to φ as well.[21]

---

[20] I do not want to endorse this suggestion myself, for I am unsure whether desires, as opposed to intentions, need to satisfy any condition of co-satisfiability at all. My concern is rather to show that *even if* desires must satisfy some such condition, it will not help.

[21] Note that the logical possibility of co-satisfiability does not tell us that it is

The logical possibility of co-satisfiability simply tells us that *some* change has to be made that brings about the logical possibility of co-satisfiability. It doesn't tell us that one of his desires is to be rationally preferred to the other, and thus it certainly doesn't tell us which of his desires is to be rationally preferred to the other.

Let's therefore forget co-satisfiability. There is another option. For in order to make the reduction of valuing to desiring to desire consistent with the claim that an agent rationally should desire in accordance with the normative reason claims he accepts, we could simply add to the reduction the following principle:

(D) If an agent desires to desire to φ then he rationally should desire to φ, and if he desires to desire to φ and desires not to φ then he rationally should get rid of the desire not to φ and acquire the desire to φ instead.

But this response misses the point.

(C1) is supposed to act as a constraint on an adequate account of normative reasons. The hope is that, if we can reduce accepting a normative reason to desiring to desire, then the reduction, in conjunction with other plausible assumptions, will actually entail this principle. But (D) is hardly an additional plausible assumption. It is a theoretically motivated principle that we should accept only if we are given an adequate argument. But the only argument we have been given is that it must be true if the reduction of valuing to desiring to desire is correct. And, in this context, that is not a good argument.

Another way of putting the same point is this. The reduction of valuing to desiring to desire in conjunction with (D) does indeed capture the spirit of (C1). But the reduction itself plays no significant role in this. The spirit of (C1) is captured by the conjunction of even the most implausible reduction with a

irrational to have the desire to desire to φ and the desire not to φ. For these desires *are* co-satisfiable. If having this pair of desires is irrational then we need a further principle to explain why, presumably: 'It is irrational to have a pair of desires if their co-satisfaction brings about the having of a pair of desires that it is logically impossible to co-satisfy.' Thus the added qualification that the agent may have to rid himself of his desire to desire to φ as well.

principle, like (D), that stipulates the very connection we want to derive. Things would, of course, be different if we had some *independent* reason to accept the reduction. The point is just that, in the absence of such reasons, we have no reason to prop up the reduction by accepting (D). Let's therefore consider Lewis's reduction on its own terms to see whether any independent reasons are forthcoming.

Those who seek to reduce valuing to higher-order desiring face a formidable objection.[22] Since they seek to reduce valuing to higher-order desiring, they must come clean and identify valuing with higher-order desiring *at some particular level or other*. Lewis does come clean in this way. He identifies valuing with second-order desiring. But now the quite general problem such theorists face can be put in the form of a question for Lewis in particular. Why identify valuing with second-order desiring? Why not third-order, or fourth-order, or . . . ?

The implication of the question is, of course, that each identification is as plausible as any other. But if each is as plausible as any other, then *all* such identifications are equally implausible. Therefore, no plausible reduction has been effected.

Lewis confronts this objection fairly and squarely. However, his response is less than convincing. He tells us that his reason for favouring the second over the first is that 'a thoughtful addict may desire his euphoric daze, but not value it'.[23] And he tells us that his reason for favouring some level other than the highest order at which an agent desires is that 'if we go for the highest order, we automatically rule out the case of someone who desires to value differently than he does, yet this case is not obviously impossible'.[24] So far this line of reasoning seems perfectly sound. However, and unfortunately, there are no more premises to Lewis's argument. From these premises he concludes that valuing is second-order desiring.

The problem isn't just that there is a gap between Lewis's

---

[22] This objection is forcefully developed by Gary Watson in 'Free Agency', 107–9. The target of his attack is Harry Frankfurt in 'Freedom of the Will and the Concept of a Person'. Frankfurt attempts to respond to Watson's criticism, unsuccessfully I think, in 'Identification and Externality', in his *The Importance of What We Care About* (Cambridge: Cambridge University Press, 1988).

[23] 'Dispositional Theories of Value', 115.

[24] Ibid. 116.

premisses and his conclusion. The problem is that his argument demonstrates how formidable the original objection which it is supposed to answer really is. For his conclusion is simply arbitrary, given his premisses. He could equally well have chosen any level other than the first or the highest. And that just *is* the original objection.

If this is right then it follows that we cannot identify valuing with desiring to desire *at any level*. This is not to say that someone who values φing may not, even perhaps usually, desire to desire to φ. It is merely to insist that we not mistake this contingent fact for a conceptual necessity.

8. VALUING AS BELIEVING

If we cannot reduce valuing to desiring then we have no alternative but to consider reducing valuing to believing. Now Lewis, like Davidson, rejects the idea that valuing is believing. But why does he reject this idea?

Lewis reasons as follows:

What is valuing? It is some sort of mental state, directed toward that which is valued. It might be a feeling, or a belief, or a desire. . . . A feeling?—Evidently not, because the feelings we have when we value things are too diverse. A belief? . . . if valuing something just meant having a certain belief about it, then it seems that there would be no conceptual reason why valuing is a favourable attitude. We might not have favoured the things we value. We might have opposed them, or been entirely indifferent. So we turn to desires.[25]

Lewis's argument against identifying valuing with believing thus depends crucially on the idea that there is some sort of conceptual connection between valuing and desiring. But does granting that connection really preclude identifying valuing with believing valuable?

Lewis seems to think it does, but it is not at all clear why. After all, as he himself notes, the addict may desire his euphoric daze, but not value it; and he may value an unaltered, mundane state of consciousness, but not desire it. And to these examples we may add Watson's woman with a

[25] Ibid.

bawling baby; his angry, defeated squash player; and Stocker's depressives. In other words, it isn't just a conceptual possibility, it actually happens that we are indifferent, or opposed, to what we value! Whatever the precise nature of the conceptual connection between valuing and desiring, then, it does not obviously preclude the sort of indifference or opposition to what we value that the identification of valuing with believing valuable makes possible.

What is the nature of the conceptual connection between believing valuable and desiring? The answer supported by the discussion thus far is that the conceptual connection is simply the defeasible connection described in (C1): we *rationally should* desire what we value. If valuing is believing valuable, and believing valuable is believing that we have a normative reason, then the connection we are after is this:

(C2) If an agent believes that he has a normative reason to ϕ, he rationally should desire to ϕ.

And now we have to face the real problem. For how are we to demonstrate the possibility of this kind of conceptual connection between our beliefs and desires?

Plainly our strategy must be to provide an analysis of our concept of a normative reason and then show that that analysis, in conjunction with other plausible assumptions, actually entails (C2). But can we do this?

Certainly there have been attempts. Consider, for example, the following suggestion of Mark Johnston's:

As for securing an internal or conceptual connection between value and the will, *this* at least is true: to the extent that one is not weak-willed one will desire . . . as one judges valuable. So much is part of the definition of weakness of will. As far as making the connection between judging valuable and desiring . . . particularly intelligible, this seems to me achieved by the observation that 'valuable' and 'desire-worthy' are near synonyms. If judging valuable is pretty much judging desire-worthy then it is readily intelligible why judging valuable should lead to desiring.[26]

This argument might well be convincing if we were to accept the claim to near synonymy. But should we? Are 'valuable' and 'desire-worthy' near synonyms?

[26] Johnston, 'Dispositional Theories of Value', 161.

Certainly, they are not actual synonyms. For whereas if φing is valuable then φing is worth doing, if φing is desire-worthy then φing is worth desiring. But 'worth doing' means something different from 'worth desiring'.

However, though not actual synonyms, Johnston may still be right that they are near synonyms. For he might think that it follows from the fact that something is worth doing that it is worth desiring, and that it follows from the fact that something is worth desiring that it is worth doing. But even this seems quite wrong to me. For, as Derek Parfit has recently pointed out, it may not be desirable that we desire to do what it is desirable that we do, and it may not be desirable that we do what it is desirable that we desire to do.[27] Consider Parfit's example.

The self-interest theory tells me that the desirability of an action or a desire is a function of the contribution that that action or desire makes to my long-term self-interest. Thus it is desirable that I *do* just one thing: promote my long-term self-interest. However, as Parfit points out, it does not follow that it is desirable that I desire to promote my long-term self-interest. Indeed, it may well be undesirable that I desire to promote my long-term self-interest. It all depends on whether having that desire is necessary in order for me to have the set of desires the having of which will contribute most to my long-term self-interest. And that desire may well not be necessary, for my long-term self-interest may be best served by my desiring to act for the sake of family and friends, write books, advance humanity, and so on, without having any direct concern whatever for my own long-term self-interest.

If this seems right, then it follows that the self-interest theory tells me that it is desirable that I desire to do what it is not desirable that I do. And it also tells me that it is desirable to do what it is not desirable that I desire to do. However unlikely this may seem, the point to emphasize is that the issue is an *empirical* one, and so requires an empirical answer. The answer is not determined by 'near' conceptual fiat.

The self-interest theory is, of course, just an example. But what is true of the self-interest theory may well be true of other

[27] D. Parfit, *Reasons and Persons* (Oxford: Oxford University Press, 1984), pt. I.

substantive theories of practical rationality, even the correct
theory. Johnston's argument overlooks the possibility of this
sort of split between what it is desirable that we do and what it
is desirable that we desire to do. As such, it fails as an attempt
to make 'readily intelligible why judging valuable should lead
to desiring'.

However, though Johnston's argument rests on a false claim
to near synonymy it is, I think, on exactly the right track. If
anything can make intelligible the connection between judging
desirable and desiring it is an analysis of our concept of desirability. Let's therefore see whether we can formulate an
argument along his lines in a way that avoids Parfit's objection.

We have seen that to say an action is desirable is to say
that we have a reason to do it, where the relevant norms of
assessment are the norms of rationality. Now note that we can
further explicate this concept, the concept of what we have
normative reason to do, though in a way rather different from
that suggested by Johnston. For it is a platitude to say that *what
it is desirable that we do*—that is, what we have reason to do—is
what we would desire to do if we were rational.

If an argument along Johnston's lines is to be found, then
the argument will have to be that this platitude somehow
suffices to make readily intelligible why believing desirable
should lead to desiring. I believe that we can provide such an
argument. However, before giving the argument, let me say
a little about the platitude itself in order to forestall some
objections.

9. FORESTALLING SOME OBJECTIONS

The platitude tells us that what it is desirable to do is what we
would desire to do if we were rational. But is this really a
platitude? Is it too vulnerable to Parfit's objection? It might be
thought so: 'To say that we would desire to φ if we were
rational is to say that desiring to φ is rationally appropriate. But
the claim that *desiring to* φ is rationally appropriate is different
from the claim that φ*ing* is rationally appropriate. Yet what we
want is an explication of the latter idea, not the former.'

Suppose, for the sake of argument, that what we have
reason to do, in our actual circumstances, is promote our long-

term self-interest. According to the platitude it follows that, if I were rational, I would desire that, when in my actual circumstances, I promote my long-term self-interest. But this is not to say that that desire is rationally appropriate in a way that is vulnerable to Parfit's objection.

In order to see this, note that the platitude concerns a desire I would have, if I were rational, about what I am to *do*, in my actual circumstances. It does not concern a desire I actually have in my actual circumstances. And nor does it concern a desire I would have, if I were rational, about what I am to *desire* in my actual circumstances. Thus, for all the platitude tells us, what it is rational for me to do and what it is rational for me to desire may be quite different. It all depends on whether, if I were rational, what I would desire that I do, in a given set of circumstances, and what I would desire that I desire, in a given set of circumstances, are the same.

Desirability is, then, a function of our rationally appropriate desires. But what is desirable is not the having of those desires themselves, but rather the *objects* of those desires. It thus seems to me quite safe to say that the platitude avoids Parfit's objection.

Even if the platitude avoids Parfit's objection, it might be thought vulnerable to an objection from another direction: 'If the platitude is right, "ϕing is what I would desire if I were rational" gives the content of the thought "ϕing is desirable". Thoughts about our values thus turn out to be thoughts about our desires! But this seems wrong. When we deliberate we do not focus our attention in on ourselves and our own desires, we focus our attention out on the value of what we desire. Value judgements are not introspective claims about our desires, they are claims about a standard against which our desires are measured.' This objection is wrong in two ways.

First, the platitude does not tell us that thoughts about our values focus in on ourselves and our own desires. Instead, it offers us a striking contrast between introspective judgements about our own desires and our value judgements. In order to see this, contrast two ways in which a desire may figure in deliberation if, as the objector supposes, the platitude gives the content of our thoughts about our values (I question this assumption presently).

Suppose *A* very much wants to dance a jig. His desire may be taken into account in his deliberations in the following way. Recognizing his desire, he considers it and decides that it is a desire both worth having and worth acting upon. It will be fun to dance a jig, for it is fun to give one's body over to the music and move in the regular pattern that it dictates.

When *A* deliberates in this way, how does desire figure in his decision-making? Desire figures in his decision-making in at least two ways. First, introspected, his desire to dance a jig figures as an object of positive evaluation. This is indeed a case in which *A* focuses in on himself and his own desires. However, that is hardly surprising given that it is, *inter alia*, his desire to dance a jig that is being evaluated. Secondly, however, the fact that *A* would desire that, in his actual circumstances, he both desires to dance a jig and acts on that desire also figures in his decision-making. But is this an introspective judgement? Certainly not. For what makes the judgement true is not an introspectible fact about *A*; rather, it is a hypothetical fact about *A*: that is, a fact about what he would want if he were rational.

Moreover, whereas the introspective claim about *A* that he has a certain desire, say the desire to dance a jig, gives us no reason to suppose that his desire is worth having or worth acting upon, the fact that, if he were rational, *A* would want that, in his actual circumstances, he both has that desire and acts upon it does give us such a reason. This hypothetical fact about *A*'s desire, then, does seem to offer us a standard against which his introspectible desires may be measured, just as the objector insists.

Even if the platitude does give the content of our evaluative thoughts, then, our evaluative thoughts are not thereby made introspective judgements. They are introspective only if the *object* of evaluation is an introspectible item. Moreover, as we have just seen, the platitude does suffice to show how values constitute a standard against which our introspectible desires may be measured. It thus seems to me that the objection simply misses the mark.[28]

[28] There is, in fact, a third way in which desire may figure in decision-making. Suppose *B* has had a strict puritanical upbringing. He has been taught, and he believes, that bodily pleasures are to be avoided, that they

I said that the objection is wrong in two ways. The second is in the assumption that the platitude constitutes, or holds the place for, a *reductive analysis* of our concept of desirability. This assumption is implicit in the claim that the platitude gives the content of our thoughts about desirability. But quite the opposite is in fact true. Though the platitude can be refined, it cannot be turned into a reductive analysis. Thus, contrary to the objection, the platitude does not even entail that evaluative thoughts are thoughts about our own hypothetical desires.

The idea that the platitude holds the place for a reductive analysis of our concept of desirability, or a normative reason, is a common one. The idea seems to be that we can turn the platitude into a reductive analysis by giving a substantive account of what is required in order to be 'rational'. Perhaps the best-known recent attempt is Bernard Williams's in his 'Internal and External Reasons'.[29] He offers us the following:

A has a reason to φ in circumstances *C* if and only if *A* would desire that he φ's, in circumstances *C*, if:

(1) *A* had no false beliefs,
(2) *A* had all relevant true beliefs,
(3) *A* deliberated correctly.

Williams motivates the claim that these conditions constrain what counts as a reason by focusing on particular examples.

corrupt. Moreover, suppose he believes, plausibly, that dancing a jig is a way of getting bodily pleasure. And suppose further that *B* finds himself wanting desperately to dance a jig. Imagine how his desire would be taken into account in his deliberations. *B*'s desire certainly doesn't figure in his deliberations as the object of a positive evaluation. Indeed, if anything, it figures in his deliberations as the object of a negative evaluation. In deciding what he can justify doing, *B* may well have to conclude, therefore, that he cannot justify acting on his desire to dance a jig. Indeed, he may have to conclude that he cannot even justify having the desire. This may be the conclusion to which his deliberations lead him. However, the fact remains that *B* has the desire. And, alienated from it though he may be, he may find it simply irresistible. Now, it seems, we have a desire figuring in decision-making quite *independently* of deliberation. For in this case *B*'s recognition of the fact that he has the desire seems to determine his decision about what he will do *independently* of his judgements of value. This case is, of course, only one of many. The Ayer–Frankfurt–Watson cases all suggest that desires may figure in decision-making in something like this way. Philip Pettit and I mention cases of this kind in our discussion of capriciousness in 'Backgrounding Desire', §3.4. We hope to discuss these cases in greater detail elsewhere.

[29] B. Williams, 'Internal and External Reasons', in B. Williams, *Moral Luck* (Cambridge: Cambridge University Press, 1981).

Consider (1). Suppose an agent desires to mix some stuff from a certain bottle with tonic and drink it. However, he has this desire only because he desires to drink a gin and tonic and believes that the bottle contains gin, whereas in fact the bottle contains petrol. As Williams points out: 'it is just very odd to say that he has a reason to drink this stuff, and natural to say that he has no reason to drink it, although he thinks that he has'.[30] Why? Because he would not have the desire if he were rational: that is, *if he had no false beliefs*.

Consider (2). Suppose I desire to buy a Picasso. Moreover, suppose that, without my knowing, there is a Picasso for sale very cheap in the local second-hand shop. It would certainly be both true and appropriate for a friend to tell me that I have a reason to buy something from that shop. For, quite in general, as Williams says, an agent 'may be ignorant of some fact such that if he did know it he would, in virtue of some element in [his set of desires] . . . be disposed to φ: we can say that he has a reason to φ, though he does not know it'.[31] Why? Because he would desire to φ if he were rational: that is, *if he had all relevant true beliefs*.

Now consider (3). So far we have taken it for granted that desires and beliefs interact in ways that generate new desires. But this is, of course, a substantive claim about practical reason. Our desires and beliefs only generate new desires if we deliberate correctly: that is, *inter alia*, according to the means–ends principle. Moreover, as Williams points out, means–ends reasoning is only one mode of rational deliberation among many. Another example is

practical reasoning . . . leading to the conclusion that one has reason to φ because φing would be the most convenient, economical, pleasant etc. way of satisfying some element in [one's set of desires] . . . and this of course is controlled by other elements in [one's set of desires] . . . if not necessarily in a very clear or determinate way. [And] . . . there are much wider possibilities for deliberation, such as: thinking how the satisfaction of elements in [one's set of desires] . . . can be combined: eg. by time-ordering; where there is some irresoluble conflict among the elements of [one's set of desires] . . .

---

[30] Ibid. 102.
[31] Ibid. 103.

considering which one attaches most weight to . . . or, again, finding constitutive solutions, such as deciding what would make for an entertaining evening, granted that one wants entertainment.[32]

I will return to this point presently. For now, simply note that, given the wide variety of principles that govern rational deliberation, an agent has a reason to φ only if he would desire to if, in addition to the other constraints, his deliberations conform to these principles: that is, *if he deliberates correctly*.

So far so good. However, Williams doesn't offer us any more constraints on what is to count as a reason. But, as should be evident given the concerns of this paper, more constraints are certainly needed if we are to succeed in giving a reduction.

Consider, for example, Watson's woman who desires to drown her bawling baby in the bathwater. As we saw earlier, her desires are, even by her own lights, *unreasonable*. She desires to do what she believes she has no reason to do. But Williams's reduction does not have this conclusion. Her desire is not the result of any false belief; it would not go away if she were to acquire some further true belief; and nor does she seem to be suffering from some deliberative failure, or at least, not any failure of the kind Williams describes. And, of course, there are other examples as well: Watson's defeated squash player, not to mention Stocker's depressives.

It might be thought that these examples simply require the addition of a further condition:

(4) *A* is in a normal emotional state.

Nor, it might be said, is this *ad hoc*. It merely assumes, rightly, that we give rational privilege to the desires we would have if we were in such a state.

The additional condition certainly succeeds in telling us that Watson's woman with a bawling baby has no reason to drown her baby. For though she actually desires to drown her baby, if she were in a normal emotional state, she would not desire that, when suffering severe emotional distress due to the bawling of her baby, she actually drowns it. And perhaps the

---

[32] Ibid. 104.

additional condition would let us deal with Watson's angry, defeated squash player and Stocker's depressives too.

However, though not at all *ad hoc*, and even if successful at dealing with these examples, it seems to me that the need for a condition like (4) signals the end of the search for a reductive analysis. For the analysis is truly *reductive* only if, in specifying what is to count as a 'normal' emotional state, we need make no reference to what we have reason to do. But I see no reason to suppose that this could be done. For we have no grip on what is to count as a 'normal' emotional state except in the context of our practice of giving reasons and excusing failures.[33] That this is so is manifest in the fact that we simply add to our list of what is to count as a 'normal' emotional state as further examples crop up. What guides us is our conception of what is to count as a good reason or an excuse, not the intrinsic nature of the emotional state itself.

And matters are, of course, in fact much worse. For other examples force further revisions. If the heroin addict's and the kleptomaniac's desires do not provide them with reasons, and if we have no reason to suppose that their desires would disappear if they satisfied conditions (1) to (4), then we need to add a further condition, presumably:

(5) *A* is in a normal physical state.

And, once again, though not at all *ad hoc*, and even if successful at dealing with these examples, the need for a condition like (5) signals the end of the search for a reductive analysis. For, again, we have no grip on what is to count as a 'normal' physical state outside of our practice of giving reasons and excusing failures.

It is important to note what this implies. It does not imply that the platitude is not a platitude. For, equally, just as the platitude tells us, we have no grip on what is to count as a reason except in terms of what we would desire if we were rational. What it implies is rather that this platitude cannot be honed into a reductive analysis. What we have is, if you like, a non-reductive 'explication' of our concept of a reason.

---

[33] Stocker makes a similar point at the end of 'Desiring the Bad: An Essay in Moral Psychology'.

If this is right then, significantly, a central theme in Williams's work on reasons is shown to be fundamentally flawed. For, in embracing the platitude, Williams takes himself to be defending a *relativized* conception of reasons. As he puts it:

the truth of the sentence ['*A* has a reason to φ'] . . . implies, very roughly, that *A* has some motive which will be served or furthered by his φing, and if this turns out not to be so the sentence is false: there is a condition relating to the agent's aims, and if this is not satisfied it is not true to say . . . that he has a reason to φ.[34]

And again later:

Basically, and by definition, [an analysis of reasons] . . . must display a relativity of [a] . . . reason statement to the agent's *subjective motivational set* . . .[35]

But what is the relativity?

Agreeing that an agent has a reason to φ only if he would desire to φ if he were rational, Williams insists that what an agent would desire if he were rational is relative to the desires he actually has; his rational desires are, as it were, *functions from* his actual desires, where the functions are those described in conditions (1) to (3). Thus, he claims, we cannot expect that, if we were all rational, different agents would converge upon a unique set of desires. This is why Williams claims to be defending a Humean conception of reasons.[36] For he denies that rational agents all have the *same* reasons.[37]

If (1) to (3) constituted a reductive analysis of a reason then it seems to me that we can see why Williams makes this assertion. For the only element in the analysis that holds out the hope for a convergence in the desires of rational agents is condition (3): the requirement that agents deliberate correctly. But if we give this condition a reductive construal, then that hope simply fades away.

Consider, for example, the most revisionary of the forms of deliberation Williams proposes. He tells us that 'where there

---

[34] Williams, 'Internal and External Reasons', 101.
[35] Ibid. 102.
[36] Ibid.
[37] This comes out most clearly in his discussion of the Owen Wingrave example: ibid. 108–11.

is some irresoluble conflict among the elements' of one's set of desires one must consider 'which one attaches most weight to'. Now this sounds like a familiar overall consistency and coherence requirement. Construed as a function performed on an agent's actual desires, we can imagine that, in the interests of overall consistency and coherence, the agent may lose certain desires and acquire others. But the scope for this sort of revision is, we might think, severely limited. For what the agent is after is a consistent and coherent set of desires, given his actual desires as the starting-point. Thus, once we add in the fact that agents differ wildly in the desires that they actually have, we see no reason to suppose that, even as a matter of *empirical* fact, when this function is performed on the desires of agents with diverse sets of desires, they will end up with the same set of desires. Still less do we see reason to suppose that they would converge on a set of desires as a matter of *rational* fact. In other words, rational agents may yet differ in the desires that they have.

However, note how different things look when we construe condition (3) non-reductively. For the starting-point of deliberation is not now the agent's actual desires, but the value judgements he actually believes. And, according to condition (3), what he is required to do is to revise them so as to make for overall consistency and coherence.

Here, again, there is scope for the agent to give up some of his values, on the grounds that they are false, and acquire new values, on the grounds that they allow him to make better sense of the rest of his values. But it seems that, in this case, the scope for massive revisions in an agent's evaluative beliefs is much greater. Equip the agent with a robust sense of his own fallibility and a disposition to consider the evaluative beliefs of others as in conflict with his own, as opposed to merely different from his own, and we are well on the way to the possibility of a convergence, a convergence mandated by reason itself.[38]

Now there is certainly no proof that rational agents would actually end up converging on a single set of values. But,

---

[38] Myself I think that this is one way of reading Rawls's argument in his 'Outline of a Decision Procedure for Ethics', *Philosophical Review*, 60 (1951).

equally, there is no proof that they would not. There is simply no way of telling in advance. We must give the justifications and see where the arguments lead. But, if this is right, then it is simply a bald assertion to claim, as Williams does, that the platitude itself implies that our reasons are *relative*.[39]

10. THE PUZZLE SOLVED

I said the platitude that desirability is simply a matter of what we would desire if we were rational suffices for making sense of (C2): the claim that if I believe that I have a normative reason to φ, then I rationally should desire to φ. Let me now explain why that is so.

(C2) tells us that if we believe we have a normative reason to φ then we rationally should desire to φ. And that is surely no surprise if believing that we have a normative reason to φ, or that it is desirable that we φ, amounts to the belief that we would desire to φ if we were rational. For suppose we believe that we would desire to φ if we were rational and yet fail to desire to φ. Are we irrational? We most certainly are. And by our own lights! For we fail to have a desire that we believe it is rational for us to have. In other words, if we believe that we

---

[39] More formally the point can be put like this. Suppose that the proper analysis of the claim 'It is desirable that p' is relative. Thus: 'It is desirable$_x$ that p iff x would desire that p if x were rational', where 'desirable$_x$' is to be read as 'desirable-from-x's-point-of-view'. The relativization is not idle so long as a convergence in judgements of desirability does not emerge under conditions of full rationality. But if such a convergence were to emerge, the relativization would become idle; for then everyone's point of view would be the same as everyone else's. And now the point can be put like this: we can discover whether relative reasons are *the only reasons that there are* by seeing whether the arguments for and against our judgements of desirability lead us to converge on a single set of judgements of desirability. (Note that I have here abstracted away from the purely conceptual question 'Do we think of our judgements of desirability as relative (that is, as implicitly indexed to individuals) or as non-relative (that is, as implicitly universally quantified)?' My own view is that we think of our judgements of desirability as non-relative: that is, that the proper analysis of our judgements of desirability would have them concern what *we* would want if we were fully rational. Only so can we explain why we think of ourselves as in disagreement with, as opposed to merely different from, each other, in so far as we accept different evaluations. For more on this see my 'Dispositional Theories of Value' and 'Realism'.)

would desire to φ if we were rational then we rationally should desire to φ. And that is just (C2).

In this way we capture the letter of (C2), but can we capture its spirit? If we believe that we would desire to φ if we were rational, and yet desire not to φ, can we see why we should get rid of the desire not to φ and acquire the desire to φ instead, rather than, for example, change our evaluative belief? (Here we recall the problem facing the reduction of valuing to desiring to desire.)

We certainly can. Remember, φing is desirable just in case we would desire to φ if we were rational. Now, by hypothesis, what we believe is that we would desire to φ if we were rational. We do not believe that we would desire *not* to φ if we were rational. And the mere fact that we actually desire not to φ gives us no reason to change this belief. Believing what we believe, it therefore follows that we rationally should get rid of the desire not to φ and acquire the desire to φ instead.[40]

This argument is admittedly very simple. As with many simple arguments, its real power may therefore be overlooked; it might be thought 'too simple'. So let me add further support for this argument by showing that a structurally similar argument allows us to explain a similar phenomenon in the case of belief.

---

[40] Is this argument consistent with the earlier argument against Johnston? It is. Indeed it helps to explain why a theory like the self-interest theory may be self-effacing. Suppose it is rational for me to do just one thing: promote my long-term self-interest. And suppose further that it is not rational for me to desire to promote my long-term self-interest; that my long-term self-interest would be best served by my desiring to act for the sake of family and friends, write books, advance humanity, and so on, without having any direct concern whatever for my own long-term self-interest. What it is desirable that I do is, in this case, not what it is desirable that I desire that I do. But now suppose I come to *believe* the self-interest theory. I come to believe that it is desirable to promote my long-term self-interest and undesirable to desire to promote my long-term self-interest. From the argument just given, having these beliefs makes it rational for me to desire to promote my long-term self-interest and to desire not to desire to promote my own long-term self-interest. Since the reason I have the desire to promote my long-term self-interest, something we know independently that I rationally shouldn't desire, is that I *believe* the self-interest theory, it is no surprise to learn that I rationally shouldn't believe the self-interest theory. The theory is self-effacing. And since I desire not to desire to promote my long-term self-interest, it is no surprise that I am motivated to get rid of that belief. I am indeed moved to do what the theory tells me it is rational to do.

Note that the following principle, itself much like (C2), governs our beliefs:

(C3) If an agent believes he has (most) reason to believe that p then he rationally should believe that p.

And note, furthermore, that we can explain (C3) via an argument that strictly parallels the argument just given to explain (C2).

That argument trades on a platitude about reasons for action. So consider a platitude about reasons for believing. Just as, if we have a reason for ϕing, we can say that ϕing is 'desirable', where desirability is fixed by norms of rationality, if we have (most) reason to believe that p, we can say that p is (most) 'believable', where believability is fixed by norms of rationality. But now note that just as it is a platitude to say that if ϕing is desirable then ϕing is what we would desire if we were rational, it is also a platitude to say that if p is (most) believable then p is what we would believe if we were rational. Equipped with these platitudes, we have enough to explain (C3).

Suppose an agent believes that he would believe that p if he were rational and yet fails to believe that p. Is he irrational? He certainly is. And by his own lights! For he fails to believe something he believes he has good reason to believe. Indeed, this must surely be a paradigmatic case of irrationality.

Moreover, note that we can also explain why someone who believes that p is (most) believable, but who also finds himself believing that not-p, rationally should get rid of his belief that not-p and acquire the belief that p instead. For p is (most) believable just in case he would believe that p if he were rational. And, by hypothesis, that is what he believes. He does not believe that he would believe that not-p if he were rational. And the mere fact that he actually believes that not-p gives him no reason to change this belief. Thus he rationally should get rid of his belief that not-p and acquire the belief that p instead. And that is just (C3).

Given the structural similarity between this argument and the argument for (C2), and given the success of the argument in the case of belief, I conclude that both arguments are successful. The platitude that desirability is a matter of what we would desire if we were rational suffices to show how it can be that our beliefs about our reasons rationally require us to have corresponding desires.

11. RECONCILIATION

It seemed difficult to reconcile the claim that deliberation on the basis of our values is practical in its issue to just the extent that it is with two further claims, the claim that deliberation normally reflects our evaluative *beliefs* and the claim that our actions are produced by our *desires*. However, we have seen that these claims are not in conflict. Instead they simply reflect a substantive fact about human agents: namely, that we are rational creatures who are sometimes more rational, sometimes less. Deliberation on the basis of our evaluative beliefs is practical in its issue *to just the extent that it is* because *that* is precisely the extent to which we are rational.

The point is not that this answer is in any way surprising. It was always the only answer available. The point is rather that now we know *why* this is the answer—what the *role* of our being rational is. For if, when we deliberate, we take into account what we have reason to do, and what we have reason to do is a matter of what we would desire to do if we were rational, and to the extent that we are rational we will desire to do what we believe we would desire to do if we were rational, then nothing else but the contingent fact that we are rational to just the extent that we are *could* explain why deliberation on the basis of our values is practical in its issue to just the extent that it is. Our contingent rationality is the only variable. The contingent fact that we are rational thus matches our motivating reasons with our beliefs about our normative reasons.

Given this reconciliation, it follows that there is no conflict in the two perspectives on the explanation of action described at the outset: the intentional and the deliberative. All intentional actions are indeed explicable from the intentional perspective in terms of our underlying desires and beliefs. But, to the extent that we are rational, our actions are also explicable from the deliberative perspective. For when we deliberate we concern ourselves with our normative reasons, and, to the extent that we are rational, our underlying desires will match our beliefs about the normative reasons that we have. It is thus our substantive rationality that explains why the connection between deliberation and action is not entirely contingent and fortuitous.

Finally, despite the central importance of the platitude linking what is desirable with what we would desire if we were rational in effecting this reconciliation, we have seen that we cannot turn this platitude into a fully reductive account of our concept of desirability. This has important implications for how we conceive of the reasons that we have, for it holds out the possibility of a convergence in our judgements about what it is desirable that we do under conditions of full rationality. The conception of ourselves as deliberating agents described at the outset does not require such a convergence. However, it is fitting, given the central importance of that conception of ourselves in Kantian circles, that in defending it, we come to see a non-relative account of our reasons for action as a real possibility.

13

Reductionism and First-Person Thinking*

Quassim Cassam

1

According to Derek Parfit, the existence of a person just consists in the existence of a brain and body and the occurrence of an interrelated series of mental and physical events.[1] Parfit calls his view 'reductionism', but there is more to this view than is suggested by the initial formulation. What distinguishes 'reductionism' from other non-Cartesian conceptions of the self is its commitment to the idea that the life of a subject can be described in an *impersonal* way. As Parfit puts it, 'We could describe what, at different times, was thought and felt and observed and done, and how these various events were interrelated. Persons would be mentioned here only in the descriptions of the contents of many thoughts, desires, memories and so on. Persons need not be claimed to be the thinkers of any of these thoughts.'[2] In other words, what is possible is a description which abstracts from the ownership of mental states or events by a subject.

Sydney Shoemaker has pressed the question whether Parfit's impersonal description is simply one in which there is no actual reference to persons, or whether the entities referred to in impersonal descriptions are thought of as capable of existing without there being persons.[3] For Parfit, it seems, the force of the thesis that a life can be described impersonally is that it is

© Quassim Cassam 1992

* I am much indebted to John Campbell and David Charles for their comments on an earlier version of this paper

[1] See his *Reasons and Persons* (Oxford: Oxford University Press, 1984), ch. 10.
[2] Ibid. 251.
[3] See Sydney Shoemaker's Critical Notice of *Reasons and Persons*, *Mind*, 44 (1985), 443–53.

not essential to the individual events that combine to constitute the life of a person that they are events in the life of a person, just as it is not essential to the individual bricks of a building that they are parts of a building. On this view, mental events have something like the ontological status of Humean perceptions, that is, entities which do not, by their very nature, require subjects.[4] Henceforth, Parfit's view will be referred to as strong reductionism.

In what follows, I will attempt to develop what might be called a weak reductionist response to Parfit. The weak reductionist accepts that the existence of a person consists in the existence of a brain and body and the occurrence of a series of interrelated mental and physical events. Weak reductionism is, to this extent, anti-Cartesian, but it differs from strong reductionism in the following respect: it denies that all the mental states or events which constitute the life of a person can be adequately described in impersonal terms, for the life of a person will include the occurrence of events which are *essentially* events in the life of a person. To anticipate, it will be argued that it is distinctive of the life of a person or subject to be self-conscious, and hence to include the thinking of first-person or I-thoughts. What makes a thought a first-person thought is that it has a distinctive role in the life of a person or subject, and the content of a *particular* I-thought cannot adequately be characterized without ascribing it, or drawing upon the possibility of ascribing it, to a *particular* person or subject. Thus, a Parfitian impersonal description will fail to make proper sense of thoughts the possible occurrence of which is demanded by our ordinary conception of what a person is.[5]

2

Lichtenberg is widely reported to have objected to the Cartesian cogito argument that Descartes failed to establish his

---

[4] Parfit remarks at one point that he prefers to describe a mental life as consisting of a series of mental *events* because this 'avoids . . . the misleading implications of the words "mental state". While a state must be a state *of* some entity, this is not true of an event' (*Reasons and Persons*, 211).

[5] Something like weak reductionism may have been Kant's position. For a

right to the thought 'I think'. According to this objection, the most that Descartes was entitled to was 'There is thinking going on', that is, a thought which is impersonal in content. Following Bernard Williams,[6] Parfit notes that a Lichtenbergian substitute for the cogito need not be wholly impersonal. Another possibility would be 'It is thought: I am thinking'. For the strong reductionist, this is an appealing formulation, for it allows him to concede that there are first-person thoughts, and even that the mental events in the occurrence of which the existence of a person partially consists must include the thinking of such thoughts, without giving up the claim that the life of a person can be described impersonally. The statement 'It is thought: I am thinking' reports the occurrence of a first-person thought in impersonal terms, for, as Parfit puts it, 'Since the subject of experiences is here mentioned only in the *content* of the thought, this sentence does not ascribe this thought to a thinker.'[7]

The point of introducing an impersonal level of description is not to deny the legitimacy of ascribing thoughts to thinkers (as long as thinkers are not thought of as Cartesian subjects) but to make room for a reductionist account of the unity of consciousness. The unity of consciousness at a time is explained by the fact that simultaneous experiences can be co-conscious, that is, the objects of a single state of awareness. The unity of consciousness across time is explained by the fact that successive thoughts or experiences are related by the relations of psychological continuity or connectedness.[8] These relations can be described without claiming that the thoughts and experiences are states of a subject. It is because the thoughts and experiences themselves and the relations between them can be described in impersonal terms that facts about the ownership of mental states or events by a subject may be said to have received a reductive explanation.

---

discussion of the relationship between Kant's position and Parfit's, see my 'Kant and Reductionism', *Review of Metaphysics*, 43 (Sept. 1989), 72–106.

[6] See Williams's discussion of Lichtenberg's point in *Descartes: The Project of Pure Enquiry* (Harmondsworth: Penguin, 1978), 95–101, and Parfit's reply to Williams in *Reasons and Persons*, §§ 81–2.

[7] *Reasons and Persons*, 225.

[8] Ibid., § 88.

In his discussion of the cogito argument, Williams proposes the following objection to the modified Lichtenbergian substitute for the cogito favoured by Parfit: in order to make sense of the possibility that there might occur at a given time a thought with the content 'I doubt whether p' and also a thought with the content 'I do not doubt whether p', what is required is the notion that these thoughts might occur in, as it were, different 'places'. The notion of place is, however, totally figurative in the present context. What is required is a less figurative way of 'locating' thoughts, and if one concludes that nothing less than the ascription of the thoughts to (different) subjects will do, then the programme of describing a mental life in impersonal terms must be deemed a failure. Of course, the subjects to which thoughts are ascribed need not be thought of as Cartesian subjects; even someone who insists that subjects are essentially physical things can accept Williams's argument. The challenge for the modified Lichtenbergian position, then, is to find an effective way of placing thoughts which does not go so far as to introduce a subject who thinks.[9]

This is not a challenge which the strong reductionist finds very threatening. Parfit's response is to suggest that thoughts might be located by reference to the *bodies* upon which they are causally dependent.[10] Hence it might be thought 'I doubt whether p' in the life which is directly causally dependent upon body A, and 'I do not doubt whether p' in the life which is causally dependent upon body B, where A and B are distinct bodies. The force of this proposal is, of course, that relating thoughts to bodies is not the same as ascribing them to subjects, even if subjects are not thought of as Cartesian subjects.

Is there any reason for thinking that this way of meeting Williams's challenge is unsatisfactory? An affirmative answer to this question might be prompted by the following line of argument: as already noted, the strong reductionist claims to be in a position to do justice to the connection between I-thinking and personhood. He claims to be under no obligation to dispute the thesis that, in Jonathan Glover's words,

---

[9] See esp. p. 100 of Williams's discussion.
[10] *Reasons and Persons*, 226.

'A person is someone who can have thoughts whose natural expression uses the word "I".'[11] If it can be shown that the strong reductionist's way of responding to Williams's challenge is incompatible with an adequate account of what a first-person thought is, then, given the importance of I-thinking, strong reductionism will clearly be under threat. Unlike some other well-known objections to Humean theories of the mind,[12] the present proposal is that I-thoughts constitute a *special* problem for strong reductionism. It will be argued that such thoughts cannot be made sense of in impersonal terms and that this is what decisively undermines strong reductionism.

A simple objection to strong reductionism is suggested by the following analogy: suppose that it is reported that at time *t* a given subject thinks a thought expressed by the words 'That tree is burning'. On the face of it, the content of the thought cannot be said to have been fully specified unless it is made clear *which* tree is said or thought to be burning. If thoughts are individuated by their truth conditions, then unless it is made clear which tree is claimed to be burning the truth condition of the thought will not have been fixed and its content not adequately specified. Suppose next that it is reported that at *t* it is thought 'I am in pain'. If this is genuinely a self-ascriptive, subject–predicate thought, it would be natural to say that it is true if and only if the *person* to which the use of 'I' refers is in pain. Just as the content of a demonstrative thought is a function of the object referred to, so the truth condition and hence the content of a first-person thought is a function of the person referred to by the subject-term. In order to know *what* the thought is one must know *who* the thinker is. If *S* is the thinker then it is whether *S* is in pain or not that is relevant to the truth or falsity of the thought.

What this argument appears to show is that there is no level at which it is possible to abstract from the ownership of a first-

[11] J. Glover, *The Philosophy and Psychology of Personal Identity* (London: Allen Lane, 1988), i. 60–1.

[12] P. F. Strawson has claimed that 'States, or experiences . . . *owe* their identity as particulars to the identity of the person whose states or experiences they are' (*Individuals* (London: Methuen, 1959), 97). The present objection to strong reductionism is concerned with the individuation of *thoughts* of a specific type rather than with the individuation of *experiences*.

person thought by a particular person whilst maintaining a fix upon the content of the thought. In the case of I-thoughts, what might be called the *ascriptive* and *content*-specifying levels of description are inseparable. This is not a Cartesian point but it does call into question the atomism of the strong reductionist. The strong reductionist holds that the existence of a person consists in the existence of the appropriate mental and physical 'atoms' (a brain and body and a series of mental and physical events) and that the atoms are individuable and characterizable without presupposing their location in a given collection of atoms. It is this form of atomism which the weak reductionist seeks to resist by emphasizing that some, at least, of the supposed mental atoms can only be individuated via their ascription to a particular person.

There are a number of responses open to the strong reductionist at this point. The first would be to deny that I-thoughts are genuinely subject–predicate. Instead, the thought expressed by 'I am in pain' might be claimed to be equivalent to the thought expressed by 'It hurts', that is, a thought which is impersonal in *content*. It may be that this is ultimately the only option available to the strong reductionist but it will be set aside for the moment, both because it is unappealing and because Parfit explicitly distances himself from this position.

As indicated earlier, the response favoured by Parfit is to concede that when first-person thoughts are reported in impersonal terms it needs to be made clear whether they occur in the same or in different lives, but to insist that the *relativization* or *particularization* of I-thoughts need not take the form of ascribing them to persons. Apart from the possibility of appealing to the role of the body, another way of relativizing would be 'In the particular life that contains the thinking of the thought expressed by the utterance of this sentence, it is thought that . . .'.[13] A related point is made by David Pears, who claims that when I say that I am in pain, the mouth which utters the sentence has a vital part to play in fixing the content of what is said or of the thought expressed. I do not need to use the first-person pronoun in order to get

---

[13] *Reasons and Persons*, 226.

my message across to others 'because my mouth makes the necessary contribution to the sense of my message. It signifies me because it is part of me.'[14] What these remarks suggest is that the satisfaction of what might be called a *weak relativization requirement* suffices to fix the content of a first-person thought, where the weak requirement states that an I-thought must be relativized or particularized by being related to a particular body or mouth. Opposed to this is the view that nothing short of the satisfaction of a *strong relativization requirement* will do, that is, the ascription of the thought to a person or subject. It is the strong relativization requirement which the strong reductionist rejects, and to which the weak reductionist is committed.

In defending the strong requirement it is important to begin by separating two questions about first-person content. Firstly, there is the question of what makes it the case that a thought is a first-person thought at all, a thought belonging to the first-person type. Secondly, there is the question of what makes it the case that a thought belonging to that type has the particular first-person content which it has. To bring out the difference, consider the case in which two people, *A* and *B*, both think thoughts expressed by the words 'I am *F*'. There is a sense in which *A* and *B* think of themselves in the same type of way— what Peacocke calls the '[self]' type—but their thoughts concern different objects.[15] Hence, their thoughts have different truth conditions and different contents. Any adequate theory of first-person thought must yield an account of what makes it the case that an I-thought has the particular content it has which fits our conception of what, in general, a first-person thought *is*. An answer to the question which relativization requirement is the correct one must be *informed* by an underlying conception of what is distinctive of thoughts belonging to the first-person type.

---

[14] D. Pears, *The False Prison: A Study in the Development of Wittgenstein's Philosophy*, ii (Oxford: Clarendon Press, 1988), 240.

[15] Peacocke proposes that 'The constituent of all Peter's first-person thoughts is called a token mode of presentation; it can be taken to consist of the type [self] indexed by Peter, that person himself' (*Sense and Content: Experience, Thought, and their Relations* (Oxford: Oxford University Press, 1983), 108). The suggestion that the type [self] is indexed by a *person* is in line with the strong relativization requirement.

Earlier, it was suggested that persons must be able to think
thoughts in the first person. What now needs to be considered
is the thesis that first-person thoughts are *only* properly ascribable to persons. To regard a form of words as giving expression to a thought of the first-person type is, on this view, at
the very least to be prepared to ascribe the thought thus
expressed to a person. If this is correct, then it is plausible
that in specifying the content of a *particular* I-thought it is
necessary to ascribe the thought to a *particular person*. The
truth or falsity of the thought expressed by 'I am *F*' depends
upon whether the person who thinks the thought is *F*, for
only persons can think first-person thoughts. This is the force
of the strong relativization requirement. This defence of the
requirement meets the constraint that it should be informed
by a conception of what is distinctive of thoughts of the first-
person type.

In sharp contrast, the strong reductionist's defence of the
weak relativization requirement seems to rest upon no plausible account of what a first-person thought *is*. The strong
reductionist simply helps himself to the idea that a given
thought belongs to the first-person type and then particularizes
the thought by relating it to a particular mouth or body. It is
difficult to see how this can be the appropriate form of relativization once it is accepted that it is persons and not bodies
which are capable of thinking I-thoughts. This is especially
clear when an attempt is made to specify the truth condition
of an I-thought using only the weak relativization requirement,
for if the truth or falsity of the thought expressed by 'I am *F*'
does not depend upon whether or not the *person* to which the
use of 'I' refers is *F*, then it is not clear how the truth condition
is to be specified in a manner which accords with our usual
understanding of what an I-thought is.

The strong reductionist may reply that it is enough to describe a first-person thought as one expressed by a certain
form of words, and that this is what underlies the importance
attached to the mouth which utters the appropriate words.
For reasons which will emerge shortly, this is not an adequate
account of what a first-person thought is. A more immediate
point is that the upshot of insisting upon the adequacy of the
weak relativization requirement is to call into question the

strong reductionist's commitment to viewing I-thoughts as genuinely subject–predicate. The sentence 'I am in pain' is not equivalent to 'This body is in pain'.[16] If 'I' is a referring expression, then what uses of it refer to are persons. As Pears concedes, the use of the first-person pronoun in the utterance 'I am in pain' is superfluous. If the crucial factor is the mouth which produces the utterance then 'It hurts' really would do just as well. If it is replied that the Pearsian account is only intended to illuminate the role of 'I' in communication rather than thought, then the strong reductionist has yet to meet the challenge posed by the need for first-person *thoughts* to be relativized.[17]

3

The central claim which underpins the argument of Section 2 is that first-person thoughts are only correctly ascribable to persons. Hence it will not be correct to ascribe I-thoughts to non-human animals, robots, and Martians unless we view them as persons. The strong reductionist may dispute the claim that there is a constitutive connection between person-hood and a capacity for I-thinking. Consider the following list of six necessary conditions of personhood suggested by Daniel Dennett: persons are (1) rational, (2) subjects of intentional ascriptions, (3) the objects of moral judgements, (4) moral agents, (5) language-users, (6) self-conscious.[18] There are difficult questions about the weighting of these conditions, but suppose that failure on counts (3) and (4) is sufficient to disqualify something from counting as a person. Yet failure on these counts alone cannot plausibly be regarded as dis-qualifying something from being a thinker of I-thoughts. If only persons can think I-thoughts then such thoughts will be denied to creatures simply on the ground that they fail to

[16] See Pears, *The False Prison*, ii. 252.

[17] Pears does seem to be concerned exclusively with the role of 'I' in communication. To this extent, the argument of this section does not bear directly on Pears' concerns. John Campbell and David Charles have pressed this point in discussion.

[18] See Dennett's 'Conditions of Personhood', in D. Dennett, *Brainstorms: Philosophical Essays of Mind and Psychology* (Brighton: Harvester Press, 1981).

meet the ethical conditions on personhood. This is surely a counter-intuitive result.

In order to meet this objection it will be necessary to introduce a distinction between persons and what might be called subjects of experience. Parfit treats these concepts as interchangeable, but the concept of a subject might be thought to lack some or all of the ethical baggage of the ordinary concept of a person. In any event, whether or not ordinary usage supports such a distinction, it will henceforth be assumed that subjects are like persons except that they do not necessarily meet the ethical conditions of personhood. So the thesis which is now to be considered is that I-thoughts are only properly ascribable to subjects. Earlier it was suggested that it is not enough to say that an I-thought is simply one expressed by a certain form of words. It now needs to be argued that our conception of what I-thoughts are draws upon and is informed by a certain conception of the role of such thoughts in the life of a subject. This would make it intelligible that in specifying the content of a particular I-thought it should be necessary to ascribe it to a subject.

In *The Varieties of Reference* Gareth Evans provides what he calls a functional characterization of various Idea-types, including I-Ideas. In general, an Idea of an object is 'something which makes it possible for a subject to think of an object in a series of indefinitely many thoughts, in each of which he will be thinking of the object in the same way'.[19] A functional account of an Idea-type characterizes it in terms of the special relation of thoughts involving it to certain sorts of evidence and to behaviour,[20] although Evans adds that such an account does not constitute a complete account of an Idea-type. In the case of I-Ideas the functional account includes an *informational* and an *action* component. A thinker of an I-thought must realize the relevance to such thoughts of various special ways of gaining knowledge of his mental states and physical properties, and his I-thoughts must have the appropriate connections with his actions.[21] A particularly important feature

---

[19] G. Evans, *The Varieties of Reference*, ed. J. McDowell (Oxford: Clarendon Press, 1982), 104.

[20] See *The Varieties of Reference*, ch. 7, app. 2.

[21] The connections between I-thinking and action are discussed by John

of I-Ideas is the way in which they give rise to thoughts dependent upon information received over a period of time. As Evans remarks, 'It is possible to regard this feature of I-Ideas as part of the informational component of a functional characterization. A possessor of an I-Idea has a capacity to ascribe past-tense properties to himself on a special basis: namely the memory of the basis appropriate for an earlier present-tense judgement.'[22] *Cognitive dynamics*[23] is the study of the way in which the belief system of a subject deals with the passage of time. According to Evans, the cognitive dynamics of I-Ideas are peculiarly simple:

if a subject has at t a belief which he might then manifest in judging 'I am now F', then there is a non-negligible probability of his having, at a later time t^1, a disposition to judge 'I was previously F' . . . so far as the I-Idea is concerned, the later dispositions to judge flow out of the earlier dispositions to judge, without the need for any *skill* or *care* (not to lose track of something) on the part of the subject. We can put this point by using . . . the terminology of immunity to error through misidentification: a past-tense judgement 'I was F' is not based upon a pair of propositions ⟨That person was F⟩ and ⟨I am that person⟩.[24]

This account of I-Ideas might suggest the following way of connecting the capacity for I-thinking with subjecthood: to begin with, it is important to recognize that the functional account of I-Ideas is intended as a *constitutive* account. Thus, for a thought to *count* as an I-thought, it must be a thought one of whose components is a particular I-Idea, and for an idea to *count* as an I-Idea, it must possess the various features set out in the functional account. What this suggests is that it will only be correct to ascribe I-thoughts to a system which is organized in a certain way; the system must be organized in such a way that its I-thoughts stand in the appropriate relations to each other, to certain kinds of evidence and to action, where the 'appropriate' relations are those set out in the functional account. What is the best way of characterizing such a system? At this point, it is tempting to claim that a

Perry in his important 'The Problem of the Essential Indexical', *Nous*, 13 (1979).
[22] *The Varieties of Reference*, 238.
[23] Evans borrows the label from David Kaplan.
[24] *The Varieties of Reference*, 237.

system which is organized in the required manner is bound to qualify as, if not a person, then at least a subject. Thus, a willingness to ascribe I-thoughts to a given creature must go hand in hand with a willingness to ascribe to it a certain kind of internal organization, and that is in effect to be prepared to ascribe to it the status of a subject.

This line of argument raises a number of fundamental questions. In the first place, it might be objected that the argument reaches the desired conclusion simply by resorting to arbitrary stipulation at the crucial point. It might be tempting to say that a system which meets the Evansian conditions is bound to qualify as a subject, but is this really a temptation to which one ought to succumb? The charge of arbitrary stipulation might be resisted as follows: on the one hand, it is plausible that self-consciousness, rationality, and agency lie at the heart of the notion of a subject, where self-consciousness is understood as a matter of a subject's being able to conceive of itself as temporally extended and spatially located. On the other hand, it would seem that no creature could satisfy the constraints set out in the functional account of I-Ideas without being, in the relevant sense, self-conscious and capable of rational action. So it is no surprise that the ascription of I-thoughts goes hand in hand with the conception of that to which the thoughts are ascribed as a subject.

It may be that the force of the earlier objection was not to deny that in ascribing I-thoughts to a creature one must be prepared to ascribe to it the appropriate surrounding capacities, but to suggest that these capacities will not *necessarily* be such as to mark it out as a subject. It may be that, in practice, I-thinking and subjecthood are ascribed as elements of a single package, but it is a *non sequitur* to conclude that the elements of the package are, in principle, inseparable. There are, in fact, several ways of taking this objection. It may be denying that the Evansian account of the background required for I-thinking is the right account. If it were, I-thinking would only be possible for subjects, but I-thinking can in fact be sustained by something far less rich. Alternatively, the objection may be accepting the earlier account of the cognitive dynamics of I-Ideas, but denying that a system whose I-thoughts satisfy the Evansian constraints thereby qualifies as a subject. Finally, and most subtly, the objection may be understood as accepting these constraints and accepting that a system which satisfies the constraints will thereby qualify as a subject, but as denying that the latter fact does any explanatory work. That is to say, it is possible to maintain a grip on the structure and context required for I-thinking whilst *abstracting* from the fact that a system capable of sustaining I-thinking will count as a subject. The idea is that our understanding of the constraints does not *derive* from or is not *informed* by the conception of how the life of a subject is organized. The fact that something capable of I-thinking is a subject is an interesting consequence of the functional account but not fundamental to it, something without which the functional account would cease to be intelligible.

The first version of the objection is hardly convincing as it stands. If the earlier account of the cognitive dynamics of I-Ideas is to be rejected, what is required is an argument for rejection and at least a sketch of an alternative. I will return to this matter in the concluding section. Neither is the second version of the objection very threatening without further work, for it prompts the question what more is required for something to count as a subject than is provided for by its meeting the earlier conditions on I-thinking. As it stands, the objection is merely a piece of hand-waving. The final version of the objection is one which deserves to be taken more seriously. This version accepts the earlier account of the constraints on I-thinking, but in that case what is required is an answer to the question what makes that particular conception of the constraints on I-thinking the *right* conception; *why* is it necessary that I-thoughts should stand in the specified relations with one another and to action? What the objection denies is that the only way of making sense of and *explaining* the specific constraints on the capacities required for I-thinking is to draw upon the concept of a subject; but what is the alternative? It is all very well denying that what renders the constraints intelligible is the concept of a subject, but it is far from clear how else the constraints are to be grounded.

Consider, for example, the idea that if someone judges 'I am F', then there is a non-negligible probability that he will later be disposed to judge 'I was F'. Why should there be such a connection between a past- and present-tense I-thought? The beginning of an answer to this question is provided by Locke's suggestion that a person 'can consider itself as itself, the same thinking thing, in different times and places'.[25] In other words, a person must be capable of conceiving of itself as temporally extended. This is also an important theme in Kant, on behalf of whom Jonathan Bennett writes that 'The notion of oneself is necessarily that of a possessor of a history: I can judge that this is how it is with me now only if I can also judge that this is how it was with me then.'[26] These remarks suggest the following line of argument: what explains the intimate connection between a present-tense I-thought and a corresponding past-tense thought is the fact that the systems to which the thoughts are ascribed must be able to think of themselves as having a history, in virtue of the fact that they are persons or subjects, and one can only think of oneself as temporally extended if one's I-thoughts at a given time flow out of one's earlier I-thoughts without the need for any skill or care. Our understanding of the constitutive dynamic relations between I-thoughts draws upon the way in which the related thoughts help to sustain the idea of their subject as temporally extended.

These remarks are intended not as a conclusive argument, but as giving a rough indication of how our understanding of what a subject is might help to ground and render intelligible a particular constraint on I-thinking. Of course, much work remains to be done. Clearly, it needs to be explained in much greater detail why the idea of oneself as having a history should require I-thoughts to stand in *precisely* those relations set out in the earlier functional account. This is not a task which will be undertaken here. The present point is to insist that our understanding of the structure required to sustain I-thinking needs to be anchored in some way, and to suggest that what provides the anchor is the fact that it is subjects to whom I-thoughts are properly ascribable, where a subject is conceived of as—to paraphrase a remark of Strawson's—the embodiment of a *temporally extended* point of view on the world.[27]

[25] Locke, *An Essay Concerning Human Understanding*, II. xxvii.

[26] J. Bennett, *Kant's Analytic* (Cambridge: Cambridge University Press, 1966), 117.

[27] See *The Bounds of Sense* (London: Methuen, 1966), 104.

These considerations also have a bearing on the earlier objections. For example, it might be said that the Evansian constraints on I-thinking cannot be the right ones, because we do after all ascribe I-thoughts to those with severe brain damage, even though it is doubtful whether they meet all those constraints. Nevertheless, it remains the case that even in these difficult cases we are not inclined to deny that those to whom the thoughts are ascribed are subjects. Neither is this merely a superficial feature of the way in which we talk. The fact that, even in the problematic cases, the ascription of I-thoughts goes hand in hand with the attribution of subject status is a reflection of the fact that we rapidly lose grip on what an I-thought is in isolation from our understanding of the nature of the thinkers of such thoughts. The problem of severely impaired subjects may prompt the observation that the conception of what counts as a subject needs to be a fairly liberal one, but on its own it is powerless to establish the conclusion that the concept of a subject does not anchor our understanding of the normative requirements on I-thinking, as the third version of the objection requires.

The difficulty with the weak relativization requirement is that its conception of what suffices to particularize a first-person thought fails to respect the constitutive connection between I-thinking and subjecthood. If what makes it the case that a thought is of the first-person type is the fact that it has a distinctive role in the life of a subject, then it cannot be correct to say that what makes it the particular thought it is is its causal dependence upon a particular body, for subjects are not bodies. Bodily considerations have an important part to play in individuating persons or subjects, but if talk of the causal dependence of a thought upon a body is simply a peculiar way of ascribing the thought to the subject whose body it is, then the position is no longer compatible with strong reductionism. Even if the existence of a subject consists in the existence of a brain and body and the occurrence of an interrelated series of mental and physical events, the individual I-thoughts should not, given the inseparability of the ascriptive and content-specifying levels, be thought of as analogous to the bricks of a building, for the bricks do not owe their identity to the building of which they are a part. The thinking of a first-person thought is essentially an event in the life of a subject, and *which* thought it is depends upon *which* subject's life it is a part of.

4

According to the argument of the preceding section, the challenge facing the strong reductionist is to explain the constitutive-dynamic constraints on I-thinking in impersonal terms. What now needs to be considered is a response to this challenge which appeals to a functionalist account of the mind. According to functionalism, mental states are individuated by reference to their place in a complex causal network of states. Shoemaker sees functionalism as calling Parfitian reductionism into question, for will not the existence of such a system or network amount to the existence of a person?[28] Indeed, functional definitions seem to draw quite explicitly on the concept of a person, for, as Shoemaker puts it, 'it is in conjunction with other mental states *of the same person* that a mental state produces the effects it does; and its immediate effects, those the having of which is definitive of its being the mental state it is, will be states (or behaviour) on the part of the *very same person* who had the mental state in question'.[29]

The difficulty with this line of argument is that even if what makes it the case that a given state is the belief that *p* is its causal relations to inputs, outputs, and other mental states, why should it be necessary that such content-yielding causal relations should hold between states of a person? The funcionalist account of content is certainly anti-isolationist, but this anti-isolationism appears compatible with holding that a state may have the content of the belief that *p* even if the network by reference to which it is individuated is, say, a sophisticated computer and not a person at all. Indeed, the reference to persons in Shoemaker's specification of the form of a functional definition seems curiously unmotivated. What functionalism requires is the notion that something counts as the realization of a given state if, in conjunction with other

---

[28] Critical Notice of *Reasons and Persons*, 446.
[29] 'Personal Identity: A Materialist's Account', in S. Shoemaker and R. Swinburne, *Personal Identity* (Oxford: Blackwell, 1984), 93.

states in what might be called the same 'psychological space', it produces certain effects in that same space. What makes it the case that given states belong in a single space is just the fact that they have the functionally appropriate effects. As cases of 'divided minds' illustrate, psychological spaces cannot be equated outright with persons. A belief and a desire may be assigned to distinct spaces or subsystems on the grounds that they do not have the effect that one would expect if they were elements of a single space or subsystem. It is important to note that the distinct spaces to which the belief and desire are assigned need not always be thought of as distinct persons or subjects, for they may be too transient for such a characterization to be plausible. Functional definitions may need to draw upon the concept of a single psychological space, but this is compatible with individuating particular spaces in functional terms. The phrase 'psychological space' was introduced in order to emphasize the extent to which the functionalist can remain neutral on ontological questions. On the face of it, the concept 'same person' is doing no special work in functional definitions, work which could not be done by the more neutral and abstract concept of a space within which various states are appropriately functionally related.

In connection with the cognitive dynamics of I-Ideas, it might be wondered how far the Evansian account is from a functionalist account. It is true that in the characterization of the cognitive dynamics, use was made of the idea that when a subject judges 'I am F', there is a non-negligible probability that he—the very same *subject*—should later be disposed to judge 'I was F'. How much genuine *explanatory* work is the reference to the subject doing? Consider, in this connection, Shoemaker's notion of a 'successor state'.[30] The idea here is that while the content of a person's belief or intention will depend to a certain extent on the nature of all his states at earlier times, there will often be a particular state on whose content its content especially depends. It is of that earlier state that the current state is the 'successor state'. For functionalism, 'a mental state is defined in part in terms of what successor state it is liable to give rise to in combination with various

[30] Ibid. 95.

other states'.[31] Suppose, then, that the functionalist were to attempt to capture the cognitive dynamics of I-thinking by claiming that what makes a thought a present-tense self-ascriptive thought of the form 'I am *F*' is the fact that it is liable to cause a particular type of successor 'state', namely a thought with the content 'I was *F*'. This is not Shoemaker's own account of what is distinctive of first-person thought,[32] but it is a recognizably functionalist way of handling the cognitive dynamics. If it is objected that the successive 'states' must be states of the same person, it may be replied by the functionalist with strong reductionist sympathies that it is only required that the successive thoughts occupy a single psychological space, where such spaces are themselves delineated in functional terms. There is an element of circularity here, but there are familiar functionalist strategies for defusing the apparent circularity of functional definitions.[33] Even if it turns out that the successive thoughts are related as events in the life of a single person, this fact would be doing no special work in the account. Is there really such a gap between an Evansian functional account of I-Ideas and an impersonal functional*ist* story?

This reply to the argument of Section 3 faces the following difficulty: the point of that argument was that it is not enough to say that a present-tense I-thought must be liable to give rise to a corresponding past-tense I-thought. The point of the argument was that this requirement needs to be *explained*. The recent functionalist argument does not address the second task. The earlier suggestion was that the 'normative' relation between the successive thoughts can only properly be understood by reference to the concept of a self-conscious, temporally extended subject. The concept of a psychological space cannot itself explain the constraints because it is not clear what the constraints are on the organization and development of a space. It is only if such spaces are modelled on the lives of subjects that the full force of the claim that a given element in

---

[31] Ibid.

[32] In § 8 of his discussion Shoemaker stresses the role of I-thoughts in the determination of action.

[33] See Shoemaker's discussion of the Ramsey–Lewis strategy in 'Personal Identity: A Materialist's Account', 98–101.

the space 'ought' to give rise to specific further elements is captured. The question is whether the strong reductionist can explain this 'ought' without implicitly drawing upon the concept of the mental life of a subject. His case is not advanced by appealing to functionalism; if functionalist accounts of I-thoughts are informed by a conception of what is distinctive of the life of a subject—where the reference to a subject is not thought of as dispensable[34]—then such accounts are of no use to the strong reductionist. If functionalism allows no explanatory work to be done by the concept of a subject in its treatment of first-person thoughts, then it stands accused, along with strong reductionism, of failing to provide the constraints on such thoughts with an adequate explanatory foundation.[35]

The strong reductionist has a number of options at this stage. One would be to reject the demand for an explanation of the constraints on I-thinking. It is enough that the existence of such constraints should be recognized and that they should be statable without reference to persons, perhaps by exploiting the concept of a psychological space. Alternatively, he may insist that the constraints are genuinely explicable in impersonal terms. He may dispute the earlier suggestion that the Lockean–Kantian conception of a subject is what grounds the constraints, or he may argue that it does ground the constraints but not in a manner which is incompatible with strong reductionism. These rejoinders are worthy of detailed

[34] To be fair to Shoemaker, he certainly does not regard his version of functionalism as congenial to strong reductionism. The question is whether the functionalist is entitled to insist that special explanatory work is done by the concept of a person or subject.

[35] In a highly suggestive discussion, John McDowell claims that in attempting to do justice to the constitutive role of the notion of rationality in our thought about propositional attitudes, functionalism commits a kind of naturalistic fallacy ('Functionalism and Anomalous Monism', in E. LePore and B. McLaughlin (eds.), *Actions and Events: Perspectives on the Philosophy of Donald Davidson* (Oxford: Blackwell, 1985, 389)). The present argument against strong reductionism is intended faintly to echo McDowell's argument. The point is that the strong reductionist and, arguably, the functionalist fail to recognize the constitutive role of the concept of a subject in our conception of first-person thoughts and are therefore in no position to explain the sense in which one I-thought 'ought' to follow another, *given* our understanding of the nature of those to whom such thoughts are properly ascribable. Without this anchor the 'ought' is rendered highly problematic.

investigation, although it should be clear that some of them begin to call into question the distinctiveness of the strong reductionist position. The prospects for strong reductionism do not appear bright if it is committed to disputing the suggestion that the most basic way of understanding what a first-person thought is is to see it as having a distinctive role in the life of a person or subject, and that such thoughts are therefore to be particularized by being ascribed to particular subjects. If the strong reductionist claims to be able to accommodate these suggestions, then serious questions must arise about just what strong reductionism *is*.

14

The First Person: The Reductionist View of the Self*

John Campbell

1

Rousseau said: 'He who pretends to look on death without fear lies. All men are afraid of dying, this is the great law of sentient beings, without which the entire human species would soon be destroyed.'[1] But we are accustomed to oscillate on the topic of our own death. On the one hand, looked at from our immersion in our ordinary activities, death is something terrifying, something it is hard to think about with clarity. The problem is not the expectation of the pain and suffering that may be associated with death; it seems to be even more fundamental than that. Death is the end of everything, and that is what is terrifying. On the other hand, looking at the matter objectively, it is hard to see what is so very bad about it. One's plans and projects may be pursued by others, in so far as they are worth pursuing. Life for most people will go on just as before, and we are certainly considering a very small disturbance in the cosmos.[2]

It is sometimes said that the subjective view of the topic of death has its own inherent instability, and that what we deeply care about in survival can be had even if we do not ourselves

* Thanks to Bill Brewer, Quassim Cassam, David Charles, and Naomi Eilan. Earlier versions were presented to a discussion group in Oxford, and given as special lectures at University College, London, and I am indebted to participants for their comments. This paper was written while on leave at King's College Research Centre, and I owe a great deal to the stimulus of the Centre

[1] Jean-Jacques Rousseau, *Julie; or, The New Eloise.*
[2] For extended discussion of this oscillation, see T. Nagel, *The View from Nowhere* (New York and Oxford: Oxford University Press, 1986), ch. 11: 'Birth, Death and the Meaning of Life'. See also D. Wiggins, 'The Concern to Survive', in D. Wiggins, *Needs, Values, Truth* (Oxford: Blackwell, 1987).

continue in existence. That is, even if we stick with the 'participant' viewpoint, the perspective from our immersion in our ordinary activities, death as such actually holds no deep fear for us. This can be brought out, the claim is, by reflection on the following type of case. Consider the way in which an amoeba divides by fission. It may be that, after the fission, we cannot identify either of the amoeba that are around then with the original organism. For they may be qualitatively similar, and there may be no way in which we can justify supposing that one rather than the other is identical to the original. It may also be, though, that the two products of the fission are causally related to the original organism, and sufficiently similar to it, that the following condition is met: if only one 'branch' had taken, so that one of the fission-products never came into existence, we would have been happy to say that the original organism had survived. Now, as a thought experiment, consider the supposition that humans might divide like that. That is, they split spontaneously into two humans. We have no reason to justify supposing that one rather than another of the products is identical to the original. And we cannot suppose that they are both identical to the original, because there are two of them and there was only one original. So the original has ceased to exist. But suppose we look at this situation from the participant standpoint. Suppose you assume that this is about to happen to you: you are about to fission. The situation does not at all seem as bad as ordinary death. Of course there may be practical problems; but the prospect of having to deal with them is not at all as bad as the subjective panic, the terror that the thought of one's own death can induce. Nevertheless, someone who fissions ceases to exist. This implies that the subjective panic can be subverted from within, as it were: without moving to the standpoint of a transcendent objectivity, from which no one's survival matters any more than anyone else's survival, one could reach an accommodation with death.

Ultimately I shall try to show that this line of thinking is in fact not correct, that the attempt to subvert the subjective panic by appealing to fission cases does not work. But I want to begin by looking at Derek Parfit's attempt to set this argument on deeper foundations, by formulating a view of the self, an account of what the self *is*, which would directly undermine the subjective panic occasioned by the thought of one's own death. This position asks what it is whose survival we are concerned about, and, by giving a kind of 'exploded view' of it, tries to convince us that what we subjectively care about is not an all-or-nothing matter—we can, for example, make sense of the notion of degrees of survival. So that even if one ceases to exist, the things one subjectively cared about may be largely attained.

This reductionist view of the self demands that it should be possible to give a non-circular definition of the identities of persons, in terms of the relations holding between certain more fundamental entities than persons. It demands that it should be possible to give a non-circular definition of the identities of persons, in terms of the more fundamental relations holding between more basic particulars. In particular, the reductionist appeals to bodies, experiences causally dependent upon them, and causal relations between those experiences. The reductionist is explaining what a person is, in these more fundamental terms.

This approach will give us a kind of exploded view of oneself, so that when one expresses the panic of the thought of one's death, one is in a position, from the standpoint of immersion in one's own life, to reflect on just what it is whose survival concerns one. Now the crucial point about the exploded view of oneself is that it is, in a sense, 'impersonal'. That is, one can describe all the components of the exploded view, and the way in which they are all related, without using terms which refer to persons, or which presuppose that persons exist. In particular, one can think of oneself, in the exploded view, without having to use the first person at any point. One can identify all the particular experiences, and the ways in which they are all related to each other and to the body, without having to think of them as '*my* experiences'. This means that one can reflect on the survival of this congeries of experiences and the physical body, and on just why it matters, at a level that is more fundamental than the level at which one uses the first person. Once we move to this deeper, impersonal level, the claim is, we can see that concern to survive is not properly put as the desire that *I* should continue to exist. The concern to survive would be better put as the desire that there should be further experiences which are suitably related to a particular set of current experiences and this body. But now, once we have attained the deeper level, it is apparent that ordinary concern to survive tends to be put in overly dramatic terms. Even after my death, there may be future experiences which are suitably related to those current ones. The case of fission makes this vivid. In the case of fission, there is a plethora of experiences which are suitably related to those present ones, and this body, even though I have ceased to exist. So everything that I care about in survival is had here, even though I have ceased to exist. Notice that this view has fought off the terror of death without moving to a 'transcendent' or 'objective' standpoint from which no one's survival matters any more than anyone else's. We are still operating as subjective participants; it is still acknowledged that one attaches special weight to there being, in the future, experiences which are suitably related to these current experiences.

The crucial move here is evidently in the claim that it is possible to move to a level of thought about oneself and one's future which is more fundamental than anything involving the use of the first person. Everything depends on the idea that we really can dig down to such a level.

We ought to remark on the reductionist's use of 'the body' as a primitive in his reduction. This means that we have to resist the plausibility of the idea that the identity of a person just is the identity of a body; for then bodies are not more basic entities than persons. The simplest way for the reductionist to do this is to point to the possibility of bodily transfer—of a person occupying one body at one time and a different body at a later time. There is constant pressure, though, for the reductionist to renege on this: to exploit the difficulty of supposing that bodily transfer can happen, so as to make the notion of a body do work in the reduction that it really can do only if bodies just are persons.

The reductionist has also to give an impersonal characterization of the 'unity relation' for persons: the relations between the various psychological states and the body of a single person.[3] The aim is to give a description of various causal connections which at no point makes use of the notion of a person. 'Fission' cases play a deep role in the argument here. They make it seem that it must be possible to give an impersonal description of the unity relation for persons. For each product of the fission seems to be psychologically connected to the original self in all the ways that matter for personal identity. But neither product is identical to the original. So it must be possible to describe the psychological connections between the fission products and the original self without presupposing sameness of person; and that will give us our impersonal characterization of the unity relation for persons. Using the description of these causal connections, between things which are more basic than persons, we arrive at our exploded view of a person. We can use it to say what a person is—that is, we can use it to say when a particular collection of things constitutes a person. Or, to put the point somewhat differently, we can say that we are defining the identity of a person in terms of more primitive relations between more primitive items. The idea then is that the exploded view will allow us to see exactly what it is whose survival we care about subjectively, and it will show us that what we deeply care about is not simply the survival of the whole aggregate: with the reductive analysis, we can engage in more exact and discriminating judgements as to what we care about.

I want first to focus on the idea that there is an 'impersonal' level at which we can talk about experiences, a deeper level than the level at which we have the use of the first person, or any talk of persons in general.

2

Ordinarily I think of my experiences as *mine*; so how am I to achieve an impersonal way of thinking and talking about

---

[3] The term 'unity relation' comes from J. Perry, 'Can the Self Divide?', *Journal of Philosophy*, 73 (1972), 463–88.

them? It is often supposed that the reductionist has at this point to suppose that experiences can in principle exist unowned, so that it is simply a contingency that all my experiences are in fact bound together as the experiences of a single individual. Experiences are concrete particulars which could perfectly well exist without the person who has them. But this view does not seem to be intelligible; we can make nothing of the idea of unowned experiences. So the reductionist has to do without it.[4]

The reductionist might acknowledge that once we move to a level of discourse at which we do have talk of persons, nothing can be made of the notion of an unowned experience. He may still hold that there is a more primitive, subjectless use of psychological predicates. This is the kind of construction identified by Lichtenberg, such as 'There is thinking' or 'There is pain'. Here there is no subject. Similarly, the use of 'it' is a grammatical dummy in the subjectless 'It is raining'. There is no subject to which the thinking or the pain is being ascribed, in these formulations. But that is not to say that we can make sense of the possibility of thinking or pain without a person who is thinking, or is in pain. Rather, the subjectless formulation belongs to a level of language more primitive than any at which there is reference to persons. So we cannot, at this primitive level, so much as state the proposition that a particular experience is unowned. Similarly, suppose we have a child who is taught to say 'It is raining' as a substitute for its protests when rained upon or its cries when it sees rain. This child need not have the conception of a place at which it is raining; it might be unable to make anything of the notion of its raining somewhere else, for instance. So the talk of rain here is prior to talk of places. But that is not to say that we can make sense of the idea of there being rain, without there being any particular place at which it is raining. Once we move to the level at which rain can be assigned to places, we can acknowledge that rain must always happen somewhere or other. So we can say that talk of rain is more basic than ascrip-

---

[4] This point is often held to be devastating to the reductionist's appeal to experiences. See e.g. S. Shoemaker, Critical Notice of *Reasons and Persons*, *Mind*, 44 (1985), 443–53, and H. Noonan, *Personal Identity* (London and New York: Routledge, 1989), 120–1.

tions of rain to places, without being committed to the possibility of locationless rain. Similarly, we can take the subjectless
'There is thinking' or 'There is pain' to be primitive, and to
involve no reference to persons, while still holding that once
we move to the level of discourse at which we do have talk of
persons, nothing can be made of the notion of an unowned
experience.

There is, though, a problem for this approach. Suppose I am
using these subjectless formulations to report psychological
states. Of course, I cannot use them to say who is having a
particular experience. But none the less, there is a question
about whether I can use the subjectless formulations only to
report upon what are in fact my own states; or whether I can
use them to report both my own states and the states of other
people. On one reading, the proposal is that our reductive
base will be provided by using them to replace both first-
person and third-person psychological predications. So when
I say 'There is pain', this may be reporting either my own
experience or that of another, though the distinction between
one person and another is something of which I may be presumed to have no grasp. Still, there are distinctions that I
must be able to mark. I may want simultaneously to say 'There
is pain' and 'There is no pain', without falling into contradiction. If I can use the construction to report what are in fact
the states of different people, I need to be able to manage some
kind of relativization of it. Moreover, we have to relativize in
such a way that suitable pairs of psychological ascriptions are
relativized to the *same* thing. This is particularly obvious if we
consider ascriptions of emotion or temperament, which are
characteristically made as part of a whole complex of ascriptions of psychological state. We have to relativize in such a
way that the whole series of such ascriptions can be relative to
the same thing, over a period of time. The same point holds
when we consider the rationality constraints on ascriptions of
belief and desire.

There is an obvious problem about this. On the face of it, we
want the effect of the relativization being to persons, in that
two correct reports of psychological state will be relativized to
the same thing just if they are states of the same person. But,
of course, the reductionist cannot use the notion of a person in

giving the relativization. Parfit's solution is to relativize a report of psychological state to what he calls a 'life'.[5] A life is, apparently, a series of mental and physical events; he speaks of 'the interrelations between all the mental and physical events that together constitute a person's life.'[6] But plainly, not just any series of mental and physical events can be taken to constitute a life, if the coherence constraints on ascription of psychological state are to be applied to the ascriptions made relative to a single life. We need some explanation of when a series of mental and physical events constitute one life. The explanation might be that a life is the totality of things that happen to a single person. But then, in relativizing ascriptions of mental state to lives of persons, we abandon reductionism. We manage only a superficial juggling with grammatical categories if we insist that mental states be given subjectless reports and relativized to lives of persons, rather than being predicated of persons directly.

The reductionist holds, though, that an impersonal characterization can be given of the unity relation for the life of a person. So he may say that reports of mental state are understood only when they are grasped as being made relative to one or another life; and that one has grasped this notion of a life only when one has grasped the unity relation for persons. This obviously abandons the idea that ascriptions of mental state are more primitive than talk of persons, for to grasp the ascriptions, one must grasp the unity relation for persons. What remains of the reductionism is only the demand for an impersonal characterization of the unity relation. The reductionist may protest that he does not accept that two correct reports of psychological state will be relativized to the same thing just if they are states of the same person. The relativization might rather be to bodies. We might take it, in effect, that the notion of a life that we need is the notion of the life of a body. This has some initial plausibility when we consider ascriptions of psychological predicates to others. But that initial plausibility owes everything to the plausibility of the idea that the boundaries of the body just are the boundaries of the

---

[5] D. Parfit, *Reasons and Persons* (Oxford: Oxford University Press, 1984), 226.
[6] Ibid.

person. If we suppose that bodily transfer is possible, then we have to acknowledge that the constraints of coherence on the ascription of psychological states may apply across bodies, so that relativization to a body does not give us what we need.

At this point, I want to consider a motivation for reductionism not mentioned by Parfit. This is the desire to view persons as a kind of animal, continuous with the rest of nature. One factor here is the desire to understand how psychological predicates can be applicable to both humans and animals which are not persons. Obviously, both persons and animals can suffer pain and anxiety, for instance, even if we find it difficult to know where the boundaries are between species capable of suffering and species which are not. It is because of this that animal experimentation is controversial.[7] This means that there is a question about whether predicates such as 'is in pain' are best understood as predicates specifically of persons, or should not rather be thought of as predicates applying to animals, some of which are persons and some of which are not. That is, in grasping what it is for something to be in pain, we may not need to use the notion of a person at all, any more than we need to use the notion 'wears a hat'. It is just that once we do grasp the predicate, we can see that some of the things to which it applies are persons, just as some of the things to which it applies wear hats. Of course, at this point we have abandoned the original motivation for using subjectless predications. It was anyhow never easy to see why we should bother to introduce subjectless predications if we are then going to relativize the predications. The question for the reductionist was whether he believes it is possible for experiences to exist unowned. The response suggested by the use of subjectless predications was that there is a level of discourse about experiences at which the question of ownership or non-ownership does not arise. But once we acknowledge a need for relativization, the question could be put in terms of whether there are experiences that are not relativized to one or another thing. For the reductionist who accepts a need for relativiza-

---

[7] For discussion of the epistemology of animal pain, cf. M. S. Dawkins, 'From an Animal's Point of View: Motivation, Fitness, and Animal Welfare', *Behavioural and Brain Sciences*, 13 (1990), 1–61.

tion, the appropriate reaction would not have been an appeal to subjectless formulations. The correct response would have been an appeal to the existence of experiences which do exist unowned by any person, but which are owned by the things to which he is making his relativization. And these are not necessarily persons, but may rather be animals which are not persons.

If we do take this approach, then the unity relation for persons will be defined over psychological states which both persons and animals can have. It would not, then, be defined over emotions such as pride or shame, which can be enjoyed only by creatures which are self-conscious, which are capable of first-person thought. This, though, would mean that we were defining an impoverished psychological life, since much of what we think of as characteristic of a human mental life is first-personal. In particular, we could not appeal to auto-biographical memory as a psychological state over which the unity relation was defined. We could not do so, for just the same reason that we could not ascribe shame or pride to an animal that was not a person. These states are first-personal. For a creature to be in such a state demands that it can, in Locke's phrase, 'consider itself as itself, the same thinking thing, in different times and places'.[8]

Does this matter? Could we not explain what a person is by defining the unity relation only over states which both persons and animals which are not persons can have—states such as pain or perception? It might be said that the identity of a person is quite different from the identity of an animal, because the identity of a person is not the identity of a body whereas the identity of an animal just is the identity of a body. But the reductionist may resist this. No doubt there are many species for which identity is sameness of body—that certainly seems to be the right criterion to apply to jellyfish, for example. But in the case of other animals, things are not so clear. Suppose, for instance, that Rover, the aged family dog, has failing kidneys and a transplant is arranged. The relief one might feel here is quite different to the reaction one would

---

[8] John Locke, *An Essay Concerning Human Understanding*, ed. P. H. Nidditch (Oxford: Oxford University Press, 1975), II. xxvii. 9.

have to the news that Rover's brain is failing but that a transplant has been arranged. The thought that it won't be Rover after the operation is hard to resist. But it will be the same body, with only an organ transplant. The point is easy to miss because we are very often not concerned at all with the identities of individual animals. If there is a principle here, it is that animals with centrally organized, and relatively high-level cognitive faculties cannot be identified with their bodies, whereas simpler creatures can. This means that even animals which are not persons cannot be identified with their bodies, so the reductionist who is drawn by the idea of giving a common explanation of the identities of persons and animals is so far not compelled to give up his view.

To be a reductionist, though, it is not enough simply that one hold that persons are animals. One must also be willing to give a reductionist account of what it is to be an animal; a reductionist account of the unity relation that has to hold between a number of entities for them to constitute a single animal. Otherwise, merely saying that persons are animals does nothing to show how they can be regarded as reducible to networks of constituent objects.

One way of being a reductionist, then, would be to hold that an explanation can be given of the unity relation for 'higher' animals generally, which would make no use of the notion of a person, and which would be defined over constituents, such as bodies and psychological states such as suffering, which are not unique to persons. The appeal of this view is that it would do something to show how persons can be part of nature; though of course, a number of problems would remain, such as the mind–body problem for animals. As I said, Parfit does not give this motivation for his view; but it does none the less seem to be a reason for supporting reductionism.

The general problem with the whole approach of supposing that the relativized formulations can give the reductionist his reductive base emerges when we reflect that for them to work in this way, it must be plausible that they do indeed constitute a primitive layer of language: a layer which is more fundamental than our ordinary ascriptions of psychological states to persons. For suppose we ask what the most fundamental types of pain-ascription look like. Among the most primitive types we must include ascriptions of pain made otherwise than on the basis of observation; ascriptions which, in so far as they can be said to have a basis at all, are made because one is in pain, rather than because one observes anyone's pain. In general, when reporting what are in fact one's own psychological states, the judgements are not made on the basis of observation. Now we are acknowledging the need for relativization of one's ascriptions of psychological state. And there is certainly a unity in all one's judgements about what are in fact one's own mental states, the judgements about psychological state that one makes otherwise than on the basis of observation. They must all be relativized to just the same thing. But that unity is secured by the fact that these judgements are, as we might say, implicitly first-personal. They unite all the psychological states that one ascribes in this way as the states of a single person. The fact that it is the same body that is involved is grasped only derivatively, through the realization that the person has not changed bodies. The unity of the states reported otherwise than on the basis of observation is a personal unity. This destroys the reductionist's hope of finding a way of ascribing psychological states that does not involve any appeal to the notion of a person, yet which is more primitive than our ordinary ascriptions of psychological state. Ascriptions of animal pain are conceptually dependent upon ascriptions of pain to persons.

We can here contrast the case of ascriptions of pain which are made otherwise than on the basis of observation with the case of ascriptions of physical condition made otherwise than on the basis of observation. For example, there is my knowledge of the position of my own limbs, as when I think 'I am cross-legged' or 'My arms are behind my back'. Using my sense of balance, I may think 'I am about to fall over'. Or again, I may think 'I am being jostled', 'I am cold and wet', 'My back is stiff', 'Something is biting me', and so on. These ways of knowing one's own physical characteristics are all implicitly first-personal; the thing of which they are all properties is identified as a person, not, if there is a difference, as a body. This comes out in many ways. The various physical predications which one makes in this way are all true of a single thing—it is not as if one has knowledge merely that, somewhere or other, there is something which is looking out of the window. One knows that it is the very same thing that is looking out of the window as has something sticking into its foot. If there is a difference between persons and bodies, then, obviously, these physical properties are united as properties of a single person, rather than as properties of a single body. The same point can be made for the ability to self-ascribe these properties over a period of time. If bodily transfer is possible, then the totality of physical predicates I know to apply and to have applied, in these special ways, are predicates which I know to be true of a single person, rather than a single body. Finally, these ways of knowing of physical characteristics are integrated with one's knowledge of one's own psychological states. If I know, in this special way, that I am in front of a window, and that I am thinking about Vienna, then I know, without any need for further premises, but only a single inferential step, that I am both in front of a window and thinking about Vienna. All this means that these ways of knowing about physical properties cannot be expressed at the level of the reductionist's reductive base, for there would then be an implicit reference to persons. But it does not show that the physical properties themselves cannot be mentioned at the level of the reductive base. For there surely is a primitive use of talk of these properties which does not depend on the ability to ascribe them otherwise than on the basis of observation. The case is quite different for psychological predicates. For all other uses of these predicates depend upon the most primitive level at which one can ascribe them otherwise than on the basis of observation. There is no such thing as a level at which one uses the concept of pain, but in such a primitive way that one cannot yet ascribe it to oneself simply on the strength of being in pain. There is no primitive level at which all one's ascriptions of pain depend upon observation.

The effect of this point is to put pressure on the reductionist's conception of one thing's being 'more primitive' than another. What we have just seen is that all ascriptions of pain, even to animals which are not self-conscious, are conceptually dependent upon a level of thought at which there is reference to persons. If we want to say that such ascriptions of pain are nevertheless more basic than reference to persons; that they nevertheless are available at an impersonal level of description; then we had better be prepared to say what we mean by 'more basic'. For evidently it cannot mean 'conceptually more basic'. In fact, though, an alternative formulation is at this point not difficult to find. We can simply use a modal formulation: these states could exist even though there had never been any persons. The existence of such states is independent of the existence of persons. The problem with this kind of formulation is that, as it is usually used, it implies the possibility of ownerless experiences. But here there is no commitment to ownerless experience. It is just that the experiences may not be owned by a person; they may rather be the experiences of some other kind of creature. Notice also that the modality here relates to types of experience, rather than particular tokens. The owner of an experience may be essential to it: if a pain is had by a particular person, it may be that it is essential to that pain that it was had by that very person. Nevertheless, that type of psychological state could have existed even if there had never been any persons. In that way, talk of such states is available for the reductionist's reductive base.

The first problem with this approach is that it does not seem to give us the kind of reduction we were initially promised—a deep, impersonal level of thought at which we had abandoned the use of the first person. For in acknowledging that there is no level of thought about psychological states that is conceptually more primitive than the level at which we have the use of the first person, we acknowledge that the first person is always in play, and we always have to hand the materials whereby to formulate the concern for personal survival that the reductionist sought to finesse. The kind of metaphysical reductionism that is now on offer does not speak to our initial concerns.

Once we have reached this stage, moreover, it is apparent that it is crucial to the reductionist that it be possible to characterize the unity relation for persons without appealing to such first-personal states as pride, or shame, or autobiographical memory. For it is not possible that there could be such states even though there had never been any persons. This belies the practice of reductionists—Parfit evidently assumes that psychological connectedness will be defined over states such as autobiographical memory, rather than being confined exclusively to states which could equally be had by creatures which are not persons, such as pain or suffering.[9] And it is not credible that the unity relation for persons can be defined only over states which do not involve the first person. Even though we should want to acknowledge the possibility of amnesia, so that autobiographical memory is not our only concern, we still do not want, in giving a psychological version of the unity relation, simply to set aside autobiographical memory.

These problems arose only because we were considering a reductionism which not only used subjectless formulations to characterize its reductive base, but which held that these formulations could be used indifferently to report upon one's own mental states and the mental states of other people. We have seen that it is not possible to sustain a position on which this use of the subjectless formulation is conceptually more basic than our ordinary talk of persons. The reductionist might instead propose, though, to use the subjectless formulation in such a way that it could not be used indifferently to report upon one's own mental states and the states of other people. This would certainly be closer to the use advocated by Lichtenberg and Wittgenstein, who plainly had in mind a use of the form on which it could report only the mental states of at most one person.[10] The reductionist could hold that this use of these subjectless ascriptions of psychological state is genuinely more basic than their use at the level of talk of persons. This use of 'It hurts' or 'There is thinking' is one on which it can be used only to report what are in fact one's own mental states; it relates to a level of thought at which the conception of assigning mental states to persons, and, in particular, the thought of assigning mental states to other people, has simply not come into play. It is a cry with which one's own thoughts are greeted.

On this interpretation, if a particular use of 'There is thinking' expresses a truth, then so too would a use by that speaker of 'I am thinking'; and conversely. How are we to explain this logical link? We might take 'I am thinking' to be the basic form,

---

[9] *Reasons and Persons*, 204–9.

[10] Ludwig Wittgenstein, *Philosophical Remarks*, trans. R. Hargreaves and R. White (Oxford: Blackwell, 1975), §58.

and say that 'There is thinking' is, as it were, a primitive sketch of it: it is implicitly egocentric, and really only makes full sense when we grasp it as elliptical for 'I am thinking'. But of course, on this understanding of it, the formulation 'There is thinking' is of no use to a reductionist: it already implicitly uses the language of persons; it makes sense only as a crude approximation towards 'I am thinking'.

The alternative gloss on 'There is thinking' is to suppose that it is the primitive form, fully comprehensible as it stands. The reductionist has to start from this solipsistic base, at which he has only the capacity to greet thoughts with a cry; develop the conception of himself as the whole network of these thoughts; and then somehow win his way out to the conception of himself as one among a possible plurality of subjects, all of whom can have these thoughts. This construction is what will ultimately explain the relation between 'There is thinking' and 'I am thinking'. The reductionist thus faces the problems which classically lead to solipsism: given that, in the first instance, I understand psychological predicates in such a way that they cannot be applied to a plurality of subjects, how can I then find intelligible their application to other people? He also has the problem of understanding how there could be subjects other than himself. For in developing his conception of himself, the thinker has no need to appeal to the idea of a particular relation between thoughts; every single thought that he can greet with 'There is thinking' just is one of his, and there is no need for him to appeal to a particular type of relation which one thought must bear to certain of his thoughts for it to be one of his. But then we have no grip on how the thinker might find it intelligible that there are other subjects, internally structured in just the same way as him. The classical response to solipsism is to say that its starting-point is wrong; that we have to begin with the ascription of thoughts to a plurality of subjects. That response seems correct, but it is obviously inconsistent with reductionism.

3

There are other aspects of the reductionist's position which are still of interest. In particular, we can ask whether he is right in thinking that he can give an impersonal description of the unity relation: the relation that has to hold among a collection of experiences and a particular body for them to constitute a person. Another way we can put the point is to say that the reductionist may still be able to give an impersonal description of the relation that must hold among a particular set of experiences for them to constitute a single person. That is, he may be able to give an impersonal description of the way in which the constituents of the exploded view are to be assembled to give a person.[11] I want to connect this thesis with a point already remarked. We saw that there is one way in which the reductionist might try to sustain his view of experience. This would be to suppose that the kind of reduction he is providing is not one which gives a level of thought conceptually more fundamental than that at which the first person is used. It is, rather, a reduction which appeals only to psychological states which could have been had by animals which are not persons, even if there never had been any persons—states such as perceptions and pains. As we saw, this does not seem to provide a perspective from which the concern to survive can be reformulated, because it is not a conceptual reduction, and the first person is still in play. But that does not in any case accord with the practice of reductionists. They accord a central place to states such as autobiographical memory or first-personal plans and intentions, in giving their exploded view. These states cannot be had by creatures which are not persons, because they require self-consciousness. I want to propose an explanation of the centrality reductionists give to these first-personal states.

Suppose we consider how the reductionist is to go about giving an impersonal report of a first-personal state, such as recalling that one heard the chimes at midnight. If we give the report in the form 'John is thinking: I heard the chimes at midnight' then we run into the obvious difficulty that the reference to John is precisely reference to a person, whereas we were trying to give an impersonal description of the state. But we can here use the 'subjectless' formulations discussed

---

[11] This is the position recommended to the reductionist by Shoemaker, Critical Notice of *Reasons and Persons*.

earlier, and instead say, 'It is thought: I heard the chimes at midnight'. Of course, here we shall really need some kind of relativization of the ascription; but, it may be held, the relativization need not be relativization to persons. It may, for example, be relativization to a particular body. There is also a slightly subtler kind of appeal to persons that the reductionist has to avoid. Suppose the ascription we consider is not 'It is thought: I heard the chimes at midnight', but 'It is re-membered: I heard the chimes at midnight'. Here we do not have a direct ascription of the thought to a person, but the notion of a person seems to be involved nevertheless. The notion of remembering being used here is one which seems to depend upon the notion of a person. For it is not really being remembered, 'I heard the chimes at midnight', unless the person who is now thinking 'I heard the chimes at mid-night' is the same person as did hear the chimes at midnight. The obvious response to this would be for the reductionist to refrain from using the notion of memory in giving the kinds of reports of psychological state which he wants to use in defining the unity relation for persons. But as we have seen, reductionists do not in fact want to abandon talk of autobio-graphical memory altogether in giving their analysis. The route taken by Parfit is to define a notion of quasi-memory that does not depend upon the notion of a person. He says:

an apparent memory is an accurate quasi-memory if

1. the apparent memory is of a certain past experience,
2. this experience occurred,

and

3. the apparent memory is causally dependent, in the right kind of way, on this experience.[12]

It then has to be shown that the 'right kind' of causal depen-dence can be characterized without any appeal to the notion of a person. In general, then, the thesis is that the unity relation is a distinctive causal relation we can define over psychological states. Even if we acknowledge that this description will have to describe relations between first-person psychological states, which are neither conceptually nor, in the sense given above,

---

[12] Parfit, *Reasons and Persons*, 226.

ontologically more basic than the notion of a person, still, the purely causal relations between those states may be describable without appealing to the notion of a person. We can do better than simply saying that the relations in question are the causal relations which characteristically hold between the states of a single person. So the reductionist says.

There seems in fact to be no reason to suppose that there is any causal relation, or set of causal relations, which characteristically holds among the psychological states of a single person. No such explicit reductive description has ever been given. And when one considers the wide variety of pathological cases there are, in which there is causal disintegration consistently with the presence of a single person, it is hard to believe that an informative boundary line could be drawn, in reductive terms, between cases in which the causal breakdown means we no longer have a single person and cases in which there is still but one person.

The very notion of a causal connection between two mental states does not involve the notion of a person. There is, however, another kind of connection between psychological states which does involve the notion of a person. One reason why it can seem possible to give an impersonal description of the unity relation for persons is a failure to distinguish sufficiently between these two types of connection.

Consider the I-thoughts of a single thinker. They are inferentially integrated, in the following sense: from any two premisses, both stated using the first person, the thinker is entitled to draw inferences which trade upon the identity of the thing referred to in the two premisses. For example, from 'I am F' and 'I am G', the thinker is entitled to move directly to the conclusion, 'I am both F and G'. There is no need for a further premiss asserting the identity of the thing referred to by those two uses of 'I'. In contrast, if one thinker thinks 'I am F', and another thinks 'I am G', there is no question of either being entitled to conclude that anyone is both F and G. So suppose that we consider the Lichtenbergian reports of thoughts, 'It is thought: I am F' and 'It is thought: I am G'. In order to know whether we can trade upon identity in inferences involving these two thoughts, we have to know whether it is the same thing that is being referred to. But to know that, we have to know whether it is the same person who is thinking both thoughts. This point does not apply only to inferences involving propositions entertained simultaneously by a thinker. It applies also to the logical relations between first-person propositions entertained by the same thinker at different times. For example, it applies to the relation between a first-person present-tense judgement and the subsequent memory deriving from it; and to the relation between a plan I form at one time and my later decision that I should put the plan into action then. If I think at one time 'I am *F*', I can judge at a later time 'I was *F*', without needing to use any premiss asserting the identity of my earlier and later self. What we have here is a kind of temporally extended inference. It is, of course, necessary for the correctness of the transition that the two uses of 'I' be by the same person.

It might be said that this does show the need for a kind of relativization of Lichtenbergian reports of thoughts, but that this need not be a relativization to persons. For example, it might be said that these two I-thoughts have each to be relativized to a body. And if they are relativized to the same body, then it is legitimate to trade upon identity in inference involving them. But this response only even seems to work because it exploits uncertainties that most of us would feel when considering questions of personal identity. Perhaps the identity of a person just is the identity of a body. In that case, the relativization just mentioned will certainly work, but only because we are relativizing thoughts to persons, and reductionism is abandoned. Suppose, on the other hand, that the identity of a person is not the identity of a body: that a prince can wake up in the body of a cobbler. In that case, the relativization will not work. Two I-thoughts might be dependent upon different bodies, and yet be inferentially related, being thoughts had by the same person. Two I-thoughts, had at different times, might be dependent upon the same body, and yet not be inferentially related, because the body is at different times inhabited by different people. We shall not be able to get the relativization right until we make it relativization precisely to a person. Notice, incidentally, that the relativization to a person is enough. That is, if a single person grasps two I-thoughts, then they just are inferentially related—there is no further question about whether the thinker is using both I-thoughts to think of himself in the same way. This is what is correct about the thesis that 'I' lacks a Fregean sense.

The reductionist will deny that he has any responsibility at all to give a relativization here, on the grounds that he has no need to characterize the inferential relations among first-person thoughts. The only connections among thoughts which concern him, he will say, are causal connections; in particular, relations of psychological continuity and connectedness.[13]

If the account is purely causal, though, it is unlikely to work. A great deal of causal fragmentation is possible in the life of a person, consistently with there being a single person there. In contrast, the norms of inference serve precisely to draw together the unity of a person. The unity relation for persons has to be thought of as a normative relation. The problems that we encounter when we try to give a causal characterization of it are problems not of detail, but of principle.

I focus on first-person thoughts, because they evidently play a central role in the psychological connectedness that is distinctive of persons. I think it would be possible to give a description of the connectedness in the psychological life of a creature which was not a person in purely causal terms. One might appeal to the direct causal connections between the psychological state of the creature at one moment and its psychological state a moment later. And one might try to characterize more specialized causal relations between particular states and their effects. In giving a description of the connectedness of persons, however, we cannot rest with this kind of account. It is distinctive of persons that they are capable of first-person thinking, and that their psychological lives are organized around first-person thinking; they are organized around autobiographical thought. A merely causal description of this type of connectedness faces serious difficulties.

The charge is that it is guilty of confusing causal with normative relations. We can draw a parallel here between reductionism about the self and a functionalist view of propositional attitudes.[14] It is sometimes objected to a functionalist

[13] Ibid. 204–9; cf. p. 226.
[14] The parallel is proposed by Quassim Cassam in his contribution to this volume. He takes it in a rather different direction.

theory of thoughts that it treats as causal relations between thoughts connections that are in fact irreducibly normative.[15] So, for example, consider the relation between the thought that p, the thought that q, and the thought that p and q. This is not properly described as a propensity of the first two thoughts to produce the third. The correct way to describe the relation between them is to say that the first two entail the third; and this is what we need in giving an account of what individuates the thought that p and q, what makes it the thought that it is. If this parallel is correct, then we can say that what is central to the identity of a person is not the causal relation between the thought 'I am F' and the thought 'I am G', namely that they have the propensity to produce the thought 'I am both F and G'. What is central to the identity of the person is rather the normative relation between the thoughts, that the first two entail the third, without the need for any further premisses. The same point can evidently be made about the first-person thoughts of a single thinker over a period of time. What is central to the identity of the person is not the causal relation between the thought 'I am F' and the later thought 'I was F'. What matters for identity is rather the normative relation between the two thoughts, that the correctness of the earlier one entails the correctness of the later one.

We can pursue the point by considering the classical cases of 'multiple personality'. The fact that it is a single human being that is involved in such a case means that the various personalities cannot be entirely causally isolated from one another. If one personality damages the arm of the body, that will affect the activities of another personality, which has to operate with a damaged arm (so to speak). But we can envisage a kind of limiting case, in which the various personalities are, so far as is possible, causally isolated. In practice, this limiting case is not encountered: typically one personality will have direct knowledge of the actions or thoughts of another. But the causal isolation may be sufficiently advanced, as in the case, reported by Prince, of 'Christine Beauchamp', that we want to

---

[15] J. McDowell, 'Functionalism and Anomalous Monism', in E. LePore and B. McLaughlin (eds.), *Actions and Events: Perspectives on the Philosophy of Donald Davidson* (Oxford: Blackwell, 1985).

say that there are different people inhabiting a single body.[16] So we might say that 'Sally' and *'B1'*, different personalities of Christine Beauchamp, are different people using the same body at different times. If we take this line, then when Sally says 'I have been to Vienna', and *B1* says 'I have never been to Vienna', the two uses of 'I' refer to different people, and both statements may be true.[17]

Even in this case, though, we may think the causal disintegration cannot be so extreme as to warrant such a description. And certainly there are cases of less complete breakdowns of integration where we may wish to distinguish between personalities, because of the causal fragmentation, but resist saying there are different people inhabiting the same body. But then, how are we to distinguish between the statements of one personality, and the statements of another, given that we cannot ascribe them to different subjects? In this kind of case we can use an adverbial approach to the ascription of beliefs and statements. We have to form adverbs from 'Sally' and *'B1'*; so suppose we use 'Sallywise' and *'B1*-ly'. Then we can say: 'C.B. says$_\text{Sallywise}$ that she has been to Vienna', and 'C.B. says$_{B1\text{-ly}}$ that she has never been to Vienna'. Both ascriptions might be true—that is, C.B. might have made just those statements, in just the ways indicated. But the two statements ascribed cannot both be true, for C.B. cannot have both been to Vienna and not visited it; and the truth of the two statements just depends upon whether C.B. was there.[18]

The point here is that there is still a normative connection between C.B.'s two statements—they are contradictory—even if there are no direct causal connections between them. The project of trying to define the kind of causal relations that would be required for the connection to hold seems at least difficult; and perhaps it is impossible. Perhaps whether the normative relation holds is something that depends, that supervenes upon causal relatedness; but that might be so without a reductive definition being possible.

[16] M. Prince, *The Dissociation of a Personality* (London: Longmans, 1905).

[17] For discussion of such cases, cf. K. V. Wilkes, *Real People* (Oxford: Oxford University Press, 1988), ch. 4: 'Fugues, Hypnosis, and Multiple Personality'.

[18] An adverbial analysis of cases of multiple personality was proposed in lectures by J. J. MacIntosh in Calgary, in 1978.

It might be held that unless two propositional attitudes of a subject are directly causally related, there is no normative relation between them. For example, if two different personalities of the same thinker are causally highly insulated, so that while one thinks 'I have never been to Vienna' and the other thinks 'I have been to Vienna', the propositions cannot be simultaneously apprehended and their contradictory character grasped by the thinker, then perhaps they are not normatively related. This position seems to have little to recommend it. It is quite obvious that if the thinker could simultaneously grasp the two propositions, he would appreciate that they are contradictory, and the reason for that is that they are contradictory, that the normative relation does hold between them. To say this is to repeat the point made above, that there is a way in which we do not need the notion of the Fregean sense of the first person. Given two uses of 'I', the question whether they are inferentially related, in that their user can trade upon the identity of reference in inferences involving them, depends only upon whether it is the same person who produced both tokens of 'I'. There is no further question whether he was thinking of himself in the same way both times. He was thinking of himself in the first-person way both times; and there is no finer discrimination to be made among the ways in which he might have been thinking of himself.

The point can be made vivid by considering the case of self-deception. We may want to think of self-deception in terms of a 'main system' of belief and a 'protective system', which are in some ways causally interactive, but in some ways causally insulated from each other.[19] In doing so we need not be supposing a network of homunculi, so that the different systems are different subjects of thought. We might rather be using an adverbial analysis, on which the distinction is between X's believing$_{\text{main-systemly}}$ that p, and X's believing$_{\text{protective-systemly}}$ that not-p. Of course, whether one uses such an adverbial analysis is independent of what view one takes of the rationality of self-deception. But what we can say is that it is a fallacy to suppose that a view on which self-deception is motivated, and to be understood in terms of the distinction between main

[19] Cf. D. Pears, *Motivated Irrationality* (Oxford: Oxford University Press, 1984).

system and protective system, is committed to viewing those systems as the subjects of propositional attitudes.

These propositional attitudes, believing$_{main-systemly}$ that p, and believing$_{protective-systemly}$ that not-p, despite their causal isolation, are obviously normatively connected: indeed, that is the whole point of their causal insulation, in this model of self-deception, that their normative connection must not be made vivid. So suppose now we consider the first-person attitudes, believing$_{main-systemly}$ that one has not been to Vienna, and believing$_{protective-systemly}$ that one has been to Vienna. The question whether these attitudes are attitudes of the same person, and the question whether they are normatively related, as contradictories, are one and the same. But it would plainly be wrong to conclude from this that we could give a reductive account of the unity relation by appealing to such normative connections. The normative connections are no more funda-mental than the question whether it is a single person that is involved. The only thing that might make this seem un-problematic would be a failure to distinguish between the normative relations, which are definitionally tied to personal identity, and the causal relations between propositional atti-tudes, which have no such definitional tie to personal identity, but can be characterized without appeal to it.

Once we realize the tangle of causal relatedness and causal isolation that can hold between the various mental states of a single thinker, we might well question whether we can reasonably hope to give a definition of just what the needed causal relations are that must hold between two states for them to be states of the same thinker. If there is a rule, perhaps it is simply: one animal, one person. In that case, the normative relation always holds between I-statements made by the same animal, whatever the degree of internal causal fragmentation, and sameness of animal just is sameness of person. The project of characterizing relations between mental states, while appeal-ing only to the identities of entities more fundamental than persons, has been abandoned—for, on this approach, same-ness of animal just is sameness of person. Alternatively, we might hold that different subjects of thought can inhabit the same animal, and that, when this happens, we can always point to the specific causal breakdowns which make the diagnosis compelling, without acknowledging the possibility of giving a general formulation of necessary and sufficient conditions for causal integration in a single subject. Perhaps no such definition is possible. Perhaps all we can say is that the various first-person thoughts are normatively related, in that inferences between them which trade upon the identity of the subject are legitimate, without being able to give any necessary and sufficient conditions in terms of the causal structure of the subject which are required for these normative conditions to hold. If we have to appeal directly to these normative relations, though, then, as we have seen, sameness of person is the only relativization that will do to secure them, and the reductionist cannot characterize the relations between mental states which are supposed to constitute identity without making reference to persons.

This section began with the question why reductionists give the centrality they do to first-person psychological states, in giving a description of the unity relation for persons. For, as we saw, it would on the face of it be more consonant with the thrust of the reductionist view to confine attention to the states which persons have in common with other animals, and to attempt to define the unity relation only over such states. On the face of it, certainly, animals which are not persons have less complexity in their psychological lives than do animals which are persons; so perhaps we can give a reductionist account of the unity relation for them. The insight that makes the reductionist depart from this model in the case of persons is the insight that the relations between first-personal states are constitutive of the identity of the person. The reductionist's mistake is to suppose that these relations can be characterized as merely causal. In fact, as we have seen, the relations that matter here are normative, inferential relations. And in describing why these norms of inference hold between first-person thoughts, we have no choice but to appeal to the notion of sameness of person.

4

Let us bring these points to bear on the role of fission cases in the argument over reductionism. One role they play is to make it seem unquestionable that the notions of psychological connectedness that we need in characterizing the unity relation for persons can be described in impersonal terms. For it seems that an original self is psychologically connected to each of its two successor selves in all the ways relevant to personal identity, yet it can hardly be identical to both of them. So we must be able to describe those psychological connections without appealing to the notion of personal identity. One reply to this line of thought would be the multiple occupancy thesis: that in a fission case, what transpires is that even before the fission, there were two different people, qualitatively identical no doubt, in the same place at the same time, who merely went their separate ways after the fission. Here I want to note only that this is a way of resisting the reductionist's reading of fission. For on the multiple occupancy thesis, the psychological connectedness between fission products and the original selves just does require personal identity. The products are connected psychologically only to earlier stages of the very same person; 'fission product' and 'original self' are phase sortals.[20]

Suppose that, with the reductionist, we resist the multiple occupancy thesis, so that a case of fission is understood as involving three different people, the original self and the fission products. How are we to use fission, so interpreted, as a guide in providing an impersonal characterization of psychological connectedness? It might be thought, in fact, that we already have a high-level description of connectedness: the relation which holds between an original self and its fission products. But this is not in fact impersonal. For what is a fission case? It is precisely a case in which, had either fission product not existed, the original person would have persisted. So we shall need a direct characterization of connectedness, if it is to be given an impersonal description.

It is, however, not at all obvious, once we begin on the task of giving such a direct description, that it can be done in impersonal terms. Any credible account will begin with a memory of one's own past—but will such memory really be

[20] For defence of the multiple occupancy thesis, see Noonan, *Personal Identity*, 164–8 and 196–8; D. Lewis, 'Survival and Identity', in D. Lewis, *Philosophical Papers*, i (Oxford: Oxford University Press, 1983).

distributed to the products of fission? Suppose that I remember taking the children to the zoo one Sunday. And then I fission. Can it be true of both products of the fission that each has the memory they would express by saying 'I took the children to the zoo one Sunday'? If both really do remember this, then both must have taken the children to the zoo that Sunday; but in fact there was only one person who took them then. The fact is that both fission products have memories which are false. Each seems to remember taking the children to the zoo that Sunday, but in fact neither did. If both understand the situation, that there has been a fission which resulted in two duplicates of the original, so far as is possible consistently with there being fission, then both may conclude that X took the children to the zoo that Sunday. But neither would be right to suppose that this is something that he himself did. (We could resist this conclusion only by endorsing the multiple occupancy thesis. For then both products really could claim to have taken the children to the zoo that Sunday. But endorsing the multiple occupancy thesis makes the fission case useless for the purposes of grounding an impersonal characterization of psychological connectedness.) It thus appears that fission products are not psychologically connected to original selves in the way that people are usually psychologically connected to their earlier selves. For people usually remember what they did and experienced earlier. Fission products, however, cannot take their memories at face value, but have to distance themselves from them. They have to regard their memories as relating not to what they themselves did earlier, but to what someone else did earlier. Here we see very plainly what is wrong in the reductionist's use of causal rather than normative relations between first-person thoughts. It is true that the causal relation between the apparent memory of a fission product and the first-person thoughts of the original subject is similar to the causal relation between the memories of an ordinary person and his earlier thoughts and experiences. We can bring this out by remarking that if either side of the fission had not 'taken' at the time of the split, then we would have had but a single person, with an ordinary set of memories. This does not, of course, do anything to show that we can give an explicit reductive account of the causal relation. And the crucial point remains that, despite this causal similarity, the fission product, on realizing the situation, has to distance himself from his apparent memories. They are not memories of things which he himself has done.

It might be replied that this failure of psychological connectedness between an original self and its fission products is relatively unimportant. It depends on an extrinsic fact—that there was fission. Had it not been for the fission, either product would have been identical to the original, so the relevant relations of psychological connectedness would have held. But whether the relevant psychological relations hold between a given product and the original surely cannot depend on the extrinsic issue of whether the other product is around. This response, though, simply misses the importance of the first person as a determinant of whether the relevant psychological relations hold. The extrinsic fact controls whether the memories the later subject has of the earlier subject can really be taken by him to be memories of what he himself did. And nothing could be more crucial than that to whether the relevant psychological connectedness holds. It is not an unimportant feature of our memories that they are organized autobiographically, as the memories of the thoughts and deeds of a single person, as the memories of what I thought and did. Anything that disturbs that organization, extrinsic or not, disturbs psychological connectedness.

It is here that the reductionist may appeal to the notion of 'what matters' in survival. The reductionist may question precisely the importance of the autobiographical organization of our memories. The psychological connections which matter to us, he may say, are preserved through fission. So what we have to do is characterize those connections that are preserved. This can be done in an impersonal way (since identity is not preserved through fission), and this will give us at any rate part of the unity relation for persons. If this line of thought is to work, the reductionist has first to convince us that the psychological connections which matter to us are indeed preserved through fission. The kind of case we need is one in which I am, for example, lying in a hospital bed wondering whether the fission has in fact succeeded. If it has, then I have a double on Mars, say, who will in the future be causally isolated from me, so that he and I can in no way affect each other's lives. On the face of it, it is hard to see why this should matter to me. In fact, even if I can see this coming, it is hard to see why I should care about it. So the psychological relations we do care about are preserved through fission. The task is then to characterize them, which must be possible impersonally, since they are preserved when identity is not, and identity can then be characterized in terms of them plus, perhaps, a non-branching condition. So the reductionist argues.

But are the psychological relations which matter really preserved through fission? It seems to me that, in fact, fission is not a matter of indifference. Consider the following remarks by Nabokov in the Afterword to *Lolita*: 'Every serious writer, I dare say, is aware of this or that published book of his as of a constant comforting presence. Its pilot light is steadily burning somewhere in the basement and a mere touch applied to one's private thermostat instantly results in a quiet little explosion of familiar warmth.'[21] If this is an accurate report of his condition, then he ought not to be indifferent to fission. For, after fission, there would be no one who had the right to say 'I wrote *Lolita*'. Of course, it would still be true that *Lolita* was written; but that is not the same thing at all.

On first encounter, it can seem that fission cases provide a way of pin-pointing what we deeply care about in ordinary survival, and that they show that what we deeply care about does not require identity. This appearance is brought about entirely by a failure to spot the fact that fission would mean loss of the right to one's autobiographical memories; my memories of what I have seen and done. The accessibility of one's own autobiographical memories, from every part of one's life, increases steadily with age, and there is an obvious point to this.[22] Autobiographical memories are not valued principally as guides to future action. They are valued for their own sake. The fact is that identity is central to what we care about in our lives: one thing I care about is simply what I have made

[21] Vladimir Nabokov, *Lolita* (Harmondsworth: Penguin, 1980), 314.
[22] D. C. Rubin, S. E. Wetzler, and R. D. Nebes, 'Autobiographical Memory Across the Lifespan', in D. C. Rubin (ed.), *Autobiographical Memory* (Cambridge: Cambridge University Press, 1986).

of my life. Fission would force reorganization of the picture I have of life so far, even if my principal achievements have been of a quite different order to writing *Lolita*; perhaps they were entirely domestic, along the lines of taking the children to the zoo one Sunday when I did not want to go. Indeed, the basic point here does not have to do with achievement as such— it has to do with the way in which various incidents stack together to make a life. Fission would mean there could be no thinking of such things as things I had done; it would deprive me of one of the consolations of age. Perhaps it is wrong to look for this consolation; perhaps it is wrong to want a sense of the significance, of the pattern, in one's life. But that can hardly be shown by considering fission. Of course, there can be such a thing as seeing the pattern in someone else's life, in viewing their life as a sort of picaresque novel. But there is precisely the distance in this that makes all the difference between it and a sense of what I have done with *my* life.

Parallel points to these could be made for the case of intention. I may intend to write a novel—I may feel that it will vindicate all the sacrifices I have made so far if I do that, I may plan to marry Jane—I may feel that that would make sense of everything. If I fission, the best I can hope for is that someone else will do these things. That may make everything worth while for them, which is all very well, but it is not at all the same thing as everything being made worth while for me, which was the whole idea. The psychological connections which matter do not hold between me and my fission products. The reductionist might try to amend things here by introducing a notion of 'quasi-intention', which might link me to my fission products, but there simply is no coherent notion here which both describes our ordinary intentions, and which might operate as a link in fission cases. Parfit makes the attempt:

It may be a logical truth that we can intend to perform only our own actions. But we can use a new concept of *quasi-intention*. One person could quasi-intend to perform another person's actions. When this relation holds, it does not presuppose personal identity. The case of division shows what this involves. I could quasi-intend both that one resulting person roams the world, and that the other stays at home.

What I quasi-intend will be done not by me, but by the two resulting people.[23]

It is exceedingly difficult to grasp what Parfit has in mind here. The first person has a special link with motivation and action— it is because of this link that one's intention that one should oneself do something is connected to one's doing it in a way quite different to the way in which my intention that someone else should do something is related to their finally doing it. A quasi-intention cannot be an intention that one should oneself do something, because it can be acted upon after the division. But it is not simply an intention that someone else should do something either. That would obviously not yield any kind of psychological connectedness between the person who has the intention and the person who performs the action, and it is not what Parfit wants. He says:

Normally, if I intend that someone else should do something, I cannot get him to do it simply by forming this intention. But, if I am about to divide, it would be enough simply to form quasi-intentions. Both of the resulting people would inherit these quasi-intentions, and, unless they changed their minds, they would carry them out.[24]

On one reading of this, a quasi-intention is simply a first-person intention, such as the intention that one should take the children to the zoo. After the division, both duplicates would apparently have that intention, as they might both apparently have the memory of having taken the children to the zoo already. But given that both products of the division understand the situation, they should be as distanced from the intention as they are from the memory. It is no more an intention that *they* should do something than the memories are memories of what they did. So there would still not be the psychological continuity between an intention and its being acted upon that there ordinarily is. In any case, this does not seem to be what Parfit wants. He wants it to be the case that the products of the division should be differentially affected by the original subject's quasi-intentions—that they of themselves should bring it about that Lefty should roam while Righty stays

[23] *Reasons and Persons*, 261.
[24] Ibid.

at home. If one were about to divide, it would be extremely useful to be able to do this, but the project in detail seems incoherent. If the intention is to have the required direct connection with action, it must be first-personal; but if it is to affect Lefty and Righty differentially, it must be an intention that *Lefty* should do this and *Righty* should do that—that is, it must be an intention that other people should do these things. But then it does not have the required direct connection with action—why should Lefty and Righty be particularly moved by what someone else wants them to do, even supposing that they recognize themselves as the Lefty and Righty mentioned in the contents of those intentions?

Let us review the position. The argument we have been considering runs as follows. All the psychological connections relevant to personal identity are preserved through fission. Since identity is not preserved through fission, the argument runs, it must be possible to describe these psychological connections without assuming sameness of person. That is, we can give an impersonal description of psychological connectedness. In reply to this, we have seen that the psychological connections we have to consider include the ability to keep one's autobiographical memories; and that is not preserved through fission. Further, it is evident that a description of what is required, for the right to keep one's autobiographical memories, will have to appeal to the notion of sameness of person. Parallel points, as we have seen, can be made for the case of intention.

There is, however, another way in which the case of fission can be used. As we saw at the outset, one motive for reductionism is the desire to show how, from a subjective viewpoint, the concern to survive might be freed from a concern with identity, so that, for example, one's own death seems less terrifying a prospect. The strategy was to provide an exploded view of oneself, the reductive analysis, which would enable one to attain a more precise and discriminating analysis of what one valued in one's own survival. We have seen that fission cases give no reason to suppose that such a reductive analysis might be possible, and that the only way for a reductive account seems to be to define personal identity in terms of relations between states which both persons and animals which are not persons can be in. This is an approach which few reductionists have advocated. However, there is another way in which fission cases could be used. We have seen that through fission much would be lost of what a person values: autobiographical memory, and the possibility of acting on one's own intentions. But we might use fission cases in another way. Rather than using the first person to articulate one's subjective view of the prospect of fission, we might introduce another term, 'I*', which articulates a subjective view from which fission really is a matter of indifference. Using 'I*', we might elaborate a subjective viewpoint from which the panic of one's own death vanishes. This would be in contrast to our actual subjective viewpoint, which is expressed by the ordinary first person. The possibility of introducing such a term, 'I*', does not constitute a way of defending reductionism, since persons do not, as things stand, actually use any such term, and there is not much point in trying to give a reductive account of creatures quite different from us who use 'I*' rather than 'I' in expressing their points of view. The possibility of introducing such a term is of interest rather for the possibility it raises of adopting a quite different subjective attitude to death. The proposal is, then, that we could elaborate this attitude to death without going by way of reductionism.

We must not minimize the depth of the change that is being proposed here, in the replacement of 'I' by 'I*'. We can immediately remark some difficulties that arise in explaining how 'I*' operates. Is it to be a referring term? If it is, how does it differ from 'I'? One strategy would be to hold that 'I*' is a singular term, but that, while it refers, it does not refer to a person. Perhaps what it refers to is simply a path in a tree of fissionings and fusions. The problem with this strategy is to understand why it is not simply a notational variant on a view which equates persons with paths in trees of fissionings and fusions. After all, 'I*' is functioning in every other way like the first person. Of course, putting things in this way would involve commitment to the multiple occupancy thesis. For two paths might coincide for a time. But that in itself would not explain why the strategy suggested is not one which simply uses the ordinary first person, but understands the notion of a person in such a way that the multiple occupancy thesis holds.

In general, any view which holds that 'I*' is a term, referring to
Fs, which replaces our ordinary use of 'I', will be a notational
variant on a view which retains our ordinary use of the first
person, but holds that persons are Fs.

An alternative strategy is to hold that while the use of the
first person is replaced by the use of 'I*', 'I*' is not itself
a referring term. It simply 'expresses' certain psychological
relations. In that case, we are envisaging a scenario in which
the creatures involved do not grasp the first person, and
they have no comparable way of referring to themselves. That
means that we are dealing with creatures which are not self-
conscious—they have no ability to refer to themselves, in the
knowledge that that is what they are doing; they cannot consider themselves as themselves, at different times and places.
That in turn means that we are dealing with creatures which
are not persons. It certainly does seem possible to envisage
such creatures, but it is not so easy to see how one might go
about taking up their subjective stance oneself.

It might be held that the use of 'I*' is to be thought of as
supplementing, rather than as replacing, our ordinary use of
the first person. This would mesh with a response to fission
cases which begins with the following observation. It can
happen that the mere fact that someone else wants me to do
something gives me a reason to do that thing. For example, if
my father wants me to do something, there are background
points which mean that that already gives me some reason to
do it. First, there is the mere fact of his closeness to me. This is
a matter of his causal relation to me—that he is my father, after
all. There may also be shared interests and values between us,
so that if he has on reflection formed the view that I should do
this, that already gives me some reason to think that I would
myself on mature reflection also think that I should do it;
perhaps I even think that he is a better judge than I am of how
to serve those interests and values. These are independent
factors. Even if his interests and values are different to mine,
I may feel that the causal connection between him and me
gives me some reason, however slight, to do the thing. Alternatively, a public figure whose views I trust, though he bears
no such causal relation to me, might have some capacity to
affect my plans simply by recommending a particular course of

action to me. Now an earlier self is connected to its fission products in both of the ways just identified. So given that fission products can have knowledge of what the original self wanted them to do, and that they have these kinds of connection to the original self, these wants of the original self should carry some weight in influencing the plans and actions of the fission products. The use of 'I*' would merely express this special relationship between the original self and the products. In this kind of case, the use of the first person remains the basic, uneliminated connection between plans and action. If I am a fission product, I may well have a number of intentions that I* should do something; but that only shows me that someone close to me would like me to do those things. They have no bearing on what I actually do until I decide that I will act upon them. As I have said, I do have some reason to form the intention that I will act on them; but that is not the same thing as having the intention. And the point remains that it is the linkage between what I plan to do and what I actually do that gives us the psychological connectedness characteristic of personal identity. Similarly, the role of the first person in autobiographical memory remains fundamental—it is what connects earlier and later judgements by the same person. Indeed, we can go further than saying that the use of 'I' has not in fact been eliminated by this proposal. The use of 'I' could not be eliminated without making it quite unintelligible why the kinds of connectedness described above should matter. The reason why my father's wishes matter to me is precisely his connection to me; the reason why I might be guided by a public figure is precisely the relation between his interests and values and mine. Just so, the only reason why the intentions of my earlier self should matter to me as a fission product is the causal connection, and similarities, of that earlier self to me. The use of the first person is needed to explain why these psychological relations matter; abandon the use of the first person, and there would be no reason at all why the plans and ambitions of the earlier self should matter to the fission product.

In elaborating an alternative to our ordinary subjective viewpoint, then, we do better to consider uses of 'I*' which replace our ordinary use of the first person. But how are we to explain the term thus introduced? One way would be to say that 'I*' is subject to the following rule: each token of it may refer to the person who produced it, or to any person psychologically connected to the producer. The term could function as a restricted demonstrative, like 'that tree', which can apply to any one of a particular range of individuals.[25] So there is a substantive question to ask about how the term can be used to refer to the person who produced it. This is the price we pay for distancing ourselves from the ordinary first person, which is simply governed by the rule that any token of it refers to the person who produced it. Once we are considering a term not governed by that rule, there is a question about how its reference can be directed to the person who produced it. But perhaps the correct picture is that on some occasions of its use 'I*' is subject to that rule, whereas on other occasions of its use it operates in a different way. There is also the question how psychological predicates are to be introduced and explained, if we do not have the ordinary first person. One answer would be that they are introduced and explained as predicates of persons, using ordinary proper names. This, however, means that we have to consider a language which has no place for the psychological statements which are made otherwise than on the basis of observation; it will have no counterpart to our ordinary use of 'I am in pain', for example, a statement which does not require the identification of an individual, but is made simply on the strength of the fact that one is in pain. In this language, all psychological statements will involve the use of proper names, and so require the identification of an individual. It might be held that we can use 'I*' to plug this gap. We have only to consider the way in which it is used when it identifies the person who produced it; and that use of 'I*' will enable us to make statements such as 'I* am in pain', otherwise than on the basis of observation. The problem now is that this use of 'I*' seems to be exactly synonymous with the ordinary first person. And, as before, given the centrality it has in our psychological lives, it will seem that all other uses of 'I*'

---

[25] Something like this use of 'I*' is proposed by Carol Rovane, 'Branching Self-Consciousness', *Philosophical Review*, 99 (1990), 355–95; but the semantic description is sketchy, and it is not clear whether users of 'I*' also use the first person.

have their motivational force because of their connection with this fundamental use of 'I*', on which it is a version of the first person. There will have been no deep conceptual change. If we want to elaborate a genuinely subjective view on which identity does not matter in survival, we shall need a deeply articulated account of 'I*' and its role in the explanation of psychological predicates. Until we have such an account, of course, there is always the response from the standpoint of a transcendent objectivity—that no one matters any more than anyone else, and that identity does not matter because survival does not matter.

This connects with the final remark I wish to make, on the bearing of these points on reductionism. I have stressed the central place of the first person. And, at some points, the reductionist will no doubt have wished to protest that what I have done or plan to do is of no cosmic significance, and that there is something almost unbearably egocentric about assigning the first person the central place I have given it. Though I have some sympathy with the protest, it reflects a poor grasp of the place that I have assigned to the first person, and it gives no comfort to the reductionist. We have been trying to establish the character of the psychological connectedness that typifies persons, and it is here that I have said we must give central place to the first person. It is, of course, quite right to say that we often give ourselves more weight than we ought to in our deliberations, and perhaps we always give ourselves more weight than we ought to. This point is indifferent to the specific account that is given of the notion of a person and the psychological connectedness characteristic of persons: the point could be made whether or not reductionism about persons was true. Our present concern is not with that issue. We have been trying to do something rather different: to explore the question whether the possibility of fission cases gives any reason to suppose that psychological connectedness can be described in impersonal terms. We have been considering a line of thought which says that the psychological connections which matter subjectively in survival are all preserved through fission, even though personal identity is not, so that it must be possible to describe those connections impersonally. I have been pointing out that the psychological connections which matter in survival have an ineliminably first-person character, and consequently cannot be preserved through fission. It would be quite consistent with this to hold that, in the end, survival does not matter at all, from the standpoint of the cosmos. Survival is one thing, the cosmos another.

15

The Autonomy of Colour*

Justin Broackes

This essay takes two notions of autonomy and two notions of explanation and argues that colours occur in explanations that fall under all of them. The claim that colours can be used to explain anything at all may seem to some people an outrage. But their pessimism is unjustified and the orthodox dispositional view which may seem to support it, I shall argue, itself has difficulties. In broad terms, Section 2 shows that there exist good straight scientific laws of colour, constituting what one might call a phenomenal science. Section 3 offers a larger view of what we are doing when we attribute colours to things, a view which makes it a case of holistic explanation, similar in many ways to psychological explanation. Section 2 emphasizes the model of scientific explanation, and Section 3 the holistic model found in rational explanation; but it will emerge that colour explanation in different ways fits both models, as it also does the two principal notions of autonomy that the first section identifies.

1. ARE COLOURS EXPLANATORILY IDLE?

Philosophers often say that colours are explanatorily idle. As McGinn has put it:

© Justin Broackes 1992

* For discussion and comments on earlier versions of this paper, I am grateful to David Bell, Quassim Cassam, William Child, Larry Hardin, Kathleen Lennon, Michael Martin, Peter Smith, Paul Snowdon, Helen Steward, and Tim Williamson, as well as to other members of audiences where I have presented it. I owe a special debt to John Campbell: without his own writings on colour this would have been very different work, and without our many discussions, it would have been a good deal less enjoyable. To David Charles I am grateful for criticism and encouragement that go way beyond those of a generous editor

First, these qualities are not ascribed to things as part of the enterprise of explaining the causal interactions of objects with each other: colour and taste do not contribute to the causal powers of things. Primary qualities are precisely the qualities that figure in such explanations . . . Secondly, secondary qualities do not explain our perception of them; primary qualities are what do that.[1]

On the other hand, some philosophers have thought the contrary,[2] and they have painters[3] and much of everyday speech on their side. We regularly hear claims like these:

> (1) The red paint turned pink because he added white to it.
> (2) The house gets hot in summer because it is painted black.
> (3) The orange light of the evening sun made the façades of the buildings seem to glow.
> (4) The yellow of a life-jacket caught his eye as he looked across the water into the distance.
> (5) He stopped at the traffic lights because they were red.

Colours are invited to explain the appearance of things (3), human perception (4), action (5), and even the characteristics of non-sentient items, like the colour of a paint (1) and the temperature of a house (2).

Why then deny that colours explain what they seem to? Of

---

[1] C. McGinn, *The Subjective View: Secondary Qualities and Indexical Thoughts* (Oxford: Oxford University Press, 1983), 14–15. Cf. J. Bennett, *Locke, Berkeley, Hume: Central Themes* (Oxford: Oxford University Press, 1971), 102 f.; J. McDowell, 'Values and Secondary Qualities', in T. Honderich (ed.), *Morality and Objectivity: A Tribute to J. L. Mackie* (London: Routledge & Kegan Paul, 1985), 118.

[2] 'Colours have characteristic causes and effects—that we do know' (Wittgenstein, *Remarks on Colour*, ed. G. E. M. Anscombe, trans. L. L. McAlister and M. Schättle (Oxford: Blackwell, 1977), III. 82).

[3] The painter Philipp Otto Runge said in a letter to Goethe: 'This has driven me on at least to study the characteristics of the colours, and whether it would be possible to penetrate so deeply into their powers, that it would be clearer to me what they achieve, or what can be produced by means of them, or what affects them'. (Runge, as quoted in Goethe's *Farbenlehre*, in the *Zugabe* that follows §920, my translation; J. W. Goethe, *Sämtliche Werke*, ed. K. Richter, H. G. Göpfert, N. Miller, and G. Sauder (Munich: Carl Hanser, 1989), x. 266). There is a translation of virtually all of the *Didaktischer Teil* (Didactic Part) of the *Farbenlehre*, by Charles Eastlake (Goethe, *Theory of Colours* (London: John Murray, 1840), repr. with intro. by D. B. Judd (Cambridge, Mass.: MIT Press, 1970)). Unfortunately Runge's letter is not translated by Eastlake.

course they are not fundamental physical properties, like mass and charge. But we should not need reminding that good explanation is not always explanation in the terms of basic physics. As Putnam has said, we can explain why a square peg will not fit into a round hole, by saying the board and the peg are rigid, and the round hole is smaller than the peg. An 'explanation' in quantum mechanics, or whatever other basic terms, would miss the relevant features. For 'the same [higher-level] explanation will go in any world (whatever the microstructure) in which those *higher level* structural features [rigidity and size] are present. In that sense *this explanation is autonomous.'*[4]

Why shouldn't colours occur in explanations that are auton-omous in a similar way? Autonomy means different things to different people, and it may be helpful to clarify the two main senses I shall be giving it. The first involves no more than is introduced in the last quotation from Putnam: the same explanation would go through in any world where the same higher-level properties were present. It is no part of an auton-omy claim in this sense, therefore, that properties invoked in an autonomous explanation are in every way independent of properties at other levels. The squareness of the peg is, for example, supervenient on the basic physical properties and arrangement of the peg's constituent parts. Colours simi-larly will be supervenient upon physical properties. In this usage, therefore, interdependence is not, as it is for Patricia Churchland, 'autonomy's opposite'.[5] Colour explanations will be autonomous in this sense if they are indifferent to the underlying realization of the property—if the same explana-tion would go through if the object's redness, for example, were realized in some microstructurally different way. But that does not imply that the explanation is independent of other properties in every way. It means that it is independent of microstructural variations that would result in the same macroproperty.

[4] H. Putnam, 'Philosophy and our Mental Life', in H. Putnam, *Philosophical Papers*, ii: *Mind, Language and Reality* (Cambridge: Cambridge University Press, 1975), 296.
[5] P. S. Churchland, *Neurophilosophy* (Cambridge, Mass.: MIT Press, 1986), 380.

In what is probably a different sense, explanations are autonomous if they rule themselves, in that they are responsible to, and to be judged by, criteria internal to that style of explanation—and not by criteria from another domain. On this understanding, an autonomous explanation will typically (though not necessarily) be 'epistemically independent' of other explanations, in that knowledge that it meets the appropriate internal standards of success will be independent of knowledge concerning any other form of explanation. But it may still (and typically will) be the case that the explanation fails to be 'ontologically independent', in the sense that the higher-level causal relations would hold even if the underlying lower-level causal relations did not. In between these two senses of independence there is a third issue, of whether for any higher-level *classification* there has to be at a lower level a classification that corresponds (a type-identity, or restricted type-identity); and a fourth issue, of whether every higher-level *causal generalization* must correspond to (or be reducible to) one or more lower-level causal generalizations. But to claim that a property figures in autonomous explanations in the sense explained at the start of this paragraph is not to claim independence in any sense stronger than the first of these four.

I shall be exploring the prospects that colours figure in explanations that are autonomous in these two senses. Why should one resist the idea? Localized error, so to speak, is of course unavoidable: individual explanatory claims are bound sometimes to turn out false—as I shall later suggest is actually the case with (4). But some people may still suspect a global error—a mistake in the very idea that colours can occur in 'autonomous explanations'. The resistance must have a theoretical source, and I shall briefly consider four.

One might suspect that colour explanation, if there were such a thing, would compete for space with physics, and each would crowd the other out. The obvious reply is that explanatory schemes at different levels may peacefully coexist if they stand in appropriate relations. It is widely believed that mental and physical schemes of explanation can peacefully coexist if mental phenomena are supervenient upon physical phenomena. Could not colour explanation in a similar way coexist with the physical sciences, if a corresponding supervenience relation held there too?[6] The suggestion is plausible. My present perception of blue, for example, would be explained by the blueness of the mug in front of me, while the underlying visual processes were explained by whatever physical features are relevant. There will be no competition between the explanations, if the colour, as seems plausible, supervenes on the physical features.

[6] Though no definition of supervenience is uncontroversial, a first approximation would be: f-properties supervene on g-properties iff it is metaphysically necessary that situations indiscernible in g-terms are also indiscernible in f-terms, but not vice versa. The case for peaceful coexistence of mental and physical discourses has been made in different ways by Davidson, Fodor, and Dennett. There are people who have argued for the elimination of the mental. But the most notable proposals (like that of Churchland, *Neurophilosophy*, esp. chs. 7–9) attack the mental scheme of discourse not on the a priori ground that different levels of discourse can never coexist peacefully (Churchland is herself a defender of a plurality of levels of scientific discourse—see p. 358), but rather on the a posteriori ground that 'folk psychology' is not the best candidate for the job it is intended for, and looks set to be replaced by an ideally developed neuroscience (see e.g. p. 396). So the belief in a plurality of legitimate levels of discourse is I think not a contentious one. The second issue—raised by the claim that folk psychology should be replaced by neuroscience—is not one which I can pretend to discuss properly here. But since the issue lurks in the background of discussions later in this paper, it may help to say now that my own response would be to call into question Churchland's view of what the aim of mental discourse *is*. If its aim is not to 'explain and predict' in the manner of the physical sciences, then failure *at that job* is not a reason to abandon it. (For alternative views of the domain and methods of rational explanation, see e.g. Davidson, 'Mental Events' and 'Psychology as Philosophy', repr. in D. Davidson, *Essays on Actions and Events* (Oxford: Clarendon Press, 1980); J. McDowell, 'Functionalism and Anomalous Monism', in E. LePore and B. McLaughlin (eds.), *Actions and Events: Perspectives on the Philosophy of Donald Davidson* (Oxford: Blackwell, 1985); K. Lennon, *Explaining Human Action* (London: Duckworth, 1990).) A third and different matter is Churchland's claim that 'cognitive psychology' looks unlikely to succeed in isolation from neural science (or if it persuades itself that it is 'autonomous with respect to neuroscience' (p. 362)). On this issue, Churchland's view seems completely persuasive, if the domain of cognitive psychology includes such questions as why we sleep, and why we forget as much as we do. But that does not immediately lend support to the second claim, unless the aims of ordinary mental discourse and 'folk psychology' are the same as those of cognitive psychology. For the comparison between the relation of mental and physical explanations and that of colour explanation and physical explanation, see J. Campbell, 'A Simple View of Colour', in J. Haldane and C. Wright (eds.), *Realism and Reason* (Oxford: Oxford University Press, forthcoming), §3. I urged the same point in J. Broackes, 'The Identity of Properties' (D.Phil. thesis, Oxford University, 1986), 228. Not being able to argue all points at once, the succeeding discussion presumes the peaceful coexistence of the first pair, and considers the suitability of using that as a model for the relation of the second pair.

One might worry about the fact that the putative effects of colour are primarily on humans, or, if on other things, on their colour, rather than on, say, their size and shape.[7] But that is hardly a reason to deny them causal efficacy: the primary effects of economic factors like an increase in the money supply are also on humans and other economic factors (rather than directly on the size and shape of physical objects); but we do not treat that as a reason to say they are causally idle.

A third worry might be that colours are parochial: there are totally colour-blind humans, and if they had been the only ones around, then they would hardly have felt they were missing something. But we can admit the parochiality of something without denying it causal efficacy. Economic factors, again, are parochial (there are societies without money, and a view of our own existence that makes money an irrelevance); but that does not make us deny the reality of economic causes.

Perhaps the most serious concern is that colours are dispositions, and dispositions neither cause nor explain. The issues are too complex to discuss properly here,[8] but there are problems at each stage of the argument. First, one may doubt whether colours are in fact dispositions. I shall later be giving reasons to deny the orthodox view of them as dispositions to produce experiences in us, while suggesting that they are dispositions of a different kind. But we can certainly not simply presume that colours are dispositions of any kind, in the face of the substantial body of philosophers who have recently argued that they are not.[9] Secondly, it is doubtful whether dispositions are explanatorily idle. There is a tradition of scoffing at explanations in terms of *virtus dormitiva*. But dispositions are not all like dormitive virtue (what about the engineer's properties of capacitance, inductance, resistance, and elasticity?), and even dormitive virtue has its explanatory uses. (The man fell asleep at the controls of the machine because he had drunk

---

[7] The effect of the black paint on the temperature of the house seems an exception to this. But we will shortly have reasons to doubt whether the claim is strictly true.

[8] I discuss them more fully in my book *The Nature of Colour* (in preparation).

[9] e.g. P. M. S. Hacker, *Appearance and Reality* (Oxford: Blackwell, 1987), chs. 3 and 4; Campbell, 'A Simple View of Colour'; and Barry Stroud in his John Locke lectures in Oxford.

too much of a cough mixture with a dormitive virtue.) The issues can hardly even be aired here, but even if colours are dispositions, we cannot assume that they are explanatorily idle for that reason, any more than for the other reasons I have considered.

2. COLOUR LAWS AND COLOUR SCIENCE

What are the prospects of finding good straight scientific explanations that employ colours? What can colours be used scientifically to explain? We might distinguish three possible uses of colours: to explain (1) the effects of bodies (and light) on humans and other animals (notably in perception), (2) the effects of bodies (and light) on the colour properties of other bodies, and (3) the effects of bodies (and light) on the non-colour properties of other bodies (like their temperature, motion, or size).

The last category is the least promising. The most conspicuous cases where colour affects the non-colour properties of non-sentient things are cases where they do so only by affecting sentient beings, who in turn produce the effects in the non-sentient things. (The colour of the traffic-lights affects the motion of the cars, but only as it is seen by the drivers.) These cases therefore reduce to the first category. There may seem to be cases where colour is directly responsible for the non-colour properties of something: the warehouse walls, we may say, are heating up in the sun because they are painted black. But on closer inspection, the explanation seems to be invalidated by lower-level facts. The walls, we find out, are really heating up because they fail to reflect the infra-red light from the sun, rather than because they fail to reflect the visible light in the way that makes us call them black. It is not the blackness proper that explains the effect. Black things commonly absorb infra-red as well as visible light, so we naturally say 'if it hadn't been black, it wouldn't have heated up like that'. But the counterfactual is strictly false: the house could well have been some other colour and still heated up like that (if, say, it was painted in a green paint that also absorbed in the infra-red); and it could well have been black and not heated up like that (if the paint absorbed light in the visible range but not in the infra-red). The threat of invalidation by lower-level explanation may well be endemic to purported explanations of this kind. We have reason to believe that non-colour physical phenomena can in principle be explained in physical terms; we know (par-ticularly from the existence of metamerism, described below) that colours are (often quite strikingly) variably realizable in physical terms; so it seems likely that for any physical effect produced by an object of one colour, there could be another object of the same colour that did not have that effect. The prospects, therefore, of finding laws by which colours could be treated as causes of the instantiation of other physical pro-perties (other than via perception) seem remote—though the argument does not rule out the possibility in principle.

The initial prospects look better of giving scientific expla-nations on the basis of colour for the other two ranges of phenomena: human perceptions and the colours of things. Here a similar challenge arises, but in this case I think it can, at least often, be met. Quite aside from any general prejudice that the only decent explanation is explanation in the terms of physics, there is a worry that these phenomena are simply (as a matter of fact) better explained in terms of physical properties more basic than colour. The main reason for saying this is the existence of metamerism. Because of the limited sensitivity of the eye, two lights may have the same colour though their spectral composition is different. Two objects may look the same colour though the light coming from them is spectrally different, and their spectral reflectance profiles are different. This in itself is no reason to say that colours are unexplanatory: so far it seems a standard case of variable realizability. But many of the effects that we commonly ascribe to the colours turn out too to be determined not by the colours but rather by their realizations. We may say that the tomato looked brown because it was in green light. But it turns out that the *colour* of the object and the *colour* of the light are not sufficient to determine the object's appearance: it is the *spectral reflectance* of the object and the *spectral composition* of the light that determine the character of light reflected from the object, and hence its appearance. As is well known, a shirt and a pair of trousers may match in the midday sun, but differ in fluorescent lighting. Clearly, therefore, the appearance of the objects in the fluorescent light cannot be determined by the *colour* of the light and the *colour* of the objects.[10] The threat is not that there is lower-level explanation which goes deeper than the higher-level account (that in itself would not invalidate the account), but rather that the lower-level explanations show us that the purported higher-level account rests on claims that are just not true. It is simply *not true*, the challenge runs, that the reason the tomato looked that shade is that it was in green light of just that colour: for that shade of green illumination is neither necessary in the circumstances nor sufficient for the thing with that shade of red to look that shade of brown. A proper explanation will have to refer to the lower-level spectral characteristics of the object and the light. This threat, that the variable realizability of colours will invalidate purported colour explanations, I shall call 'the challenge of metamerism'.

If the threat seems to be realized in the case just described, that does not mean that it is in all colour explanations. Maybe some colour explanations can defeat the challenge of metamerism, and some cannot. This will be so if some but not all colour explanation is 'autonomous' in Putnam's sense: 'the same explanation will go in any world (whatever the microstructure) in which those *higher level* . . . features are present'.[11] Some explanations do seem to meet this condition. The mug looks blue to John because it is blue and John is looking at it in decent lighting, and he has good colour vision. The claim cannot be undermined by considering objects whose blueness is realized in a different spectral reflectance profile: whatever its spectral profile, as long as the mug is blue, then it will look blue to John in the circumstances described. It is the blueness that nomologically correlates with the effect, not just some

---

[10] Cf. R. M. Evans, *An Introduction to Color* (first pub. 1948; New York: Wiley, 1965), 59: 'The whole key to the solution of any *color* problem lies in a knowledge of what has happened to the relative *energy* distribution of the light . . . Two light sources having completely different energy distributions may look exactly alike to an observer and yet may produce entirely different colors if the light from them falls on the same object. It is apparent that no description of these lights in terms of *colors* can ever explain the situation, but knowledge of the energy distributions may make it entirely obvious' (my emphasis in the first sentence).

[11] 'Philosophy and our Mental Life', quoted above.

lower-lying property that happens to be coinstantiated with the blueness. Other candidates for autonomy status come to mind: the object is opaque because it is white;[12] the paint is this particular green because it was mixed from paints of this blue and this yellow, in these particular proportions; the yellow book looks brown because it is in violet light. But are all these explanations in fact autonomous? Are they in fact immune to the challenge of metamerism? To see which are and which aren't, it will help to review some of the attempts of colour theorists to come up with serious laws.

I shall put aside the theory of the aesthetic qualities of colours in various combinations. Working often to develop a discipline parallel to those of harmony and counterpoint in music, Alberti, Goethe, Munsell, and Itten, to name only some of the more prominent, have tried to set out principles of the harmony of colours.[13] Some of the attempts have bordered on the fanatical: Munsell, trained as a painter, conceived his system of colour notation, with its numerical measures of hue, chroma, and value, as a prerequisite for the proper state-

---

[12] Cf. J. Westphal, *Colour* (Oxford: Blackwell, 1987), 37–8.

[13] Alberti, for example writes: 'Grace will be found, when one colour is greatly different from the others near it . . . This contrast will be beautiful where the colours are clear and bright. There is a certain friendship of colours so that one joined with another gives dignity and grace. Rose near green and sky blue gives both honour and life. White not only near ash and crocus yellow but placed near almost any other gives gladness. Dark colours stand among light with dignity and the light colours turn about among the darks. Thus, as I have said, the painter will dispose his colours' (Leon Battista Alberti, *Della Pittura*, book II, near end; in J. R. Spencer's translation, *On Painting*, rev. edn. (New Haven, Conn. and London: Yale University Press, 1966), 84–5). (John Spencer's reference in his notes to 'the colour chords' of 'the Albertian colour system' (p. 130 n. 83, cf. p. 105 n. 23), however, finds more systematicity in Alberti's comments than I can find there.) Goethe's *Farbenlehre*, pt. 6, esp. §§803 ff., sets out principles of colour harmony, and traces them to the eye's 'tendency to universality' (§805). The same tendency as he uses to explain contrast effects (when the eye 'spontaneously and of necessity . . . produce[s]' the complementary colour) is responsible also, he thinks, for our finding combinations of complementary colours harmonious (§§805–7, cf. §61). Munsell carefully distinguishes the aesthetic characteristics of three typical paths one may take from a given colour: the 'vertical' path (taking lighter and darker values of the same hue), the 'lateral' path (changing the hue without changing either value or chroma) and the 'inward' path (towards the centre of the colour solid and beyond to the opposite hue). Describing their uses, he adds that the third is 'full of pitfalls for the inexpert' (A. H. Munsell, *A Color Notation*, 8th edn. (The Munsell Color Company, 1905, 1936), 38).

ment of the principles of colour harmony. 'COLOR ANARCHY IS REPLACED BY SYSTEMATIC COLOR DESCRIPTION,' he exclaimed in capital letters.[14] The status of such principles of harmony is a matter of such complexity that I shall set it aside for another time.[15]

In the field of straight experimental science, there is a fine body of explanation of colour phenomena. The work straddles areas which are otherwise often separated, like optics, quantum electrodynamics, chemistry, psychology, and psychophysics. The best-known work—like that of Newton in optics, and of Helmholtz and Maxwell in psychophysics—is on the explanation of colour phenomena in terms of physics. The kinds of explanation and law that are our present concern, on the other hand, are those that explain colour phenomena in terms of other colour phenomena. From a wide possible range, I shall consider five types of law, as developed in the work of the nineteenth-century colour theorists Grassmann, Chevreul, and Rood.

One might take Newton's 'centre of gravity' law of additive colour mixing to be the first straight scientific law where

---

[14] Munsell, *A Color Notation*, 24.

[15] One point, however, may be worth raising. There is a tendency to think that aesthetic responses to colour are direct and unaffected by reasoning, training, and cultural influence. But this (like the 'tingle-immersion' view of aesthetic response in general) will not survive scrutiny. Aesthetic judgement, with respect to colour as anything else, is always open to revision, at least in its details, as a result of aesthetic experience of other situations, reflection, and *thought*. None the less, it is remarkable that there is such a discipline as harmony and counterpoint at all—and it seems therefore that, at least with respect to what might be called a strictly delimited aesthetic language, it is possible to make rough-and-ready aesthetic judgements on the basis of rules: 'this is not (for the language of Haydn and Mozart) discordant', 'the chord progressions of this chorale harmonization are more or less in the style of Bach'. Something similar in the case of colour seems promising: you cannot tell in advance that this particular colour combination will never, in any context, look good. (Maybe the four colours look terrible together on the walls of a room, and awful used in a particular textile design for a dress. But when employed in a particular way on a book jacket, they suddenly look right.) It is a matter of continual artistic discovery that things that people once assumed would never look right or sound right can suddenly begin to do so, employed in a new way—a way which may itself change the artistic or musical language. But we can none the less come up with limited rules of thumb: for example, that any employment of this combination of colours, if seen pretty much with present eyes, will look a bit unpleasant.

colours are among the explanantia.[16] Newton claims that if the colours of the spectrum are arranged in a circle, with white in the centre, then if you know the colours of the component spectral lights out of which a compound light is composed, then you can predict the colour of the mixture. If you consider the points on the colour circle representing the spectral lights in the mixture, and assign to each of them a weight proportional to the intensity of light of that kind, then the centre of gravity of the resultant figure will represent the colour of the mixture of lights, as illustrated in Fig. 15.1. But though Newton talks of predicting the colour of the mixture from 'each Colour in the given Mixture', he is using 'colour', I think, really for refrangibility or, as we would now say, wavelength. He is giving a rule to allow us, from the relative amounts of light at each *wavelength*, to predict the colour of the result. It was only with Grassmann's Third Law 150 years later that it became clear that the explanantia in this kind of colour mixture law could be colours rather than wavelengths.[17] For, as a matter of empirical fact, the results of mixing a green light and a blue light of a particular hue and saturation will be perceptually indistinguishable, whatever the spectral composition of the two lights—however the green and blue are 'realized'. In the laws on the results of mixing coloured lights, the 'challenge of metamerism' can be met: in so far as Grassmann's Third Law is true (and that is within wide limits) variation in the spectral composition of the lights which does not change their colour will not change the colour of the mixture. Explanation of the

---

[16] Isaac Newton, *Opticks* (first pub. 1704, 4th edn. 1730; New York: Dover, 1979), book I, pt. 2, prop. vi, prob. ii (pp. 154–8).

[17] 'Two colours, both of which have the same hue and the same proportion of intermixed white, also give identical mixed colours, no matter of what homogeneous colours they may be composed.' (H. G. Grassmann, 'Theory of Compound Colours', *Philosophical Magazine*, 4 (1854); repr. in D. L. MacAdam (ed.), *Sources of Color Science* (Cambridge, Mass.: MIT Press, 1970), 60.) Some qualifications should be noted. Maxwell's triangle and the subsequent empirical research leading to the 1931 CIE x,y chromaticity diagram showed that in place of Newton's circle, the locus of spectral points in this kind of mixing diagram needs rather to be in the shape of a plectrum or tongue. Secondly, each point on a modern chromaticity diagram represents a certain hue and saturation, but brightness is not taken into account, as it needs to be in a full explanation of additive mixing. (For further details, see e.g. R. W. G. Hunt, *Measuring Colour* (Chichester: Ellis Horwood, 1987), 58–60.)

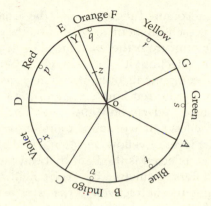

FIG. 15.1. *Newton's colour wheel: to predict the colour of mixtures of light*

The circumference DEFGABCD represents 'the whole Series of Colours from one end of the Sun's colour'd Image to the other'. Let p, q, r, s, t, v, x *be the 'Centers of Gravity of the Arches' DE, EF, FG, GA, AB, BC, and CD respectively; 'and about those Centers of Gravity let Circles proportional to the Number of Rays of each Colour in the given Mixture be describ'd'. 'Find the common Center of Gravity of all those Circles,* p, q, r, s, t, v, x. *Let that Center be Z; and from the Center of the Circle ADF, through Z to the Circumference, drawing the Right Line OY, the Place of the Point Y in the Circumference shall shew the Colour arising from the Composition of all the Colours in the given Mixture.' The ratio of OZ to the radius of the circle gives the relative saturation of the colour. (From Newton,* Opticks, *154–5.)*

colour of the mixture in terms of the *colour* of the lights combined is, in Putnam's terms, autonomous.

In the mid-nineteenth century, Chevreul, a chemist working at the Gobelins tapestry factory, tried to formulate other scientific laws of colour. Out of the many which he offered in his *Principles of Harmony and Contrast of Colours*,[18] I shall consider three important types: laws on the mixing of coloured pigments; laws for what appearance is produced when light of one colour falls on objects of a second colour; and laws of colour contrast, either simultaneous or successive. Two of these turn out, I think, not to meet the initial challenge of metamerism.

[18] M.-E. Chevreul, *The Principles of Harmony and Contrast of Colours, and their Applications to the Arts*, 2nd edn. (1st French edn. 1838; trans. Charles Martel (London: Longmans, 1855)).

The mixture of coloured pigments is today called subtractive mixing, because each pigment may be thought of as subtracting a certain amount from the incident light in the process of (only partially) reflecting it. Crudely considering only red, green, and blue components of light, we may say that a yellow object reflects only the red and the green (and filters out the blue), a blue object reflects only the green and the blue (and filters out the yellow). If we paint, therefore, a layer of blue paint on top of a layer of yellow on some white paper, then the only light that is reflected is the light that can pass so to speak through both filters, namely, the green light. The effect of mixing two pigments subtractively is the same as that of superimposing two filters, so we seem to have an explanation here of why, when we mix yellow and blue paint, we get green.[19]

The trouble is, however, that this kind of explanation is not well equipped to resist the challenge of metamerism. It turns out that the colour of a pigment mixture is not determined solely by the *colours* and quantities of the components, but also by their spectral reflectance characteristics. It was a simplification to think of the filtering action of a blue pigment as simply removing the yellow. Two pigments of different spectral characteristics may look the same colour in a certain form of daylight. But now imagine we also have a coloured celluloid filter, and look at the metameric samples through it. It may well happen that, through the filter, the samples now look different from each other.[20] And the situation is essentially the same if, instead of having a celluloid filter in front of the eyes, we paint a layer of colour on top of the sample, as in subtrac-

---

[19] Some forms of colour mixing are neither precisely subtractive nor precisely additive. In colour printing, if dots of different colours are printed *on top of* one another, the mixing can be considered subtractive; if dots too small to be individually seen are printed *next to* one another, then the mixing can be considered additive.

[20] Mathematically, to get the character of light reaching the eye we would (at each wavelength λ) multiply the power of the illuminant at λ by the reflectance of the sample at λ and then by the transmittance of the filter at λ. Now (as far as the character of light reaching the eye is concerned) it does not make any difference whether the filter comes between the illuminant and the object, or between the object and the eye. (The two cases may be perceptually different, if the context results in different adaptation.) Since we already know that two metameric samples may become distinguishable in colour when the illumination is varied, it is not surprising then that the same happens when the samples are seen through a filter.

tive mixing of pigments. The result is, then, that we cannot pretend that it is colour alone that determines the outcome of subtractive mixing: there may be differences between the result of mixing one yellow paint with blue and the result of mixing another yellow paint with it, even if the two paints look the same colour in daylight. In this area, it seems, rough-and-ready generalizations are all we can hope for.[21]

Chevreul extensively studied the effects of seeing an object of one colour in light of another colour. Pages of his *Principles of Harmony and Contrast* are filled with experimental generalizations like these:

Yellow rays falling upon a Black stuff, make it appear of a Yellow-Olive.
Yellow rays falling upon a White stuff, make it appear of a light Yellow. . . .
Yellow rays falling upon a Blue stuff, make it appear Yellow-Green, if it is light, and of a Green-Slate if it is deep.

(Chevreul, *Principles*, 92)

Violet rays falling upon a Yellow stuff, make it appear Brown with an excessively pale tint of Red.

(Ibid. 94)

Unfortunately, these laboriously-collected generalizations are simply not reliable. Recognizing some of their shortcomings, theorists later in the nineteenth century (like Ogden Rood) tried to amend them. But there is a problem of principle: the existence of metamers makes it impossible to predict accurately the apparent colour of an object of one colour seen in light of another. There will be metameric yellow objects, for example, that in daylight are indistinguishable in colour, but in the same violet light no longer match each other. It therefore cannot be simply the *colour* of the object and the *colour* of the light

[21] F. W. Billmeyer and M. Saltzman, *Principles of Color Technology*, 2nd edn. (New York: Wiley, 1981), 130, gives a remarkable CIE diagram (after Johnston, 1973) showing the results of mixing various paints with increasing amounts of titanium dioxide white. The colour changes often show up as lines that are anything but straight, and in some cases the result of adding a small quantity of white is to move the colour not in the direction of white but at 90° to it. In certain circumstances, there will also be chemical reactions in colorant mixing, and then clearly no mixing rule that attended only to the colours of the colorants and not to their chemistry could hope to account for the results.

that determine the appearance. I shall return to the question whether this conclusively scotches claims of lawlike autonomous status for all colour generalizations of this sort, but the initial challenge of metamerism has not been met.

The third category of colour law in Chevreul which I shall consider is laws of colour contrast. The appearance of a region of colour is affected both by the colours of objects that were in the field of view a short time before, and by the colours of other objects which are in the field of view at the same time. After-images are dramatic examples of the first phenomenon. Leonardo noted cases of the second: 'white garments make the flesh tints dark, and yellow garments make them seem coloured, while red garments show them pale.'[22] The phenomena were studied widely in the eighteenth century,[23] but it was Goethe and Chevreul who made them famous. Goethe explained that in both cases, it is 'the colours *diametrically opposed* to each other which reciprocally evoke each other in the eye' (*Farbenlehre*, §50, my emphasis). Each colour evokes its complementary—hence the names *successive contrast* and *simultaneous contrast*.[24] An object seen as red will leave a green after-image, one seen as turquoise will leave a yellow one.[25]

---

[22] *The Notebooks of Leonardo da Vinci*, ed. I. A. Richter (Oxford: Oxford University Press, 1952), 136.

[23] Chevreul (*Principles*, pt. 1, sect. 2, ch. 2) acknowledges that Buffon (1743) noticed examples of both types, and also mentions Scherffer (1754), Œrpinus (1785), Darwin (1785), and Count Rumford (1802).

[24] Chevreul gives the impression that he invented the terms. (In *Principles*, p. 374, he talks of earlier writers who lacked 'the fundamental distinction which I had made between two sorts of contrast under the names of *simultaneous contrast* and *successive contrast* of colours'.) But Goethe had grasped the distinction quite clearly (e.g. in the *Farbenlehre*, §56). I have not seen any reference in Chevreul to Goethe's work, and I do not know what the relation between them was. But there is a fundamental agreement between them, notably on the universality of these contrast effects (Chevreul: '*every* colour seen simultaneously with another, appears with the modification of an accidental colour' (*Principles*, p. 376, my emphasis); Goethe, *Farbenlehre*, §51) and in the view that an understanding of contrast is the foundation for understanding the laws of colour harmony (Chevreul, *Principles*, 376–7; Goethe, *Farbenlehre*, §§60–1, §§805–7). This is why both of them attack earlier writers' descriptions of contrast effects as 'accidental colours' or 'adventitious colours' (Goethe, *Farbenlehre*, §§1–2, Chevreul, *Principles*, p. 376), whereas in fact 'they are the foundation of the whole doctrine' (Goethe, *Farbenlehre*, §1).

[25] One description of the phenomenon in the *Farbenlehre* is almost as remarkable as the event it describes: 'I had entered an inn towards evening, and, as a well-favoured girl, with a brilliantly fair complexion, black hair, and a

'A grey building seen through green pallisades appears . . . reddish.' (Goethe, *Farbenlehre*, §57.)

The laws here are precisely ones of colour: the colour of the after-image is the complementary of the colour of the original appearance, and is not affected by the spectral realization of that colour.[26] The robustness of these laws is easy to understand given a knowledge of the causal processes involved; given that the cones in the retina respond in indistinguishable ways to two metameric red objects, and that our after-images and simultaneous contrast effects causally depend on our retinal responses, we would expect metameric red objects to be indistinguishable in their contrast effects. The challenge of metamerism in this case is therefore fully met.

Now for the final type of law. Ogden Rood worked on all forms of colour science at Columbia in the 1870s, and his *Modern Chromatics*[27] is still well worth reading. He offers one type of causal colour generalization that we have not considered before: describing how hue changes with saturation. One of several tables details 'the effects of mixing white with coloured light':

Name of colour	Effect of adding white
Vermilion	More purplish
Orange	More red
Chrome-yellow	More orange-yellow
Pure yellow	More orange-yellow
Greenish-yellow	Paler (unchanged)
Green	More blue-green
Emerald-green	More blue-green

scarlet bodice, came into the room, I looked attentively at her as she stood before me at some distance in half shadow. As she presently afterwards turned away, I saw on the white wall, which was now before me, a black face surrounded with a bright light, while the dress of the perfectly distinct figure appeared of a beautiful sea-green' (Goethe, *Farbenlehre*, §52, p. 22).

[26] It is worth noting however, as Goethe and Chevreul did not, that after-image complementaries are not always the same as mixture complementaries: the colour of the after-image produced by a coloured light may not be the same as the colour of a second light that when mixed with the first yields white. Perhaps unfortunately for Goethe, the eye's 'tendency to universality' (*Farbenlehre*, §805) is not entirely precise. See M. H. Wilson and R. W. Brocklebank, 'Complementary Hues of After-Images', *Journal of the Optical Society of America*, 45 (1955), 293–9.

[27] (London: C. Kegan Paul, 1879.)

Cyan-blue	More bluish
Cobalt-blue	A little more violet
Ultramarine (artificial)	More violet
Violet	Unchanged
Purple	Less red, more violet

(p. 197)

The general formula covering these effects is this: 'when we mix white with coloured light, the effect produced is the same as though we at the same time mixed with our white light a small quantity of violet light.' (p. 197.) And this generalization again seems able to meet the challenge of metamerism. The process of mixing white with a coloured light is one of additive mixing, which we have seen already is unaffected by change of spectral composition. So if one orange of one spectral type turns redder on the addition of white, then a metameric orange of another spectral type will do so too.

Of the five types of law considered, three immediately meet the challenge of metamerism: the laws of additive mixing, of colour contrast, and of change of hue as a colour is desaturated. Only the first is readily expressed in mathematical terms (when developed for example in connection with a CIE x,y diagram). But they are all of them robust in the sense that substitution of metamers will not invalidate them. We can accept without worry, therefore, the autonomy in Putnam's sense of a wide variety of explanations that invoke colour.

Two of the types of law considered fail the test for robustness. Laws of subtractive mixing and of the appearance of objects seen in light of another colour are at risk of being invalidated by substitution of metamers. But the challenge may be being exaggerated. The existence of metamers certainly means that we will not be able to find absolutely precise and indefinitely refinable generalizations on these issues that are also true. But that does not mean that there cannot in this area be broad generalizations which are quite literally *true* and *lawlike* in the sense that they are supported by their instances and support counterfactuals. (There is a difference between a narrow claim that is only partly true, and a broad claim that is precisely true.) Though the appearance of a yellow object in violet light may not be determined exactly by the colours of the

object and the light, it may still be determined roughly by
them, for example, to lie somewhere in the brown region.
Similarly, even if we cannot predict the exact appearance of a
mix of yellow and blue paint, we may none the less be able to
predict that it will be some form of green. And if this is so,
then explanations that use precisely these deliberately broad
terms will still be autonomous in Putnam's sense.[28]

How far exactly this objection is valid is an empirical matter.
If we employ sufficiently broad colour classifications, then it
will be fairly easy to find true generalizations about them. If we
employ colour classifications that are too narrow, then it will

[28] Davidson makes a telling admission when discussing psychophysical
generalizations. He admits that, notwithstanding his denial of psychophysical
laws, it would be embarrassing to deny that there are any 'inductively established correlations between physical and psychological events' ('The Material
Mind', in his *Essays on Actions and Events*, 250). 'The burned child avoids the
flame' is his example; one even less susceptible of counter-example might be:
'A conscious person with no otherwise detectable abnormality, holding a hand
in a flame, will begin to feel pain'. Davidson's comment is that such generalizations 'are lawlike in that instances make it reasonable to expect other instances
to follow suit without being lawlike *in the sense of being indefinitely refinable*'
('Mental Events', 224, my emphasis). If what Davidson says here is right, then
the broad generalizations about colour contemplated at this point in the main
text will be 'lawlike' only in the weaker of two senses of the term. But
Davidson's stronger sense of 'lawlike' may itself be anomalous. Why should
being lawlike in any sense be a matter of being 'indefinitely refinable' or
'sharpen[able] without limit'? Davidson's original explanation of the notion
was that 'Lawlike statements are general statements that support counterfactual and subjunctive claims, and are supported by their instances' ('Mental
Events', 217). But it is not clear that this notion of law has any internal
connection with that of indefinite refinability. If this is right, then Davidson's
denial of psychophysical laws is rather weaker than at first appears (strictly
all it denies is *indefinitely refinable* psychophysical laws, *sharpenable without
limit*); and his argument for the identity theory would require not just the
Nomological Character of Causality as naturally interpreted, but the stronger
principle that 'events related as cause and effect fall under strict deterministic
laws, *indefinitely refinable and sharpenable without limit*' ('Mental Events', 208,
amended by the addition of the words in italics). A further difficulty with
Davidson's view comes to the surface here: if on his view there are two senses
of 'lawlike', and it is in only one of these that he wishes to deny the existence
of lawlike psychophysical connections, then it is odd that the argument for that
denial actually seems to make no play with the difference between those two
senses. To rephrase the point: if the criterial and evidential differences between
the nature of mental and physical discourse do not rule out the existence of
lawlike psychophysical connections in the weaker sense, it is not clear that
they can rule out the existence of lawlike psychophysical connections in the
stronger sense—given that Davidson's argument for the latter claim shows no
obvious sensitivity to the difference between these two senses.

be easy to find metameric counter-examples. How broad the classifications must be in order to be 'sufficiently broad' is an empirical question to which I do not know the answer. But the apparent availability of broad generalizations suggests that the challenge of metamerism is not an objection in principle to the idea of lawlike colour generalizations, even in those cases where colour does not determine *all* the colour properties at issue in the outcome. Even if the generalizations are broad and intrinsically incapable of indefinite refinement, they may still be lawlike, unobvious, and non-trivial.

In this section we have considered the prospects of good scientific laws about colours. The challenge to be met was not that lower-level explanation would be available as well (for that is innocuous), but that the proposed colour laws would actually be invalidated by metamerism: colour effects could only be explained in terms of information at the level of wavelengths, rather than colours. We considered five types of law as examples. Three of them conclusively meet the challenge: laws of additive mixture, of colour contrast, and of change of hue with saturation. Two of them on the other hand do not: laws of subtractive mixture, and of how objects of one colour appear in light of another. But even in these cases, there are still prospects at least of broad generalizations that are lawlike, and of correspondingly broad causal explanations. The case for the autonomy of at least some scientific colour explanations seems complete.

3. COLOUR INTERPRETATION

We raised earlier the possibility that colours might have their home in a holistic interpretative scheme like that of rational explanation. The scheme might even be an extension of the scheme of rational explanation. This would certainly seem right if the traditional dispositional thesis were correct. If colours were dispositions to produce experiences in us, and if experiences were ascribed to people in the course of interpreting them as (more or less) rational creatures, then colours would figure in an extension of rational explanation. One striking consequence would be that a second form of *autonomy*, mentioned in Section 1, would then seem to attach to ascriptions of colour. On one familiar picture, the ascription of psychological states is autonomous in the sense that it is responsible only to assessment by standards internal to that form of explanation. In one form of this view, set out by Davidson and developed by McDowell, psychological explanation is explanation of a special sort, namely 'rational explanation', which has different aims from those of broadly 'physical' explanation.[29] The ascription of psychological states has 'its proper source of evidence' only 'in terms of the vocabulary of the propositional attitudes'.[30] If colours were simply dispositions to produce psychological occurrences, then we might expect the former to inherit the same sort of autonomy as attaches to the latter—though the line of inheritance might not be direct. Though of course colours would not themselves be psychological states, they would in a sense be 'offshoots of the psychological'.

This is a powerful picture, but things are not that simple. Though the main figures are already recognizable, much will need to be repainted. The traditional dispositional thesis fails to make sense of some of our colour attributions, and this shows, so I shall argue, that we have a deeper conception of the nature of colours—namely, as (in the case of surfaces) ways in which objects change the light. This might threaten to remove any essential connection of colour with the psychological, but that depends on how exactly we characterize the 'ways' in which objects change the light. The ascription of colours does indeed prove to be part of the implementation of a scheme of explanation of everyday experience. That, by itself, might be said equally of other characteristics of external objects, like their size and shape, and does not guarantee that the qualities ascribed are themselves interestingly 'psycho-

---

[29] 'To recognize the ideal status of the constitutive concept [of rationality] is to appreciate that the concepts of the propositional attitudes have their proper home in explanations *of a special sort*: explanations in which things are made intelligible by being revealed to be, or to approximate to being, as they rationally ought to be.' By contrast, what might roughly be called 'physical' explanation is characterized as 'a style of explanation in which one makes things intelligible by representing their coming into being as a particular instance of how things generally tend to happen' (McDowell, 'Functionalism and Anomalous Monism', 389, my emphasis).

[30] Davidson, 'Mental Events', 222, 216.

logical'. None the less, it will turn out to be not just a prejudice that there is something both 'relative' and 'subjective' about colours which puts them in a different position: they really are connected with the psychological in a way that size and shape are not. The view of psychological ascription as the employment of a scheme of *rational* interpretation will turn out to need qualification; but the claim to autonomy in the special sense of this section will survive.

3.1. *Away from the Dispositional Thesis*

I shall set aside criticisms of the dispositional thesis on grounds of circularity or triviality, since these are not, I think, conclusive against versions that make no pretence at a reduction of colour. There is a more telling criticism that touches even the truth of the coextensiveness claim that something is red, yellow, or whatever iff it would look red, yellow, or whatever to normal observers under normal circumstances.[31] The problem is this. There are, we may imagine, killer yellow objects that kill anyone who looks at them.[32] Far from having a disposition to produce experiences of yellow in normal observers, they have a disposition to end all experience in them whatever. A defender of the dispositional thesis might insist: 'Such an object would still look yellow *if only it could be seen* by normal observers under normal circumstances.' But this does not need to be true: there is a difference between the nearby possible worlds in which an object is visible, and the nearby possible worlds in which it is visible and also has its actual present colour. Imagine a situation where there are a lot of killer yellow objects around, but we have learnt to deal with them: they tend to be small, they emit a distinctive bleeping sound, and (taking care not to look at them) we can easily cover them with thick black paint which the death-rays cannot penetrate.

---

[31] There are good reasons for adding 'actually' and perhaps also 'now' operators to this. But I shall not go into these here, and they are independent of my present concerns.

[32] I have heard the killer yellow example ascribed to Saul Kripke and Michael Smith. I do not know how either of them has used the example, however, and I can only apologize if I have distorted it or omitted the best bits.

In such a situation the sentence 'If only the object could be seen . . . then it would look yellow' will be false, simply because, if only the object could be seen, it would be covered in black paint.

The natural response is to plug the gap: instead of saying 'If only it could be seen . . .', the dispositionalist will say 'If only it could be seen *without changing its colour* . . .'. This is progress, but not enough. There will be situations where an object can be seen and its colour is unchanged, but the colour itself cannot be seen. It may be a very short and faint flash of light; it may put our cones out of order but not the rods; it may be visible but only through a dark filter (and otherwise the death-rays get us). It looks as though we have to ensure not only that the object is visible and its colour unchanged, but that *the colour itself is visible*. We seem to have arrived at this:

(D1) x is yellow iff if only x's colour could be seen by a normal observer y, then x would look yellow to y.

This is true but trivial. It is tantamount to:

(D2) x is yellow iff if only a normal observer y could see what colour x is, then y would see x to be yellow.

And the same of course could be said of other properties too:

(D3) x is a dog iff if only a normal observer y could see what kind of animal x is, then y would see x to be a dog.

and even:

(D4) x is a piece of platinum iff if only a normal observer y could see what kind of substance x is, then y would see x to be a piece of platinum.

Of course there is a difference between these claims. The 'if only' clauses become progressively harder for humans to satisfy: we can often tell at sight whether something is yellow, perhaps less often whether it is a dog, and very seldom whether it is platinum. But by the time the dispositional thesis has been reduced to (D1), the interest lies not in what it says, but in any surrounding commentary that can be given to explain what part it plays in our thought about colours, and what else plays a part in addition.

A deeper problem should also be evident. The puzzle cases are ones in which a normal observer *cannot* in fact see the colour (or chemical composition) of the object, but (struggling to maintain a version of the dispositional thesis) we insist on talking about how he *would* see the object if only he *could* see its colour (or chemical composition). But obviously if we take a view on this issue in any particular case, this can only be because we have already—quite independently of these dispositional theses—taken a view on what is necessary for an object to count as yellow or whatever. (In the parallel case, if we say 'if only he were able to see what substance it is, he would see it as platinum', then this can only be because we know already, for reasons other than its appearance, that the sample really is platinum.) If, therefore, we make sense of these cases of killer yellow, it can only be because we have— independently of the dispositional thesis (D1)—a view on what it takes for something to be yellow. We must have, therefore, a conception of the nature of colours, just as we have a conception of the nature of platinum and of other chemical substances.[33]

What is this conception? What is the common factor between a visibly yellow object and one that is yellow but not visibly so? We cannot say simply: the primary qualities of the objects and their parts. Something that had exactly the same primary qualities (of all constituent parts) as a killer yellow object would kill people just as surely as the killer yellow object does. (Interestingly, even an ordinary yellow object in the dark cannot be said to have exactly the same primary qualities as a similar object in the light: a yellow book cover, for example, will in the light be absorbing photons and emitting photons, which it will not be doing in pitch darkness. If in the dark it were literally in the same primary quality state as it is normally in when illuminated, then it would be glowing!) If it has to be some physical property, then the common factor to all yellow

---

[33] I bracket here questions of what Putnam has called the 'division of linguistic labor'. It may be that individual users do not need such a conception, if others in the community, to whom they are prepared to defer, have one. So I talk here of what 'we' need. Our conception may itself be 'obscure and relative'—like a definite description of which we only later identify the satisfier.

objects will at best be some subset of primary qualities, or some relatively complex high-level primary quality. This of course is the physicalist proposal of Armstrong,[34] much criticized in the recent writings of Hardin and Westphal. It turns out that it is much harder to find a physical property common and peculiar to yellow things than one might imagine. There plainly is no one structural property responsible for the yellowness of all yellow objects. Neither is there any simple physical characteristic common to the light they give off, even when normally illuminated. (They will not, for example, merely give off light from the 'yellow' part of the spectrum: something that only reflected light of wavelengths from 565 to 575 nanometres would look so dark it would be black.) But on the other hand the suggestion that there might well be no physical property at all common and peculiar to yellow things is an odd one: for more than a century, psychophysics has investigated the physical characteristics of things that look yellow without obviously wasting its time. The idea of building a machine to tell the colour of any object from a 'purely physical' specification of it is hardly in the same class as the idea of building one to identify sentimental poems or baroque façades.

There are both phenomenal and non-phenomenal elements in our conception of colours; the difficulty is to see their interconnection. At one extreme there is the temptation to recognize only the phenomenal element: to say for example, as the dispositional thesis does, that being yellow is solely a matter of how a thing looks to people. But we know from killer yellow that this is not true. At the other extreme there is the temptation to recognize only the non-phenomenal element: to say for example that being yellow is solely a physical property.[35] But apart from the difficulty of saying how ordinary observers could (on this conception) have any confidence in their own ability to tell the colour of something at sight (why should unaided perception be a reliable guide to a 'physical property' of yellowness any more than it is to alkalinity, or to being

---

[34] See D. M. Armstrong, *A Materialist Theory of the Mind* (London: Routledge & Kegan Paul, 1968), ch. 12.

[35] Abstracting from a number of contentious issues, I shall offer as a first elucidation of the notion of a physical property: 'a property that can be introduced in the language of physics'.

made of platinum?), there is the difficulty of identifying the
'physical property' in question, and in offering an account of
why we should wish to dignify with the title 'yellow' the items
that have that physical property. A promising compromise is to
make colour a non-phenomenal property identified phenomenally: 'yellowness is picked out and rigidly designated as that
external physical property of the object which we sense by
means of the *visual impression of yellowness*.'[36] This instantly
accommodates killer yellow: killer yellow objects have the same
underlying non-phenomenal property as those which produce
impressions of yellow, though they do not themselves produce
that impression because of the death-rays they give off as well.

But we should not let our minds be narrowed by the thought
that the only range of properties available for our fundamental
conception of colour is the range of physical properties. There
are, at least at first sight, many properties that are not physical
properties: mental, economic, functional, aesthetic, and moral
properties, to cite only a few of the more striking (and perhaps
overlapping) categories. Of course philosophers will take different attitudes to the apparent diversity: some will accept it
whole-heartedly; others will deny it outright, insisting that
there are no genuine classifications other than those of physics.
In the middle will be people who accept certain ranges and try
to reduce the others. To assure one's title to any of these views
is not the task of a paragraph or two. The pressure towards
a pluralism of types of property will be great for anyone impressed with Strawson and Grice's observation[37] that where
there is agreement on the use of expressions with respect to an
open class, there must necessarily be some kind of distinction

---

[36] S. Kripke, *Naming and Necessity*, rev. edn. (Oxford: Blackwell, 1980), 128
n. 66. I take it here that Kripke means by 'physical property' a property introduced by the predicates of physics. He also says, however, that yellowness is
'a manifest physical property of an object' (128 n. 66; cf. 140 n. 71), and it
would be possible to take 'manifest physical properties' to be something other
than properties of physics: perhaps physical in a broad sense (part of the
natural world) but also 'manifest' in the sense *fully open to view, fully grasped by
anyone who understands the term*, so that colour would be a phenomenal property
rather than one of physical science. This would make the view closer to the
'simple view' of John Campbell, the non-reductive realisms of Hacker, Stroud,
and Putnam, and the view which I defend myself.

[37] See P. F. Strawson and H. P. Grice, 'In Defence of a Dogma', *Philosophical
Review*, 65 (1956), 141–58.

present—unless one also believes that every distinction made with any predicate can be identified with a physical distinction, quite unrestrictedly[38] and without massaging the extensions of the terms. The arguments that this kind of physicalist property-identity is unlikely to be available are known well enough from the works of Davidson and Fodor not to need repeating here. Accepting a pluralism of properties, the principal challenge is then, I think, to show how this pluralism is compatible with a belief in the fundamentality of physics. Again, I think the essential moves have been made by Davidson and Fodor, showing that the irreducibility of, for example, mental to physical classifications is no obstacle to a broader physicalism that treats the former as supervenient upon the latter.

None of these views is uncontroversial. But given the prima facie availability of a view of mental properties of this general type, the possibility is open of regarding colours in a similar way: as properties that figure in an autonomous explanatory space (or subspace), irreducible to physical science, but supervenient upon it. Colours would figure in a distinctive form of colour explanation. The concerns of colour attribution would be different from those that govern the attribution of other ranges of property, though there would no doubt be points of contact.

3.2. Colour Interpretation

To say this is not to be relieved of the burden of doing something more to characterize the nature of the properties that

---

[38] Note that even those who (like Lewis) advocate restricted type-identity must (if Grice and Strawson are right) allow that there is some property common, say, to Martians in pain and humans in pain, even if it is not what these theorists call 'pain'. This may be the property of being in a physical state which plays the role of pain for that kind of organism, and we can call it a second-order physical property if we like. But it should be noted that it is not definable in the language of physics alone, unless the specification of the higher-level *functional role* is itself definable in the language of physics—which there is reason to doubt. Some would take refuge at this point in a metaphysically charged use of the world 'property', designed not to apply to just any classification that people are capable of coherently effecting. But that still leaves the problem of making sense of a plurality of classifications, to replace that of making sense of a plurality of properties.

colours, thus conceived, are, or to characterize the scheme of explanation which equips us thus to conceive them. I shall take the latter question first, and the former in the section that follows.

On the present suggestion, colours are in some ways parallel to mental properties, figuring in their own explanatory discourse. It may help, therefore, to employ some of the same techniques to elucidate colour discourse as have been used elsewhere to characterize mental discourse. In Davidson, and in a different way, in functionalists like Lewis and Shoemaker, one can find the suggestion that psychological discourse is the employment of an explanatory theory governed by certain constitutive principles. To characterize that discourse, we need to articulate some of the constitutive principles, and make clear how the overall explanatory scheme is applied to empirical cases.[39]

In Davidson's procedure of holistically interpreting either aliens or fellows, we make use of a priori principles which, for example, link belief, desire, and action, or (in another famous example) belief, meaning, and holding true. In Lewis and Shoemaker, there is a parallel idea that each psychological state can be characterized by the role it plays in a functional organization implicit in the platitudes and other a priori claims of common-sense psychology. What will be the parallel principles for colour explanation? Some of them will indicate relations between the various colour concepts; others will indicate their relations to the phenomena which they are used to explain.

Perhaps the fullest articulation of such principles is provided in Wittgenstein. In the *Remarks on Colour*, he considered a variety of propositions which seem to characterize a kind of 'logic' of colour. 'Pure yellow is lighter than pure, saturated red, or blue.' (III. 4.) 'A *shine*, a "high-light" cannot be black.'

---

[39] There are of course notable differences in these philosophers' attitudes to the constitutive principles. Lewis and Shoemaker, for example, believe that the significant interrelations between psychological states can be captured in *topic-neutral* causal terms (which yet are sufficient to form an individuating description of each such state), whereas Wittgenstein would not: the constitutive principles might themselves embody a particular 'point of view', the grasp of which was not available to just anyone. The idea of treating colour discourse in parallel to mental discourse can be found in Wittgenstein: 'The colour concepts are to be treated like the concepts of sensations.' (*Remarks on Colour*, III. 72.)

(III. 22.) 'Yellow is more akin to red than to blue.' (III. 50.) '[We don't] speak of a "pure" brown.' (II. 60.) 'Grey is between two extremes (black and white), and can take on the hue of any other colour.' (III. 83.) 'Black seems to make a colour cloudy, but darkness doesn't' (III. 156.) The source of many of the most interesting remarks is the letter from the painter Runge, which Goethe reproduced in his *Farbenlehre*—which in turn Wittgenstein had before him as he wrote some of the *Remarks*.[40] 'If we were to think of a bluish orange, a reddish green or a yellowish violet, we would have the same feeling as in the case of a southwesterly north wind.' 'Both white and black are opaque or solid.' 'White water which is pure is as inconceivable as clear milk.' (Runge's letter, §§2 and 11; cp. Wittgenstein, *Remarks* III. 94.) 'Black makes all colours dirty, and if it also makes them darker, then they equally lose their purity and clarity.' (Runge's letter, §5.) 'The opaque colours lie between white and black; they cannot be either as light as white or as dark as black.' (Runge's letter, §12, my translation.) A particularly important claim in Wittgenstein links the notions of surface colour and film colour: 'Something white behind a coloured transparent medium appears in the colour of the medium, something black appears black.'[41]

Wittgenstein's *Remarks* contain a fascinating discussion of the ways in which our mastery of such principles depends upon our natural capacities and our innate endowment—as also, we might add, does our mastery of parallel principles connecting psychological states. A fuller account of colour classification than my own would have to investigate this issue. But for present purposes, it will be sufficient to draw out other types of parallel between colour explanation and psychological explanation.

The ascription of psychological states to people is part of the holistic explanation of behaviour; similarly, the ascription of

---

[40] It is a great pity that the letter is omitted from Eastlake's translation, and even from some German collected editions of Goethe's works. The letter follows §920 of the *Didaktischer Teil* of Goethe's text (Munich edn., 264–71).

[41] *Remarks on Colour*, III. 173; cf. Goethe, *Farbenlehre*, §582. Wittgenstein may have unconsciously remembered Goethe's comment, or he may have independently rediscovered it. In general Wittgenstein seems to have paid more careful attention to Runge's letter than to the rest of Goethe's text.

colours to things is part of the holistic explanation of our
perception. To describe just one small element in the picture:
rather as beliefs and desires (in a certain context) produce
action, the colours of objects, the lighting conditions, and the
presence of observers together (in a certain context) produce
perceptions of colour. The explanation is holistic: one and the
same perception may have been produced by say, a blue object
in white light, or by a white object in blue light, just as one
piece of behaviour may be caused by alternative combinations
of beliefs and desires; and only the accumulation of evidence
can allow us to choose between such alternatives. Most importantly, the mastery of the holistic scheme depends on mastery
of a range of a priori principles which together constitute a
kind of theory. It is of course a posteriori that any particular
system can be interpreted as having beliefs and desires, but it
is a priori that if a system has beliefs and desires, then they
relate in various particular ways to each other, and to inputs
and outputs. (In the hackneyed example, if someone desires
that p and believes that her ϕing will bring it about that p, then
other things being equal, she will tend to ϕ.) In similar fashion,
though it is a posteriori that any particular region of the universe is coloured, it is a priori that colours relate in various
ways to each other, and to things that they cause and are
caused by. (For example: 'Nothing can be red and green all
over.' 'If there is something blue at place p, and a person is
present with p in front of her, conscious and with a normally functioning perceptual system, then (subject to various
provisos) she will have an impression as of a blue object in
front of her.'[42])

Most interesting is the way the parallel lends support to both
the subjectivity and (in a different sense) the objectivity of
colour. We are used to the idea that the states we ascribe
to people when we employ the psychological scheme are
'subjective' in the sense not just that they are states *of* subjects,
but also that the states are themselves perspective-dependent:
only a theorist who has a particular point of view (embodied in

---

[42] For parallels between the explanation of action and the explanation of
perception (though he is not talking of colour in particular) see C. Peacocke,
Holistic Explanation (Oxford: Clarendon Press, 1979), esp. ch. 1.

his grasp of the a priori theory) will so much as comprehend the states thus ascribed. (Martians might make nothing of our talk of jealousy, through lacking the constitution necessary to grasp the theory, or to feel jealous.)[43] And yet the ascription of such states is perfectly objective in the sense that those ascriptions can perfectly well be really (and not merely 'apparently' or 'for practical purposes') true. (It may be a perfectly objective fact that person *a* is jealous.) In a similar way, the employment of colour terms is subjective in the sense that it embodies a particular point of view, inaccessible to certain perfect rational people. At the same time, the colour ascriptions of people who have that 'point of view' are objective, in the sense of being assessable as genuinely true or not.[44]

Of course there is more than merely a parallel between the psychological scheme and the colour scheme. There are direct connections between them, because of the fact that colours give rise to experiences of colour, and (to put the matter carefully) variations in physiology determine simultaneously variations in the colours of which we are capable of being aware, and variations in the perceptual experiences in which we are aware of them.

How exactly does this picture of colour explanation relate to the issue of autonomy? In the second usage which I have distinguished, the term 'autonomy' is used for the status of a discipline or explanatory scheme which is self-governing, in the sense that it sets its own standards of correctness and is open to critical assessment only from within the discipline or explanatory scheme. In this sense, everyday classification of metals recognizes its own non-autonomy: we recognize that, on whether something is gold, common-sense judgements make claims that can only be fully justified (and may in fact be

---

[43] A further form of subjectivity lies in the fact that, in the case of ordinary psychological descriptions, the scheme employed by the theorist is also a scheme employed by the object of the theory: persons are in a special sense self-interpreting systems. This form of subjectivity clearly does not have a direct parallel in the case of colour.

[44] Of course there are other senses of 'subjectivity' and 'objectivity' of which I am not here speaking. The particular combination of forms of subjectivity and objectivity which I propose receives a fuller defence in McDowell, 'Values and Secondary Qualities', and D. Wiggins, 'A Sensible Subjectivism?', in D. Wiggins, *Needs, Values, Truth* (Oxford: Blackwell, 1987).

overturned) by going outside everyday methods of judging and turning to the metallurgists. Whether an explanatory scheme is autonomous or not is highly sensitive to the delimitation of the explanatory scheme: taken together, everyday classification of metals and metallurgy might count as autonomous, though the first alone did not. The notion is not easy to apply: psychological explanation might be presented as autonomous, in the sense that it sets its own standards; but yet it may turn out that those standards themselves make essential reference to physical and externalist considerations. So autonomy in this sense does not mean 'independence of the physical'. A claim of autonomy in itself carries no anti-scientific bias either: the physical sciences themselves could be described as autonomous. But what autonomy does mean is that if the *internal standards* of a field leave no place for criticism on scientific grounds of judgements in that field, then there is no place *simpliciter* for criticism of such judgements on those grounds. The claim of autonomy in itself is usually a trivial one, a demand to recognize an explanatory scheme for what it is: to recognize the relevance of certain kinds of consideration to judgements made in it, and the intrinsic irrelevance of other kinds of consideration. Whether the claim is news to anyone will depend on what kinds of consideration exactly are mentioned when the claim is developed in detail.

The role of colours as properties used in interpretation suggests that they occur in explanations that are autonomous in this second sense. How exactly? The most important point is that nothing outside the methods of colour discourse can force us to abandon a colour judgement: if on looking at an object in a variety of circumstances and checking with other people, we conclude that it is red, then there is no place provided for correction of this judgement on other grounds. So far, this is a pretty high-grade form of self-government. What we have also provided for, however, is the possibility that on occasion it may be impossible to tell by looking what colour something is (for example, because it would kill you first), and then it will often only be information about the physical (for example, the object's spectral reflectance curve) that can conclusively underwrite a colour attribution. Is this a departure from 'autonomy'? It is a little hard to know how to answer. Not if the internal rules on colour ascription themselves provide for this. It is only possible to apply colours to objects that cannot be seen if you already have a view on what colours *are*. I would suggest that it is now an integral part of colour ascription that anything which has the property that underlies our ordinary perceptions of red will itself be red. It is of the nature of a discovery, though a fairly obvious one, that the property in question, in the case of surfaces, is a way of changing the light (as I shall argue in the next subsection); but which spectral reflectance curves correspond to this way of changing the light will be a piece of *recherché* information. On this view, it is integral to colour explanation that there will be cases where the colour of something can only be determined by means other than simple perception: so colour explanation is autonomous precisely by itself making provision for reference to the areas outside superficial perception. By now this is a fairly modest claim of autonomy; but less turns on the employment of the label than on the understanding of the reasons for which it is employed.

Two further issues are worth a few quick comments. To describe colour explanation and psychological explanation as forms of 'interpretation' should not be taken as suggesting (as it does sometimes in Davidson) an instrumentalist or anti-realist view of the items ascribed in such explanation. Unless the occurrence of a term in a theory used to explain or interpret phenomena automatically forces an anti-realist understanding of that term, then the use of the word 'interpretation' here will not do so. Secondly, I have sometimes used the term 'rational explanation' where 'psychological explanation' would in some respects have been less misleading. I used the former term to allude to a view of the nature of psychological explanation found in Davidson and McDowell, which I wished to use as a model for colour explanation. But the term may have short-comings even in its original context. The domain of psychological explanation seems to be wider than that of rational explanation, if the latter is defined by the 'constitutive ideal of rationality'. We may on occasion explain what people are doing by saying they are playing football, doodling, or dancing. The explanations are perspective-dependent (and may be impenetrable to the Martians), but it is not clear that the concept of *rationality* is central either to the activities or to our recognition of them. One might well say that we can describe people as engaging in such activities only if we treat them *also* as subjects of belief and desire, that is, as subjects of explanation that really is governed by the constitutive ideal of rationality. But even if this is true, it concedes that rationality is only one dimension of assessment of the distinctive lives of sentient beings. Even if the 'constitutive ideal of rationality' is the clearest source of the combination of subjectivity, autonomy, and realism that we find in psychological explanation, it is not to be assumed that it is the only one.

If this section has described some of the nature of colour discourse, it leaves us with the unfinished business of describing the nature of the items that this discourse actually equips us to talk about—that is, the nature of colours themselves. A recent suggestion is that of Jonathan Westphal: the colours of surfaces are ways in which they change the light.[45] The suggestion is immensely valuable, but it needs care to develop it in a satisfactory way.

3.3. *The Colour of a Surface as a Way in which it Changes the Light*

There is a difference between the light reflected from a surface and the light incident on it. At or around any one wavelength the surface will reflect a certain proportion of the light, transmit a certain proportion, and absorb the remainder. And it is a high-level empirical fact about objects in our environment that these proportions, for any one surface, usually stay roughly constant from one time to another, regardless of how much light is falling on the object.[46] It is therefore usually possible to describe how a surface changes the light by giving a 'spectral reflectance curve' for it, showing the proportion of light it reflects at each wavelength (see Fig. 15.2). The spectral reflectance curve for a surface determines its colour, on at least one natural understanding of that term, according to which the

---

[45] A physical colour is defined by Westphal as 'the alteration of a complete spectrum'. A green object, for example, is 'an object which will absorb or darken almost all of any incident red light and reflect or not darken higher proportions of light of the other colours' (*Colour*, 84).

[46] Exceptions include objects that change colour with temperature, those that fade in the light, and things like light-sensitive sunglasses. Fluorescent, iridescent, and glossy surfaces also need special treatment.

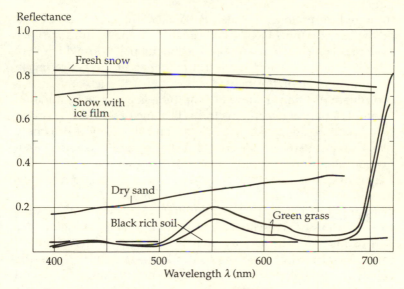

FIG. 15.2. *Spectral reflectance curves of some typical natural objects*

Source: *G. Wyszecki and W. S. Stiles,* Color Science—Concepts and Methods, Quantitative Data and Formulae *(New York: Wiley, 1967, 2nd edn. 1982), p. 63.*

colour of, for example, a British post-box is red—even if it is being mistaken for brown because the light is bad, or for green by a person who is colour-blind or a recent victim of spectrum-inversion, or it is invisible because there is no light on it at all.

Though spectral reflectance curves determine colours, they are not identical with them. There are two problems. First, the space of spectral reflectance curves differs from colour space: spectral reflectances vary in an infinite number of dimensions (corresponding to the proportion of light reflected at each of an infinite number of wavelengths of visible light), whereas on a natural interpretation, colours vary in just three dimensions of hue, saturation, and brightness or lightness. The loss of dimensions corresponds to the fact that there are only three kinds of cone in the retina, and objects with physically different spectral reflectances may be indistinguishable in colour. Secondly, the phrase 'the colour of the object' is indeterminate: the object may be at one and the same time red, vermilion, a highly saturated vermilion, and also R10Y 3080 (to pick a figure out of the air for the object's coordinates in the Natural Colour System). The colour of an object is like its position, which may be at one and the same time: in the house, in the bedroom, in the top drawer of the bedside table, and at such-and-such a coordinate position. Plainly at best there is going to be a many-to-one relation between spectral reflectance and even a colour coordinate position like R10Y 3080; and it will be even more many-to-one between spectral reflectance and a colour classification like *red*.

This does not mean that the colours of surfaces are not ways in which they change the light; it means only that ways of changing the light can be individuated in ways other than those of physics. Westphal's suggestion in his book *Colour* has two distinctive features; my own will emerge in discussion of them. First, Westphal seems to think we can characterize the colour of an object by taking its spectral reflectance curve and 'phenomenalizing' it—that is, reading it so that 'the *x*-axis is illuminant colour, not wavelength' (p. 32). (A surface colour itself might then be characterized by a certain *type* of thus phenomenalized spectral reflectance curve.) Secondly, following a suggestion of Wilson and Brocklebank, Westphal says that the significant property of objects 'is not the colour . . . of the light they reflect, but rather the colour of the light they *don't* reflect' (p. 80). So a green object will be one which 'refuses to reflect a significant proportion of red light' (p. 81); a yellow object will be one that refuses to reflect much blue light (p. 80). When defining the colour of lights, Westphal mentions how lights of different colours will 'darken' objects—that is, I think, make them appear dark (compared with other objects illuminated with the same light). Thus a red light is one that is 'disposed to darken green objects' (p. 85), and a blue one that will darken yellow objects. Putting the two types of definition together, we have a medium-sized if not small circle: objects are green if they refuse to reflect red light, and light is red if it darkens green objects.

Neither of the two distinctive features of Westphal's suggestion will quite do. First, if we simply read the *x*-axis of a spectral reflectance graph as illuminant colour, then it is most unlikely that for any one *x*-value a single *y*-value can be recorded as the proportion of light of that colour which the object is disposed to reflect. For, given the facts of metamerism, it is quite possible for an object to reflect, say, 85 per cent of incident light of 570 nm, but only 75 per cent of a mixture of light of 550 and 600 nm which looks (and is) exactly the same colour. Secondly, specifying kinds of light which an object fails to reflect is not enough to determine its colour, unless we add that those are the *only* kinds of light which it fails to reflect[47]— and that of course would then be equivalent to telling us that it does reflect significant amounts of other kinds. So I cannot see any advantage in talking of the kinds of light that objects *fail* to reflect rather than the kinds that they succeed in reflecting.[48]

But this should not discourage us from working for a conception of colours as ways in which objects change the light, which is phenomenal but not quite in the way that Westphal suggests. Abandoning the two-step procedure that defines surface colour in terms of the (complementary) colour of light which such surfaces refuse to reflect, we might talk instead of the light that the surfaces succeed in reflecting. Holding to the aim of characterizing colour phenomenally, we might say: the red surfaces are those that when illuminated with normal white light tend to reflect light that is, phenomenally, red (whatever the spectral composition of that light)—where for

[47] This is significant, for example, for Westphal's project of explaining why nothing can be red and green all over. The incompatibility is only a straight logical incompatibility, as Westphal wishes, if it is the incompatibility of an object's reflecting a low proportion of green light *but not of red light*, and also reflecting a low proportion of red light *but not of green light*. Without the italicized clauses, it would be open to someone to think an object could be both red and green, by being black.

[48] Westphal's motive, I think, is that the results of subtractive colour mixing are more directly predicted from the former kind of information than from the latter (though, as we have seen in Sect. 2, they will not be exactly predictable from colour information at all without recourse to spectral data). This of course does not show how ordinary people (as opposed perhaps to dyers) *think* of colours; and if Westphal is not making a claim at the level of thought (or Fregean sense), then there seems no reason for preferring his kind of characterization to an equivalent one in terms of colours reflected. As a matter of fact, grass actually reflects what one might well think a significant proportion of red light: approaching 80% at the extreme red end of the spectrum, as Fig. 15.2 illustrates. It none the less looks green partly because of the relatively low sensitivity of the eye at that point, and also because the effect of increasing by just a small amount the reflectance of the complementary colour red will only be to *lighten* or desaturate the green.

accuracy that must be interpreted: the surfaces tend in normal
white light to reflect light that results in normal people when
normally affected by it having a perception as of a red material
object.[49] But by then it seems no less illuminating to say, quite
non-reductively, that red things are ones that change the light
in a certain way, and that way is the way in which red things
change the light. Does this make a pointless detour? No: for
the route brings to light the fact that surface colours are ways
of changing the light. What red surfaces have in common is
what they do to the light: a factor that remains constant, however the character of the incident and reflected light vary
individually. It is like the elasticity of a spring, a constant factor
characterizing the way the length varies with the force to
which the spring is subjected.[50]

Are there other ways to characterize this way of changing
the light? We can say a lot within the everyday language of
colour, employing either a priori or a posteriori connections:
red things look darker than yellow ones; red is a deep colour;
the most saturated reds seem more saturated than the most
saturated yellows; red shades into orange in one direction and
into purple in the other; a lightened red becomes a pink; red is
a 'unique' hue: there are reds that seem to contain no hint of
any other colour; nothing can be red and green all over. We
can produce samples: *these* things are red, we may explain, and
those are not, and there are borderline cases like *these*—though
the samples will only be of use to people who can perceive
pretty much as non-colour-blind humans do.

Can red be characterized in non-colour terms? We can clearly
go a long way. We can characterize it as the colour corresponding to spectral light of approximately wavelengths 650 to 750

---

[49] I talk of 'normal' white light, to count out, for example, light that is
composed of two very narrow complementary bands around, say, 480 and
580 nm. Such light is phenomenally detectable for the reason that coloured
objects illuminated by it look quite different from normal. A defence of the
employment of the notion of normality must wait for another occasion.

[50] I should perhaps make clear that the claim is that (all) surface colours are
ways of changing the light, not that (all) ways of changing the light are surface
colours. There will be some objects that change the light in ways that preclude our ascribing any simple colour to them—e.g. mirrors, highly metameric
objects, oil films—except perhaps relative to a particular angle or position of
view, or of illumination.

nanometres. But that of course uses the predicate 'colour'. We can do better: psychophysics and colorimetry have, I think, put us in a position where we can tell of any newly presented object what colour it is, simply from its spectral reflectance curve (together with standard data culled from human subjects).[51] It should therefore be possible to find a 'physical' property coextensive with 'red'. The questions remain whether this physical property will be *necessarily* coextensive with the colour, and whether it will be identical with it—and I cannot pretend to answer these here. But it must be obvious that the view of colours as introduced by a distinctively subjective scheme of explanation, and as phenomenally characterized ways of changing the light (as the present section has suggested), does nothing to rule out the idea that they might be characterizable a posteriori in other ways as well.

The attractions of taking colours as ways of changing the light are tremendous. I shall mention several.

First, consider a red car on a bright day. It clearly looks red. But you will also be able to see in it the reflections of other things around, from the road and the other cars to the sky above. The surface in one sense looks a perfectly uniform colour, but almost every point on it is, in another sense, presenting a different appearance. What is it that it constantly looks to be, when in this sense it constantly looks red? Why does it 'look the same'? Because there are in the visual array cues[52] that enable us to recognize it as a presentation of an object across whose surface there is a constant *relation* between incident and reflected light: there is a constant *way in which the surface changes the incident light*.

Secondly, this conception explains how it is that in order to tell what colour an object is, we may try it in a number of different lighting environments. It is not that we are trying to get it into one single 'standard' lighting condition, at which point it will, so to speak, shine in its true colours. Rather, we are looking, in the way it handles a variety of different illumina-

---

[51] I describe the method to be employed in *The Nature of Colour*.

[52] Here and elsewhere I employ some of the language and the doctrine of Gibson's ecological optics. See e.g. J. J. Gibson, *The Ecological Approach to Visual Perception* (first pub. 1979; Hillsdale, NJ: Lawrence Erlbaum, 1986), ch. 5 and pp. 97–9.

tions (all of which are more or less 'normal'), for its constant capacity to modify the light.

Thirdly, this makes sense also of what might otherwise be thought a strange phenomenon: aspect-shift in colour perception. I have had the experience of looking at a book cover from just one angle, uncertain whether it is dark blue or black. At that point I can see it alternately as dark blue, and then as black, shifting at will between appearances. The effect goes as soon as I turn the book at a new angle to the light: it is suddenly clear that the object is dark blue. To count a transient perception as a perception of a dark blue object is to be prepared to count some different perceptions as perceptions of the same enduring object with the same colour; if such different perceptions do not in fact materialize as expected, then the object after all is not dark blue.[53] To be dark blue is not crudely to have a disposition to present a single appearance in a single kind of lighting; it is to present a variety of appearances in a variety of kinds of lighting, according to a constant pattern. And if it is puzzling how a *dynamic* property can make itself manifest in a *static* perception ('how can a disposition to present a variety of appearances be visible in a single appearance?'), then we already have, in familiar discussions of aspect-shift, the theoretical apparatus for a solution. It is because there is 'the echo of a thought in sight':[54] our perception of an object as having a certain colour is 'soaked with or animated by, or infused with'—the metaphors are Strawson's—'the thought of other past or possible perceptions of the same object'.[55] If it is a shock to find even colour appearances treated as soaked with thought—rather than being the

---

[53] Cf. Strawson: 'there would be no question of counting any transient perception as a perception of an enduring and distinct object unless we were prepared or ready to count some different perceptions as perceptions of one and the same enduring and distinct object . . . To see [a newly presented object] as a dog, silent and stationary, is to see it as a possible mover and barker, even though you give yourself no actual images of it as moving and barking' ('Imagination and Perception', in P. F. Strawson, *Freedom and Resentment and Other Essays* (London: Methuen, 1974), 52–3).

[54] The phrase is Wittgenstein's (*Philosophical Investigations*, II. xi., p. 212). Strawson makes much of it in 'Imagination and Perception'.

[55] 'Imagination and Perception', 53.

brutely given *qualia* of today's descendants of sense-data—then that is a shock worth undergoing.[56]

A remarkable related phenomenon occurs with various forms of partial colour-blindness. The impression is often given that people classed as 'red–green colour-blind' (namely, the roughly 8 per cent of men and 0.5 per cent of women who have impaired colour discrimination of reds and greens, usually in the form of deuteranomaly) have one and the same type of perception when looking at red, green, and grey objects.[57] Nothing could be farther from the truth. I myself have red–green deficiencies of vision, according to the Ishihara colour tests.[58] I confuse certain reds and greens in certain circumstances. But I do not have a single kind of perception from red, green, and grey things in general. I have no difficulty in seeing the red of a post-box, or the green of the grass, and my identification of their colour is not due to knowing already what kind of thing I am looking at. (I am equally good on large blobs of paint.) So I plainly do not have just one *concept*, applicable equally to red, green, and grey things. My problem is that occasionally I take something to be red (or brown) which turns out later to be green. What is interesting is that, when told of my mistake (or recognizing it myself, for example after trying the object in slightly different lighting), I can usually come to see the object *as* having its true colour. This involves what I earlier called an aspect-shift: the object actually comes to *look different*, even when the physical sensory stimulation is the same. Even in the lighting situation where I originally took the

[56] There are some interesting consequences of applying this outlook to the inverted-spectrum puzzles, but I cannot go into these here.

[57] 'To about 5 per cent of all men, green and red are both indistinguishable from grey' (Hazel Rossotti, *Colour* (Harmondsworth: Penguin, 1983), 123). Such people have 'an inability to discriminate red, green and grey' (Hacker, *Appearance and Reality*, 151).

[58] These are the cards devised by Shinobu Ishihara, Professor of Ophthalmology at the University of Tokyo, in 1917. Each card carries a circle made up, like a *pointilliste* painting, of small blobs of different colour. Normal trichromats will see one numeral in the pattern of blobs; the colour-blind, according to their pattern of non-discrimination, will see a different numeral, or sometimes none at all. More sophisticated tests are available now, though I have not seen them myself, and the Ishihara test is still rated as efficient in detecting red–green defects. My own deficiency is, I think, deuteranomaly.

object to be brown, I do not 'get one and the same impression' as before if I later take the object to be dark green.

This makes perfectly good sense if colours are ways of changing the light. The person with red–green deficiencies is simply less good at telling from one viewing what is the object's *way of changing the light*; but by getting a variety of views of it, he may none the less recognize that property. There is no reason to say he lacks proper colour concepts; he is simply less good in applying them. His experience is, so to speak, ambiguous where other people's is not—in rather the same way as the experience of a person who sees with only one eye will be ambiguous, where that of a person who sees with two eyes is not. Most of the time those with monocular vision have no difficulty in recognizing the three-dimensional shape of objects around them—resolving cases of ambiguity by seeing the object from different angles. We certainly have no temptation to say that they lack a concept of shape in three dimensions.[59] And something parallel can be said of people with anomalies of colour vision.

This conception of colour also makes good sense of how colour perception could have evolutionary significance: the ways in which a surface changes the light will be a constant factor the tracking of which can easily be of benefit to an organism that is tracking that surface.[60]

---

[59] There is another source of difficulty for the view that those with red–green anomalies lack normal colour concepts. They are said to be capable of recognizing variation in saturation and in brightness (obviously enough in, for example, the case of yellow and blue objects); they also (if they are not deuteranopes) see a full variation of spectral hues. But in that case, putting together the concepts of saturation, brightness, and hue, they ought to have a full conceptual grasp of the variation of colour within the red and green regions too—whatever their difficulties may be in recognizing it. There are more serious deficiencies of colour perception which result in certain spectral lights being seen as achromatic—which one would naturally suppose was bound to result in misapprehension of the hue circle. But there is still, even with such people, a real question (and I mean just that) whether they may none the less have learned our own colour concepts properly, by appreciating the abstract structure of colour space (which other people in the community can tell them about) and recognizing as much of their colour perception as is sound as the (more than usually fallible) presentation of *certain* colours in restricted regions of that space—which can serve as points of reference allowing them to 'place' other colours which they actually cannot see.

[60] By contrast it is hard on the orthodox dispositional view to see any reason why colour-vision should have had adaptive value. Why on earth should our

The attractions of regarding colour as a way of changing the light are clear, though (particularly in the case of evolution, ecology, and colour-blindness) they raise questions that demand attention at much greater length. None the less, this cannot be a full conception of colour, simply because colours apply not only to objects that change the light, but also to objects that emit light. 'Yellow' is not simply ambiguous, as applied to surfaces, lights, illumination, films, after-images, and so on. But in at least some of these cases, the colour plainly cannot be a 'way of changing the light', so if yellow is a single feature, it cannot strictly ever be literally a way of changing the light.

The beginnings of a solution of the problem are not hard to find. There are a number of links between the yellowness of light and the yellowness of a surface. Yellow light falling on a white object will make it look yellow or yellowish, depending on the degree of adaptation possible to the light. Yellow light shining through a white translucent glass (like the globe of an old station waiting-room) will look similar to white light shining through a yellow globe. The exact connection of the two categories (surface colour and light colour), however, is complex, as Wittgenstein has taught us. Why is there no brown light? Why are there no grey lights?[61] What exactly are the parallels between the two areas of colour application? My own answer, which I think is also Wittgenstein's, involves both language and innate endowment, including physiology. To put the answer schematically: it is part of our language that some terms and not others apply to both lights and surfaces; someone who failed to grasp this would count as using different concepts from us. Other species might act differently from us in this, but then they would be using colour-concepts that were at best analogues of our own. But what we are here characterizing as similarities embedded in the language cannot be separated from our innate predispositions: it may, for example,

ancestors have evolved so as to be good at tracking the disposition of objects to cause a sensation of red in normal humans under normal circumstances? Human beings didn't even exist then!

[61] And remember: 'If we taught a child the colour concepts by pointing to coloured flames, or coloured transparent bodies, the peculiarity of white, grey and black would show up more clearly.' (Wittgenstein, *Remarks on Colour*, III. 240.)

be necessary to have a certain kind of neurophysiology in order to be capable of learning a language of this type. As always with rule-following, the ability to 'go on' in a certain way, given a certain training, is something that depends upon a certain natural endowment (and incidentally also upon environmental conditions, like certain kinds of constancy in the objects around us). Human beings to a large extent share with other humans these natural endowments, but there are conspicuous cases where, for example in the case of colour-blindness, a person is unable to learn a concept that others try to teach him.

The suggestion is that colours of surfaces are ways in which they change the light. The colours of lights are intimately connected with them: at one level, we may say, the same colours apply in parallel cases 'because such cases look similar'; but if pushed to say *in what respect* the cases look similar, we could only say 'in colour', and that was the very similarity we were (perhaps misguidedly) trying to explain. If on the other hand we say only 'the cases strike us similarly' then that is clearly correct: the very fact that we react by applying the same term shows that. But it is not a deep explanation of why the colour applies as widely as it does. Changing levels, we may indeed look at neurophysiological characteristics that are similar between human perception of the two cases. But in the most general terms, we may say that the similarity resides as much in our reactions to the things as in the things.

Section 2 defended autonomy in Putnam's sense: independence from mode of realization. The present section has defended autonomy in a second sense. A third sense might come to mind: explanatory independence from the objects of other explanatory schemes. I should make clear that I am not claiming autonomy in this third sense, either for colours or for psychological states. Psychological states do not form an explanatorily closed system, and the defence of psychological explanation as a form of holistic explanation autonomous in the other two senses does not need to pretend otherwise. There are a mass of psychological phenomena that are not explicable by the methods of rational explanation. 'Why do human beings forget as much as they do?' 'Why is a person who has just lost his job more susceptible to illness than one who hasn't?'

'Why do people become schizophrenic?' 'Why do people with Alzheimer's disease lose their mental faculties?' Maybe part of the answer to these questions will involve rational explanation invoking psychological states like imagining and desiring. But in most cases, what explanation is available will cross into other areas, like (at different levels, more than one of which may be relevant to a single puzzle) physiology, evolutionary biology, scientific psychology, and others.

In similar fashion, colour phenomena, though sometimes explained by other colour phenomena, will not always be. A mass of questions come to mind the answers to which force us to turn to other disciplines. 'Why do colours fade?' 'Why does red seem to advance in front of green?' 'Why is the sky blue?' 'Why is grass green?' 'Why do colour contrast effects occur?' 'Why do blue objects come to seem relatively brighter *vis-à-vis* red objects as the light goes in the evening?' (The Purkinje phenomenon.) 'Why does hue change with brightness?' (The Bezold-Brücke effect.) Only physics, physiology, chemistry, and various forms of scientific psychology can tell us. But the admission that colour phenomena form anything but an explanatorily closed set is perfectly compatible with claims of autonomy in the other two senses.

SELECT BIBLIOGRAPHY

ANTONY, L., 'Anomalous Monism and the Problem of Explanatory Force', *Philosophical Review*, 98 (1989).

ARMSTRONG, D. M., *A Materialist Theory of Mind* (London: Routledge & Kegan Paul, 1968).

—— *A Theory of Universals* (Cambridge: Cambridge University Press, 1978).

AVERILL, E. A., 'Color and the Anthropocentric Problem', *Journal of Philosophy*, 82 (1985).

—— 'The Primary–Secondary Quality Distinction', *Philosophical Review*, 91 (1982).

BENNETT, J., *Linguistic Behaviour* (Cambridge: Cambridge University Press, 1976).

BLACKBURN, S., 'Moral Realism', in J. Casey (ed.), *Morality and Moral Reasoning* (London: Methuen, 1971).

—— 'Rule-Following and Moral Realism', in S. Holtzmann and C. Leich (eds.), *Wittgenstein: To Follow a Rule* (London: Routledge & Kegan Paul, 1981).

—— *Spreading the Word* (Oxford: Clarendon Press, 1984).

—— 'Supervenience Revisited', in I. Hacking (ed.), *Exercises in Analysis: Essays by Students of Casimir Leroy* (Cambridge: Cambridge University Press, 1985).

BLOCK, N. (ed.), *Readings in the Philosophy of Psychology*, i and ii (Cambridge, Mass.: Harvard University Press, 1980–1).

—— and FODOR, J., 'What Psychological States Are Not', *Philosophical Review*, 81 (1972).

BOGHOSSIAN, P., and VELLEMAN, J. D., 'Colour as a Secondary Quality', *Mind*, 98 (1989).

BOYD, R., 'Materialism without Reductionism', in Block (ed.), *Readings in Philosophical Psychology*.

BURGE, T., 'Cartesian Error and the Objectivity of Perception', in R. Grimm and D. Merrill (eds.), *Contents of Thought* (Tucson, Ariz.: University of Arizona Press, 1988).

—— 'Individualism and the Mental', in P. French, T. Uehling, Jr., and H. Wettstein (eds.), *Midwest Studies in Philosophy*, iv (Minneapolis, Minn.: University of Minnesota Press, 1979).

CAMPBELL, J., 'A Simple View of Colour', in J. Haldane and C. Wright (eds.), *Reality, Representation, and Projection* (Oxford: Oxford University Press, forthcoming).

CASSAM, Q., 'Kant and Reductionism', *Review of Metaphysics*, 43 (Sept. 1989).

CHURCHLAND, P. M., 'Eliminative Materialism and the Propositional Attitudes', *Journal of Philosophy*, 78 (1981).

—— *Matter and Consciousness* (Cambridge, Mass.: MIT Press, Bradford Books, 1986).

CHURCHLAND, P. S., *Neurophilosophy* (Cambridge, Mass.: MIT Press, 1986).

COHEN, G. A., *Karl Marx's Theory of History* (Oxford: Oxford University Press, 1979).

COPP, D., and ZIMMERMAN, D. (eds.), *Morality, Reason and Truth* (Totowa, NJ: Rowman and Allanheld, 1985).

CRANE, T., 'Why Indeed? Papineau on Supervenience and the Completeness of Physics', *Analysis*, 51 (1990).

—— and MELLOR, D. H., 'There Is No Question of Physicalism', *Mind*, 99 (1990).

CUMMINS, R., *The Nature of Psychological Explanation* (Cambridge, Mass.: MIT Press, 1983).

CURRIE, G., 'Individualism and Global Supervenience', *British Journal for the Philosophy of Science*, 35 (1984).

—— and MUSGRAVE, A. (eds.), *Popper and the Human Sciences* (Dordrecht: Nijhoff, 1985).

CUSSINS, A., 'The Connectionist Construction of Concepts', in M. Boden (ed.), *The Philosophy of Artificial Intelligence*, Oxford Readings in Philosophy (Oxford: Oxford University Press, 1989).

—— 'Varieties of Psychologism', *Synthese*, 70 (1987).

DANCY, J., 'Moral Properties', *Mind*, 90 (1981).

DAVIDSON, D., *Essays on Actions and Events* (Oxford: Clarendon Press, 1980).

—— 'Rational Animals', *Dialectica*, 36 (1982); and in E. LePore and B. McLaughlin (eds.), *Actions and Events: Perspectives on the Philosophy of Donald Davidson* (Oxford: Blackwell, 1985).

DAVIES, M., 'Externality, Psychological Explanation, and Narrow Content', *Proceedings of the Aristotelian Society*, Supp. Vol. (1986).

DAWKINS, R., *The Blind Watchmaker* (Harlow: Longman Scientific and Technical, 1986).

—— *The Selfish Gene* (Oxford: Oxford University Press, 1976).

DENNETT, D., 'Conditions of Personhood', in D. Dennett, *Brainstorms: Philosophical Essays on Mind and Psychology* (Brighton: Harvester Press, 1981).

—— *Content and Consciousness* (London: Routledge & Kegan Paul, 1969).

—— *The Intentional Stance* (Cambridge, Mass.: MIT Press, 1987).

DRETSKE, F., *Explaining Behaviour* (Cambridge, Mass.: MIT Press, Bradford Books, 1988).

—— *Knowledge and the Flow of Information* (Cambridge, Mass.: MIT Press, 1981).

DUMMETT, M., *Truth and Other Enigmas* (London: Duckworth, 1978).

DUPRÉ, J., 'The Disunity of Science', *Mind*, 92 (1983).

ELSTER, J., *Explaining Technical Change* (Cambridge: Cambridge University Press, 1983).

—— *Making Sense of Marx* (Cambridge: Cambridge University Press, 1985).

EVANS, G., 'Things without the Mind', in Van Straaten (ed.), *Philosophical Subjects*.

—— *The Varieties of Reference*, ed. J. McDowell (Oxford: Clarendon Press, 1982).

FEIGL, H., 'Physicalism, Unity of Science and the Foundations of Psychology', in H. Feigl, *Inquiries and Provocations*, ed. R. Cohen (Dordrecht: Reidel, 1981).

—— and MAXWELL, G. (eds.), *Minnesota Studies in the Philosophy of Science*, ii (Minneapolis, Minn.: University of Minnesota Press, 1958).

FEYERABEND, P. K., 'Explanation, Reduction and Empiricism', in H. Feigl and G. Maxwell (eds.), *Minnesota Studies in the Philosophy of Science*, iii (Minneapolis, Minn.: University of Minnesota Press, 1962); repr. in P. K. Feyerabend, *Realism, Rationalism and Scientific Method* (Cambridge: Cambridge University Press, 1981).

FIELD, H., 'Conventionalism and Instrumentalism in Semantics', *Nous*, 9 (1975).

—— 'Mental Representation', in Block (ed.), *Readings in the Philosophy of Psychology*, ii.

FODOR, J. A., 'Individualism and Supervenience', *Proceedings of the Aristotelian Society*, Supp. Vol. 60 (1986).

—— *The Language of Thought* (Sussex: Harvester Press, 1976).

—— 'Making Mind Matter More', *Philosophical Topics*, 17(1) (Spring 1989).

—— *The Modularity of Mind* (Cambridge, Mass.: MIT Press, 1983).

—— *Representations* (Cambridge, Mass.: MIT Press; Brighton: Harvester Press, 1981).

—— 'Special Sciences (or: The Disunity of Science as a Working Hypothesis)', *Synthese*, 28 (1974); repr. in Fodor, *Representations*.

GIBSON, J. J., *The Ecological Approach to Visual Perception* (first pub. 1979; Hillsdale, NJ: Lawrence Erlbaum, 1986).

GOLDMAN, A., *A Theory of Human Action* (Princeton, NJ: Princeton University Press, 1980).

GOLDMAN, A. H., *Moral Knowledge* (London: Routledge, 1988).

GRENE, M. (ed.), *Dimensions of Darwinism* (Cambridge: Cambridge

University Press, 1983).

GRIFFIN, J., *Well-Being* (Oxford: Clarendon Press, 1986).

HACKER, P. M. S., *Appearance and Reality* (Oxford: Blackwell, 1987).

—— 'Locke and the Meaning of Colour Words', in G. Vesey (ed.), *Impressions of Empiricism* (London: Macmillan, 1976).

HACKING, I. (ed.), *Exercises in Analysis* (Cambridge: Cambridge University Press, 1985).

HALDANE, J., 'Understanding Folk', *Proceedings of the Aristotelian Society*, Supp. Vol. 62 (1988).

HARDIN, C. L., *Color for Philosophers: Unweaving the Rainbow* (Indianapolis, Ind.: Hackett, 1988).

HARDIN, R., *Collective Action* (Baltimore, Md.: Johns Hopkins University Press, 1982).

HARE, R. M., *The Language of Morals* (Oxford: Clarendon Press, 1952).

—— 'Supervenience', *Proceedings of the Aristotelian Society*, Supp. Vol. 58 (1984).

HAUGELAND, J., 'Weak Supervenience', *American Philosophical Quarterly*, 19 (1982).

HEIL, J. (ed.), *Cause, Mind, and Reality: Essays Honouring C. B. Martin* (Dordrecht: Kluwer Academic Publishers, 1989).

HELLMAN, G., and THOMPSON, F., 'Physicalism: Ontology, Determination and Reduction', *Journal of Philosophy*, 72 (1975).

HONDERICH, T., 'Psychophysical Lawlike Connections and their Problem', *Inquiry*, 24 (1981).

HOOKER, C., 'Towards a General Theory of Reduction', *Dialogue*, 20 (1981).

HORGAN, T., 'Supervenience and Microphysics', *Pacific Philosophical Quarterly*, 63 (1982).

—— 'Which Physical Events are Mental Events?', *Proceedings of the Aristotelian Society*, 81 (1980–1).

HORNSBY, J., 'Physicalism, Events and Part–Whole Relations', in E. LePore and B. McLaughlin (eds.), *Actions and Events: Perspectives on the Philosophy of Donald Davidson* (Oxford: Blackwell, 1985).

—— 'Physicalist Thinking and Conceptions of Behaviour', in P. Pettit and J. McDowell (eds.), *Subject, Thought, and Context*.

JACKSON, F., *Perception* (Cambridge: Cambridge University Press, 1977).

—— and PETTIT, P., 'Functionalism and Broad Content', *Mind*, 97 (1988).

—— 'In Defence of Folk Psychology', *Philosophical Studies*, 57 (1990).

—— —— 'Program Explanation: A General Perspective', *Analysis*, 50(2) (1990).

JAMES, S., *The Content of Social Explanation* (Cambridge: Cambridge University Press, 1984).

JOHNSTON, M., 'Dispositional Theories of Value', *Proceedings of the Aristotelian Society*, Supp. Vol. 62 (1989).

KIM, J., 'Causality, Identity, and Supervenience in the Mind–Body Problem', in P. French, T. Uehling, Jr., and H. Wettstein (eds.), *Midwest Studies in Philosophy*, iv (Minneapolis, Minn.: University of Minnesota Press, 1979).

—— 'Concepts of Supervenience', *Philosophy and Phenomenological Research*, 65 (1984).

—— 'Epiphenomenal and Supervenient Causation', in P. French, T. Uehling, Jr. and H. Wettstein (eds.), *Midwest Studies in Philosophy*, ix (Minneapolis, Minn.: University of Minnesota Press, 1984).

—— 'Explanatory Exclusion and the Problem of Mental Causation', in E. Villanueve (ed.), *Information, Semantics and Epistemology* (Oxford: Blackwell, 1990).

—— 'Explanatory Realism, Causal Realism, and Explanatory Exclusion', in P. French, T. Uehling, and H. Wettstein (eds.), *Midwest Studies in Philosophy*, xii (Minneapolis, Minn.: University of Minneapolis Press, 1987).

—— 'The Myth of Non-reductive Materialism', *Proceedings of the American Philosophical Association*, 3 (1989).

—— 'Psychophysical Laws', in E. LePore and B. McLaughlin (eds.), *Actions and Events: Perspectives on the Philosophy of Donald Davidson* (Oxford: Blackwell, 1985).

—— 'Psychophysical Supervenience', *Philosophical Studies*, 4 (1982).

—— '"Strong" and "Global" Supervenience Revisited', *Philosophy and Phenomenological Research*, 48(2) (1987).

—— 'Supervenience and Nomological Incommensurables', *American Philosophical Quarterly*, 15 (1978).

—— 'Supervenience and Supervenient Causation', in *Southern Journal of Philosophy*, 22, Supp. (1984) (Spindel Conference: The Concept of Supervenience in Contemporary Philosophy).

—— 'Supervenience as a Philosophical Concept', *Metaphilosophy*, 21 (1990).

KINCAID, H., 'Supervenience and Explanation', *Synthese*, 65 (1988).

KLAGGE, J., 'Supervenience, Ontological and Ascriptive', *Australasian Journal of Philosophy*, 66 (1988).

LENNON, K., 'Anti-reductionist Materialism', *Inquiry*, 27 (1984).

—— *Explaining Human Action* (London: Duckworth, 1990).

LEWIS, D., 'An Argument for the Identity Theory', *Journal of Philosophy*, 63 (1966).

—— 'Dispositional Theories of Value', *Proceedings of the Aristotelian Society*, Supp. Vol. 62 (1989).

LEWIS, D., 'Mad Pain and Martian Pain', in N. Block (ed.), *Readings in the Philosophy of Psychology*, i.

LEWIS, H. A., 'Is the Mental Supervenient on the Physical?', in B. Vermazen and M. Hintikka (eds.), *Essays on Davidson: Actions and Events*.

LOAR, B., *Mind and Meaning* (Cambridge: Cambridge University Press, 1981).

—— 'A New Kind of Content', in R. Grimm and D. Merrill (eds.), *Contents of Thought* (Tucson, Ariz.: University of Arizona Press, 1988).

LYCAN, W. G., *Mind and Cognition* (Oxford: Blackwell, 1990).

MACKIE, J. L., *Ethics* (Harmondsworth: Penguin, 1977).

—— *Problems from Locke* (Oxford: Oxford University Press, 1976).

MACDONALD, C., *Mind–Body Identity Theories* (London: Routledge, 1989).

—— and MACDONALD, G., 'Mental Causes and Explanation of Action', *Philosophical Quarterly*, 36 (1986).

MACDONALD, G., and PETTIT, P., *Semantics and Social Science* (London: Routledge & Kegan Paul, 1981).

—— 'Modified Methodological Individualism', *Proceedings of the Aristotelian Society*, 86 (1985–6).

—— 'The Possibility of the Disunity of Science', in G. Macdonald and C. Wright (eds.), *Fact, Science, and Morality* (Oxford: Blackwell, 1986).

—— *Special Explanations* (Oxford: Blackwell, forthcoming).

McCULLOCH, G., 'Dennett's Little Grains of Salt', *Philosophical Quarterly*, 40 (1990).

—— Reply to Peter Smith, 'Subjectivity and Colour Vision', *Proceedings of the Aristotelian Society*, Supp. Vol. 60 (1987).

McDOWELL, J., 'Aesthetic Value, Objectivity, and the Fabric of the World', in E. Schaper (ed.), *Pleasure, Preference and Value* (Cambridge: Cambridge University Press, 1983).

—— 'Functionalism and Anomalous Monism', in E. LePore and B. McLaughlin (eds.), *Actions and Events: Perspectives on the Philosophy of Donald Davidson* (Oxford: Blackwell, 1985).

—— 'Singular Thought and the Extent of Inner Space', in P. Pettit and J. McDowell (eds.), *Subject, Thought, and Context*.

—— 'Values and Secondary Qualities', in T. Honderich (ed.), *Morality and Objectivity: A Tribute to J. L. Mackie* (London: Routledge & Kegan Paul, 1985).

McFETRIDGE, I., 'Supervenience, Realism and Necessity', *Philosophical Quarterly*, 35 (1985).

McGINN, C., *The Character of Mind* (Oxford: Oxford University Press, 1982).

—— *Mental Content* (Oxford: Blackwell, 1989).

—— 'Mental States, Natural Kinds, and Psychophysical Laws', *Pro-

ceedings of the Aristotelian Society, Supp. Vol. 52 (1978).
—— 'Philosophical Materialism', Synthese, 44 (1980).
—— The Subjective View: Secondary Qualities and Indexical Thoughts (Oxford: Oxford University Press, 1983).
McLAUGHLIN, B., 'Anomalous Monism and the Irreducibility of the Mental', in E. LePore and B. McLaughlin (eds.), Actions and Events: Perspectives on the Philosophy of Donald Davidson (Oxford: Blackwell, 1985).
MARR, D., Vision (New York: Freeman, 1982).
MELLOR, D. H., 'The Reduction of Society', Philosophy, 57 (1982).
MENZIES, P., 'Against Causal Reductionism', Mind, 97 (1988).
MILLER, R., 'Methodological Individualism and Social Explanation', Philosophy of Science, 45 (1978).
MILLIKAN, R., Language, Thought and Other Biological Categories (Cambridge, Mass.: MIT Press, 1984).
MOORE, G. E., Principia Ethica (Cambridge: Cambridge University Press, 1903).
NAGEL, E., The Structure of Science (London: Routledge & Kegan Paul, 1961).
NAGEL, T., Mortal Questions (Cambridge: Cambridge University Press, 1979).
—— The View from Nowhere (New York and Oxford: Oxford University Press, 1986).
NEANDER, K., and MENZIES, P., 'David Owens on Levels of Explanation', Mind, 99 (1990).
O'NEILL, J. (ed.), Modes of Individualism and Collectivism (New York: Heinemann, 1973).
OPPENHEIM, P., and PUTNAM, H., 'The Unity of Science as a Working Hypothesis', in H. Feigl and G. Maxwell (eds.), Minnesota Studies in the Philosophy of Science, ii. (Minneapolis, Minn.: University of Minnesota Press, 1958).
OWENS, D., 'Levels of Explanation', Mind, 98 (1989).
PAPINEAU, D., For Science in the Social Sciences (London: Macmillan, 1978).
—— 'Social Facts and Psychological Facts', in Currie and Musgrave (eds.), Popper and the Human Sciences.
—— 'Why Supervenience?' Analysis, 50(2) (1990).
PARFIT, D., Reasons and Persons (Oxford: Oxford University Press, 1984).
PEACOCKE, C., Holistic Explanation (Oxford: Clarendon Press, 1979).
—— 'Demonstrative Reference and Psychological Explanation', Synthese, 49 (1981).
—— 'No Resting Place: A Critical Notice of The View from Nowhere, by Thomas Nagel', Philosophical Review, 98 (Jan. 1989).

PETRIE, B., 'Global Supervenience and Reduction', *Philosophy and Phenomenological Research*, 48 (1987).

PETTIT, P., 'Broad-Minded Explanation and Psychology', in P. Pettit and J. McDowell (eds.), *Subject, Thought, and Context*.

—— 'Social Holism without Collectivism', in E. Margalit (ed.), *The Israel Colloquium: Studies in the History, Philosophy and Sociology of Science*, v (Dordrecht: Reidel, forthcoming).

—— and McDOWELL, J., *Subject, Thought, and Context* (Oxford: Clarendon Press, 1986).

—— and SMITH, M., 'Backgrounding Desire', *Philosophical Review*, 99 (1990).

PUTNAM, H., *Philosophical Papers*, i: *Mathematics, Matter and Method* (Cambridge: Cambridge University Press, 1975).

—— *Philosophical Papers*, ii: *Mind, Language, and Reality* (Cambridge: Cambridge University Press, 1975).

—— *Representation and Reality* (Cambridge, Mass.: MIT Press).

RAILTON, P., 'Moral Realism', *Philosophical Review*, 95 (1986).

ROSENBERG, A., *The Structure of Biological Science* (Cambridge: Cambridge University Press, 1985).

—— 'The Supervenience of Biological Concepts', *Philosophy of Science*, 45 (1978).

ROTHBEARD, M. N., *Individualism and the Philosophy of the Social Sciences* (San Francisco, Calif.: Cato Institute, 1979).

RUBEN, D. H., *The Metaphysics of the Social World* (London: Routledge & Kegan Paul, 1985).

RYAN, A., *The Philosophy of the Social Sciences* (London: Macmillan, 1970).

SCHAFFNER, K. F., 'Approaches to Reduction', *Philosophy of Science*, 34 (1967).

SCHIFFER, S., *Remnants of Meaning* (Cambridge, Mass.: MIT Press, Bradford Books, 1987).

SEARLE, J., *Minds, Brains and Science* (London: British Broadcasting Corporation, 1984).

SELLARS, W., 'Empiricism and the Philosophy of Mind', in Sellars, *Science, Perception and Reality* (London: Routledge & Kegan Paul, 1963).

SHOEMAKER, S., 'Functionalism and Qualia', *Philosophical Studies*, 27 (1975).

—— 'Personal Identity: A Materialist's Account', in S. Shoemaker and R. Swinburne, *Personal Identity* (Oxford: Blackwell, 1984).

SMITH, M., 'The Humean Theory of Motivation', *Mind*, 96 (1987).

SMITH, P., 'Anomalous Monism and Epiphenomenalism: A Reply to Honderich', *Analysis*, 44 (1984).

—— 'Bad News for Anomalous Monism?', *Analysis*, 42 (1982).

—— 'Subjectivity and Colour Vision', *Proceedings of the Aristotelian Society*, Supp. Vol. 60 (1987).

SNOWDON, P., 'On Formulating Materialism and Dualism', in J. Heil (ed.), *Cause, Mind and Reality*.

SOBER, E., *The Nature of Selection* (Cambridge, Mass.: MIT Press, 1984).

STRAWSON, P. F., *Individuals* (London: Methuen, 1959).

STROUD, B., 'The Physical World', *Proceedings of the Aristotelian Society*, 87 (1986–7).

TOMBERLIN, J. (ed.), *Philosophical Perspectives*, iii and iv (Ridgeview, Calif.: Atascadero, 1989 and 1990).

VAN STRAATEN, Z. (ed.), *Philosophical Subjects* (Oxford: Oxford University Press, 1980).

VERMAZEN, B., and HINTIKKA, M. (eds.), *Essays on Davidson* (Oxford: Oxford University Press, 1985).

WALTON, K., 'Categories of Art', *Philosophical Review*, 79 (1970).

WESTPHAL, J., *Colour* (Oxford: Blackwell, 1987).

WIGGINS, D., *Needs, Values, Truth* (Oxford: Blackwell, 1987).

WILLIAMS, B., 'Internal and External Reasons', in B. Williams, *Moral Luck* (Cambridge: Cambridge University Press, 1981).

WOODFIELD, A., *Thought and Object* (Oxford: Clarendon Press, 1982).

WRIGHT, C., 'Moral Values, Projectivism and Secondary Qualities', *Proceedings of the Aristotelian Society*, Supp. Vol. 61 (1988).

WRIGHT, L., 'Functions', *Philosophical Review*, 82 (1973).

YOSHIDA, R. M., *Reduction in the Physical Sciences* (Halifax, NS: Dalhousie University Press, 1977).

INDEX OF NAMES